FRONT LINE AFRICA
THE RIGHT TO A FUTURE

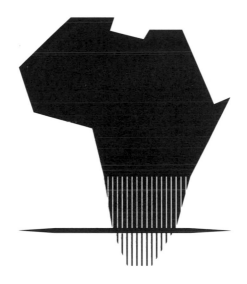

AN OXFAM REPORT ON CONFLICT AND POVERTY IN
SOUTHERN AFRICA

S U S A N N A   S M I T H

British Library Cataloguing in Publication Data

Smith, Susanna, *1951—*
    Front Line Africa: the right to a future
    Southern Africa. Social conditions
    I. Title
    968.06'3

    ISBN 0-85598-103-2
    ISBN 0-85598-104-0 pbk

Front cover & page heading illustration by Alison Moreton
Back cover photograph: Sumve Primary School, Mwanza Region, Tanzania
(Geoff Sayer / Oxfam)

Published by Oxfam, 274 Banbury Road, Oxford OX2 7DZ
Designed by Oxfam Design Studio 797 DMH 89
Printed by Alden Press, Oxford
Typeset in 10 point Times Roman

Contents

Acknowledgements

I am grateful to the many people who have given their time and the benefit of their experience to the research for this book. Those who deserve special thanks are the people in southern Africa whom we interviewed and consulted, who are too numerous to mention. In addition, I should like to thank the people who undertook research: Rona Alexander (on the European Community Special Programme), Akwe Amosu (Angola), Bornwell Chakaodza (eastern Zimbabwe), Justin Forsyth (Namibia), Paul Goodison (EC policy), Liz Holmes, Robin Palmer (Zimbabwe), Julian Quan (Mozambique and Zimbabwe), and Geoff Sayer (illustrations).

This book draws on the collective experience over time of Oxfam's work in Angola, Malawi, Mozambique, Namibia, South Africa, Tanzania, Zambia, and Zimbabwe. I have therefore been greatly helped by the active collaboration of many Oxfam staff members and trustees.

I am also indebted to a number of other people who have helped with advice and editing. Special thanks go to Reg Green, Malcolm Harper, Prudence Smith, Sithembiso Nyoni, Colin Stoneman, Nicola Swainson, Ian Linden, Ken Wilson, Bruce Coles, and Chris Dammers.

Officials in a wide range of organisations and governmental departments have also helped by supplying information. These include a number of departments within the governments of Angola, Malawi, Mozambique, Tanzania, Zambia, and Zimbabwe; the British Department of Trade and Industry, Foreign And Commonwealth Office, and Overseas Development Administration; the British embassies in Angola and Mozambique; the South African embassy in London; the Commission of the European Community;

the library of the US embassy in London; UNHCR, UNICEF, and the United Nations Council for Namibia; the World Bank and the International Monetary Fund; the African National Congress of South Africa; the International Committee of the Red Cross and the League of Red Cross Societies; the Quaker Office at the United Nations; the Overseas Development Institute; the International Defence and Aid Fund; the Anti-Apartheid Movement; Business International; and the library of Queen Elizabeth House, Oxford.

Lastly, Prudence Smith and Catherine Unia deserve special thanks for their help with childcare, as do the staff of the Oxfam workplace nursery. The book could not have been written without their support.

Susanna Smith
February 1990

General notes

Geographical focus

Oxfam's current programme in southern Africa supports a wide range of work in Angola, Malawi, Mozambique, Namibia, South Africa, Tanzania, Zambia, and Zimbabwe. This book concentrates on those countries where we have up-to-date, direct experience. This is why the book does not deal in depth with developments in Botswana, Lesotho, and Swaziland.

'Front Line States'

The 'Front Line States' are those states in southern Africa which have formed an alliance to fight apartheid and white minority rule in South Africa. They are formally constituted as a group led by one of the Presidents, elected periodically, and they meet regularly to coordinate their policies. The member states are Angola, Botswana, Mozambique, Tanzania, Zambia, and Zimbabwe.

SADCC

The members of the Southern African Development Coordination Conference (SADCC), at the end of 1989, were Angola, Botswana, Lesotho, Malawi, Mozambique, Swaziland, Tanzania, Zambia, and Zimbabwe. Namibia is expected to join on independence.

Currency conversions

Pounds sterling, US dollars, the South African Rand, and European Currency Units (ECUs) are used throughout this book according to normal convention. Where other currencies are used, a sterling equivalent has been provided alongside, at the official rate of exchange for the month or year in question.

Abbreviations

ACP	:	African, Caribbean, Pacific
ANC	:	African National Congress (South Africa)
ARMSCOR	:	Armaments Corporation (South Africa)
AZAPO	:	Azanian People's Organisation (South Africa)
BLS	:	Botswana, Lesotho, Swaziland
CMEA	:	Council for Mutual Economic Assistance
CONSAS	:	Constellation of Southern African States
COSATU	:	Council of South African Trade Unions
ESAF	:	Enhanced Structural Adjustment Facility
FLS	:	Front Line States
FNLA	:	National Front for the Liberation of Angola
FRELIMO	:	Mozambique Liberation Front
GDP	:	Gross Domestic Product
GNP	:	Gross National Product
IBRD	:	International Bank for Reconstruction and Development (World Bank)
IDA	:	International Development Association (World Bank)
IMF	:	International Monetary Fund
MDM	:	Mass Democratic Movement (South Africa)
MNR	:	Mozambique National Resistance
MPLA	:	People's Movement for the Liberation of Angola

NACTU	:	National Confederation of Trade Unions
NF	:	National Forum
OAU	:	Organisation of African Unity
OECD	:	Organisation for Economic Cooperation and Development
PAC	:	Pan-Africanist Congress
PTA	:	Preferential Trade Agreement
RENAMO	:	Mozambique National Resistance
SACBC	:	Southern African Catholic Bishops' Conference
SACC	:	South African Council of Churches
SACU	:	Southern African Customs Union
SADCC	:	Southern African Development Coordination Conference
SADF	:	South African Defence Force
SATS	:	South African Transport Services
SWAPO	:	South West Africa People's Organisation
UDF	:	United Democratic Front
UNCTAD	:	United Nations Conference on Trade and Development
UNHCR	:	United Nations High Commissioner for Refugees
UNITA	:	National Union for the Total Independence of Angola
ZANU	:	Zimbabwe African National Union
ZAPU	:	Zimbabwe African People's Union

SOUTHERN AFRICA

Introduction

February 1990 was a significant month for southern Africa. Watched by the world, Nelson Mandela walked free after 27 years as a political prisoner in South Africa. He was released just days after President de Klerk had announced important initial reforms, including the unbanning of the African National Congress and other key organisations, and the lifting of some aspects of the State of Emergency.

At the same time, Oxfam workers in South Africa, Mozambique, and Angola were facing less newsworthy developments. In South Africa, Oxfam fieldworkers learned that President de Klerk had refused to meet representatives of several rural communities which we have supported in their battle to resist forced incorporation into the South African 'homelands'. In Mozambique, there was growing concern that another outbreak of famine would occur, because armed conflict was preventing relief aid from reaching large numbers of people. In Angola, the delivery of relief aid to people in the drought-affected areas in the south was hampered by the continuing war.

This book aims to inform the public debate on southern Africa from our viewpoint and experience as a relief and development agency. Oxfam has been working in the region for over thirty years. A fifth of all our overseas grants is spent there. Our work is directly affected by the massive scale of human suffering and the daunting obstacles to peace and just development which we witness.

Drawing on Oxfam's direct experience, this book focuses on southern Africa during the 1980s, tracing developments up until the end of 1989. It examines the range of pressures — global, regional, and national — which lie behind conflict and poverty, and which have impeded development. It shows how these pressures combine to affect poor people in their struggle for a better life. In particular, we identify three major obstacles in the fight against poverty, underdevelopment, and oppression. They are apartheid in South Africa, the unequal economic relationship between the underdeveloped South and the industrialised North, and the marked failure of southern African nations to promote equitable development.

Front Line Africa: The Right to a Future goes on to look at the policies of Britain and the European Community towards the region's complex array of problems. The book ends with a number of recommendations to the British government, the European Community, and the governments of southern Africa, which we believe could contribute to the relief of poverty and suffering.

We argue that the 1990s bring an unprecedented opportunity for the international community to help establish a non-racial democracy in South Africa. This would not only remove a central cause of regional instability, but it could also boost the economic prospects of the wider region. Further, more far-reaching measures are needed to support increased levels of production and fairer trading terms, to promote debt reduction, and to improve debt-management strategies in southern African states. Much depends on the international community, and whether it has sufficient political will to match this challenge. It is also vital that development policy errors are addressed by the southern African governments. More responsive and accountable systems of government are essential to the fight against poverty.

Britain has a key role to play. Indeed, its extensive, deeply-rooted links with South Africa and the wider region mean that if it is not going to be part of the solution, it will remain part of the problem.

Section I
Regional constraints on development

Background to South Africa's policy of regional destabilisation

Growth of nationalism in southern Africa, 1948-1975

From 1948 onwards (when the National Party first came to power in South Africa) apartheid, colonialism, and white-minority rule came into increasingly direct conflict with the political tenets of the mass nationalist movements emerging throughout Africa. Inside South Africa, throughout the region, and across the continent the nationalist cause was growing on a significant scale.

International opinion against South Africa was boosted by African leaders as independence came to the colonial territories of the continent. In March 1961, during the Commonwealth Prime Ministers' Conference, the London *Observer* published an article by Julius Nyerere in which he laid out the fundamental reasons why South Africa's continued membership of the Commonwealth was unacceptable to the people of Tanganyika, as mainland Tanzania was then called.

His article remains an eloquent statement of the moral and political issues at stake, and its timely publication was an early example of diplomatic pressure against South Africa. It is widely thought that the publication of his article strongly influenced the climate of opinion among the then Commonwealth heads of government. South Africa withdrew its application for re-admission, apparently preferring this course to facing almost certain rejection.

President Julius Nyerere in 1968, seven years after Tanzania's independence,
addressing a rally in Dar es Salaam.   (Camera Press)

> The people of Tanganyika are working to build a non-racial democratic
> society ... what we want is a society where the individual matters, and not the
> colour of his skin, or the shape of his nose. Racial group privileges or
> discriminations are incompatible with this.
>
> The policies of apartheid now being practised in the Union of South Africa
> are a daily affront to this belief in individual human dignity. They are, in
> addition, a constantly reiterated insult to our own dignity as Africans, about
> which we cannot be expected to remain indifferent, and which could inflame
> our own passions if not otherwise dealt with ... [1]

The southern African 'front line' — a metaphor often used to denote the
(geographical and political) boundary between the independent, black-ruled
states of the region and the colonial or minority-ruled ones — started with
independent Tanzania's southern border and President Nyerere's
uncompromising condemnation of apartheid. Today, the 'Front Line States'
(FLS) is a political alliance comprising Tanzania, Zambia, Angola,
Mozambique, Zimbabwe, and Botswana. Namibia is expected to join on
independence.

Tanzania was the first of today's Front Line States to reach full
independence, in 1961. The 'front line' moved southwards when Zambia
(formerly Northern Rhodesia) came to independence in 1964, on the break-up
of the settler-ruled Central African Federation which had been created by

Britain, the colonial power.

The other two states freed from the Federation, Southern Rhodesia and Malawi, took different political paths. The Smith regime in Southern Rhodesia, wanting to maintain the political supremacy of the white settlers, unilaterally declared independence from Britain in 1965, thus prolonging the Zimbabwean nationalist struggle for majority rule, and strengthening the country's links with South Africa. Independent Malawi established diplomatic relations with South Africa in 1967. To date, this is the only such link between South Africa and another African country. Malawi's particular relationship with South Africa means that it is not a member of the FLS alliance. However, it is a full member of the Southern Africa Development Coordination Conference (SADCC — a regional organisation formed in 1980 primarily to reduce economic dependence on South Africa).

Of the former British High Commission territories, Botswana and Lesotho came to independence in 1966, and Swaziland in 1968. In 1963, having failed to incorporate these territories with a view to including them in the 'homelands' design,[2] South Africa proposed instead to establish a southern African common market — a regional political and economic institution with South Africa as the dominant member. Although this proposal fell through, it was the early conceptual forebear of the Constellation of Southern African States (CONSAS), a South African regional policy objective relevant to the later destabilisation phase (see below).

Instead, once independent, these countries were incorporated into the Rand monetary area (from which Botswana subsequently withdrew), and the Southern African Customs Union, which ensured that South Africa had considerable economic leverage over them.

In 1969, independent Africa's opposition to apartheid and colonialism in southern Africa was formally coordinated in the form of the 'Lusaka Manifesto', a document on relations with Portugal, Rhodesia, and South Africa which remains the touchstone of the Front Line States political alliance. Led by Tanzania and Zambia, fourteen states from east and southern Africa signed it in April; it was adopted by the Organisation of African Unity (OAU) in September, and subsequently approved by the UN General Assembly. The document is very moderate in tone, advocating peaceful change to majority rule unless all such attempts fail. But it warns that without progress, "patience will be exhausted". The document rejects black as well as white racism, acknowledges that whites in southern Africa have strong ties to the land, as many of them have made their home there for generations, and notes that they are therefore entitled to be considered Africans, regardless of their skin colour. Thus, cooperation between all peoples of southern Africa for the benefit of all was stated as the ultimate goal of the FLS alliance, with the warning that this cannot be achieved if the white Africans refuse to recognise the legitimate aspirations of black Africans.

Until the mid-1970s, however, South Africa was well insulated from proximity with its independent, anti-apartheid neighbours by a buffer zone of colonial territories. While this buffer zone was in place, South Africa's regional policy centred on efforts to reinforce the protective barrier by forming alliances with the colonial governments of these territories.

Increasing regional and international pressure, 1975-1978

The regional outlook changed dramatically from the mid-1970s onwards. Various factors combined to create a regional environment which became increasingly unfavourable to the South African government's interests, and which therefore led to a shift in its regional strategy.

South Africa's 'buffer zone' suddenly began to disintegrate when Angola and Mozambique became independent in 1975, following a coup in Portugal (led by disaffected army officers who had become politicised by their experience of Portugal's colonial wars in Angola, Mozambique, and Guinea Bissau). Mozambique and Angola joined the FLS alliance. South Africa became militarily involved in Angola in an unsuccessful attempt to prevent the pro-Soviet Popular Movement for the Liberation of Angola (MPLA) from becoming the independent country's first government.

The fact that the Angolan and Mozambican nationalist movements had come to power, after long and bitter warfare, gave a boost to the mounting popular resistance within South Africa. The 1976 Soweto uprising, and the brutal state repression of the young people involved, refocused international criticism against South Africa, and further radicalised urban youth, many of whom had become politicised through the Black Consciousness Movement of the time. Hundreds of young people left South Africa in the aftermath of Soweto, and many joined the African National Congress (ANC) in exile. Others remained and became more politically active inside South Africa. The death of the young black activist Steve Biko while in detention in 1977 also heightened international censure and further catalysed internal opposition.

The southward march of national independence also helped the ANC, the South West African People's Organisation (SWAPO — fighting for the independence of Namibia from South Africa), and the Zimbabwe African National Union (ZANU). On joining the FLS alliance, Mozambique and Angola set about extending support to these liberation movements.

The Soweto Uprising, 1976 - a watershed event in the recent history of mass resistance against apartheid. 10,000 school pupils protesting against 'Bantu education', in particular the use of Afrikaans in schools, marched through Soweto. They were confronted by the police, who provoked violent clashes. The demonstrations spread to other townships, copying the pattern of attacks on police patrols and symbolic buildings. The official death toll was 575, with 2,389 wounded. Many politicised young people went into exile after 'Soweto', and many community organisations were subsequently formed inside South Africa. (IDAF)

Independent Angola offered refuge and military bases to the ANC and SWAPO. Luanda became the headquarters of SWAPO in exile, and SWAPO guerrillas were able to move more easily across Namibia's northern border, using Angolan territory as a rear base. Mozambique offered military rear-base support to ZANU, and hospitality to the ANC, although its headquarters remained in Lusaka.

The failure of various internationally sponsored efforts at mediation in Rhodesia during the mid-1970s meant that the war for independence continued, threatening what remained of South Africa's buffer zone. However, South African business interests profited from the situation because of the captive export market created by mandatory UN sanctions against Rhodesia.

South Africa's relations with the West deteriorated over the granting of 'independence' to the Transkei 'homeland' in 1976, and the impasse over Namibia's future after the UN Plan for its independence was agreed in 1978.

It was against this background of increasing internal, regional and international pressure on apartheid that South Africa shaped the regional strategy which it pursued for most of the 1980s. Its overriding preoccupation was with the defence and security of the apartheid state.

'Total onslaught' and the 'total strategy'

We are today involved in a war, whether we wish to accept it or not.

(South African White Paper on Defence, 1977)

Reflecting the growing involvement of the military in formulating both foreign and domestic policy in South Africa, the 1973 White Paper on Defence first introduced the concept of the 'total strategy', which was further elaborated in the succeeding White Papers on Defence of 1975 and 1977.

The government argued that South Africa faced a "total onslaught", the aim of which was "the overthrow of the present constitutional order and its replacement by a subject, communist-oriented, black government".[3] Although the onslaught was described as "communist inspired", it was also seen to embrace a wide range of forces, including not only the FLS, the ANC and SWAPO, but also the UN, the OAU, and "the West". To counter the perceived threat of a concerted attack on South African society, the concept of the 'Total National Strategy' was developed, and was adopted as official policy in 1978 following P.W. Botha's rise from Defence Minister to Prime Minister, later to become State President.

In 1977, the 'total strategy' was officially defined as

the comprehensive plan to utilize all the means available to a state according to an integrated pattern in order to achieve the national aims within the framework of specific policies. [4]

In his preface to the 1977 White Paper on Defence, P.W. Botha —

then Minister of Defence — explained why the new strategy had arisen:

During the past two years there have been far-reaching political, economic, and military developments in both the global and regional context, with direct implications for the Republic of South Africa. Marxist militarism is casting a shadow over Africa. Nevertheless the Western countries still take part in a senseless arms embargo against the RSA.

... the principle of the right of self-determination of the White nation must not be regarded as being negotiable.

Military strategy forms part of a broader national strategy to ensure this.

Regional cooperation — on whose terms?

South Africa's terms

In so far as regional policy is concerned, the aims of the 'total strategy' have been reformulated over time. In 1979, the idea of a regional constellation of states (CONSAS) was reintroduced, and its creation was a major policy objective. CONSAS members were to share economic, political, and defence interests, with South Africa as the key member determining the regional order.

CONSAS membership was intended to include as many independent states in the region as would join, together with Namibia and the 'independent' bantustans in South Africa, under a client grouping of minority parties. Since the notion of CONSAS was revamped in 1979, it has been adapted in the light of subsequent events. But some observers believe that it remained a background policy objective throughout the 1980s.

The Front Line States' terms

By 1979, the FLS had laid firm plans for their alternative regional economic cooperation body, the Southern African Development Coordination Conference, widely known by its acronym SADCC. In direct contrast to CONSAS, SADCC was conceived as a vehicle for restructuring regional economic relations. Its primary aim was to reduce dependence on South Africa.

The first ZANU (PF) rally to be held in Rhodesia as the liberation war drew to a close, Salisbury, 1979.   (Neil Libbert/Camera Press)

Both sides needed Zimbabwe to come to an internationally recognised independence suitable for their different purposes. Situated right in the centre of the region, straddling the major transport routes, with the most developed economy after South Africa's, an independent Zimbabwe was the missing part of the regional jigsaw necessary to fall into place before any regional economic grouping could be developed, CONSAS or SADCC.

South Africa hoped Zimbabwe would come to independence under the leadership of Bishop Muzorewa (then installed as the caretaker leader under the terms of the March 1978 internal settlement), while the FLS needed a victory by the Patriotic Front alliance (the tactical alliance between ZANU and ZAPU formed in October 1976). [5]

In the event, ZANU PF's landslide electoral victory in 1980 and Zimbabwe's immediate accession to the FLS alliance meant that SADCC was established within weeks, and plans for CONSAS were undermined. At its first full inaugural meeting, in Lusaka on 1 April 1980, SADCC defined four main strategic objectives. Firstly, the reduction of economic dependence, particularly, but not only, on the Republic of South Africa. Secondly, the forging of links to create genuine and equitable regional integration. Thirdly, the mobilisation of resources to promote the implementation of national, interstate, and regional policies. And fourthly, concerted action to secure international cooperation within the framework of a strategy for economic liberation.

The formation of SADCC represented a setback to the South African government's plans for the region on many different fronts. As regards membership, not only had the nine independent states of the region refused to join CONSAS, but they were also quick to join its political and economic rival — SADCC. As a result, CONSAS went ahead on a very limited scale which fell far short of South Africa's original plan for a regional organisation. An 'inner constellation' was formed, comprising South Africa and the four 'independent' bantustans (Transkei, Bophuthatswana, Venda and Ciskei) with elaborate structures for cooperation.[6] South Africa's plans to develop this 'inner constellation' into the originally envisaged 'wider constellation' were deferred to the future.

The establishment of SADCC revealed the Front Line States' open intention to transform the existing economic order, in defiance of South Africa's regional economic domination. SADCC's first priority was to reduce the region's transport dependency on South Africa by strengthening regional alternatives. The South African-backed conflicts in Mozambique and Angola have targetted the region's east-west trade corridors. This strategy increased regional dependence on South Africa's trade routes, thereby attacking the political tenets of SADCC.

Thus, regional economic cooperation became a key factor as the South African government's regional behaviour grew distinctly more aggressive and coercive. Its plan to shape regional relations through CONSAS was blocked. Its buffer zone had been finally replaced by Front Line States (with the exception of Namibia). There was mounting internal pressure and resistance to apartheid, all of which stimulated international censure against South Africa. The destabilisation phase of South Africa's regional policy, which began with that country's invasion of Angola in 1975, intensified, until signs of a shift in strategy became apparent in 1988.

Internal developments, 1983 — 1987

During the 1980s, with the 'total national strategy' in place, the apartheid system of government was entering a decade of heightened crisis, one which led inexorably to what many observers now believe to be the early 'transition' phase towards the final end of apartheid. Key developments took place inside South Africa. These, together with South Africa's hostile actions in the region, focused renewed international condemnation of the South African government.

State repression of extra-parliamentary opposition in South Africa was stepped up following the imposition, in 1985, of the State of Emergency. During 1988, 32 anti-apartheid organisations were restricted from all political activities.　(IDAF)

During 1983, there was a significant growth of anti-apartheid organisations within South Africa. The United Democratic Front (UDF) and the National Forum (NF) were formed as umbrella organisations to link local and national groups; the trade union movement also began to develop umbrella organisational structures at this time. This was a key element behind the high-profile and well-rooted 'popular uprising' which surfaced in 1984.

From 1984 to 1986, popular resistance inside South Africa increased on an unprecedented scale. It was focused on education and housing; and on issues such as the deployment of the South African Defence Force (SADF) in the townships, and forced removals of black people from their land; and on mass rejection of the state's 'reform and repress' strategy. In particular, resistance coalesced around the government's proposals to 'reform' apartheid by introducing a tricameral parliament, which excluded blacks, and gave severely limited powers to the 'Coloureds' and 'Asians' in their 'own' separate parliamentary chambers.

Illustrating the view that the apartheid system provokes a cyclical round of violence — one of black rebellion and state repression[7] — the 1984 increase in popular resistance provoked a backlash, also on an unprecedented scale. In July 1985, the government declared a State of Emergency covering 36 magisterial districts. This was temporarily lifted in March 1986, but during those seven months it has been estimated that at least 853 people were killed in nationwide political violence, that 7,992 people were detained under Emergency regulations, and a further 4,152 under other laws.[8]

Another State of Emergency was declared in June 1986. This time it was nationwide, and it was annually renewed with increased restrictions in 1987, 1988, and 1989. Between September 1984 and December 1988, political violence cost over 4,000 lives (mostly black).[9]

Between 1986 and 1988, state repression continued. Thirty-two anti-apartheid organisations were restricted, effectively banned from all activities, during 1988. Detentions under Emergency regulations continued. In the first year of the total State of Emergency (as from June 1986), some 20,000 people were detained; in the second year, some 8,500; and estimates of the numbers held over the following year give a figure of 2,000.[10] Yet organised resistance was not contained by the government actions, even though many organisations and activists in the resistance network had been affected by the repression. Work stayaways, rent, consumer and transport boycotts, and armed resistance continued.

Media restrictions

Increased controls on media reporting of all political conflict were introduced

THE WEEKLY MAIL

PRICES: JOHANNESBURG, PRETORIA & REEF R1,00 (plus 12c GST) | ELSEWHERE IN SA R1,12 (excl. GST)

Volume 2, Number 24 FRIDAY JUNE 20 to THURSDAY JUNE 26, 1986

THE PAPER FOR A CHANGING SOUTH AFRICA

WE'RE BACK ON THE STREETS! The paper that was seized last week will be on sale as usual from today

The EPG report: An extraordinary document made **ordinary** by our extr aordinary times **8**

A leaf-munching plan to **beat** malnutrition **7**

FRONT PAGE COMMENT

Our lawyers tell us we can say almost nothing critical about the Emergency

But we'll try:

PIK BOTHA, the Minister of Foreign Affairs, told US television audiences this week that the South African press remained free.

We hope that ▉▉▉▉▉▉▉▉▉▉▉▉▉▉, ▉▉▉▉▉▉▉▉▉▉▉▉▉▉▉▉▉▉▉▉▉▉▉▉▉ ▉▉▉▉▉, was listening.

They considered our publication subversive.
● If it is subversive to speak out against ▉▉▉▉▉, we plead guilty.
● If it is subversive to express concern about ▉▉▉▉▉, we plead guilty.
● If it is subversive to believe that there are better routes to peace than the ▉▉▉▉▉▉▉, we plead guilty.

● To PAGE 2

RESTRICTED | Reports on these pages have been censored to comply with emergency regulations

The front page of the South African "Weekly Mail", announcing the government's sweeping media restrictions under the 1986 State of Emergency. International public opinion was numbed when the images of resistance disappeared from regular TV coverage. Free association and a free press are key prerequisites for negotiations.

in December 1986, and further restrictions followed.[11]   The effects of these restrictions have been far-reaching.   In particular the restricted TV coverage largely succeeded in reducing international public awareness of the struggle in South Africa.

The 1986 White Paper on Defence and Armaments Supply explained the powerful Defence Department's analysis of the role of the foreign media under the heading 'Propaganda Onslaught'.   Having attacked the 'negative' radio broadcasts about South Africa emanating from various African countries, the paper went on to state:

> The transmissions from Western transmitters such as the Voice of America, the British Broadcasting Corporation, Deutsche Welle, France and the Netherlands were more subtle, and a higher degree of hostility towards the present dispensation was at times noticed.

> In support of some local media, foreign media attempt to create a climate for negotiation with the ANC ... The SA Defence Force was one of the main targets of this (foreign) radio propaganda. Broadcasts focused especially on accusations of so-called aggression against neighbouring states, so-called destabilisation and so-called support to resistance movements. The role of the SA Defence Force in containing internal unrest also figured strongly in recent broadcasts, and a smear campaign is being conducted concerning alleged atrocities against the local population.[12]

By 1986, the network of resistance organisations had sustained serious setbacks due to the repression unleashed against them.   There are numerous records detailing state repression.[13]

Oxfam's experience

During the 1980s, Oxfam's programme of support in South Africa has had to respond to the great tidal waves of internal developments, and in particular to the cyclical pattern of resistance and repression.

The growth of internal anti-apartheid organisations generated a pressing need for financial support to a wide range of newly formed groups active on social issues. Once launched, these organisations were to face the effects of severe repression. As Oxfam field workers have been stressing since the early 1980s, working in South Africa during a time of increasing state repression has been especially difficult. In this respect, Oxfam and other foreign non-governmental agencies have experienced how state repression has affected people's organisations and everyday life.

Direct effects of state repression

Organisations have been shut down or severely restricted, and key people have been detained or have gone into hiding to avoid detention.   Many organisations supported by Oxfam have been affected in this way — including Trade Unions, Advice Centres, paralegal organisations, organisations resisting removals, education organisations, community newspapers, crisis, welfare, and emergency relief organisations, and rural communities, especially those in the 'homelands'.

In February 1988, The Detainees' Parents Support Committee, a key organisation which campaigned against detentions, was restricted, effectively banned. For a while afterwards, independently-assessed, up-to-date information on Emergency detentions was harder to obtain. However, as has happened with so many popular organisations, soon after one was restricted, another was formed to take over its role. The Human Rights Commission, under the South African Council of Churches and the Southern African Catholic Bishops' Conference, is now a key source of reliable information.

Another example is the Chesterville Residents Association in Durban. The

Abraham Maja, a church worker in the Transvaal, was detained for eight months without trial under Emergency regulations. He helps to run advice centres which support people who face the many legal, economic, and employment problems created by apartheid. This work was seriously disrupted by his arbitrary detention.
(Rona Alexander)

membership of its Executive Committee had to change composition four times in two years, due to detentions of its workers under emergency regulations which severely hampered working links with the community, and the continuity of work.

For Abraham Maja, who worked with the Northern Transvaal Council of Churches, arrest came completely out of the blue. Part of his work was to support Oxfam-funded community advisers. He was arrested on 13 June 1986, on the day the State of Emergency was announced. He was eventually released on bail in February 1987, and all charges against him were later dropped. He explained to an Oxfam fieldworker the effects of his arrest and that of a colleague, and the impact of a police raid on their office: "With the detention of the fieldworker, only two new staff remained. They were intimidated by the police attention, and quickly resigned. The office came to a standstill. This was the situation I found on my release eight months later."[14]

Indirect effects of state repression

Because of the way in which community organisations have been targeted — restricted by the state, and attacked by right-wing vigilante organisations — many community structures have been severely disrupted. This means that the work of their local community service organisations (advice centres, for example) is hampered. This has happened in two related ways. Firstly, because a repressive crackdown often creates a sharp upturn in the need for help — perhaps legal advice, medical assistance, or help with a housing crisis — which stretches the capacity of the service organisation. And secondly, because community service organisations have to operate within a framework of community representation on their management committees. So when the community leadership has been detained or is in hiding, it is frequently impossible for working links of this sort to be maintained.

An example is the advice centre in the semi-rural area of Inchanga, a quiet spot in Natal. Large areas of Natal are dominated by conflict between Inkatha (the quasi-cultural movement, based only in Natal, led by Chief Gatsha Buthelezi) and members of the United Democratic Front (the UDF) and the Confederation of South African Trade Unions (COSATU).[15] The peace of Inchanga was shattered in early 1988 when a number of youths fled there, followed by Inkatha, police and defence forces. Suddenly, Inchanga became a hot-spot. The advice centre (based in a mission) found itself surrounded by conflict — with troops all around, and helicopters hovering overhead. The Chairperson of the Centre was arrested, and the relationships which had grown up between the Centre and the community were badly affected. People became afraid and suspicious, and the Centre's management were unable to meet for nine months because of tensions in the community. They were scared to meet in case Inkatha vigilantes decided the Centre was a UDF or COSATU organisation, which could have sparked off a chain of tit-for-tat funeral killings.

Another example is the Durban Crisis Network, a service organisation which does relief work, helping people with such things as legal aid and urgent cash needs. It is linked with some 40 different community organisations. The disruption of the grass-roots community organisations meant that the services of the Crisis Network were severely curtailed.

Effects on development workers

A typical case is that of Alex Mbatha, a South African development fieldworker supported by Oxfam and working with the Southern African Catholic Bishops' Conference. In 1981 he was detained during an early morning police raid on his Soweto home. His wife Khosi and their two-year-old daughter Dudu were also arrested. They were held for seven months without trial, and no charges were ever brought against them. During this time they were tortured. Following his release, Alex recounted his experiences while in detention, which have been so typical of others. He said,

> On 22 October 1981, the police came into my house, smashed open my door with a crowbar, and rushed in as if there was a criminal in the house. They woke us up. They threw suitcases all over our bed and we were rushed out of

Vigil for Alex and Khosi Mbatha, held outside the South African Embassy in London during their 7 months' detention without trial in 1981/2. Alex was a development worker in South Africa for the Southern African Catholic Bishops Conference and Oxfam. The Mbathas fled into exile on their release.   (Oxfam)

the house in only a few minutes. I shall never forget how we were rushed out of the house, as if it was on fire. They had me by the scruff of my neck, and I had Dudu, our baby, in my hands. We were pushed into a car. Little did I know that I would never see my home again. [The family fled into exile on their release.]

On 19 November they started taking me to the torture chamber ... They started on me by putting a hood over my head when I was naked. They would beat the daylights out of me, pouring water over the hood at the same time. Later they used electric gadgets on my private parts, and over my whole body.

They would come into my cell at any time, preferably at night, and just kick me and say I am still stubborn.

I pitied them because I could see they were part of a machine, part of a system that is so inflexible and not prepared to listen, part of a system that smashes black families.[16]

Conclusion

All these internal developments were reflected in South Africa's regional policy. Having stimulated conflict, tension, and military expenditure both inside South Africa and within the wider region, the state's 'total onslaught' analysis easily perpetuated itself. In 1986, for example, just a month before the South African air raids on Gaborone, Harare, and Lusaka which were especially timed to undermine the Commonwealth Eminent Persons' mission, the South African Minister of Defence argued that the SADF and Armscor (the parastatal armaments industry established because of the UN arms embargo) needed increased resources, because "... the internal security situation has worsened; the conventional arms build-up in neighbouring countries continues; and the SA Defence Force must adapt its posture within the new dispensation." He continued:

It is not only in the interests of the RSA, but undoubtedly also of our neighbouring states and the subcontinent, that the excessive build-up of forces and the escalation of terrorist activity be stopped. It is of the greatest importance for the well-being and security of all the Southern African countries that all parties strive towards actively establishing a common interstate forum where matters of common security and welfare may be dealt with to the benefit of all. The SA Defence Force is prepared to participate in the activities of such a forum at any time and place.[17]

However, developments from 1983 onwards caused the tide to turn slowly against South Africa. The government began the 1980s with the hawkish view that apartheid could be defended intact by external aggression and internal 'reform and repression'. But by the end of the decade, mounting pressures on apartheid were to lead to a change of strategy.

The 'destabilisation' phase of South Africa's regional policy

In its dealings with the surrounding states, the South African government has wielded the stick of military and economic sanctions to bend neighbouring nations to its will.

This, the external face of apartheid, is of importance in defending the system and in holding at bay pressure from the international community for ending it.[1]

(Excerpt from the report of the Commonwealth Eminent Persons Group, following their mission to South and southern Africa in May 1986.)

The external face of apartheid: destabilisation

During the 1980s, South Africa's foreign policy towards its neighbours became widely known as 'destabilisation'. It was a policy of aggressive military and economic interventions (both direct and indirect) in the region.

Destabilisation is a deliberate policy which has clear, political objectives. As one leading South African academic and policy analyst has stated,

The (political) objective of destabilisation is to effect profound political changes in the 'target state'. These may or may not involve structural change — which means dislodging the regime in power — but certainly involve major changes in the target state's behaviour, specifically towards the 'destabiliser'.[2]

South Africa's regional policy uses a mix of military, economic, political and diplomatic elements, combining coercive with persuasive tactics (the 'carrot and stick' approach). These have been used in different combinations at different times, and have played on the different characteristics and

Mozambican mother and child on the move — arriving at a settlement for displaced people at Alto Moloque in Zambezia Province after MNR attacks on their home area.

(Jenny Matthews / Oxfam)

vulnerabilities of the countries in the region.

From 1989 onwards, with a new configuration of international and internal pressure on apartheid, it is widely believed that South Africa's regional policy is adapting to meet new circumstances. Most observers believe there is a shift away from predominant military aggression towards a largely economic and diplomatic offensive.[3]

Because the situation is now more fluid than it has been for years, the pace of change is difficult to predict. As one leading member of the United Democratic Front (UDF) explained, "Experience shows that the South African government only moves when pressure is applied. Although we have paid a very high price for the pressure we have put on the government, it is more needed now than ever."[4]

Defending the system — foreign policy begins at home

Like any government's foreign policy, South Africa's overall aim is to further its view of the 'national interest'. In this case, it is clear that the survival of an embattled system of white supremacy was the foremost element of 'national interest' during the 1980s. Until apartheid is ended, this will remain the overall aim, although strategy will alter to meet new developments. The specific objectives of South Africa's regional policy can be divided into three main categories — security, economic considerations, and political factors.

As far as security is concerned, South Africa's pressure throughout the 1980s on neighbouring states ensured a geographical barrier to protect against infiltration from guerrillas loyal to the African National Congress (ANC). Reportedly, no nearby state now accords the ANC military training bases. The Nkomati Accord of 1984 provided for the withdrawal of Mozambican support for the ANC, apart from a small diplomatic presence. A similar non-aggression treaty is reported to have been reached with Swaziland. ANC personnel were expelled from Lesotho, following the South African-backed coup in January 1986. Some reports in August 1989 stated that Zambia had insisted on a scaled down ANC presence, although these were later denied. As part of the bargaining process involved in the tripartite peace agreement on Angola and Namibia in 1988, Angola agreed to withdraw its ANC military training facilities. (It has since been reported that the ANC military personnel who have had to leave Angola have been accommodated instead in Uganda, Ethiopia, and Tanzania.[5])

Economic considerations have been central to South Africa's relationship with the wider region, for two main reasons. Firstly, a constant element of South Africa's regional policy over the years has been to ensure that its poorer neighbours continue to serve its domestic economic requirements. The region is important for South Africa's economy — providing markets for its exports, some imports (mostly primary produce), transport revenue, and labour. South Africa's determination to form and dominate a regional organisation for economic cooperation (as well as cooperation in other fields) has been a key element of its regional policy.

Secondly, South Africa has aimed to foster the region's economic dependence on its own economy, as a bargaining counter against increased international sanctions. For example, in March 1989 Foreign Minister Pik Botha warned against the European Community's proposals for extended coal sanctions against South Africa (principally opposed by West Germany) by saying that if South African coal mines were closed as a result, "Hundreds of thousands of black Africans, even from neighbouring countries, would lose their jobs and will be sent home."[6]

President Chissano of Mozambique replied by saying that his people were already suffering from sanctions imposed by South Africa, and that the repatriation of the small proportion of Mozambican migrant workers employed in the coal mines should be seen in the context of the 62,000 people who had then been recently released from territory held inside Mozambique by guerrillas of the Mozambican National Resistance (MNR, or RENAMO) and who were being assisted by the government. He said, "The social burden of Mozambican miners sent back from South Africa will not be unbearable. They are welcome." [7]

Taking up the point, official British statements have constantly stressed the harm which increased sanctions against South Africa would do to the rest of the region as one reason for not applying them. Sanctions, as an official Foreign Office policy statement on South Africa puts it, " ... would also damage our own economy to no avail, and those of the neighbouring states".

The paper goes on to say that the other southern Africa states "could lose from a weakened South African economy and certainly would lose if South Africa retaliated against them for measures imposed by them or by others. The losses inflicted on them would far exceed the capacity of outsiders to help."[8]

On the economic front, South Africa's policy has also experienced failures. The Southern African Development Coordination Conference (SADCC) has had a considerable measure of success, especially in opening up transport routes, and in the diplomatic sphere. The business lobby within South Africa has pointed out that destabilised states cannot provide buoyant export markets, and destabilisation has further tarnished South Africa's international image, creating increased pressure for sanctions, and exacerbating foreign investors' and lenders' lack of confidence.

Political considerations have also been important in the shaping of South Africa's regional policy. The economic and political difficulties faced by other African countries, in particular the destabilised countries, have often been invoked to justify postponement of the central political issue in South Africa — universal adult suffrage in a unitary state without special privileges based on race. Problems beyond South Africa's borders (regardless of their causes and in spite of the poverty, violence, and economic decline within South Africa) are used to 'demonstrate' that, as far as Africa is concerned, majority rule is undesirable.

For example, a 1987 pamphlet distributed by the South African Embassy in London claimed,

Child in Onvervacht, in the Orange Free State white farmlands, a 'dumping ground'
for black people who have been removed from their former homes.

(Nancy Durrell-McKenna / Oxfam)

South Africa has rejected the one man, one vote constitutional models that
have plunged Africa into so much misery and chaos ... Given the disastrous
consequences of one man, one vote in Africa - of which South Africa is an
integral part, sharing the continent's manifold socio-economic headaches -
such a political dispensation is not feasible for South Africa in the foreseeable
future.[9]

The National Party's view that majority rule has brought disaster to the
rest of Africa is important to their domestic political platform, because it
relates closely to their vision of the future constitutional shape of South
Africa (outlined in the Party's Five Year Plan of 1989 — see Appendix 1). In
February 1989, while leader of the National Party and before becoming State
President, F.W. de Klerk told reporters, "Typical one-man-one-vote leads to
majority rule ... That would be catastrophic for South Africa."[10] On the same
day, in his speech to parliament (from which blacks are excluded), he
characteristically described what would be called full constitutional
democracy anywhere else as 'domination':

Is there anyone in this chamber in favour of black domination? I doubt it ...
To the white voters I today give this assurance: in building a new
dispensation, which offers full and equal rights to all, the National Party will
jealously watch over your security and interests, and those of minority groups
... Our strong emphasis on group rights ... is based on the reality of South
Africa and not on an ideological obsession or racial prejudice.[11]

At the end of 1989, the National Party remained wedded to some form of 'group rights',[12] in direct contrast to the ANC's position, which holds that 'group rights' is the central tenet of apartheid. ('Group' in this context means racial group, and 'group rights' is a National Party shorthand term taken to mean that minority groups, as defined by the Population Registration Act, would be able to hold political and economic power in measures disproportionate to their numbers.) In an October 1989 address, Thabo Mbeki, head of the ANC's Department of International Affairs, explained the implications of this policy:

> De Klerk and the National Party went to the September elections on an apartheid platform, clearly and consistently stated as 'Group Rights'. It runs through their Five Year Plan. When de Klerk says the issue of universal franchise is no longer in dispute, he means it within the context of apartheid.[13]

Policy formulation

South Africa's policy towards the region is a synthesis created by different, often competing, interest groups within the ruling elite. The relative powers of the competing elements are also affected by changing pressures and developments.

The military has played a key role, but many observers now believe that, as far as regional policy is concerned, the influence of the 'verligte' (Afrikaans for 'enlightened') outlook is becoming increasingly important. This is mainly because the power held by the 'securocrats' (the hawkish elements normally associated with the military) was probably tempered by the SADF's defeat at Cuito Cunavale in southern Angola in 1988, and by President Botha's resignation from office in August 1989.[14] (The former Minister of Defence, and the person held most responsible for what one British government Minister has called the "infuriating" lack of progress,[15] he is widely regarded as the patron of the securocrats' political ascendance.)

Throughout the 1980s, South Africa remained a highly militarised state, with a powerful security apparatus controlling all levels of civilian society. This 'National Security Management System'[16] was designed to implement the defence of apartheid. A key issue for the coming period is how far the power of this apparatus and the 'securocrat' political interests vested in it will diminish. President de Klerk announced his intention to dismantle the NSMS in November 1989.[17]

Furthermore, although the role of parliamentary democracy in South Africa has been eroded by the militarisation of the State, nevertheless the results of the September 1989 'general' election clearly demonstrated that the white electorate wanted change.

The main elements of South Africa's regional strategy

The key aspects of South Africa's regional strategy during the 1980s were economic and military. Diplomacy re-emerged towards the end of the 1980s, most markedly during F.W. de Klerk's pre-election trips (as President-Elect) to Zambia, Zaire, Mozambique, and Lesotho in July and August 1989.

South Africa's regional strategy has also employed a combination of 'carrot and stick' tactics. In part, this is thought to reflect the fact that there are competing interests within the ruling elite,[18] as well as reflecting a deliberate strategy. In June 1987, Chester Crocker, then the US Assistant Secretary of State for African Affairs, explained,

> The South African government appears to be following a two-track policy, and the two tracks complement each other rather than contradict each other. By maintaining its links with and support for RENAMO, the South African Government controls an instrument with which to pressure the Government of Mozambique. At the same time, the South African Government provides positive incentives, such as economic incentives, to the Government of Mozambique. The South African Government's objective is to create negative and positive incentives to influence Mozambican behaviour in directions favourable to South African interests.[19]

A 1985 funeral procession at Guguletu in South Africa. Under Emergency Regulations which banned mass opposition gatherings, the funerals of those killed by political conflict became the focus for popular demonstrations.   (Dave Hartman / Afrapix)

At the end of the 1980s, in keeping with the shift in its regional strategy, South Africa was reviewing the balance between carrot and stick. Many believe that the 'carrot' will predominate. Even so, South Africa's regional behaviour will continue to be rooted in the government's perceived domestic interests, and, as the Commonwealth Heads of State put it in 1985,

> ... only the eradication of apartheid and the establishment of majority rule on the basis of free and fair exercise of universal adult suffrage by all the people in a united and non-fragmented South Africa can lead to a just and lasting solution of the explosive situation prevailing in southern Africa.[20]

Economic elements of South Africa's regional strategy

The punitive economic pressures used as part of South Africa's regional policy have created widespread hardship. Nobody knows what the long-term damage of these massive costs to the economic fabric of the region will be.

A key economic lever has been the concerted attempt — mostly through proxy military support — to sabotage the four east/west transport corridors (three in Mozambique and one in Angola) which carry the trade of the landlocked SADCC states. The aim of this was to increase economic dependence on South Africa (by increasing reliance on the trade routes running through South Africa), and thereby to sabotage the Southern African Development Coordination Conference (SADCC).

But, alongside its punitive military and economic tactics, and in keeping with its objective of remaining the dominant regional economic power, the South Africa government has also sought positive economic links. These fall into three main categories: trade and trade credit, funding for economic cooperation projects, and aid.

Trade credit

Trade credit has been an effective way of at least maintaining (and at best increasing) trading links with the region. Trade credit is a much-valued incentive in countries acutely short of foreign exchange, and has been extended by the South African government, which allows export credit guarantee cover to South African firms doing business in the region. Zambia, for example, has found that South African firms are the only ones in a position to offer this incentive.[21] For some years, Zambia's economic crisis has meant that its export credit guarantee cover rating among other trading partner nations has been negligible.

Economic cooperation projects

There are three main projects involving cooperation between South Africa and the region.[22] In addition to the direct economic benefits of each project, they also have important advantages for South African business interests and the government's international standing. In particular, the international

Transport routes in southern Africa

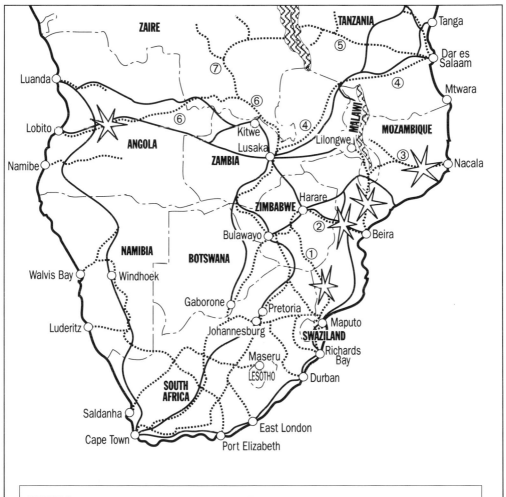

KEY				
National boundry		①	Limpopo Line	
Road		②	Beira line	
Railway		③	Nacala Line	
		④	Tanzania-Zambia Railway (TAZARA)	
		⑤	Tanzania Railways Corporation (TRC)	
Sabotaged railway		⑥	Benguela Line	
		⑦	Voie Nationale	

cooperation these projects entail breaks down the 'isolation' factor — which has been such a key preoccupation of recent South African foreign policy.[23]

In Lesotho, the Highlands Water Scheme is a large project to dam, channel and tunnel river pathways so that Lesotho can generate its own electricity and so that water — one of the few natural resources South Africa is short of — can be sold to South Africa. Money for the scheme has been raised from a diverse range of sources, including the World Bank. Although the scheme will benefit Lesotho's fragile and dependent economy, it is also bringing South Africa more than assured water supplies. Firstly, South African firms stand in a good position to tender for the internationally financed construction contracts. And secondly, both the bilateral accord with Lesotho and South Africa's involvement in the international cooperation for financing the scheme[24] help to break South Africa's isolation.

The Cabora Bassa Dam in Mozambique is the largest hydro-electric complex in Africa. It is capable of providing Mozambique and South Africa with cheap electricity, were it not for the guerrilla forces of the Mozambican National Resistance (the MNR), which regularly sabotage the transmission lines to South Africa. (This has meant that Mozambique has had to spend precious foreign exchange on repairing the lines, and importing electricity from South Africa.) Under a new agreement to reopen the project, the South African government is to make credits available to a South African construction company for the rebuilding of pylons. South Africa joins with Italy and Portugal in financing the project. In giving Mozambique 'non-lethal' military aid to defend the line, South Africa finds itelf protecting its investments against a force it is responsible for having built up.[25]

The third example of economic cooperation is the Sua Pan project in Botswana, which will provide the South African market with around 300,000 tonnes of soda ash a year.[26]

Aid

Mozambique and Malawi have both received South African economic assistance. The new capital city of Malawi, for instance, was built with South African finance. When State President Botha visited Mozambique in September 1988, he announced a gift of 'non-lethal' military aid, worth $4.5 million. Speaking at the handover ceremony a couple of months later, South Africa's Deputy Defence Minister used the opportunity to portray Pretoria as a regional benefactor. He said, "South Africa is the stabiliser of the region. The constant accusation that the SADF is destabilising Southern Africa is therefore untrue."[27]

Oil storage tanks destroyed by SADF sabotage, Namibe, Angola. Angola depends on its oil industry for almost all its foreign exchange earnings. (Keith Bernstein / Oxfam)

Military elements of South Africa's regional strategy

The most dramatic form of destabilisation has been the military dimension, as reflected in the massive suffering, displacement, and economic disruption it has caused. South Africa has used both direct and indirect military strategies to destabilise its neighbours.

As far as direct military aggression is concerned, conventional South African forces occupied southern Angola intermittently from 1975 until implementation of the tripartite peace agreement of December 1988. The testimony of one South African conscript gives a clear account of his duties when he was deployed in Angola between 1983 and 1984.

> Then our unit was sent into Angola. We went straight to Chiede, 20 km over the border (with Namibia). We were doing a lot of vehicle patrols because you don't walk once you're in Angola. We spent two or three days at Ngiva taking a lot of things out. We blew the runway, and we blew a lot of ammunition up and we bashed the buildings down, we exploded a lot of things all over the place.[28]

The SADF has launched commando raids into Angola, Botswana, Mozambique, Lesotho, Swaziland, and Zimbabwe, and has mounted air strikes into Angola, Mozambique, Zambia, Zimbabwe, and Botswana. According to press reports collated over the period December 1981 to April 1988, the SADF has acknowledged 11 raids into neighbouring states, excluding its military operations in Angola. One of these raids, where two South African soldiers were killed in Zimbabwe, was officially said to be 'unauthorised'. At least 144 people have been killed and 233 injured in these acknowledged raids. However, over the same period, there were at least 11 unacknowledged attacks on neighbouring states in which at least 20 people were killed, and five injured, according to press reports. Moreover, over the same period, a total of 46 assassination attempts on ANC members living outside South Africa were reported in the South African press. This figure does not include the acknowledged SADF raids into neighbouring states. At least 42 ANC members are reported to have been killed and at least 13 injured in these events.[29] In addition, at least ten people have been forcibly abducted from neighbouring states to South Africa over the same period.[30]

The only southern African countries which have escaped direct military aggression from South Africa to date are Tanzania and Malawi. (As the only African country with full diplomatic relations with South Africa, it is unlikely that Malawi would be attacked directly.) However, both of these countries are indirectly affected by South Africa's military destabilisation of their neighbours. Both countries host refugees from Mozambique, and have committed troops to fight there. And Malawi suffers severe economic problems as a result of MNR sabotage of its trade routes through Mozambique.

But it has been South Africa's indirect (proxy) military destabilisation, its support for rebel movements especially in Mozambique and Angola,[31] which has caused far more suffering and destruction than its direct military aggression. Before the December 1988 'Southwestern Africa tripartite peace agreement', South Africa was openly supporting the Angolan rebel movement, UNITA.[32] But there has been controversy over the issue of South African support for the Mozambican National Resistance (MNR, or RENAMO, known throughout Mozambique as the "bandidos armados" — the armed terrorists).

South African support for the MNR, 1984 — early 1989

In March 1984, the South African government scored a key success in terms of the security objectives of its regional policy when the Nkomati Accord was signed. (This was a bilateral non-aggression treaty between Mozambique and South Africa, signed at the point when Mozambique had been brought to its knees by drought and war.) The evidence suggests that between the signing of the treaty and early 1989, South Africa did not keep to its side of the bargain, and continued to support the MNR covertly.[33] Not surprisingly, given the high-profile nature of the Nkomati Accord, the South African government consistently denied that it was supporting the MNR, acknowledging only a

Working closely with the Mozambican government's disaster relief agency, Oxfam has distributed cloth, blankets, clothing, seed, and tools to people displaced by MNR attacks.
(Jenny Matthews / Oxfam)

'technical' violation in 1985.[34]

For example, in July 1987, following a BBC1 interview with one of Oxfam's emergencies officers about Oxfam's work in Mozambique and the causes of the crisis, Oxfam received a letter from an official in the South African Embassy in London which stated, "I must take strong exception to (Oxfam's) statement ... The accusation of supporting RENAMO is consistently used in this country as a handy anti-South African tool. The South African government has consistently denied assistance to RENAMO ..."[35]

Only a month earlier, however, Chester Crocker, then US Assistant Secretary of State, had given evidence to a Congressional hearing on Mozambique. He said,

> South Africa took over responsibility for training and arming RENAMO, a Rhodesian Central Intelligence Organisation creation, in 1980 following Zimbabwe's independence. South African officials made little effort to disguise their country's actions as part of an effort to put pressure on the Mozambican government. The US continues to collect and analyse information on RENAMO's relationship with South Africa from all available sources, including sensitive intelligence sources. The evidence clearly indicates a continuing relationship of communication with and support for RENAMO from the Government of South Africa.[36]

More recently, during his visit to Mozambique in September 1988,[37] P.W. Botha — then State President — announced that South Africa was to change its policy. In addition to announcing 'non-lethal' military aid to Mozambique (primarily to protect the Cabora Bassa electric power lines supplying South Africa), State President Botha was reported to have promised that South Africa would cease assistance to the MNR. President Chissano said of their meeting, "South Africa gave us guarantees that they are not going to help RENAMO." [38]

However, reports over the following months indicated that, at best, support was still coming from South Africa which the government was not taking adequate steps to prevent, or at worst, that it was coming from official sources. In March 1989, six months after President Botha's statement, the US State Department issued a communique confirming its belief that the South African government continued to support the MNR.[39] Also in March 1989, it is reported that the Soviet Deputy Foreign Minister, Anatoly Adamashin, provided proof of continued support from South Africa when he met South Africa's Foreign Minister Pik Botha.[40] Following this, in April 1989, it was reported that eyewitnesses of an MNR attack on the border town of Ressano Garcia said that South African military vehicles assisted the MNR guerrillas.[41]

Changing strategy towards Mozambique

The evidence suggests that South African support for the MNR continued after the 1984 Nkomati Accord, but probably at a reduced level. Thereafter, as the MNR grew into a force which could increasingly maintain itself from other foreign sources as well as from captured material and forced cooperation from the civilian population, official South African support probably fell away (although private sources in South Africa continue their support).

The probable reasons behind South Africa's changing strategy towards Mozambique are four-fold.

Firstly, South Africa has been under diplomatic pressure to adhere to the terms of the Nkomati Accord. Britain has played a key role in this respect (see Chapter 10). Secondly, the devastating 'success' of South Africa's destabilisation of Mozambique has meant that most of its original objectives have been achieved. Mozambique has been brought to its knees, and has had no option other than to adapt its stance towards South Africa.

The Mozambique government has kept to its side of the Nkomati Accord in restricting the ANC's presence. Mozambique has become markedly less vociferous on the issue of sanctions. Economic cooperation, on South Africa's terms, is now well under way — South African trade and investment prospects are being assisted by the opening of a South African Trade Mission

Even though it has been partly destroyed by the MNR, this clinic at Marrambula in Zambezia Province still functions.   (Keith Bernstein / Oxfam)

in Maputo; and Mozambique has entered into economic cooperation projects with South Africa.

Thirdly, having built up the MNR to the point where it is probably able to sustain itself from other sources for the time being, the hawks in the South African ruling elite can be sure that it will continue to wreak havoc. And fourthly, for the time being at least, the apparently prevalent view of the National Party is that positive regional political and economic cooperation, wherever possible, is desirable. During this critical period of flux, it is in the National Party's interests to woo its international allies and attempt to heal rifts in the region. This will help to give it maximum leverage during the coming tussle over the future shape of South Africa.

However, this period of flux and opportunity also contains real risks. In spite of the widespread optimism, the situation inside South Africa remains inflammable. Although both state and opposition showed in the peaceful mass demonstrations at the end of 1989 that restraint is possible, nevertheless the deep feelings of alienation among the black majority and the highly militarised state structures of repression remain.

And as the last decade has shown, the region is acutely vulnerable to the consequences of South Africa's internal instability. As Chris Patten, then the British Minister for Overseas Aid, put it in 1987, "The southern African region is overshadowed by crisis. A crisis brought about by the effects throughout the region of the iniquitous system in South Africa."[43]

After his visit to southern Africa in May 1989, US Assistant Secretary of State Herman Cohen said,

> Unfortunately we continue to see evidence that a certain amount of assistance is coming into Mozambique from South Africa. Now whether this is being done by elements of the SA military or by the private sector is very difficult for us to tell. But we continue to pressurise the SA government to shut off this aid. [43]

In July 1989, shortly before F.W. de Klerk was to arrive for a pre-election visit to Mozambique, President Chissano said that his government no longer believed Pretoria supported the MNR. He added, "We are prepared to believe that the South African armed forces, as such, are not in support" of the MNR. But that "... everything indicates (that some) elements inside South Africa support them."[44]

Since then, attention has focused on what steps Pretoria is taking to prevent such support. Reports of August 1989 indicated that the South African government was preparing legislation to outlaw assistance to the MNR.[45]

The MNR is reported also to receive support (channelled through South Africa) from other, private, sources in, for example, Portugal, the USA, West Germany, and Saudi Arabia.[46] In view of the diverse nature of the support base they have been able to build up, it is clear that a coordinated international effort is needed to stem the flow of resources.

What is the nature of the MNR?

The controversy surrounding the nature of alleged South African support for the MNR is likely to continue,[47] in spite of the probable shift in emphasis in South Africa's regional policy. But the enduring fact, regardless of dispute over 'smoking gun' evidence, is that South Africa built up the MNR (from the comparatively small and insignificant force they took over from Rhodesian control) into a force which has wrecked the country and is now feared by many to be beyond reining in — a sort of 'Frankinstein's monster'. Specialising in brutality against civilians and economic sabotage, the MNR and the banditry it has spawned have created the social and economic breakdown necessary for its continued survival.

Until more is known about the nature of the MNR, it is difficult to see exactly which solutions to the conflict would be lasting. Many of the MNR's most curious features derive from its origins as a purely military machine.

Augusto at school in Lichinga, his refuge since he saw his parents killed by the MNR. Every night at bed-time he wants to put his clothes close to hand under his pillow, in case the 'bandits' come.   (Keith Bernstein / Oxfam)

Numbering an estimated 15,000 men, it is well organised as a military movement, but not as a political one. Hence it is able to mount military actions in every province of the country, but it has not been able to produce a convincingly authentic political programme.[48] Although common sense indicates that the MNR must rely on widespread civilian support — whether voluntary or not (and the clearest evidence is that it is not[49]) — it depends almost entirely on forced recruitment for its fighting ranks.[50] Its central base is thought to be in the Shona-speaking Manica and Sofala Provinces of Mozambique, but it does not appear to have grown organically outwards from these areas, developing its following and ideology over time. Instead, not long after South Africa had taken over support, its military operations spread systematically throughout the country (especially where the transport corridors bisect the length of the country) as well as across borders into neighbouring states.

There are still disputes about the nature of the MNR and the factors affecting its development.[51] As one writer on Mozambique has put it, "It is in the nature of a covert war, particularly one carried out in a large country with numerous impediments to good communication, that many aspects remain obscure."[52]

There is contention over the extent to which FRELIMO actually created support for the MNR with its early agrarian transformation programme (in particular the scheme to create Communal Villages) and its early attempts to reduce the power held by traditional leaders. There is debate, too, about the quality of democracy in a one-party state, and differences of opinion over the level of popular support during FRELIMO's struggle for independence, and over the extent to which the MNR leadership is composed of disaffected FRELIMO cadres. The extent of random individualistic banditry alongside MNR sabotage remains unclear, as does the question of whether this pre-existed the MNR's military campaign.

Notwithstanding these factors, what is abundantly clear from Oxfam's experience is the extreme brutality against civilians, and the senseless destruction for which the MNR is responsible.

South African involvement in the conflict in Angola

Although South Africa has been deeply involved in conflict in both Mozambique and Angola, it is nonetheless important to note the significant differences between the two situations. For example, whereas the MNR was created by a foreign power (Rhodesia), UNITA is a genuinely indigenous rebel movement, even though its military and political power has been greatly boosted by external support. Whereas FRELIMO, the ruling party in Mozambique, can claim widespread popular support throughout the country,

An adult literacy class in Luanda, organised by OMA, the national organisation of Angolan women. (Jenny Matthews / Oxfam)

Conflict is responsible for much of the suffering in Angola. Here Selmira Salala (12 years old) learns to walk again. She stepped on a UNITA landmine during an attack on her village.

(Akwe Amosu / Oxfam)

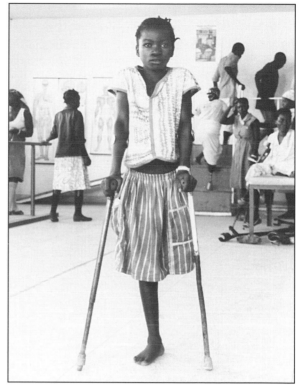

history shows that Angola's ruling party — the MPLA (PT) (the Popular Movement for the Liberation of Angola, Workers' Party) — assumed power in 1975 on a relatively narrow support base, centred on an influential stratum of educated people[53] in Luanda, the capital city.[54]

There have been two broad, linked dimensions to conflict in Angola, which have developed over the years since independence. South Africa has been embroiled in both.[55] First, between 1975 and the implementation of the December 1988 peace agreement, the SADF repeatedly invaded Angola over the border from occupied Namibia. And second, Angolan government forces have been at war with UNITA since 1975, when the 'Alvor Accord' (a flimsy tripartite transitional coalition comprising the three main liberation movements of the time) disintegrated into bitter civil conflict. The roots of this conflict date back to the 1960s, to the struggle for independence. What began as a civil war quickly escalated into an international flashpoint involving South Africa, the USA, the Soviet Union, Cuba, and Zaire, as each of the rival parties turned to foreign governments for military support and hardware.

In mid-1975 South Africa intervened in the chaos which had broken out by sending in an invading force in an attempt to install its preferred party (the rump of UNITA which had sought refuge in south-east Angola after its military defeat) into power. It failed, largely because of the last-minute arrival of Cuban troops, who came to support the MPLA, and the (temporary) withdrawal of US support to the other liberation movements.[56] What began as a 'one-off' South African invasion was to develop into a series of sustained air and ground incursions into southern Angola as the MPLA assumed power, and set about extending hospitality and military support to SWAPO and the ANC.

Alongside its own incursions, South Africa was helping to resuscitate UNITA, and by mid-1986 was reported to have spent some US$1 bn. on training and equipping the rebel forces.[57]

The human dimensions of conflict

DATE 27.7.87.

TO: OXFAM, OXFORD.

FROM: OXFAM, MAPUTO, MOZAMBIQUE.

*RE. HOMOINE MASSACRE ON SATURDAY 18.7. WE NOW HAVE
MORE INFORMATION. BY FAR THE MOST KILLED WERE
WOMEN + CHILDREN. HOSPITAL WORST HIT. ALL
EXPECTANT MOTHERS KILLED BAR 2 ESCAPEES. WOMEN
WORKERS KILLED TOGETHER WITH KIDS ON THEIR BACKS.
MOST WERE SHOT, A FEW WERE HACKED OR BAYONETTED.
APART FROM HOSPITAL, MOST WERE SHOT IN THEIR HOMES.
FOOD + CLOTHING ROBBED. HOSPITAL LOST ALL
BEDCLOTHES, MEDICINES, EQUIPMENT, DOMESTIC
UTENSILS, COMPLETE SETS OF EQUIPMENT FOR 2 HEALTH
POSTS, ETC. ETC. GOVERNMENT DISASTER RELIEF AGENCY
NEED FUNDS TO BUY URGENT NECESSITIES FOR HOMOINE.
CAN WE MAKE GRANTS FOR THIS EMERGENCY?*

*(An Oxfam telex from Mozambique. 380 people were killed by the MNR —
the rebel movement in Mozambique — in the Homoine massacre, 49 were
seriously injured, and many were kidnapped.)*

The scale of suffering

The casualties of conflict in southern Africa divide into three categories:
those directly killed in violent incidents, those who have died as a result of
war-related famine, and the babies and children who would otherwise have

lived if they had had enough to eat and adequate access to health services.[1]

Some 325,000 Mozambicans and Angolans are estimated to have been direct casualties of conflict between 1980 and 1988.[2] Many of the Mozambican casualties have been young children, deliberately killed and often mutilated first, in order to cause anguish to their parents.[3]

Another 200,000 people are estimated to have died as a result of war-related famine.[4] But perhaps the worst effects are those on children's health. Hundreds of thousands of children have died because war has destroyed their chances of survival. According to UNICEF,

> Infant and child mortality rates in Angola and Mozambique are now estimated to be the highest in the world. The underlying cause is underdevelopment compounded by war and economic destabilisation, and the resulting set-backs and dislocations. The tragic consequence is that, every four minutes, a small child who would have lived if these set-backs had not occurred is dying in Angola and Mozambique.[5]

All economically underdeveloped countries experience the chronic problem of preventable child deaths, resulting from malnutrition and inadequate health services. In Mozambique and Angola the problem is made acute by conflict — conflict in which peasant agriculture and basic public services are the rebel guerrillas' targets.

Orphaned children

In these war-stressed countries, the killing of adults leads to especially vulnerable children, many of whom are suffering from serious emotional trauma as they struggle with the memory of brutal attack.

In Mozambique, an estimated 250,000 children have been orphaned or separated from their parents as a direct result of war,[6] while in Angola the number is conservatively estimated at 300,000.[7] Accurate estimates are hard to come by, because unknown numbers of orphaned children will have been taken in by family or friends, while others will be among the Angolan refugees in the neighbouring countries of Zaire, Zambia, and Namibia. However, orphanages have become increasingly necessary because the stresses of life in a ruined economy, together with the massive population upheavals caused as people flee from areas of conflict, have broken down social cohesion and the capacity of many extended families to take responsibility for orphans.

Social workers in Angola readily admit that they cannot cope with the large numbers of war orphans. There are registered war orphans in each of the country's provinces. By mid-1988, 2,344 were being cared for in permanent state-run centres, while 26,091 were in temporary homes or

Orphaned by MNR killings, these children have been temporarily resettled in shelters close to the garrison town of Espungabera in western Mozambique.   (Chris Johnson / Oxfam)

centres for want of more places in the established children's homes. [8]

'Lar Essanjo' is a state-run orphanage in Huambo, Angola, which cares for over 130 babies and children. The children come to the centre in many different ways. Some have been found wounded with their parents and taken, along with other casualties, to hospital. If the children survive and their parents do not, they are brought from the hospital to the centre. Government troops often find children alone in the ruins of their village after a UNITA attack, and bring them into care. Sometimes the children are brought by friends of the deceased family. By whatever route they come, these children are especially vulnerable. Usually frightened and disorientated, they are often also suffering from poor health. Dominga Cesar, the centre's Director, gave an example.

> A little girl arrived today. She has oedema of the legs and her hair has turned yellow — clear signs of malnutrition. She must see the doctor and be put on a special diet. We have special foods for these cases. But she also needs lots of love and attention, and with so many children here, it's hard to give them as much as they need.[9]

Many of the children who arrive are not yet old enough to speak. If nothing is known about them, they are named anew and the orphanage staff guess at their age and give them a birthday.

The children sleep in large dormitories, but the building is old and the roof leaks. Some parts of the upstairs rooms are unusable in the rainy season because of damp. The home has a small vegetable garden at the back. The produce from it not only helps to feed the children, but is also bartered for essential items such as rice, baby milk, and porridge when supplies run out.

Dominga Cesar and her colleagues achieve much in difficult conditions. They lack the resources they would like to have, yet they know that the children in their centre are receiving better care than the many thousands of war ophans who are living in temporary homes for lack of social service resources.

War-disabled people

Accurate assessments of the total number of war-wounded in Angola and Mozambique are unavailable, because war conditions and under-resourced government services prevent any systematic census. In Angola alone, the International Committee of the Red Cross estimates the numbers at between 20,000 and 40,000.[10] This means that Angola has the highest proportion of limbless citizens in the world.[11]

Not surprisingly, civilians are often caught in the cross-fire between UNITA and government troops. However, the great majority of the war-disabled civilians have been the victims of anti-personnel mines. People have triggered these off as they go about their everyday lives — while working in their fields, for instance, or while walking to and from their homes, or perhaps while riding in a lorry on their way to market in a neighbouring town. As the UN Africa Emergency Task Force reported, "It is calculated that 85 per cent of this number (i.e. war-disabled) suffer from leg handicaps, because most of the accidents are caused by anti-personnel mines."[12]

In Angola, the use of mines in civilian areas, homes, and places of work is widespread because of the nature of the war between UNITA and the MPLA government. UNITA has reportedly pursued a two-fold military strategy. Firstly, it aims to undermine the government through economic sabotage at all levels. And secondly, in creating widespread rural insecurity — by wrecking people's access to a stable livelihood, to basic services such as schools and health facilities, and to assured protection — UNITA aims to make people feel vulnerable, and therefore alienated from the government. Thus, the gruesome logic of UNITA's focus on economic and political destabilisation by military force, in a country where the majority of people make a living from peasant agriculture and animal husbandry, has meant that rural communities have been a principal target. The widespread and unpredictable nature of UNITA's raids on rural civilians has meant that the government is indeed unable to protect civilians adequately.

Government forces have also been known to use land mines, particularly in defence of strategically important installations like airstrips and garrison towns, but also indiscriminately in some UNITA-held areas.[13] There can be no doubt that civilian casualties have resulted from both sides' use of mines.

The war-disabled have created a serious additional strain on the country's deteriorating health and rehabilitation services. As the UN Emergency Task Force for Africa reported in 1988,

> Large-scale sabotage and destruction of health facilities, creches, orphanages, social welfare centres, and existing rural and urban health posts have been registered. The remaining operational facilities are heavily taxed by the constantly expanding numbers of traumatized, mutilated, and seriously ill persons, including numerous orphans or abandoned children ...[14]

Rehabilitation of the war-disabled in Angola

Twelve-year-old Selmira Salala is one of UNITA's landmine victims. Her village was attacked in 1985. As she fled the fighting, she stepped on a mine laid to maim those trying to escape. After hospital treatment she survived, but one leg had to be amputated. She was brought to the special prosthesis centre in Huambo, called Bomba Alta, where she has been fitted with an artificial limb. A worker at the centre explained, "Because she is still a child,

Laurinda Chinginila learning to walk again after losing both legs when she stepped on a UNITA landmine. Few war-disabled people in Angola are able to benefit from such rehabilitation services. (Akwe Amosu)

growing perhaps 3-4 cm a year, we have made her artificial leg slightly too long. As she grows and starts to feel it has become too short, she will know that it is time to make her way back here and have it adjusted. She will probably need a new limb every two to three years until she is 18, when she can have an adult-sized one."[15] All this depends on whether Selmira can keep returning to the centre.

Besides a new rehabilitation centre in Luanda, Bomba Alta is the only established centre catering for civilians in Angola. It can manufacture and fit up to 100 artificial limbs a month, but clearly this capacity falls far short of the needs. Anyone coming to Bomba Alta in need of treatment is accepted and treated free of charge, but shortages of transport and supplies create problems.

Although successful treatment at Bomba Alta enables patients to be mobile, many of the most badly wounded will not be able to undertake hard physical work again, and this creates more anxiety for people with no other means of earning a living.

Laurinda Chinginila, 25 years old and a mother of two children, is a case in point. She explained, "I will be able to get about, but I will never be able to work in my fields again." Laurinda was one of the centre's most badly wounded patients. Early in 1987, she stepped on a mine as she was walking home from her fields near Longonjo, 87 km from Huambo, with her baby on her back and her older child walking a few paces in front. Miraculously, her children were unhurt, but she lost both legs. She was taken to the provincial hospital and then brought to Bomba Alta. By April 1988, she was walking on her two new limbs. Staff at the centre said she had learned to do so exceptionally quickly: it had taken her only eight months to become proficient, rather than the usual 12 months or more.

Run by the Ministry of Health and the International Committee of the Red Cross (ICRC), the centre itself has been attacked by UNITA. In 1983, guerrillas destroyed workshops and vehicles belonging to the centre. In 1984, the centre's night-duty security guards were killed, a stores warehouse was burnt down, and some local people living nearby were attacked.[16]

The long-term consequences of war disability in Angola are also shocking. The ICRC estimates that rehabilitation centres for the victims of anti-personnel mines will still be needed thirty years from now. This assessment is based not only on the future needs of the children and young people who have already been wounded and will need help for decades to come, but also on the grim awareness that Angola's countryside is littered with undetonated mines, buried, and (in the case of plastic mines) undetectable.

Refugees and displaced people — flight and impoverishment

The large and growing numbers of displaced people, refugees, and those made destitute by war are a clear indicator of the sheer scale of suffering. South Africa's regional policy has been a key factor behind the suffering of well over 12 million Mozambicans and Angolans.[17] These people have either been forced to leave their homes, or they have managed to remain in their home areas but have been reduced to extreme poverty by the economic destruction which war has brought.[18]

Of these 12 million people, 8 million have had to leave their homes. They include an estimated 6.1 million displaced within their own countries, and some 1.89 million people who have had to flee as refugees to neighbouring states. In addition, some 4 million urban people are affected by the economic breakdown which war brings.

These statistics demonstrate that the human consequences of war reached crisis proportions by 1989. Over half of Mozambique's total population and over a third of Angola's total population were directly affected by conflict.[19]

The available statistics on displacement indicate orders of magnitude only. More accurate assessments of the numbers of people whom the war has displaced are hard to come by. It is difficult to count people on the move in a zone of conflict, or to judge whether people are fleeing attacks or leaving their homes to look for better economic prospects.

The sheer numbers of internally displaced people create serious problems for the local communities and state-run services looking after them. In the war-torn countries, the massive relief operations needed to help the displaced and destitute are fraught with problems. In the neighbouring countries hosting refugees, there are enormous strains on local resources and services. In Malawi, for example, there is a national average of one Mozambican refugee for every 10 Malawians.[20] And, because the refugees are concentrated in Malawi's most populous southern region, the local proportions are even higher. A proportionately equivalent number of refugees in the UK would be about 5 million, or more than the total population of greater Manchester.

One family's story

In the course of a few weeks, Merriam Kaumphawi — the matron of Nsanje District Hospital in southern Malawi, in the heart of the area with the largest concentration of Mozambican refugees — was 'adopted' by a family of three Mozambican orphans. Merriam recounted their story:

Merriam Kaumphawi with Domingo, Milia, and Rosa, the three Mozambican orphans who have adopted her, standing by her house at dusk.

(Susanna Smith / Oxfam)

I call them my children now and I feel very lucky to have them, even though I know that one day they will return to their home.

The children fled over the border in September 1986. They had lost their parents before their village was attacked, and were living with another family. They tagged along when the survivors of the attack fled, and they walked through the bush for three days and two nights to get to the border. The two older ones took turns carrying Rosa, the baby.

A few weeks after they arrived at the refugee settlement, Rosa was admitted to our hospital for care and special feeding; she had very severe malnutrition. On my rounds, I noticed that Rosa was not being properly washed and cared for. In our country, it is the relatives attending patients who are responsible for their everyday care. Then I found out that Rosa's nine-year-old sister, Milia, was the one staying with her and doing her best to look after her, but she didn't know about baby care. So I taught Milia how to wash Rosa, how to do her hair, keep her clothes clean, and feed her. And I asked her to let me know how Rosa was getting on and if there were any problems. After that, Milia would often come to find me for a chat and to report on Rosa's progress. She looked after her sister beautifully, and Rosa made a good recovery.

And, as Rosa got better, Milia started spending more and more time at my house, which is in the hospital grounds. Then their older brother, Domingo, made his way here from the refugee camp to find his sisters, and he too started spending time at my house. Before I knew it, they were living with me, and then when Rosa was well enough to be discharged, naturally she joined us.[21]

The scale of the refugee problem

1.265 million Mozambican refugees, the largest group, have taken refuge in Malawi, Zimbabwe, Zambia, Tanzania, Swaziland, and South Africa. Over 4 million Mozambicans have been displaced in their own country.

632,000 Angolan refugees are in Zambia, Zaire, and Namibia. 1.5 million Angolans have been displaced in their own country. (For comparison, 1989 estimates for the numbers of refugees worldwide — excluding people displaced within their own countries — range between 13 and 15 million.) In

Movements of mozambican and Angolan refugees in the 1980s

Angola and Mozambique many of those registered as displaced have had to move a number of times, either to avoid direct attack or to escape the collapsed rural economy. Changing military events mean that the fighting and insecurity have constantly shifted from one area to another.

As far as Angola is concerned, an Economist Intelligence Unit report of 1987 — at the time when the South African Defence Force was occupying large tracts of territory in southern Angola —— stated that up to nine tenths of the country were considered unsafe. "This does not mean that UNITA is solidly implanted over nine tenths of the country ... it is doubtful whether more than 250,000 people in the country as a whole (well under 5 per cent of the total population) are under UNITA 'administration' in any permanent or even semi-permananent sense. However, most of the rural population is not really administered by the Luanda government either. The key point is that most of Angola is insecure." [22]

Widespread social dislocation has been created. The sheer numbers of people who, whether voluntarily or not, have left their homes hint at the extent of social breakdown. But a mere headcount cannot describe the enduring effects of displacement.

Refugees' experiences

Many relief workers, in settlements for internally displaced people and for refugees alike, have noticed the vital importance of community cohesion for those surviving an attack. Tribal, village, and family networks often serve to rescue and sustain the survivors of attack.

One typical example is a group of Angolan refugees living in the remote village of Kayombo in north-western Zambia, just a few kilometres from the Angolan border. They fled to Zambia after a UNITA attack in November 1985. These people came from a closely knit group of small village settlements, which came under the traditional leadership of Chief Chipawa, who fled with his people. On arrival in Kayombo, they were granted land and hospitality by the traditional leader on the Zambian side, who is tribally related to them and therefore obliged to offer them refuge. Chief Chipawa explained how they came to be in Kayombo.

> We were attacked at eight in the evening when it was dark. There was no time for us to collect our things, we just had to run. But we knew where to come, because we have our relations here.

> Everything was destroyed in our place. They burnt our houses and our crops; all our animals were lost. We ran to save our lives. This was the second time that UNITA attacked us. The first time, there were some government troops there to defend our village. But when the second attack came, the soldiers had gone and we were alone. UNITA attacked with guns. It was too

confusing to know how many attackers there were.

When the attack came, we all scattered into the bush, and we made our way here in different groups. The group I was with took five days to get here. We walked through the bush and didn't meet any UNITA on the way, so we were able to walk during the day. But some of our people took ten days to reach us here. By the time everyone had arrived, we saw that nobody had been lost, but we came here with nothing.

On the way here, we lived on wild honey, bush fruits, and roots. We carried honey with us as we were walking, because it was a good thing to feed to our children.

We were very happy where we lived. We had everything we needed, plenty of maize, beans, groundnuts, sweet potatoes, banana and orange trees. When we hear the war is finished, then we will go back. For now, we want to stay in Kayombo because we have been helped here by the people. The chief has given us two limas of land (i.e. half a hectare) for each family, and the local mission has given us seeds and tools. The people in the village helped us with many things, and we are allowed to use the clinic and send our children to the school.

We feel peaceful here, we know that there is no need to fear. We can live together with our families here, and grow our food as we've always done.[23]

Most victims of attack, however, are not so lucky. For example, a whole village in the area bordering Kwanza Sul and Huambo Provinces in Angola fled from a UNITA attack. They had no better option than to walk 180 km to reach the refuge of an official resettlement scheme, a journey which took them weeks. As a result of this ordeal, the people who eventually arrived were all young adult men and women. The children and old people had not been able to withstand the journey.[24]

Many rural farming families, dependent on their crops and animals, are reluctant to move away from their villages. Maria Chingossi came from a village in Angola which had already moved once. She eventually fled with the rest of the village to a resettlement centre in 1985. After the fourth assault, the villagers agreed with the army that they would not survive renewed attack and, under the leadership of their chief and the school teacher, 84 people set out in the direction of Waco Kungo, a military garrison town.[25] Maria described the journey:

After the attack, we spent a week in the bush, sleeping out in the heavy rains. It was cold. We couldn't get back to the village because they were there destroying our huts and goods. After that, the army told us we could go back to our village, but we only stayed there for four days, because the bandits came back again. So the army decided that the people should leave because of the continuous killing.

That's the reason that brought me here. On the way here, we faced a lot of suffering in the rain, feeling hunger. Sometimes we had to push the children because they couldn't go on. There was no transport. It was only walking and suffering to save our lives.[26]

The constant threat of attack creates an atmosphere of fear and insecurity throughout the conflict-ridden areas. One international aid worker reported that in the eastern part of Angola's Moxico Province, for example, people move in and out of the towns according to their perceptions of the risk of UNITA attack.

Some people will choose to leave the town at night and sleep out in the bush, feeling that this is when UNITA is most likely to attack government offices in the town, while others will choose to stay in the town at night because they think this is more secure. They are afraid of being attacked in the bush - either by UNITA or by thieves, or by government troops mistaking them for UNITA in the dark. Much depends on the latest attack, or the latest rumour.[27]

Mr Ferreira is one of the community leaders of Muloza refugee camp in southern Malawi, just over the border from the Mozambican town of Milanje. He helps to organise the distribution of relief supplies among the camp's

Mr Ferreira (second from left), a community leader at the Muloza settlement for Mozambican refugees in Malawi, where he helps to organise relief distribution. In Mozambique he was a Customs official.   (Susanna Smith / Oxfam)

9,800[28] people, but he is also concerned about their psychological needs.

> We need things to do to keep our spirits up — we need to carry on with life.
> But there's very little land for us to work, and no employment for us in this
> area. We're hoping for permission to start up a school for the children. [29]

Case-study: Mozambican refugees in South Africa

In 1986 and 1987, in an attempt to seal the border with southern
Mozambique, the South African authorities electrified long sections of the
border fence near the town of Komatipoort. Part of this fence has two
settings — lethal and non-lethal. There are warning notices posted along the
fence, but many of the refugees trying to cross are illiterate.

Some 40-50 Mozambicans, desperate to escape the fighting in their home
areas, are estimated to have been killed by the fence.[30] Others have managed
to reach the other side by putting tree trunks across the fence, or shorting the
current. The fence is just one of the many frightening obstacles the refugees
have to negotiate as they try to find refuge in South Africa. Other
impediments include minefields, armed border guards, and the wild animals
in the Kruger National Park which runs along long stretches of the border.[31]

In August 1989, it was reported that in order to avert certain disaster,
South African officials had to dismantle part of the fence temporarily. An

*The South African authorities have built an electrified fence along stretches of the
border with Mozambique. Part of the fence has two voltage settings: lethal and non-
lethal.*   (Jenny Rossiter)

The South African "Homelands" hosting Mozambican refugees

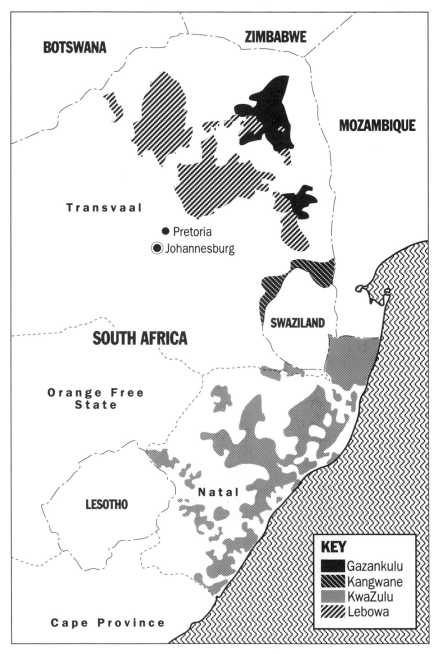

estimated 2,200 refugees, fleeing yet another MNR attack on the Mozambican border town of Ressano Garcia, were allowed through to Komatipoort.[32]

Refugee rights denied

Refugees from Mozambique have been crossing into South Africa since 1983, to escape the combined effects of war, economic breakdown, and periodic drought and flood.[33] Nobody is sure about the numbers, partly because Mozambican work-seekers have been crossing into South Africa for the last 100 years, many of them without official permission to work. By November 1989, Oxfam estimated there to be between 150,000 and 200,000 Mozambican refugees in South Africa,[34] with some 1,500 — 2,000 new arrivals coming over the border each month.[35] In addition to the refugee population, official statistics of the numbers of economic migrants from Mozambique estimate that there are 80,000 legal workers and 150,000 illegal workers.[36]

Once in South Africa, the refugees are subject to what one Oxfam fieldworker called 'transferred apartheid'. The South African government does not permit the United Nations High Commissioner for Refugees (UNHCR) to operate fully in the country, so refugees from Mozambique are not entitled to the basic protections normally provided for in refugee law. The most important right denied to them is the right to stay in the country of refuge until conditions permit fully voluntary repatriation — in technical jargon the right to 'non-refoulement'.

With no internationally protected rights, any refugees found in 'white' South Africa are considered to be 'illegal aliens', and repatriated forthwith.[37] The refugees are only allowed to stay in some of the 'homelands'. Oxfam fieldworkers reported that some 3,000 Mozambicans per month were repatriated from 'white' South Africa during 1988. In February 1989 an overloaded lorry, packed with refugees being sent back over the border, overturned, injuring several people and killing one woman.

Once they have been sent back over the border, many of the returnees find it impossible to travel back to their home areas. So they live in limbo in the border towns until they can travel back home. Elias Macundla was stranded in the Mozambican border town of Ressano Garcia for two years after he was forcibly repatriated from South Africa in 1985.

> We fled across the South African border when the 'bandidos' (MNR) attacked. Then we were arrested by the South African police and repatriated back here. But I can't get back to my home in Magude District because of the fighting, so I have to stay here and make a living doing odd jobs as best I can.[38]

Filipe Baloi from Chicualacuala also explained how he came to be living in limbo in Ressano Garcia:

> There are about 200 of us here from Gaza. We live here out in the open. I
> fled Chicualacuala with my family four weeks ago. The 'bandidos' robbed us
> of everything, including our five head of cattle. So we fled to South Africa,
> where we were captured by the police and put in prison for two weeks. Then
> we were repatriated.[39]

Although banned from 'white' South Africa, those refugees who manage
to evade capture are permitted temporary residential rights and access to relief
assistance in some of the 'homelands' nearest the border where many have
family links. Consequently, Mozambican refugees are to be found in the
'homelands' of Lebowa, Kangwane, Gazankulu, and Kwazulu.

Much of the relief assistance is provided by the churches and charities,
including Oxfam, which supports two kindergartens for refugee children in
Kangwane and Gazankulu. Although refugees also use the local 'homeland'
services (funded by Pretoria), this indirect contribution is thought to be all
that the South African government provides for the refugees.

In accordance with the 'grand apartheid' structure they have fled to, the
refugees are allowed to stay in the 'homelands' on condition they hold special
permits,[40] and do not trespass into 'white' South Africa. The 'homeland'
authorities had to seek special permission from Pretoria to allow refugees
even this limited amount of protection.[41]

Sadly, South Africa is not the only country where Mozambican refugees
have experienced the infringement of their rights. In Zimbabwe, where there
are an estimated 175,000 Mozambican refugees,[42] and despite the close ties
that exist between the Mozambican and Zimbabwean governments, an
estimated 10,000 refugees were forced to return back over the border in
1987.[43] Twelve to fifteen refugees were reported to have been killed in the
process.[44]

This 'refoulement' occurred as a result of heightened security tensions in
eastern Zimbabwe, an area which has been seriously affected by MNR cross-
border attacks from mid-1987 onwards. Further security-related restriction
measures were imposed on Zimbabwean citizens in the area, which included
the prohibition of cross-border trade, and the insistence that all border
crossings took place at the official border posts.

In November 1987, the Zimbabwean government recognised the
remaining Mozambicans as refugees entitled to protection under the relevant
instruments of the UN and Organisation of African Unity (OAU).[45] Although
a welcome move, it also meant that tens of thousands of long-settled
Mozambican economic migrants could be required to live in the designated
refugee camps, which were already greatly overcrowded.[46]

During the early months of 1988, however, further forced repatriations occurred (although they were much smaller in scale), and it is thought that some border actions aimed at MNR guerrillas had the effect of restricting new arrivals of Mozambicans.[47] Since then, the Zimbabwean government has told UNHCR that it does not condone further refoulement, and plans are under way to open up new refugee camps to relieve overcrowding in the four existing camps.[48]

Economic insecurity

Unemployment and the resulting poverty are already endemic problems in South Africa's 'homelands', and the arrival of thousands of Mozambican refugees only makes things worse. The refugees have almost no opportunity to earn a living there. Consequently, many have deliberately crossed into 'white' South Africa seeking work — often on the white farms of the Transvaal.[49]

In July 1989, local relief workers reported a recent case of gross exploitation. A white farmer had hired 30 Mozambican refugees staying in Gazankulu to work for him for three weeks. They agreed to labour on his farm for R3 (69 pence) per 12-hour day, payable weekly. After the first week, he paid them their wages. They received no money at the end of the second week. At the end of the third week, instead of paying them, the farmer reported them to the SADF as illegal aliens, whereupon they were directly deported back to Mozambique.

Economic insecurity is also a great problem for Mozambican refugees in Zimbabwe and Malawi, where land shortage and unemployment have meant there is little scope for the refugees to earn a living locally. In these countries, however, the governments have taken a much more responsible role in providing for the refugees they host.

Government responsibilities towards refugees

The plight of the Mozambican refugees in South Africa highlights two key issues. Firstly, there is an urgent need for proper international protection to be accorded to the refugees in South Africa.[50] And secondly, the refugees badly need better economic prospects, towards which the South African government should contribute.

Given the heavy burden of responsibility which the South African government bears for conflict in Mozambique, and given that an end to the war still appears remote, the South African government's treatment of the Mozambican refugees is all the more callous.

Food shortages and hunger

In Mozambique and Angola, serious food shortages, sometimes reaching famine proportions, have been caused and worsened by war. All aspects of food production, storage, marketing, and relief distribution have been adversely affected. Food imports to Mozambique and Angola are massive. For example, in 1989 the UN estimated that Mozambique needed US $237 m. worth of food aid for the following year.[51]

Food security[52] at national, regional, and household levels has been undermined, with devastating human consequences. For instance, in Mozambique a survey conducted among peasant farmers in four rural districts in early 1987 showed that some 60 per cent of households had no food stocks at all, and that only about 9 per cent had enough food to last until the next harvest. At national level, food security has closely mirrored the country's fortunes. Marketed food production rose steadily from independence in 1975 until 1982, when it began to collapse, due to drought and the disruption of the peasant agricultural economy by a number of other factors, including the government's damaging rural development policy. Production rose slightly with better rains, but recovery was reversed by war. During 1985/86 production collapsed, as conflict spread across large areas of the countryside. A modest increase in production in 1987 resulted from a rise in producer prices, and determined efforts by the government to redress previous policy errors by giving greater priority to the peasant production sector. Greatly intensified warfare in 1986/87 and erratic rains continued to disrupt food production, which rose in 1988/89 as a result of improved security.

In early 1989, war-related famine was experienced once again in Mozambique.[53] At least 3,500 people died of starvation in a coastal district of the northern Nampula Province, where drought had affected the harvest and MNR attacks had made it impossible to assess local relief needs. In addition, it was reported that 1,000 people a week were dying of hunger in the remote Gile and Ile districts of Zambezia Province. Most of them were people who had already been displaced by MNR attacks [54] and were living in relief camps whose supply routes had been cut off by the MNR. Oxfam field reports from Zambezia Province detail how MNR attacks frustrated the relief effort which had been mounted to reach the famine victims in Ile and Gile. One reported,

> The convoy which was carrying relief supplies to Ile was attacked just outside Namacurra, where it had stayed overnight. Sixteen trucks were burnt, and many goods lost. Seven of the trucks belonged to the government relief organisation. So no supplies have been getting through to Mocuba, let alone Ile. Then the train was attacked in early May, and since then there have been two more derailments. So next to nothing has been received in Mocuba for a month.[55]

Another read,

This week, all of us involved in the Zambezia emergency are feeling frustration, anger, and hopelessness at the increasingly grave situation. The horrific MNR attack on Inhassunge, made international by the barbaric killing of three Italian priests (the autopsies confirmed that they were bayonetted to death), and the disappearance of a fourth, is only part of the story.

Gile is in a pitiful state, with 87,000 displaced people who are sick and starving. A small plane airlift may begin in a week's time, but we have reports that 140 people are dying every day, and at least 750 tons of food a month are required. That would need 42 trips a day in the TTA Islander (the only plane available)! How can this District be supplied?[56]

Reliable and comprehensive statistics on the nutritional status of people in the war-torn areas are hard to come by. Oxfam, UNICEF, and other relief organisations have, however, confirmed that there are serious problems in Angola and Mozambique.[57]

People who have been displaced by conflict are particularly vulnerable to malnutrition and ill health. Having had to flee their own land, even those who are fortunate enough to have reached the safety of an official settlement find that it takes some time to re-establish food production. Relief rations are often inadequate or erratically delivered. For example, the nutritional status of the Mozambican refugees in Malawi was found to be declining in 1989, because of inadequate food rations, distribution problems, and the very limited economic options open to refugees outside the official settlements.[58]

The marketing and distribution of what food is grown is also hampered by war. Ricardo Joao is a local director for AGRICOM, the state-run agricultural production and marketing agency, in Mozambique's Zambezia Province. He explained,

Reaching the outlying districts is very difficult. The roads have been cut, which means we can't transport produce. Very often, we manage to buy and store produce only to find that the 'bandidos' (MNR guerrillas) then burn it.

AGRICOM is a target because we are responsible for marketing food in the rural areas. Our transport fleet has suffered great damage. About 30 vehicles have been destroyed, and we are left with only nine.

Even in the accessible areas, drought has reduced production. We have also had problems with the lack of goods like cloth, salt, sugar, and soap, things which people can't produce themselves and want to buy. Unless these things are in the rural shops, the peasant producers will not accept cash for their produce. At the moment we have these commodities, but we can't transport them out to the rural areas.[59]

An account of the statistics of human suffering runs the risk of dehumanising the reality of people's lives. Many Oxfam field workers agree that it has been their personal experiences which have really made an impression. One Oxfam worker in Malawi wrote,

June marks the beginning of the cold season in Mankhokwe, the largest of the camps for Mozambican refugees in Malawi. Thousands and thousands of people were crowded together in the light drizzle on the flat land alongside the Shire river. Suddenly, someone called out. I turned round and, a few yards away, I saw an elderly woman beckoning me over. She was huddled over a small fire made within a circle of stones. When I reached her, she held out her hand to help me crouch down next to her, which meant she then had to rearrange the torn piece of sacking which she had drawn round her. It was her only piece of clothing, and most probably her only possession because, as I later learned, she had just arrived at the camp after fleeing an MNR attack on her village.

We had no common language, but through the international medium of gestures and emphasised speech she described the attack, the chaos, the fear, and how she had fled into the bush, bent over to avoid being seen. She was

Down but not out, a newly-arrived refugee at Mankhokwe settlement in southern Malawi.

(Oxfam)

intent on telling her story. I think it was a way of exorcising the trauma. The thing which most struck me was her anger and defiance. She had an unmistakable proud and dignified feeling about herself. She left me in no doubt that she was down, but by no means out. When she had finished, she gestured that I should take her photograph as if to seal her meaning.[60]

Victims of brutality

Systematic brutality against civilians has been a hallmark of the conflicts in Mozambique, Angola, and Namibia.[61]

Mozambique

In Mozambique, besides attacking economic infrastructure and government services (agricultural support schemes, and health, education, and food relief services), the MNR deliberately target civilians, often using mass terror as their instrument. Their apparent objectives are to frighten the population into submission and, having caused widespread breakdown in commerce and civil administration, to ensure that large areas of the country remain ungovernable.

Villages, food stores, health centres and staff, hospitals, schools and teachers, agricultural training centres, roads and railways, government vehicles, power lines — in short, anything of any use to anyone — have all been systematically attacked and destroyed.

Although much remains to be documented about the nature of the MNR (see Chapter 2 for a fuller discussion), their calculated brutality has been recorded in detail. A 1988 US State Department research mission interviewed 200 Mozambican refugees in depth about their experiences of conflict. Interviews were conducted in 42 different locations in five countries. The final report concludes,

> First, the level of violence reported to be conducted by RENAMO (MNR) against the civilian population of rural Mozambique is extraordinarily high ... it is conservatively estimated that 100,000 civilians may have been murdered by RENAMO ...
>
> ... refugees report ... systematic forced portering, beatings, rape, looting, burning of villages, abductions, and mutilations.
>
> Second, the relationship between RENAMO and the civilian population, according to refugee accounts, revolves almost exclusively around a harsh extraction of labour and food. If these reports are accurate, it appears that the only reciprocity provided by RENAMO for the efforts of the civilians is the possibility of remaining alive ... The refugees report virtually no effort by RENAMO to explain to civilians the purpose of the insurgency, its proposed program or its aspirations ...
>
> Third, there were serious complaints about abuses by some FRELIMO

Government soldiers. But ... only three to four per cent of the complaints were attributed to FRELIMO soldiers. They tended to be isolated reports, often from the areas of the country most remote from Maputo.

Fourth, the refugees and most independent sources rejected the assertion that much of the violence in Mozambique is attributable to neither FRELIMO or RENAMO but instead to armed bandits affiliated with neither side. It appears ... that violence by 'freelance bandits' does not account for more than the occasional, isolated instances of the high level of reported violence.[62]

Mr Sandufombe is a Mozambican refugee living in Kunyinda settlement for Mozambican refugees in south-western Malawi. He was captured by the MNR and forced to be a porter and labourer.

I was taken during the attack on our Chief's village,[63] and we were made to walk and carry goods to Gorongosa in Sofala Province. We walked day and night. You can see that I have a false leg, so it was very difficult for me.

When we got to their place, I was made to farm. We were kept as prisoners, split into groups and guarded while we worked. All the food we grew was for RENAMO. They gave us rations so that we could work.[64]

Mr Sandufombe was captured by the MNR and forced to work as a porter and then as an agricultural labourer in Mozambique's Sofala Province.

(John Clark / Oxfam)

Nene Bonjes, 7 years old, was kidnapped by the MNR in August 1986, and was not reunited with his family until four months later. The day he was captured, his mother had left their hut to go and draw water. She heard gunshot sounds, and ran back to find the child gone. "He was very thin when I got him back," she recalled.[65]

Nene Bonjes (centre foreground) and his mother, with a younger child. He was captured during an MNR raid on their village, and held for four months.

(Susanna Smith / Oxfam)

Angola

In Angola, the effects of conflict on the population have not been so well documented as they have been in Mozambique. Nevertheless, it is clear that UNITA has captured and mistreated civilians. At Becon settlement for displaced people in central Angola, Francisco M'Bule, a traditional leader, told his story.

> UNITA attacked Cabolo where I used to live, and we were taken to the bush. They didn't take us far — just to the mountains some kilometres from the village. They took about half of us, some 210 people.

We had no clothing, no salt, and very little to eat. It was misery. We were naked as if we were animals. They stole our cattle, and they ate our pigs. We lived like this for five months.

Our work was to transport stolen food from nearby villages to support UNITA's operation. During that five months, many of us were wounded. We weren't at a military base, that was far away. It was just a small group of UNITA guarded by ten armed men.

These UNITA people took us to a meeting where the leaders claimed they were governing the country and that in the very near future they would give us cars, good condition houses, clothes, and food. By the end of five months, we hadn't seen any of these things.

I got away by running, even though there was heavy gunfire from UNITA ... the soldiers had intimidated us so that we wouldn't try, all the paths were mined. This is why we stayed for so long.[66]

Luisa Vita Saluta, a woman who escaped UNITA at the same time, recalled the situation of women in the UNITA-held area where she lived.

For us married women there was no problem except that we had to give 'fuba' (maize flour), bananas, sweet potatoes, anything we had to feed UNITA 'visitors', whom we never saw. But we had to make our single girls run away and hide because if we didn't they would be taken.[67]

Luisa Vita Saluta, who escaped UNITA captivity, seen here singing and dancing to welcome visitors to the resettlement camp for displaced people at Waco Kungo.

(Akwe Amosu)

In Waco Kungo transit centre for newly arrived displaced people, more people reported on their experiences. Adolfo Cupessala was held for one and a half years by UNITA at a base near Kassongue. He said,

> We were treated badly by UNITA. We had to work like slaves. They gave us no soap, no clothes, and no salt. UNITA told us that everyone who lives in an MPLA area (i.e. in an area controlled by the government) was a slave to the Cubans and Soviets. They told us we would only have to work for three years and that Angola would be independent, then everybody would dress well and have everything ... On the other hand, they threatened that if we didn't work well we would get beaten. I saw some people who didn't obey and they got 150 lashes. Some were tied to trees and shot for trying to escape, or refusing to work.[68]

Fernanda Shopeto was pregnant when she was captured, and she had her baby at a UNITA base. She later reported,

> Women who got separated from their own men were forced to join men there. If they didn't, UNITA would say they were trying to escape.[69]

Zimbabwe

In Zimbabwe, the conflict in Mozambique is also causing serious problems for the people living along the eastern border. Since mid-1987, MNR cross-border attacks have increased, causing widespread fear, and over 300 deaths.

An elderly man who lives in an area of Zimbabwe near to the border with Mozambique told Oxfam about the day when MNR guerrillas murdered his wife, his two daughters, and his granddaughter. The child was strapped to his wife's back when the MNR came. They threw the baby into the cooking fire, where she was burnt to death. Her grandmother had to watch her die, before they killed her too. He said,

> It is something which I cannot forget — the brutality and the callousness. It is one thing when you hear about MNR atrocities far away in the next District. But when it happens to you, in your own home and to your own wife and children, then it is something different. [70]

MNR attacks in eastern Zimbabwe follow a similar pattern to those in Mozambique. The attacks appear intended to instil fear and uncertainty into the local population. The guerrillas generally come into villages at night. In many of the affected areas, the villages are widely dispersed: the neighbouring village may be a kilometre away. The 'bandits' often attack people with machetes and knives; it is thought that this is done to save scarce ammunition, and in order not to raise the alarm or alert the army. They often also loot the village or homestead, and carry away any food and clothing they need. A villager in Chipinge District described the situation in his area:

> Over the last year, we know of 26 people who have been killed in this area, and more than 500 cattle have been stolen.

The last murders around here were just a few weeks ago, on 6 August (1988), when six people were hacked to death in a nearby village. We all sleep in the bush now, but spend the days at our homes. Although the army is around this area, they cannot be present in every home at night, so it is necessary to sleep out. In the morning, many families have found their homes ransacked.[71]

As more army troops have been posted to the border regions, so more MNR guerrillas are reported to have been captured. However, since most of the areas which have been attacked are within 20 km of the border, the guerrillas are easily able to escape after an attack.

Case-study: The effects of war in Namibia

Namibia has been a key part of South Africa's regional policy ever since it was first entrusted, in 1920 under a League of Nations mandate, to be administered by the government of the Union of South Africa on behalf of the 'British Crown'. However, as a colony, Namibia was not technically an object of South African destabilisation, as it had no independent government of its own to be destabilised. Nevertheless, the people of Namibia have known the worst excesses of South African domination for over 70 years, and the SADF occupied the country from 1966 until the peace agreement of December 1988 was implemented. Throughout this time, the whole of northern Namibia, the most populous part of the country, was living under military rule as the conventional forces of the SADF waged war against SWAPO guerrillas. In a country with a population of only 1.7 million,[72] the numbers of occupying troops reached 100,000 in the mid-1980s.[73] All along, it was clearly a war which needed a political solution, not a military one. Yet the South African government's intransigence on the question of independence prolonged the suffering and destruction.[74]

One of the principal strategies of the occupying forces was to prevent civilian assistance to SWAPO guerrillas by using harsh 'counter-insurgency' tactics. The police and the regular armed forces were greatly feared by civilians, but the notorious special forces known as 'Koevoet' (Afrikaans for 'crowbar') were the most feared of all. Oxfam partners have been among many Namibians harassed by the security forces. Although the overwhelming majority of human rights abuses were committed by South African forces, it must also be noted that SWAPO tortured some of the people it had detained in its camps in exile; others are still unaccounted for.[75]

The effects of war on Namibia's people have been complex and various. As Namibia's first decade of independence begins in 1990, it is important to acknowledge the high price which people have paid, and to bear in mind the enduring effects of 22 years of war.

The impact on families

Numerous Oxfam field reports have stressed the far-reaching effects of this war on family life. Families were divided as their young people left the country to join SWAPO in exile, or as they were recruited and conscripted into the South African security and military forces. At least 10,000 people lost their lives between 1966 and 1989.[76] Most families have grieved over the loss of relatives killed in the fighting. Many have been killed indiscriminately, as in the case of two-year-old Marcelina Kamulungu, who was crushed to death in 1987 by a South African armoured vehicle which drove through her family's hut.[77] Mourning became an everyday occurrence, and many of Oxfam's partners suffered personally. In a 1988 field report from northern Namibia following a bomb blast, an Oxfam worker wrote,

> It was heartbreaking to be shown two rings, a watch, and a piece of material — all that was left of Matron Shangala of Oshakati hospital and the wife of the pastor who took me to Okahao on my last trip.

Brutality, intimidation and repression

The occupying forces' brutal treatment of civilians became a hallmark of the war, and has been documented by a number of independent sources.[78] Oxfam support for a church-run Namibian human rights organisation brought us into contact with many everyday cases of abuse by the security forces against civilians. For example, in 1988 Oxfam supported the establishment of a branch in Ongwediva, in the heart of the occupied 'war zone', because of the growing number of civilian complaints. As one complainant explained,

> We need a human rights centre here because we can't take our complaints to the police. After all, you don't ask the snake which has bitten you for help.[79]

The Ongwediva centre took up the case of Mrs Nafine, whose story was typical. In September 1988 Mrs Nafine was assaulted by eight SADF soldiers. She alleged,

> They slapped me in the face, beat me with fists, kicking me in the ribs, both right and left with their boots, and one hit me hard with a rifle butt in the chest.

According to Mrs Nafine, the soldiers demanded that she submit to them sexually, but she told them to

> ... kill me rather than rape me. Then they said they were the people who hurt the civilians, and that they can do anything they want to me because I don't know them.

They took some money from her and left.[80]

Displacement and upheaval

In addition to the people (approximately 50,000[81]) who left the country to become refugees, insecurity and forced relocations meant that 300,000[82] people in the 'war zone' were displaced over the years. It has been estimated that close to 250,000 people (nearly 15 per cent of Namibia's total population, including those who were in exile) in the Ovamboland region of northern Namibia left their villages, either because of the insecurity or because they were forced to leave as the security forces created 'clear-fire zones' (where guerrillas could be 'hunted' without heed to the danger of civilians being caught in the crossfire). Most of them moved to a triangular section of land, some 30 km long and 20 km wide between Ondangua and Oshakati, which became a sprawling and squalid shanty settlement.[83]

Effects on health, education, and small-scale agriculture

The real blocks to establishing appropriate health, education, and agricultural support services for the black majority during South Africa's illegal occupation were political.[84] Nevertheless, conflict made things significantly worse for the people living in the war zone. Patients' access to hospitals and clinics was severely limited by the war-zone curfew, as well as by the everyday risks of travel: land mines and arbitrary harassment by the security forces were the main problems. Outreach health services, offering preventive health care, were also badly affected. An estimated 70,000 children and adults died from preventable causes, attributable to malnutrition and inadequate health services.[85]

Children's schooling was also affected by the war. Not only was the everyday journey to school risky, but according to reports from Oxfam partners, the security forces regularly harassed schoolchildren and teachers, and sometimes attacked school premises.[86]

A deeply resented element of South Africa's political strategy to win the 'hearts and minds' of the civilian population in the war zone was that of placing military health and education personnel in local hospitals and schools, to reinforce a crude propaganda drive to influence local people, and particularly children, against SWAPO.[87]

Small-scale peasant agriculture was also seriously undermined by the war. One reason was the population upheavals: significant numbers of people in the north were driven from their land and their farms into the no-hope existence of impoverished urban shanties, and thousands of men left the 'homeland' areas to join either SWAPO or the security forces. A second reason was that the standing crops of those who stayed on in the rural areas were frequently destroyed by the army as their armoured trucks were driven across crops, and often through homesteads.

It is impossibe to list exhaustively all the human costs of conflict and occupation in Namibia, not only because the war became a way of life for a whole generation, but also because many of the costs remain to be counted. For example, the role which the military occupation played in erosion of the !Kung people's culture cannot be quantified,[88] and the environmental damage caused by the security forces' deforestation and land clearance tactics remains to be assessed.

Perhaps the most critical issue concerns the children and young people of Namibia. The future of the newly independent country rests on them, yet the only life they know has been under apartheid or in exile.

Oxfam's work

Oxfam's work in southern Africa has developed a great deal since it started in the early 1960s, and has spanned a significant period in the history of the region. Having started with one field worker, Oxfam now has six local offices in southern Africa, and an annual grants expenditure of £4.9 million, which represents 20.6 per cent of the total worldwide grants spending.[89]

The diversion of resources from development to relief

Oxfam's work during the 1980s has been greatly affected by the devastating impact of conflict. Responding to the enormous humanitarian needs has not only stretched our resources, our staff, and volunteers, but it has grown to the point where emergency relief now accounts for 56 per cent of our total grant expenditure in the region,[90] and 20.6 per cent of our emergency relief grants worldwide. Even though it is more needed than ever before, we have had to rein in expansion of our development work in southern Africa in order to meet urgent relief needs.

The growing proportion of funds diverted to relief work from development is especially evident in Mozambique and Malawi. In Malawi, 57 per cent of Oxfam's 1988/89 grants expenditure went on the relief needs of the Mozambican refugees.[91] In Mozambique, Oxfam spent £9.6 million on relief work between 1986 and 1989,[92] and although we are not normally an agency that sends personnel into the field, we have had to recruit 30 staff to work on the emergency programme over the last five years.

Oxfam has been able to maintain a small-scale development programme in the northern Mozambican Province of Cabo Delgado. It was designed with a number of components: research into how best to support local cooperative groups of rural artisans; the provision of two trucks to service the area's need for basic supplies; the training of health workers; and several adult literacy projects. It was only possible to establish this work in the first place because the area had not been affected by conflict. However, in late 1988, the MNR moved into some of the districts where Oxfam was working, with the result that our work has had to be curtailed. Staff are not permitted to travel freely, so some training follow-up and supervisory visits have had to be called off. Security fears also hamper local meetings and the movement of supplies.[93] The health training work has been the most affected, and has been considerably reorganised as a result of the continuing fear of attack.

As war grinds on, so the human needs continue to mount, in spite of the high level of international aid which is poured into the region. In Mozambique, Oxfam's relief work has concentrated on supplying seeds, tools, clothing, blankets, and, in some cases, foodstuffs. To help overcome a major constraint facing relief work in the country, we have also assisted with transport — providing trucks and maintenance and repair facilities. Where necessary, we have also mounted airlifts to areas isolated by the MNR.[94]

Special needs

As Oxfam's relief programme continues, we have learned more about the human needs which the brutality of war in the region has created. The widespread emotional trauma suffered by so many survivors of attack deserves special attention. UNICEF reports:

> Trauma among children is widespread, although very incompletely documented and even less generally treated. In Mozambique, estimates of children traumatised, orphaned or abandoned run from 250,000 to 500,000, or up to 10 per cent of the age-group. Work in a Mozambican refugee camp in Zambia suggests a still higher percentage among refugees. For Angola, no firm estimates exist, but 250,000 would seem plausible ... Most of these children have seen relatives and friends butchered as well as their homes destroyed.[95]

While Oxfam's relief assistance has focused on physical necessities, it has become increasingly clear that the victims of terror attacks also need help to overcome emotional brutalisation. Government relief officials have stressed these special needs, particularly among children.

In the provincial Angolan town of Huambo there is a children's centre which cares for war orphans, many of whom arrived there in a deeply traumatised condition. The Director of the Centre described the case of a small boy in her care.

> This little boy arrived a few days ago. He has kwashiorkor, which is easily treated in comparison to his other problem, emotional trauma. Our children often cry in their sleep, but this little one also bursts out crying when he's awake. He hasn't talked yet. We think he's re-living the experience of seeing his parents killed.
>
> We have all the children's histories, as far as they are known, which helps us.

Francesco Mangane Sigao, who saw his family hacked to death by the MNR, has withdrawn into complete silence. He lives in a government-run centre which specialises in rehabilitating traumatised children.   (Keith Bernstein / Oxfam)

We talk to the children and we try to take away their timidness. At first, they don't speak. It can take a very long time before they begin to talk back to us.[96]

The scale of this problem is daunting. As one of Oxfam's emergency officers explained,

There is no doubt that long-term facilities for counselling and special care are needed. Obviously, material emergency assistance which Oxfam and other international agencies normally provide in disaster situations cannot deal with psychological damage. But even in the provision of material goods, there are small things we can do. For example, we have deliberately included clothing and blankets amongst the emergency relief goods going to the Mozambican refugees and displaced people.

Some people have criticised us for this, arguing that these items are not strictly essential for survival. But from talking with refugee representatives and local relief workers, we've come to learn that there are many dimensions to immediate human need. People who've survived vicious attack, who are in deep shock and distress, need and deserve the comfort of something to wrap round themselves and their children at the very least. But of course, it's no answer to their situation, it's just relief in its simplest form.

Mozambican relief workers unloading food for displaced people at Inhassunge, Zambezia Province, in February 1987.

(Keith Bernstein / Oxfam)

Relief aid under fire

But even this simplest of humanitarian gestures is affected by conflict. The logistics of moving emergency supplies to war-torn rural areas are fraught with difficulty. As outlined above, in Mozambique, shortages of fuel, vehicles, and spare parts make it difficult to move goods to isolated rural areas. Humanitarian work is attacked and deliberately disrupted by the MNR. The numerous attacks on relief warehouses and convoys, on settlements for displaced people and refugees, and on expatriate aid workers, prove that even emergency aid is considered a legitimate target.

For example, Oxfam's programme during 1987-88, to airlift seeds, agricultural tools, clothing, blankets, and other essential supplies to people in three Districts of Niassa Province in northern Mozambique, was dogged by MNR attacks. Oxfam was flying relief supplies to these areas because, as explained in an Oxfam UK telex to sister agencies,

Unloading relief supplies from an Oxfam airlift in Mozambique's Niassa Province, one of the many areas isolated by war.

(Frances Rubin / Oxfam)

THERE ARE NUMEROUS DISPLACED PEOPLE IN THESE AREAS. ADDED DIFFICULTY IS THAT SOME AREAS CAN ONLY BE REACHED BY LIGHT AIRCRAFT. RAILWAY TO COAST IS CUT (i.e. the Nacala line) WITH RESULT THAT LARGEST TOWN, LICHINGA, ALMOST WITHOUT FUEL. HENCE ONWARD DISTRIBUTION OF FOOD TO REMOTER AREAS, EVEN VIA THE FEW PASSABLE ROADS, IS VERY SLOW.[97]

As the Oxfam worker responsible for organising these airlifts explained,

We are flying supplies into Niassa Province because the MNR, the 'bandits' as everyone here calls them, deliberately attack road and rail traffic. Of course, air transport is the most expensive way of moving goods, but it was a question of necessity because drought had ruined two successive harvests and people had nothing left to plant for the following season.

Even so, on several occasions after we've flown a consignment of clothing and blankets to one of the distribution points, groups of MNR guerrillas have come soon afterwards. They scare away all the people who have gathered to

Mozambican children with their home-made toy models of Oxfam's relief planes.

(Lars Gronseth / Oxfam)

come soon afterwards. They scare away all the people who have gathered to receive our goods, and then they take things for themselves. What they don't want, they pile up and burn. That is typical of what the people here have to live with, destruction and more destruction until there is an end to the war.

We have thought deeply about this problem of attacks, and asked ourselves whether our airlifts are not just attracting more problems for the people we want to help. But it's the people themselves who say they really want us to continue, and that they don't want the MNR attacks to succeed in isolating their communities during this time of need.

It's not just that people want the relief goods, of course they do. But the thing which has struck me, which people have stressed over and over again, is that our airlifts also boost morale. To understand this, you have to imagine what it's like to live in the war-torn areas. Not only is fear of attack an everyday stress, but also war has sealed people off from the rest of the country, from normal traffic and trade. And so the arrival of the old DC3 airlift planes is a welcome break from the tedium of isolation. You only have to see the perfectly detailed little wire and wooden DC3 models the local children have made, complete with moving propellors, and the way they charge along holding them up in the air as our planes come in, to understand what I mean.

In April 1988 a fuel tanker purchased by Oxfam to help ease the transport bottlenecks which constantly hamper the distribution of relief goods in Mozambique was destroyed when MNR guerrillas ambushed an emergency relief convoy. The tanker cost £30,000, as much as a typical Oxfam shop raises in one year. The incident was reported in a telex from Oxfam Maputo to Oxfam headquarters,

28 April 1988:

ON 20 APRIL, MANDIMBA CONVOY ATTACKED.   7 VEHICLES IN CONVOY WITH MILITARY ESCORT.   ATTACKED 45 KM FROM LICHINGA.   WHEN AMBUSH TOOK PLACE DRIVER OF IVECO TRUCK WAS SHOT THROUGH FLOOR BUT KEPT GOING AND MADE IT TO LICHINGA.

FURTHER BACK IN THE CONVOY A GOVERNMENT AGRICULTURE DEPT VEHICLE TRIED TO TURN ROUND BUT WAS SHOT AT. DRIVER LOST FINGERS OF RIGHT HAND SO UNABLE DRIVE AND TRUCK STUCK ACROSS ROAD.

THE TRUCKS BEHIND HIM TURNED AND ESCAPED BUT FUEL TANKERS AND NISSAN WERE TRAPPED BETWEEN MNR AND AGRICULTURE TRUCK.   THE SECOND OXFAM FUEL TANKER WAS DESTROYED ON ITS MAIDEN VOYAGE PLUS ANOTHER LEYLAND TRUCK CARRYING PETROL.

THE NISSAN TRUCK WAS CARRYING OXFAM COOKING OIL AND RICE. IT WAS HIT BUT NOT DESTROYED.   OXFAM OIL AND RICE STOLEN BY MNR.   THE DRIVER OF FUEL TANKER ESCAPED, OTHER 2 DRIVERS STILL MISSING.   NOT SURE IF KILLED OR KIDNAPPED.

MNR attacks have also destroyed Oxfam emergency supplies in warehouses. For example, in July 1987 Oxfam staff in Mozambique telexed Oxfam's headquarters with the following news:

COASTAL TOWN OF MABALA ATTACKED ON 17 JULY. WAREHOUSE, CONTAINING GOODS EN ROUTE TO DISTRIBUTION CENTRE, WAS DESTROYED.   GOODS LOST WERE:

1 TONNE SOAP (SCF — Save the Children Fund)

47 TONNES BEANS

56 BOXES DOMESTIC UTENSILS (SCF)

10 BOXES OXFAM CLOTHES

226 BOXES COOKING OIL (OXFAM)

SEEMS DELIBERATE STRATEGY TO ATTACK WAREHOUSES CONTAINING RELIEF GOODS.[98]

Relief from relief?

As war drags on, so the need for war-related emergency relief continues. The fieldworker in charge of organising Oxfam's relief distribution programme in Mozambique's Zambezia Province says,

We are really beginning to wonder whether the outside world hasn't just got used to Mozambique's disaster - whether there is any point in hoping for international action to bring an end to this horrible war. In my job, I have to face the senselessness and misery of this war every day. The random brutality of MNR attacks makes relief work a very uncertain business. Just when you think the crisis in one area has been sorted out another one blows up, and more people are suddenly made destitute.

This year, we are asking Oxfam's fundraisers to find over £800,000 for our relief work in Zambezia Province alone. Just imagine what that amount of money could do if it were invested in a peaceful Mozambique.[99]

How conflict disrupts relief and development work

As Oxfam has learned, the effects of conflict in southern Africa are far-reaching. War in Angola and Mozambique has all but destroyed local-level development work and community services. But conflict has also affected such work even in those countries not at war. Two case studies illustrate the way this has happened.

Case-study l: Mozambican refugees in Malawi

Background

The destruction of settled communities by conflict in southern Africa creates problems which can overwhelm not only refugees and displaced people themselves, but also the host communities and local services and resources. While the largest numbers of internally displaced people in southern Africa are in Mozambique, Malawi hosts the largest number of refugees -— a burden which has created many humanitarian and development problems.

By December 1989, there were an estimated 790,000 Mozambican refugees in Malawi, most of them living in specially designated settlements along Malawi's long southern border which dips deep into northern Mozambique.

Influx peaks

The flow of refugees into Malawi responds directly to events in Mozambique. Over the last few years, the steady stream of refugees crossing the border to

*Mozambican refugees collecting food rations at Mankhokwe settlement in southern
Malawi, January 1987.*   (Mike Edwards / Oxfam)

flee 'routine' rebel attacks on their villages has suddenly risen as crisis
overtakes large numbers of people. When there have been concerted military
clashes between government troops and the Mozambican National Resistance
(MNR), increased levels of displacement are inevitable, and this has made
planning the relief effort especially difficult.

The massive increase in the number of refugees who fled into Malawi
during 1987 and 1988 was caused by the military advances into MNR-held
territory made by Mozambican government troops over that period.

As government forces moved into rebel-held territory, thousands of people
who had been confined in these areas fled from their captors,[1] thus creating a
marked increase in the numbers of displaced people needing humanitarian
assistance both inside and outside Mozambique.

For example, in September 1986 an MNR offensive on Milanje town had
sent thousands of people over the nearby border into Malawi, where Muloza
camp was established (a few hundred yards from the border, on low-lying
land prone to flooding). When government troops retook the same town, in
June 1988, an estimated 18,000 more refugees poured over the border.
According to these refugees' reports, FRELIMO officials told them to "run to
Malawi until we can assure you that Milanje will be protected on a permanent
basis".

Many of these refugees were later moved to another settlement in Malawi. According to Oxfam reports, this was done both to relieve congestion at Muloza settlement and to defuse political tension. Conflict had arisen between some of the refugees from the 1986 MNR offensive, and some of those who arrived after the 1988 government offensive. Those who 'stayed on' after the MNR took control of Milanje were held in political suspicion by many of the refugees who had fled at that time.

Another example occurred on 6 June 1988, when Mozambican government troops attacked an MNR-held area near Tengani, just south of Nsanje, Malawi's southernmost District town. The result was a sudden influx of some 23,000 refugees, bringing the total refugee population in the District up to approximately 232,000.[2] Of all the areas in Malawi where refugees are concentrated, Nsanje is the District with the highest numbers. In mid-1988 there were over 30,000 more refugees than Malawians,[3] and it is a particularly poor and drought-prone area.

Harvest time can also be particularly dangerous, as refugees have explained.[4] When standing crops are ready to eat, villages in the insecure areas are frequently raided and the harvest taken.

Mozambican refugees in southern Malawi carrying sorghum and firewood. Land shortage means that natural resources such as thatching grass, firewood, and poles for building are increasingly scarce in this area.   (Ken Wilson)

Strain on government services

The influx of refugees has put a great strain on the Malawian government's local services and administration. In Nsanje District, for example, the District Commissioner's office is responsible for government services in the area. From September 1986 onwards, when the first big influx of refugees arrived in this District, his office had to cope with the local coordination of relief work, as well as the registration of all new refugees. In mid-1987 he explained,

> The population of this District has nearly doubled, and the strain on our services is enormous, because the refugees are highly dependent on relief assistance. By the time the refugees get here, many are in a pathetic condition.

> Our health services are also under pressure. The District hospital is having to cope with the increased numbers. And we are worried by the high incidence of TB among the refugees, and the potential risk of a cholera outbreak, because clean water supplies in the camp are totally inadequate.[5]

The influx of refugees has also exacerbated Malawi's already acute land pressure, thus worsening environmental degradation. The enormous quantities of relief goods which need to be moved around the country have also damaged roads and bridges.

Sabotage of trade routes

MNR sabotage of Malawi's trade routes out through Mozambique to the coast (and, until 1987, the land route through Mozambique to Zimbabwe) presents extra logistical problems for the relief agencies.

During 1986 and 1987 Oxfam had to fly in relief supplies for the refugees, at great extra expense. The importation of food aid has also been made all the harder by the disruption of transport routes. In mid-1987, for example, as relief demands had exhausted Malawi's domestic maize stocks, the World Food Programme (WFP) was importing maize bought in Zimbabwe via Mozambique's then insecure Tete Province. The WFP representative in Lilongwe explained,

> It is cheaper to get the food aid we need to use in the southern areas of Malawi in through Tete than the long way round through Zambia, although it is more risky. Our trucks have to travel in militarily-protected convoys, and the risks mean that we can't always rely on buying food from Zimbabwe because the costs of transport either through Tete or through Zambia will escalate. We badly need the Nacala line to be repaired and made safe, which would allow us to get regular food supplies in for less cost. WFP has, therefore, taken the unusual step of providing thousands of sleepers for the rehabilitation of the Nacala line inside Mozambique. It is vital to the long-term food security of the refugees in Malawi.[6]

The effect on Oxfam's work in Malawi

Oxfam has been working in Malawi since 1964. In the 1980s, our development programme concentrated on long-term investment in three main areas: firstly, contributing to the establishment of a countrywide Primary Health Care programme relevant to the needs of the poorest; secondly, work on disability issues; and thirdly, establishing a community development programme in the Mulanje and Phalombe districts of south western Malawi. This is one of the country's poorest areas, where land hunger and the socially disastrous consequences of migrant labour are painfully evident.

But the nature of Oxfam's Malawi programme was dramatically changed from late 1985 onwards, when it became clear that a serious refugee problem was developing as a result of the conflict in Mozambique. In September 1985, Oxfam's representative for Malawi telexed Oxford his initial assessment of the situation:

> HAVE JUST VISITED MALAWI/MOZAMBIQUE BORDER IN DEDZA AREA TO
> ASSESS REFUGEE SITUATION. ALTHOUGH WE WERE PREVENTED BY
> THE MALAWIAN ARMY FROM REACHING CERTAIN AREAS DUE TO
> FRELIMO/MNR CLASHES OVER THE BORDER, SITUATION OBVIOUSLY
> SERIOUS WITH REASONABLE ESTIMATE OF 10,000 REFUGEES IN
> AREA. MOST SETTLED WITHIN MALAWIAN VILLAGES.
>
> MOST HAVE BUILT GRASS HUTS SO DON'T NEED IMMEDIATE HELP
> WITH SHELTER, HOWEVER FEW HAVE FOOD, MONEY, OR BLANKETS. WE
> ESTIMATE 25 PER CENT (OR 500 FAMILIES) ARE IN IMMEDIATE
> NEED OF ASSISTANCE, WHILE THE REST ARE BEING HELPED BY
> RELATIVES AND CAN PROBABLY GET BY FOR THE TIME BEING.[7]
>
> DUE TO ACUTE LAND SHORTAGE HERE, REFUGEES PROHIBITED FROM
> SETTLED FARMING BY MALAWIAN AUTHORITIES. UP TO NOW, SOME
> HAVE SURVIVED BY WORKING ON LOCAL FARMS AND AGRICULTURAL
> ESTATES, RECEIVING PAYMENT IN FOOD. HARVEST NOW OVER AND
> NO MORE WORK AVAILABLE, THEREFORE FOOD SITUATION BECOMING
> CRITICAL AND WILL REMAIN SO UNTIL NEXT HARVEST A YEAR FROM
> NOW.
>
> NO LIKELIHOOD OF REFUGEES RETURNING HOME UNTIL IT IS SAFE
> TO DO SO. THEREFORE PROVISION HAS TO BE MADE TO MEET
> INTERIM BASIC NEEDS ...
>
> MAIZE MEAL, MEDICAL SUPPLIES, AND BLANKETS REQUIRED IN
> FOLLOWING QUANTITIES AND COSTS ...[8]

Oxfam immediately made emergency funds available, and from this point on became increasingly involved in a programme of relief assistance, starting in the Dedza area, but spreading to other points along the south western border as and where new influxes of refugees arrived.

One of Oxfam's key concerns at this point was that, although the number of refugees was becoming critical, the Malawian authorities had not officially sanctioned an international aid effort. This meant that the scale of the problem in areas other than Dedza was not easily verifiable, and that it was not possible for the large UN organisations such as UNHCR and WFP to assist the refugees, because these organisations operate only after an official invitation from government.

The full reasons for the government's reluctance at this point to appeal for official international assistance are unclear. There is a long history of migration from Mozambique, but Malawi had never been a signatory to the international refugee conventions which permit refugees some basic rights and safeguards under international law, and open the way for UNHCR assistance. However, it was widely thought that a combination of factors lay behind the lack of action, including Malawi's political ties with South Africa, and the support which Malawi was alleged by other key Front Line States to be extending to the MNR.[9] It is also likely that the government was reluctant to attract more refugees with an official reception and relief programme.

In any event, it was to be a year before any other international relief organisations were permitted to help the refugees in Malawi. This meant that local Malawian communities and relief organisations in the refugee areas shouldered a disproportionate share of the crisis, and that the refugees did not have access to the resources to which they would otherwise have been entitled.

By January 1986, the plight of the refugees in the Dedza area had become worse. Their makeshift grass shelters - known locally as 'zitsakasa' - were not fit to withstand the rains. One of the organisers working with the mission-based relief operation wrote from Malawi,

> There is considerable sickness, malnourishment, and death among the displaced people.[10] The people are terribly at risk, as the original funds you sent have already been used up... I want to bring the distribution points nearer to the people in distress ... The hungry months are only now beginning. They have been surviving (not all) on piece work, on the generosity of their Malawian relatives, which is limited by poverty, on periodic returns to hidden maize stores in Mozambique, and by selling things of value like sewing machines or bicycles if they have them.

In spite of the enormous burden placed on this one mission station and its church workers, the relief operation was handled methodically. It was based on the knowledge and skills of local church and traditional leaders, and was carefully designed to ensure that the limited supplies of relief goods were fairly distributed. Again in January 1986, the mission reported,

*OUR SUPPLIES OF MAIZE, BLANKETS AND SMALL AMOUNTS OF CASH
FOR FOOD HAVE BEEN DISTRIBUTED THROUGH A COMMITTEE OF
CHURCH ELDERS WHO MEET THE NEEDY EVERY TUESDAY AND FRIDAY
FROM 8 A.M. TO 1 P.M. NORMALLY LETTERS ARE REQUIRED FROM
THE VILLAGE HEADMEN WHERE THE DISPLACED PEOPLE ARE
RESIDING. NAMES AND VILLAGE ARE WRITTEN DOWN, AND
ASSISTANCE IS MONITORED IN THIS WAY. URGENT CASES COMING
ON OTHER DAYS OF THE WEEK ARE HANDLED SEPARATELY.*

By March 1986, the situation had worsened. Oxfam's representative reported,

Local estimates suggest that around 180 people have been killed along the border in the last two months (the MNR is reported to have launched a major offensive against the border town of Villa Ulongwe), resulting in more refugees. The numbers are now estimated at 13,000 altogether ... There seems to be no diminution of the problem, with many reports of refugees stealing food crops from the fields of local people. Therefore, in the short term at least, we have no alternative but to continue relief assistance ... I have asked for a nutrition survey among the refugee population. The medical assistants in the nearby clinics will perform the survey.[11]

Underlining the deteriorating situation, the mission organiser wrote again to Oxfam in March 1986,

We now have upwards of 12,000 displaced people who are getting no other assistance from any official or unofficial source apart from what they can get from the local villagers who are good enough to receive them even though they are needy themselves.

I must stress the needs of these displaced people. They have come in terror of their lives. In Mozambique, they have been robbed of their maize and livestock. Sometimes their clothes have been taken, and their villages burned. Many have had relatives murdered. Many have been separated from their families and it is not known if they are alive or dead. I have met groups of children of about 12 years old, travelling together with no one to look after them. If they have Mozambican money it is of no exchange value in Malawi. They sell their possessions for food and then have to steal. Many have no relatives to give them shelter, and those that have are not welcome for long, due to local people's inability to support visitors.

By this time, the mission's arrangements for distribution and monitoring had developed with experience, and some local food supplies had been identified from which it was possible for the mission to buy maize.

We now have local committees distributing food in the six affected areas around this parish. These committee members actually visit the needy in their small huts and distribute tickets on the basis of 12 kg of maize per individual per month. The recipients then go to nearby big farmers and collect their portion. The committee are there to see they get their correct quotas.

Oliva, a Mozambican refugee staying in the Dedza area of south western Malawi. She fled from her village, which she said was controlled by the MNR, in mid-1987. "This time they came shortly after dark. They came to take the maize standing in our fields. Nobody was killed, but we were all very frightened. We hid in a ditch and then escaped over the border. We don't want to go back until the war is over. What is the use of staying there just to grow food which you don't eat?"

(John Clark / Oxfam)

By June 1986, refugee numbers were creeping up, and UN agencies were still unable to assist. Oxfam remained the only agency supporting the mission relief programme in the Dedza area, and more funds were needed. Oxfam's representative telexed the following information to headquarters:

JUST BACK FROM VISIT TO REFUGEE AREA WHERE I VISITED THE 7 DISTRIBUTION CENTRES AND HELD MEETINGS WITH 1,000 DISPLACED PERSONS IN 3 GROUPS. A FURTHER GRANT HAS BEEN REQUESTED, WHICH I SUPPORT FOR THE FOLLOWING REASONS:

NUMBER OF DISPLACED PEOPLE NOW AROUND 13,000, AT LEAST 50 PER CENT OF WHOM ARE ENTIRELY DEPENDENT ON RELIEF.

NUTRITION SURVEYS CONDUCTED LAST MONTH AMONG RECIPIENTS INDICATE OUR ASSISTANCE IS KEEPING SITUATION IN HAND ...

SYSTEMS BEING USED FOR IDENTIFICATION OF BENEFICIARIES,

*DISTRIBUTION AND MONITORING SEEM TO OPERATE VERY WELL
INDEED.*

*NO PROSPECT OF ASSISTANCE FROM ANY OTHER AID DONORS YET.
SOME PROGRESS FOLLOWING OUR REPRESENTATIONS TO UN AGENCIES,
BUT NO FIRM PROMISES. THEREFORE SEEMS NO ALTERNATIVE TO
CONTINUED OXFAM ASSISTANCE. GRATEFUL IF YOU COULD
AUTHORISE NEW GRANT OF £25,636 (ACCORDING TO DETAILED
ESTIMATES ALREADY SENT) FROM CATASTROPHE BUDGET IF FUNDS
CAN BE FOUND.*[12]

In September 1986, fresh MNR military offensives in Mozambique, just over Malawi's southernmost border, changed the situation in a matter of days. An estimated 50,000 new refugees fled from the fighting into Malawi's Nsanje and Mulanje Districts. The scale of this influx meant that the Malawian government had no option but to appeal for outside assistance, and it authorised the Malawi Red Cross Society to appeal for international support.[13] However, Malawi did not sign the relevant refugee instruments until November 1987, more than a year later.[14] The government has responded generously to the refugees ever since.

Also in September 1986, another development occurred which is thought to have helped resolve the political impasse over the official recognition of the refugees. In an unprecedented summit, Presidents Kaunda, Mugabe, and the late President Machel met President Banda. According to reports of the meeting, the Front Line States delegation pressed home their view that Malawi's support for the MNR was contributing to the destabilisation of the region, and that they would be prepared to take sanctions against Malawi if necessary. Although President Banda was reported to have denied supporting the MNR, it was agreed that Malawi and Mozambique would hold a further Ministerial meeting to discuss the problem.[15] A Joint Defence and Security Commission was duly established between Malawi and Mozambique, and two agreements were signed in December 1986, which reportedly comprised an accord on mutual cooperation and a bilateral protocol on defence, state security and public order.[16] Speaking of his hopes for the agreements, Mozambique's Minister for National Defence said there should be "maximum cooperation between the two countries in wiping out banditry".[17]

By March 1987, the number of refugees in the country had risen to 141,000. It rose steadily to 400,000 by December 1987, and to 550,000 by July 1988. By 1988 over half of Oxfam's total expenditure in Malawi was being taken up by relief assistance for Mozambican refugees.

The impact of the refugee emergency on Oxfam's Malawi programme has been considerable. Although Oxfam's long-term development programme in Malawi continues, the demands of the refugee crisis have affected our ability

The large influx of refugees into Malawi means that time and resources have to be diverted away from development work. An important part of Oxfam's long-term work in Malawi is support for Primary Health Care. The aim is to make health services accessible, and relevant to the needs of the poor. Here, Liya Chiucha, a voluntary community health worker, is weighing children at Dambule village.

(George Murray / Oxfam)

to concentrate time and resources on this side of our work. As Oxfam's representative for Malawi explained in mid-1987,

> South Africa's destabilisation has changed the whole balance and framework of Oxfam's programme in Malawi.

> As an agency committed to responding to human need, we have seen the regional conflict bringing the plight of vulnerable groups in society into sharper focus. As a result, our time and resources have been skewed towards emergency work, and relief assistance now accounts for a large proportion of our annual expenditure in Malawi. This is bound to detract from our longer-term development programme, but this is now the reality of working in Southern Africa, and there is every indication that the situation will deteriorate.[18]

Case-study 2: The effects of MNR terrorism in eastern Zimbabwe

Eastern Zimbabwe: areas affected by MNR cross-border attacks

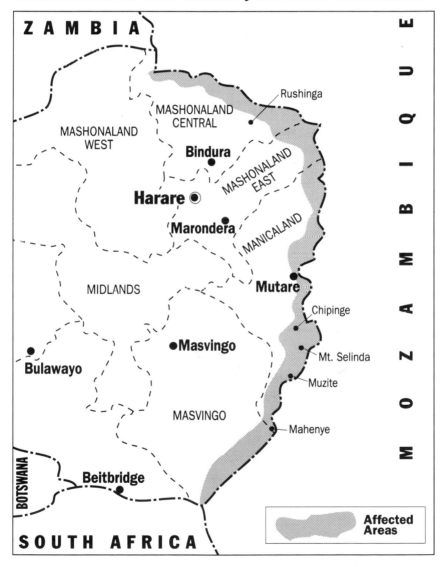

From the early 1980s until mid-1989, MNR terrorism in eastern Zimbabwe resulted in the murder of over 350 civilians, approximately 300 people injured, over 650 people kidnapped, and some 400 missing.[19] Food production suffered, and essential commercial and development activities were curtailed, including the government's Primary Health Care Programme which Oxfam has supported.

Following the commitment of Zimbabwean troops in Mozambique in late 1982, numerous brutal cross-border attacks by the MNR have taken place along the length of Zimbabwe's eastern rural border with Mozambique.[20] There has been a marked increase since June 1987.

These attacks follow a similar pattern to those inside Mozambique. They appear designed to create fear and uncertainty among the local population, through random attacks on civilians and the basic services they need. Homes, crops, livestock, shops and schools are frequently attacked. Moreover, some of the large commercial farms in the fertile eastern highlands have also been attacked. These farms produce export crops vital to Zimbabwe's national economy.

Concerned about the effects which this under-reported[21] aspect of regional conflict was having on local people and their development, Oxfam commissioned a report in late 1988. The research was conducted in Chipinge District of Manicaland Province and Rushinga District of Mashonaland East

This Zimbabwean woman, displaced by MNR cross-border attacks, walked 50 km with her three children to reach Chipote, a village farther away from the border, where she hopes to start a new life.   (Chris Johnson / Oxfam)

Province, and a range of local people and development workers were interviewed.[22]

A health worker interviewed in Rushinga District summed up the outrage felt in the community where she works and lives when she said,

> As if the poverty already prevailing here was not enough, now we are faced with another monster in the form of the MNR. Buses have stopped coming to our area. Shops have closed. It is difficult to undertake vaccination campaigns. Although the clinics are still operating, we do not know for how long. People are afraid to move — especially on foot.[23]

Background to the MNR attacks in eastern Zimbabwe

Today's situation has its roots in Zimbabwe's liberation war, which was fought from the mid-1960s until 1979, shortly before independence was finally won in 1980.

Shortly after Mozambique came to independence in 1975, it granted rear base military facilities and other forms of solidarity support to the Zimbabwe African National Liberation Army (ZANLA) forces (the military wing of the Zimbabwe African Nationalist Union (ZANU)), which were fighting for independence from settler-ruled Rhodesia.

The difficulties involved in defending Rhodesia's eastern front from guerrilla infiltration from Mozambique advanced the nationalists' military position substantially. As is now well established, Rhodesian security retaliated by creating the MNR.[24] The Rhodesian regime's aim was to undermine the military opposition to the Rhodesian Front by destabilising newly independent Mozambique in general, and by targeting Mozambique-based ZANLA personnel, bases, and communications networks in particular.

As is also well established, Rhodesian support for the MNR was taken over by South Africa from 1980 onwards, Prime Minister Ian Smith having no further use for the MNR, after negotiating at Lancaster House with the Patriotic Front (the then tactical political alliance between the two popular nationalist movements, ZANU and the Zimbabwe African People's Union — ZAPU).

Independent Zimbabwe first committed troops to Mozambique in November 1982,[25] initially to guard the Mutare-Beira oil pipeline; but the Zimbabwean 'Special Task Force' soon extended its involvement. For example, in August 1985, Zimbabwean troops launched an airborne assault on the MNR's headquarters at Casa Banana near Gorongosa, and Zimbabwean troops overran another MNR base at Nyarunyaru in November of the same year.[26] Towards the end of 1988, there were an estimated 8,000-10,000 Zimbabwean troops in Mozambique.[27]

Under the terms of its 1981 Defence Agreement with Mozambique,[28] Zimbabwe had an obligation to assist the Mozambican government's war effort. Also, landlocked Zimbabwe had strong reasons of self-interest for fielding troops in Mozambique. Zimbabwe's 'natural' trade routes run through Mozambique. There is the 'Beira Corridor', which comprises an oil pipeline, a road and a rail line, and the Limpopo rail line which connects Maputo port with central Zimbabwe. Both routes have been the object of MNR sabotage inside Mozambique since the early 1980s.

Arguing that the unity and survival of the Front Line States was threatened by insurgency in Mozambique, President Mugabe also took a leading role in persuading other Front Line States to assist Mozambique militarily.[29]   In November 1986, the month after Mozambique's President Machel was killed in an air crash on South African territory, President Mugabe said of the Front Line States' alliance, "Survival of Mozambique is our survival. The fall of Mozambique will certainly be our fall ... All and one stand together. All and one fight together."[30]

Following this, British military aid to the war against the MNR was increased. In March 1987, for example, it was agreed between Zimbabwe, Britain, and Mozambique that the number of Mozambican officers being trained by the British Military Advisory and Training Team[31] in Zimbabwe would be doubled by mid-1987. And in November 1987, Britain pledged £500,000 worth of military assistance to equip Tanzanian troops fighting in Mozambique.[32]

A village headman in Chipinge District described his experience of the MNR's motives:

> They came at night, on 6 September 1987, at around midnight. They robbed a shop which stored everything we needed, including food and agricultural equipment like ploughs. They took as much as they could carry from the shop. They could not even tell the food from the soap; the next morning we found that they had tried to eat several bars of soap while they were robbing the shop. When they had finished, they set the shop alight. Later that night, they killed a woman who refused to carry their loot. They left a note to say they would be back. In the note, they said that as long as Zimbabwean soldiers were in Mozambique, they would return.[33]

The effects of MNR aggression on community life

As described in Chapter 3, widespread fear has been one of the worst results of the MNR attacks in eastern Zimbabwe. But there have also been other extremely disruptive consequences: people's livelihoods have been affected, as has local trade, agricultural production, health services, and schooling.

Against the background of MNR-sponsored insecurity in eastern

Members of a cooperative in eastern Zimbabwe, photographed in 1982. Brutally oppressed by the Rhodesian authorities during the liberation war, they fled into Mozambique. After independence they returned to rebuild their lives, and received help from Oxfam. Now their lives are disrupted again by cross-border MNR attacks.

(John Baguley / Oxfam)

Zimbabwe, it is important to remember the recent history of the people in this area. It was the rural villagers in Rhodesia who bore the brunt of the liberation war, and people in the eastern border areas were particularly affected, because this was the area nearest to ZANLA's Mozambican rear bases. Many civilians were shot by the Rhodesian forces for assisting ZANLA guerrillas in this area, while others were killed or maimed by anti-personnel mines laid to prevent the guerrillas from infiltrating into Rhodesia.

Throughout Rhodesia, an estimated 750,000 people were forced from their homes by early 1978, and herded into 'protected villages' by the Rhodesian security forces in an attempt to cut off civilian assistance to the nationalist guerrillas. Many of the protected villages were located in the east. Now, less than a decade later, these people's lives are disrupted again. Many people in the area resent the way in which the insecurity has disrupted their family and trading links with people across the border. For security reasons, the Zimbabwe government has banned villagers from offering hospitality to Mozambicans unless they have official permission to do so. Government has also forbidden petty trading across the border, and people are banned from crossing over except at the official crossing points, which are often an inconvenient distance away.

However, it is the indiscriminate nature of the MNR attacks which is most disruptive and which has resulted in widespread fear. This is all the more marked because it has come so soon after the tremendous optimism and determination to make things work and catch up on lost development, which characterised this area directly after independence. Nowadays, people all over the insecure area are sleeping out in the bush. In Mahenye area, for instance, the local people have not slept in their houses for over a year. Nothing could make them sleep in their homes, not even the five-month long rainy season. Until the Zimbabwean security forces were reinforced in 1988, people were frequently sleeping several kilometres from their homes. With the security forces patrolling the area at night, they feel confident to sleep closer to their homes, but not inside them.

Effects on education

As in Mozambique, schools and teaching staff are a key target for the MNR. One example occurred at Nyatsato school in Rushinga District, which was attacked in September 1988. Six people were killed in the incident, and the school teachers' houses and the classrooms were gutted. The same school was attacked a couple of months later on 15 November. This time, the attack was carried out by four men armed with machetes and pangas (large knives). Again, six people were murdered, four women and two babies — one aged 18 months, and the other only seven months old.[34]

To escape fear and insecurity, many families have left their homes either to settle, or to sit it out with friends or relatives in other parts of the country. School enrolment has therefore dropped in the worst-affected areas. Staffing levels have also been difficult to maintain because of insecurity. Some teachers have left, and it is hard to find replacements for them. Surprisingly, by the end of 1988 all of the schools in Chipinge and Rushinga Districts had managed to stay open.

A villager from Rushinga District explained what had happened to his local school:

In October (1988), MNR bandits killed five people and seriously injured two others. The attack took place at our local Primary School, in spite of the close-by army camp. In our area, people have begun to dig trenches to sleep in. Nobody sleeps in their houses any more. Although the schools are protected by the army, they are still not safe.[35]

A headmaster from a school in Chipinge District described the environment he works in:

There have been several incidents of MNR attacks near our school in the last year. The last one was in July (1988) when one person was killed, and eight others were severely injured. They were hacked with pangas and stabbed with bayonets. During the raid, the bandits burned down houses and a baby was thrown alive into the fire. They also looted houses, stealing food and clothes. We feel very nervous for our children here.

The insecurity in this area has resulted in a drop in the school enrolment from 1,400 pupils last year (1987), to 1,094 this year as parents have moved away to safer areas. ... Our school also used to cater for Mozambican children and at any one time we had more than 200 children from over the border, but now the children are not able to cross over to us on a daily basis any longer.[36]

The concern about the effects of conflict on local education services expressed by people in eastern Zimbabwe has to be understood in the context of Zimbabwe's recent history. Today's generation of school children are the first to enjoy the benefits of the significantly upgraded education services now provided to all. Their parents lived through the long and painful liberation struggle, in which popular aspirations for education played a key part.

Effects on health services

Insecurity in the border areas has also affected the delivery of health services. This is another sector of public life in which the independent nation has made great achievements, and which is under threat because of MNR terrorism. Oxfam has been supporting Zimbabwe's rural health services since independence.

Helping to establish appropriate health services was one of Oxfam's key priorities in newly independent Zimbabwe. Between 1980 and 1988, Oxfam spent £1.4 million on health, nutrition, and disability programmes throughout the country.[37] Since 1984, when Oxfam began its support for the community health services in eastern Zimbabwe, our grants in MNR-destabilised areas have totalled £463,615.[38] Not surprisingly, the work which Oxfam has supported has been seriously affected.

Insecurity has affected health services in a number of ways. Several outreach clinics have had to be closed down, because staff cannot travel to them. These clinics are a vital component of the national PHC programme, especially because they provide child immunisation, child-growth monitoring, and ante-natal screening services to remote areas. Conversely, many villagers cannot easily travel to reach clinics and hospitals when they need to. An Oxfam-recruited doctor working in Chipinge District reported,

> As far as health services are concerned, it's clear that the district has been seriously affected, cancelling out a lot of hard-earned achievements. We used to have outreach workers who would travel out into the countryside and camp for several days doing their work, but this has been cancelled. Outreach clinics also used to be held once a month by nurses from the hospitals, who used to travel on bicycles, but now nobody is prepared to cycle into those dangerous areas any more.

> The abandonment of outreach services affects a number of important preventive activities. Our programme to immunise children has suffered serious setbacks. We are unable to carry out the Expanded Programme of Immunisation (EPI)[39] in several areas. Our EPI coverage is 60 per cent for the rest of the district, but less than 40 per cent in the affected area. In the Mahenye area, for example, it is less than 20 per cent.

> Also, in the insecure parts of the district our programme of spraying against the malaria mosquito is now haphazard, with some areas left out altogether because of safety considerations.

> People here have also been affected by drought, and a supplementary feeding programme for children was under way. This too has been suspended because of insecurity, so malnutrition is rife. Even for adults, the drought relief food cannot reach the affected areas. Health education services have also been curtailed.

> Because the outreach clinics no longer function, we are seeing more cases of preventable diseases like malnutrition, measles, tuberculosis, malaria and diarrhoea here at Chipinge hospital.[40]

The matron at another of the hospitals serving Chipinge District explained,

> Our outreach activities have been severely curtailed. From here we used to cover 22 different rural locations, but of those, only five areas are still considered safe, so outreach visits to the rest of the places have been cancelled. Our student nurses used to travel to these outlying areas, but they no longer felt safe.

> Our primary health care programme has suffered greatly. Children born in those areas over the past five months have not received any vaccination. As a result, there was recently an outbreak of measles among the children.[41]

Staffing shortages caused by insecurity

Insecurity also makes the recruitment of health staff for the area even harder. In spite of the growing numbers of Zimbabwean health workers now qualified, it is proving hard to attract staff to remote rural areas, partly because many prefer to take up employment opportunities in the towns and in

Mahenye health centre in eastern Zimbabwe has not been able to function effectively since it was built, because of repeated MNR attacks.   (Chris Johnson / Oxfam)

the private medicine sector. MNR terrorism makes eastern Zimbabwe even less attractive to health workers. As the Oxfam-recruited doctor explained,

> The district I work in has 300,000 people, and with the current doctor/patient ratio applying for the rest of the country, it should have more doctors. But at the moment there are only three. There are four hospitals in the District, and two of these have no doctors. We can't get doctors to come into the district because of the security situation.

> The clinics served from this hospital are also affected by understaffing.[42] For example, the clinic in Mahenye has no qualified staff. A clinic nurse at Mabe has resigned. There are no staff at Hakwato clinic, which has not been in commission since it was built because of the security situation. Gwenzi clinic has one nurse. Nurse aides have also been helping, and in places like Mahenye the army medical corps stands in for the nurses.[43]

This problem was also reported by the matron at the neighbouring hospital. She said,

> On the staffing side, we are operating with only one doctor instead of the normal three. The hospital has also lost a number of experienced nurses who could not stand the pressure and the tension of never knowing where and when the next bandit attack would be. For someone from outside this area, our hospital is the last place they would want to come and work. So although we think that the security situation here has improved somewhat,

you can't tell that to an outsider.

Describing the effects on the staff of an MNR attack on a clinic in Chipinge District, an Oxfam worker wrote,

> In Mahenye, one of the worst affected parts of the district, the health services were suspended completely for a short time earlier this year following an attack on the clinic. (When I visited the clinic, I saw holes in the window panes left by bullets.)

> Following the attack, the three nurses who were working at the clinic fled. The health services were for some time in the hands of army medics. But recently, two young women from the area went to Chipinge Hospital, where they were trained in basic nursing for two weeks. They are now running the clinic and providing basic services, such as vaccination and treating cases of malaria. The clinic has no telephone or radio contact with the hospital in Chipinge. Transport in the area is now erratic since the MNR started their attacks, so any patient who needs urgent attention has to rely on the chance of an army truck going to Chipinge or any other hospital in the urban centres.

Refugees and migrant workers from Mozambique

Additionally, the growing numbers of Mozambicans in the area — both refugees from the war and migrant workers — create a strain on local services. Talking about the way in which the refugee influx has affected health services, the Oxfam-recruited doctor explained,

> Our hospital also has to cater for the Mozambican refugees in the nearby Tongogara Camp. We don't mind treating the refugees, but our resources — equipment, drugs, and personnel — are limited. The budget we receive is only supposed to cover treatment for the local Zimbabwean population; it does not include provision for the refugees. At any one time, at least 20 per cent of the bed occupancy is taken up by refugees from the camp. We spend 35 per cent of our working hours with the refugees, and this limits what we can give to the local people.

The Mozambican migrant workers (there is a long tradition of migrant labour in this area) have particular problems.[44] They are mostly employed on the large commercial farms in the area, because they are prepared to work for wages below the legal minimum rate which must be offered to Zimbabweans. Many experience very poor living conditions on their employers' farms — overcrowding, poor sanitation, and long working hours. One Mozambican seasonal worker on a tea estate in Zimbabwe's eastern highlands said,

> Each little room here in the workers' compound has eight to ten of us living in it, and many of us will stay like that for four to five months — as long as there is work for us. It's better for a person to suffer here and earn something at the end of the month, than to stay there (in Mozambique) with nothing.

> Those of us who do not have permanent work here in Zimbabwe are afraid of being unable to return here if they're sent back to Mozambique. In

Mozambican migrant workers sorting coffee beans on a commercial farm in eastern Zimbabwe. Casual migrants generally earn well below the national minimum wage.

(Julian Quan / Oxfam)

Mozambique, the MNR robs people of their food, so many come to Zimbabwe to work and have the money to buy food, sugar, salt, soap, and clothes. Some come and go, but many stay here because of the war.[45]

Government's efforts to introduce a health worker scheme for farm labourers, along the lines of the village health-worker component of the national PHC programme, have been hampered by shortage of funds and lack of cooperation from the commercial farmers.[46] As a result of inadequate preventive services, the local curative services have to treat a high proportion of the migrant labour population,[47] many of whom cannot safely return to their homes now because of the war.

The migrant workers are not included in the headcount on which hospital budgets are fixed, so catering for them strains local health resources. As Oxfam was told at another hospital,

Most of the malnutrition cases which come to our hospital are the children of Mozambicans who are living on this side of the border, who work as labourers on the nearby coffee and tea estates. Of the 120 malnourished children we have admitted at the moment, we think 80 are Mozambicans, although it is sometimes difficult to tell. Some of the pregnant Mozambican women coming to the hospital are also malnourished, which means their babies are very often born underweight.[48]

Until the conflict in Mozambique is resolved, it will not be possible to assess the overall effects which conflict has brought to the eastern border areas of Zimbabwe. What is already clear is that the people in the eastern border areas will have borne much of the brunt. As is demonstrated by President Mugabe's active role in the current round of diplomacy to find a peace solution, Zimbabwe is desperate to find a just settlement.

South Africa's economic integration with southern Africa

Southern Africa is dependent on the Republic of South Africa as a focus of transport and communications, an exporter of goods and services and as an importer of goods and cheap labour. This dependence is not a natural phenomenon, nor is it the result of a free market economy. The nine states and one occupied territory of southern Africa ... were, in varying degrees, deliberately incorporated — by metropolitan powers, colonial rulers, and large corporations — into the colonial and sub-colonial structures centering in general on the Republic of South Africa. The development of national economies as balanced units, let alone the welfare of the people of southern Africa, played no part in the economic integration strategy. Not surprisingly, therefore, southern Africa is fragmented, grossly exploited and subject to economic manipulation by outsiders. Future development must aim at the reduction of economic dependence not only on the Republic of South Africa, but also on any single external state or group of states.

(Excerpt from the "Lusaka Declaration on Southern African Development Coordination", April 1980, the official founding document of SADCC.)

The difficulties of economic development faced by most of the SADCC states have to be understood both in their regional and global contexts. Vulnerable to the range of economic pressures currently affecting much of sub-Saharan Africa (see Chapter 8), most of the SADCC states also relate economically to South Africa. This chapter looks at some of the structural economic issues particular to the region.

The SADCC region's dependence on South Africa

The countries of this region have very difficult, entrenched, structural economic problems, largely because the South African economy was created to be the most dominant one in the region. By design, we were supposed to be economic appendices. This needs to be tackled.

(Kebby Musokatwane, former Prime Minister of Zambia[1])

Over the last century, a complex network of regional economic relationships has grown up in southern Africa, with South Africa as the dominant power. International political influence and entrepreneurial interests, especially those of Britain, have played a key role in this process, which centred on the requirements of foreign and national business interests in South Africa, and on colonial interests in the surrounding territories.

Each SADCC state has a different economic relationship with South Africa. Angola and Tanzania have insignificant economic links, but in the case of the others, apart from the 'natural' economic linkages, South Africa has also sought to impose other dependencies. As a consequence, there are now a number of different links and dependencies between the SADCC countries and South Africa.

Firstly, transport dependency on South Africa has been an important structural feature. Because of their geographical position, Botswana[2] and Lesotho have to use South African rail services for their external trade. And South Africa's military destabilisation has resulted in other SADCC states (especially Malawi, Zimbabwe, and Zambia) also having to use its transport networks because of sabotage attacks on the alternative routes. But in times of peace, the rail links passing out to the east and west coastlines would mean that little of SADCC's world trade would need to pass through South Africa.

Secondly, most of the SADCC states trade extensively with South Africa, but not with each other. Mozambique, Zimbabwe, and Swaziland, for example, have official South African trade missions in their capital cities, while others have official trade agreements with South Africa.

Thirdly, migrant labour from the SADCC states to South Africa, though diminishing, is still significant. The Overseas Development Institute claims that migrant labour employment opportunities and the workers' foreign exchange remittances are 'important' for Swaziland and Malawi, 'more important' for Botswana, and 'essential' for Mozambique and Lesotho.[3]

Fourthly, South African transnational companies have invested heavily in key SADCC economies — Zimbabwe, Zambia, Botswana, Lesotho, and Swaziland, and Namibia in particular.[4] However, Zimbabwe, which inherited an economy extremely dependent on South African investment, has made significant efforts to reduce the amount of South African investment in its economy. The only SADCC countries without extensive investment links with South Africa are Angola and Tanzania. Even in Angola, the diamond mining industry is managed by Anglo American, which (via its subsidiary de Beers) also controls sales. In Tanzania, de Beers has a 50 per cent interest in the diamond mine at Mwadui, said to be the world's largest pipe mine. [5]

Fifthly, Lesotho and Swaziland are heavily dependent on South Africa for their supplies of oil, coal, and electricity.

Historical background

In 1886 the discovery of gold in the Boer Transvaal Republic (and, previously in the mid-1860s, the discovery of diamonds at Kimberley) set off a train of events which was to make South Africa the dominant regional economy.

The ensuing mining boom (1870 onwards) provided the conditions for the development of commercial agriculture (1870 — 1920), largely because the growing mining workforce needed to be fed. And then South Africa's industrialisation process (1910 — 1940) took off on the strength of mining wealth and the international investment which gold had initially attracted to the country. External finance came from France, the Netherlands, and Germany, but the main source of capital was Britain,[6] whose imperial interests in the area dated from 1806. After the second world war, US investment came to play an increasingly important role in the South African economy. [7]

Although South Africa's gold deposits were the largest ever to have been discovered, the relatively low-grade, deep-level ore of the Witwatersrand, the main gold-bearing reef, meant that profitable exploitation depended on a plentiful supply of cheap labour, and substantial finance.

Labour recruitment soon stretched into neighbouring territories, partly because black labourers within South Africa found that the rates of pay offered by the mining houses were not as attractive as the returns to be had from the peasant farming sector.[8] Along with the development of the mines came the apparatus of control, regulation, and minimal living conditions: labour 'reserves'; contracts and their legal enforcement; pass laws; single-sex 'hostels'; mine security armies and exploitative employment practices; even liquor franchises.

The need for international finance resulted in the domination of the South African economy by a few large companies, who formed the powerful Chamber of Mines in 1889. Individual prospectors and smaller companies were squeezed out of business because they could not command the finance necessary for profitable exploitation of the gold-bearing rocks. By contrast, the companies which comprised the Chamber of Mines were large and

*The migrant workers'
hostel at City Deep Mine
in Johannesburg, in
1984. Unlike the
majority of migrant
workers (women as well
as men) in South Africa,
these people are there
legally .*

(Afrapix)

powerful enough to command ready access to the money markets of London, Berlin, and Paris.

The modern descendants of these early Rand mining companies are now sophisticated South African transnational companies (TNCs), a handful of which now dominate South Africa's economy. (The main non-state TNCs are the Anglo American Corporation, SANLAM (South African National Life Assurance Company), the Barlow Rand Group, the Volksas Group, South African Mutual, the Rembrandt Group, Anglovaal, and South African Breweries.[9]) Because they were well-placed to diversify their activities and to extend their operations into the wider region over time, they have also come to dominate key neighbouring economies. The main such company is Anglo American, which not only has key interests in neighbouring states, but also has extensive interests in the wider region and outside Africa.[10] In the early 1980s, through its subsidiary Minorco, Anglo American was reported to be the largest foreign investor in the USA.

Migrant labour

Although migrant workers are found in other parts of the world, not least in the United States as seasonal agricultural workers and in western Europe as *gastarbeiters,* there is no other country where such a system has existed for so long and has trapped so large a proportion of the labour force in a dehumanising structure.

(Excerpt from the 1989 Report for the Second Carnegie Enquiry into Poverty and Development in Southern Africa[11]*)*

The mining companies' requirement for plentiful cheap labour gave rise to the institution of migrant labour, which was to be the first layer of regional economic integration. As the need for labour in the mines grew, workers were soon recruited from neighbouring territories. As early as 1896, for example, 60 per cent of the black miners in the South African gold industry came from Mozambique. By the beginning of this century, many other workers came from the colonial territories now known as Lesotho, Swaziland, Botswana, Malawi, Zambia, and Tanzania. Once the tradition of migrancy had been established, it became a way of ensuring that labour costs were kept low, and, as the South African economy later diversified into commercial agriculture and manufacturing, migrant labour was also drawn into these sectors.

In 1891, the Chamber of Mines set up a recruiting arm known as the Witswatersrand Native Labour Association (WNLA).[12] WNLA recruiting agents travelled to villages all over southern Africa, hiring labourers, and arranging for their passage down to the mining areas.[13] The governments of the labour-supplying colonies received roughly half the miners' wages, holding the money to be paid to them at the end of their contracts. In this way, migrant labour to South Africa was a valuable source of revenue for the colonial authorities, just as it still is for the independent governments of labour-providing countries.

By 1986 40 per cent (albeit a declining proportion from the late 1970s onwards) of the labour force employed in South Africa's mines were external migrants. The proportion is declining, because since the 1970s, the South African government has been promoting strategies to reduce foreign labour. This stems from the combined political pressures of rising domestic unemployment and an unwillingness to remain dependent on foreign workers.[14] However, for the time being, the requirement for skilled labour in the mines has meant the Chamber of Mines has resisted a sharp decrease in migrant labour coming from Mozambique.

Nevertheless, the scale of migrant labour remains significant. In 1989, UNICEF estimated that between 600,000 and 750,000 families in the labour-exporting SADCC countries were highly dependent on the remittances of migrant men and women in South Africa. Put another way, this represents some four million people, approximately seven per cent of the region's population. Most of these workers come from the poor, drought-prone, rural areas of Lesotho, southern Malawi, southern and central Mozambique, and southern Botswana. [15]

The drawing of labour from neighbouring territories into South Africa and into the developing colonial economies of the region did not happen spontaneously. In Zambia (formerly Northern Rhodesia), for example, the British South Africa Company (BSAC), a chartered company formed in 1889 and backed with finance from South Africa and Britain, occupied the territory from 1891/2 until 1924,[16] intending to widen British South Africa's territory and labour control. As one leading writer on the urbanisation process in Zambia has observed,

> When power-driven machinery came into general use, factory owners in Europe had at hand large numbers of landless people uprooted from the countryside by earlier changes. This was not the position in Zambia and other African countries, whose inhabitants were largely self-sufficient landed proprietors. There was no ready-made army of unemployed persons looking for employment. One of the first aims of the British South Africa Company was to create such an army, to turn villagers into wage-workers, to separate men from their wives, families, fields, cattle, rivers, and hunting grounds. The measures adopted to bring about these changes initiated a process that gave rise to the present condition of rural displacement and urban overgrowth.[17]

In Zambia, the recruitment of labour on the required scale was achieved by a two-pronged strategy: firstly, through the introduction of waged labour; and secondly, through the imposition of various cash taxes which obliged men to seek wages, together with other measures to undermine the value of African people's agricultural and manufactured production — their accustomed means of economic survival.

As WNLA's recruiting reach developed, the contradictions between South Africa's need for labour from the surrounding territories and the increasing labour requirements of those same colonial economies sharpened.[18] In any event, that so many workers were drawn south into the South African economy was made possible by the overriding compatibility of interest between the private investment interests in South Africa and the often

Colonial magistrates collecting the 'hut tax' in South Africa. Frequent protests and revolts against such taxes took place throughout Africa.

identical business and administration interests in the surrounding British and Portuguese colonies.[19]

Enduring effects

In southern Mozambique, migrant workers' remittances from South Africa soon became a substantial and integral part of the local economy, supporting rather than merely supplementing peasant production. During the 1980s, as war and drought have further ravaged this area, migrants' remittances have become all the more important. [20]

Mozambique has been a major labour-supplying country. During the early 1970s, just before South Africa started cutting back on foreign recruitment for the mines, Mozambique was supplying 100,000 workers, some 25 per cent of the Chamber of Mines workforce. Numbers started to decrease during the 1970s, with the biggest wave of expulsions taking place during the first two years of Mozambique's independence. Numbers fell to around 40,000 by 1977, but have varied since then. For example, after the 1984 Nkomati Accord, in which South Africa pledged economic assistance to Mozambique, the number of migrant workers rose again to an estimated 55,000.

So it came as a major blow when, in October 1986, the South African government announced, not for the first time, a ban on the recruitment of Mozambican migrant workers, purportedly in retaliation for Mozambique's support for the African National Congress (ANC).[21] At the time, the Mozambican Ministry of Labour estimated that some 1,500 miners a month would return, unable to renew their contracts. [22] Although the ban (in so far as it affects skilled workers) has been partially rescinded as a result of pressure from the Chamber of Mines, nevertheless thousands of families will now have to find an alternative living in Mozambique's poor and war-ravaged economy, and there is little prospect of migrant employment opportunities in South Africa increasing.

Just six months after the 1986 ban had been announced, an Oxfam researcher interviewed Mozambican migrant workers about their experiences, in Ressano Garcia. This is a railway town just inside Mozambique's border, where tens of thousands of migrant workers come and go. Many of those disembarking from the trains there were unsure whether they would ever return. They come home laden with goods for their families, goods which are unavailable in Mozambique's shattered economy.

Raimundo Manuel Matsinhe supports his wife and seven children, who live in Matola near Maputo. Because of the ban, he is unable to return to South Africa. He said,

> It's hard. I was counting on going back there to work ... I was earning good money doing general jobs in an Anglo American mine compound. At home, there's nothing for me, there's no solution.[23]

Mozambican miners at the end of their contracts in South Africa leave the train at Ressano Garcia, carrying gifts and supplies bought in South Africa and largely unavailable in Mozambique.   (Julian Quan / Oxfam)

Former migrant mine workers wait for news of jobs outside a WNLA recruitment centre in southern Mozambique. They display certificates showing the length and type of their service in South Africa.   (Julian Quan / Oxfam)

Since the 1986 ban, workers regularly visit the recruitment centres of the Witwatersrand Native Labour Association (WNLA) in Mozambique, hoping to learn that they can renew their contracts. At a meeting outside the WNLA office at Maxixe in Mozambique's southern Inhambane Province, some of the workers who were queuing up explained their situations. Luis Sadeiro Vincent said,

> I had to return here from the mines in 1986. I haven't gone back, because I can't get work there. I'm stuck doing practically nothing now. I've got a machamba (plot of land), but because of the war I don't manage to grow much. I still hope to go back to 'Djoni' (Johannesburg). I don't know what I'll do if I can't. I have a wife and three children. At the moment we're living off my father, he has machambas. There are thousands of people here doing nothing, with no hope of getting back to the mines. [24]

Romosa Fane Chissano said,

> I have six children. Up to now we have been living off my earnings from the mines. I'll have to see what happens when the money runs out, I don't know if I'll find work, I don't know if I'll start to rob, I don't know. For the time being, my plan is still to go back to the mines. I know I can earn there. [25]

Alfaio Niwane Gwambe explained,

> The situation is serious, because I'm used to working in the mines to earn

money to support my family. Now I'm not doing anything, just working my little plot of land to grow something to feed us. It's not enough, and there are no clothes to buy. There is much hunger in our house.[26]

Hamnus Kamdlene Babaloi said,

I've worked in the mines since 1953. With things as they are now, my children cannot go to work there. One day we will have to stop, because we will be too old. How are things going to be then? Our fathers were miners, and so are we. We'd like our sons to be miners. My family has no other means of earning a living. We could farm, but it would not be enough. [27]

Development programmes to create employment for former migrant miners in southern Mozambique are under discussion. The hope is to use the varied skills, work discipline, and familiarity with a cash economy which the migrant labourers have gained from the South African mines to develop small-scale industries. But until funding is secured, and conflict resolved, the only alternative is to attempt subsistence farming.

By 1987, migrant workers' remittances earned Mozambique more than any single export crop.[28] This dependence means that the underlying trends in migrant labour policy seriously affect Mozambique's national economy as well as the livelihoods of the workers directly affected. As one writer put it,

Mozambique has been converted from a regular supplier of a substantial proportion of the mine labour force to an occasional supplier of a small proportion of 'supplementary' labour in response to irregular, unpredictable and haphazard demand from the mining industry. By contrast with Lesotho, therefore, the Mozambican economy has suffered immediately, directly, and very substantially from the cut-backs in foreign labour.[29]

The dramatic social engineering involved in the drawing of labour into South Africa changed entire local economies and traditions of economic survival in the labour-supplying countries and households. Lesotho is the most striking example, where colonial migrant-labour requirements and the incorporation of the kingdom's prime farming area into the Orange Free State were the key elements which transformed the country from a maize-exporting area into an agricultural wasteland.[30] Now dependent on the remittances of its migrant citizens for 70 per cent of its GNP,[31] Lesotho exports its structural unemployment, and some 111,000 migrant workers are officially employed in South Africa's mines.[32] Overall, Lesotho is the SADCC state most economically dependent on South Africa.

In Zambia, although the supply of migrant labour to South Africa was banned soon after independence,[33] many of the acute structural economic distortions of today relate back to the early labour recruitment for South Africa, which started the long tradition of migration away from rural production. When the official recruitment of labour to South Africa was banned from 1912 to 1933,[34] Northern Rhodesia came to be primarily used as a labour pool for the emergent economy of Southern Rhodesia. And, once the copper boom in Northern Rhodesia itself had begun, labour was required in the copperbelt towns.[35] Not surprisingly, rural subsistence production and social relations were deeply affected by the withdrawing of male labour from the rural areas.[36]

This was how Zambia got a 'head start' in the global urbanisation process. Today, after South Africa, Zambia is the most urbanised sub-Saharan African country. Less than half of its population remains in the rural areas, and this major economic and political factor has distorted national development since independence. If Zambia's economy had thrived, the extreme degree of urbanisation would not have resulted in the deep urban poverty which now accompanies the country's economic crisis. However, the government's economic mismanagement, which has included its failure to diversify the economy away from reliance on copper — an unstable commodity — and deteriorating international terms of trade have ensured the opposite. Zambia is now one of the most debt-distressed countries in sub-Saharan Africa (see Chapter 8).

By the 1980s, therefore, the pattern of migrant labour to South Africa had been woven into economic survival traditions for a century. When they became independent, Zambia, Tanzania, and Zimbabwe stopped labour out-migration and survived the process. However, in addition to Lesotho's national economic dependence (Lesotho is often called a 'suburb of the Rand'), migrants' earnings also remain important in southern Botswana, southern Malawi, and southern and central Mozambique. UNICEF reports,

> Not merely households but whole rural districts could be pushed into absolute poverty by the rapid withdrawal of employment opportunities in South Africa. This happened in Mozambique from 1974 — 1977 and again in 1987 — 1988.[37]

Investment and trade

South African trans-national companies

Over time, the handful of large foreign-owned finance companies which formed the South African Chamber of Mines in 1889 consolidated their domination of the developing South African economy as they diversified from mining into agriculture and then into manufacturing industries. They adapted to and survived the complex sequence of political developments in South Africa, not least because of the sustained western investment in the economy.[38]

As the South African economy industrialised, it drew in not only labour but also raw materials from the British and Portuguese territories in the rest of the region, and sold its manufactured goods to these nearby markets. South African companies, often in conjunction with western finance, were well placed to undertake much of this business, and so moved into mining, trading, agriculture, and finance in the region.

The case of copper in Zambia provides a good example. In the 1890s, Cecil Rhodes' British South Africa Company (BSAC) was given administrative control of Northern Rhodesia, together with mineral and land rights. The BSAC was formed by British gold and diamond interests in South Africa, and in Northern Rhodesia (Zambia) it hoped to make enough profits to cover its administrative outgoings.

However, although copper had been worked in Northern Rhodesia for centuries, and world demand for copper was booming (from the mid-1800s) as the electrical and telegraph industries expanded, Northern Rhodesian deposits were not fully exploited until the mid-1920s. This was due to a number of reasons. Firstly, the early workings were either of a low grade or difficult to exploit, and the small mining and prospecting companies were undercapitalised because British investors were more interested in financing the nearby copper deposits in the Belgian Congo. Secondly, a line of rail was extended from Southern Rhodesia up to the Congo mines in 1909, but it bypassed most of the Northern Rhodesian deposits. And thirdly, copper production and marketing was already dominated by the USA and Chile.

All this changed from 1923 onwards. Firstly, there was a new, post-war copper boom, largely due to the growing US automobile industry. This meant that the Northern Rhodesian deposits won the attention of two interconnected combines: Ernest Oppenheimer's Anglo American Corporation (of South Africa), and Chester Beatty's Selection Trust Ltd. (of the USA). Although Anglo American was a South African company, it was largely American-financed, and came in on this deal as the consulting engineers, using its experience of mining in nearby South Africa. The US concern had the finance necessary to develop and exploit the Northern Rhodesian mines.

Secondly, in 1923 the British South Africa Company changed its former loss-making economic policy and began to 'privatise' its concessions by extending rights to companies interested in Northern Rhodesia's copper. The US/South African combine was well-placed to buy.

Towards the end of the 1920s, the price of copper rose — largely due to price fixing by an American producers' cartel known as Copper Exporters Inc. This meant that the few copper supplies not controlled by the US cartel, such as those based on the cheap labour of Northern Rhodesia, became even more profitable. Despite a crash in prices (from 24 cents/lb. in April 1929 to 6.25 cents/lb twenty months later), the mines in Northern Rhodesia went on to become one of the world's most important producers.

Since then, the independent Zambian government has taken a controlling share of the copper industry, but Anglo American remains the other shareholding partner and has diversified its operations in Zambia. It now has important interests in most sectors of the Zambian economy, ranging from mining and mining supplies to catering and farming.

Today, a small number of South African TNCs hold investments in strategic sectors of the economies of all the nine SADCC states, particularly so in Zambia, Zimbabwe, Botswana, Swaziland, and Lesotho (and Namibia, expected to join SADCC on its independence).[39] And much of the international investment in the region is still based in South Africa, thus reinforcing South Africa's position as the region's economic centre of gravity.

South Africa's trade with the SADCC region

These corporate links have also been instrumental in developing the trading pattern between the SADCC states and South Africa. One feature of this trading relationship is that it is a regional cameo of a major distortion in global North/South trade. For the most part (as table 1 in Chapter 8 shows),

Workers at Durban docks in 1986 unloading rice from Thailand, and loading maize from Zimbabwe for export.   (Gideon Mendel / REFLEX)

South Africa exports its manufactured and agricultural goods to its neighbours, in return for raw materials. (Botswana, Lesotho, and Swaziland are especially important to South Africa's exports to the region.) This helps to inhibit the economic growth of many of the SADCC countries, unable as they singly are to develop and diversify their economic bases.

South Africa's own economy is also highly dependent on foreign trade: it depends on the import of machinery and complex manufactures from the west, and on the export of its raw and processed primary commodities; in particular, its gold and diamonds go all over the world.[40] But its agricultural and manufactured goods are not competitive in the markets of Europe and North America (because of protectionist trade policies), which makes the markets of Africa,[41] especially southern Africa, of key economic importance. (In the mid-1980s South Africa had a net trade surplus with the SADCC states equivalent to 44 per cent of South Africa's worldwide trade surplus.[42])

Another feature of the economy of the region is the comparative absence of intra-SADCC trade in comparison with the amount of trade each country conducts with South Africa (see table 5.1). Namibia, Lesotho, and Swaziland are isolated from intra-SADCC trade by geography and by the limitations of the regional transport network. But there are other important factors which

Table 5.1: Trade balances of the SADCC countries, 1970-84 ($m. at current prices)

| | With SADCC countries | | | | With South Africa | | | |
	1970	1979	1982	1984	1970	1979	1982	1984
Angola	1	-26	-7	-2	-8	-95	...	...
Botswana	-3	8	16	-36	-31	-426	-542	-493
Lesotho	...	...	-1	-1	-13	-426	-488	-362
Malawi	-18	-7	-1	-3	-9	-155	-90	-86
Mozambique	1	-14	-19	-7	-29	-76	-80	-56
Swaziland	3	1	5	3	-38	-344	-317	-215
Tanzania	16	26	-6	-2	...	...	...	...
Zambia	-47	3	-13	17	-63	-76	-140	-124
Zimbabwe	47	7	27	64	-60	-160	-147	28
SADCC	...	...	...	...	-251	-1,757	-1,808	-1,308

(Source: "SADCC in the 1990s: Development on the Front Line", EIU, op. cit., p. 133)

inhibit intra-SADCC trade, such as lack of foreign exchange, and consequent constraints on trade credit; and the fact that, because the SADCC countries were largely developed during the colonial era as suppliers of primary products to Europe and South Africa, there is not much mutual trading advantage between them (except for Botswana; and Zimbabwe, which has a comparatively developed manufacturing sector, and exports extensively to other SADCC states).

The Southern African Customs Union (SACU)[43] has further strengthened South Africa's trading links with the other members — Botswana, Lesotho, Swaziland, and Namibia. SACU provides for a unified customs tariff and a sharing of revenue from a common customs pool based on the levels of imports from all sources.

Because of these distorted trading relationships, SADCC has recently given priority to its 'Investment in Production' programme, which aims ultimately to increase intra-regional trade (see Chapter 8).

South Africa's need for the region's markets is likely to increase, given the present US policy towards South Africa and the gloomy export prospects which the Single European Market could mean for South Africa after 1992. This is one reason why South Africa has gone to great lengths to maintain its share of the regional markets, using a variety of export incentives.[44]

Trade in energy supplies is also an important factor in regional trading relationships, and one which has been significantly manipulated by South Africa for its political leverage and economic benefit.[45] For example, Zimbabwe's oil pipeline to Beira has been frequently sabotaged, and the routine destruction of the Cabora Bassa pylons — built so that Mozambique can sell electricity to South Africa — has meant that instead Mozambique has had to import electricity from South Africa. Although Angola's oil supplies are not traded within the region, South Africa has also sabotaged Angolan oil storage and refinery facilities.

Thus, energy supplies, particularly for Botswana, Lesotho, and Swaziland, are a key area of dependence. Accordingly, developing the region's energy sector has also been a key priority for SADCC, and one which has attracted much international support.[46]

Transport networks

Transport routes in southern Africa have always been a highly political issue, closely tied as they are to economic interests. An early example was the rail link from the gold mines in the Transvaal to Lorenzo Marques (Maputo) port, which was built by mining wealth in the 1890s. It was not only the shortest route to the coast, but it was also the first outlet to the sea from the goldmines in the Transvaal Boer Republic which could not, at the time, be controlled by the British. (At that time, the British South African colonies were Natal and Cape Colony, straddling all the other rail links to the sea.)

Because Britain's heavy engineering industry was the most advanced in the world during the boom period of European colonialism (following the 'scramble for Africa' in the 1880s), a great deal of British investment, skill, and machinery was exported to build up the transport networks of the colonies, including those in southern Africa. Even non-British colonies turned to Britain for their railways. The important Lobito (Benguela) line in Angola, for example, was completed in 1928, using British investment and equipment. Today, Angolan railway workers carefully restore the old British-made rolling stock which is so frequently blown up by UNITA guerrillas.

Another 'political' railway was the Chinese-built 'Tazara' line between Tanzania and Zambia, built in the 1970s to help landlocked Zambia during the period of sanctions against Rhodesia. For this reason it was called the 'Uhuru' (freedom) railway. During the liberation war in Zimbabwe, Rhodesian forces blew up the Chisamba railway bridge on this line, successfully cutting off Zambia's lifeline and forcing it to reopen its border with Rhodesia.

Destabilisation has made southern Africa's transport system more politically charged than ever before. As we have seen, in theory the region is well served with five east—west transport corridors. But in practice South Africa has sabotaged and manipulated SADCC trade transport in a number of ways.[47] This element of its regional destabilisation strategy has come to be known, with more than a tinge of irony, as 'transport diplomacy'.

The SADCC region's first priority has been to rehabilitate the SADCC region's five transport corridors, and the shared need to take action has formed the basis of most intra-SADCC political cooperation to date. Despite sustained sabotage, this strategy has started to bring results to the Beira line, while work on the Limpopo and Nacala lines is also beginning to bear fruit. As at the end of 1989, however, work on plans to rehabilitate the Lobito line was still held up by conflict, although international funding had been pledged.

Between 1980 and 1988 aid worth around US$1,000 m. went into rehabilitating the region's transport network.[48] Once these routes are fully rehabilitated, the SADCC region stands to save over US$300 m. a year on transport costs.[49] To date, international aid to Mozambique for transport rehabilitation, worth some US$150 m., has been blown up by MNR guerrillas.

As part of its transport and communications focus, the rehabilitation of SADCC's ports has also been a key priority, with the aim of upgrading handling efficiency and profitability.. Profits from transport routes and the use of ports are a valuable source of foreign exchange to all the seaboard SADCC countries. It is especially important to Mozambique, where the pre-independence economy was structured to take full advantage of South African and Rhodesian trade traffic, to the extent of extreme dependence. In the year before independence, this accounted for over 25 per cent of Mozambique's foreign exchange earnings, less than half of which came from exports of goods. Since then, Mozambique has paid dearly for the sealing of its borders with UDI Rhodesia, for South African-backed sabotage of its transport routes, and for South Africa's imposition of sanctions in the form of a reduction in the amount of its trade passing through Maputo port.[50]

The case of Namibia

Alongside Lesotho, Namibia is perhaps the most striking example of South Africa's economic dominance in the region. It was ruled by South Africa for 69 years, and its economy has been entirely shaped and controlled to suit South African and other foreign interests. [51] As a result, the Namibian economy is highly dependent on South Africa for both trade and transport links, and is integrated into its financial system. These dependencies and the structural economic distortions which South African occupation has created[52] pose a challenge to Namibia's independence, in all but the formal, political sense. Prospects for the kind of development which is so badly needed are slim.

Shortly before the transitional period to independence began, Andimba Toivo Ja Toivo, SWAPO's Secretary General, said that independent Namibia might elect to join SACU. He explained, "We will have to sit and talk with them, otherwise we are the ones who will suffer; even if they don't want to, we will keep knocking at their door." Citing the stranglehold which South Africa has on Namibia's economy, he said that independent Namibia would have to negotiate agreement over the use of Walvis Bay, over which South Africa insists it has sovereignty.[53]

Walvis Bay

The Walvis Bay enclave (covering 1,214 square kilometres) contains Namibia's only deep-water port. Despite eventually agreeing to decolonise Namibia, South Africa claims Walvis Bay as part of its own territory.[54] This defies world opinion, expressed clearly in 1978 when the UN Security Council ruled that the status of Walvis Bay was a matter for negotiation between an independent Namibia and South Africa, and called for the early reintegration of the territory into an independent Namibia.[55] A number of

Namibia

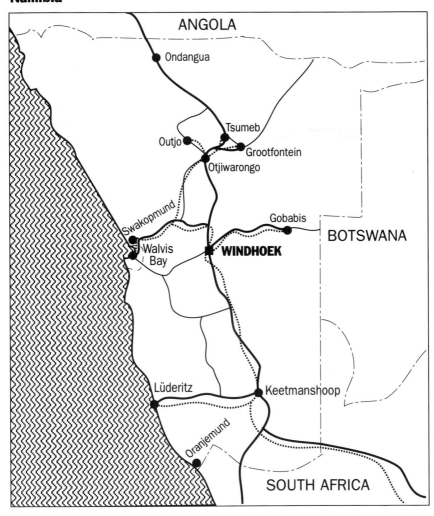

strong legal arguments have also been advanced to refute South Africa's territorial claim.[56]

Control of the Bay and the surrounding area gives South Africa a military foothold in the heart of independent Namibia (Walvis Bay has long been a South African military and naval base), and control over the fishing industry based on the Bay. But arguably the most important leverage is its control over the only port capable of handling the independent nation's trade in any quantity. Some 40 per cent of all Namibia's foreign trade passes through

Walvis Bay, December 1989. Namibia's only deep-water port is claimed by South Africa. This sign has been erected in preparation for Namibian independence.   (IDAF)

Walvis Bay (a proportion which would increase once Namibia managed to diversify its trading partners), including some 97 per cent of its sea trade. In 1989, 99 per cent of all Namibia's foreign trade passed either through or to South Africa, or through the South African-held Walvis Bay.

In other words, South Africa's grip over export and import routes will in no way be loosened by Namibia's independence. This crucial leverage is enhanced by Namibia's economic integration with South Africa and by South Africa's domination of Namibia's transport network. Regaining control of Walvis Bay will be vital to Namibia's future development. Schemes to develop an alternative port, or to channel trade through Angola, would be extremely costly.

Britain, with its historical links with Namibia and particularly its former annexation of Walvis Bay, has a responsibility to press for its reintegration into Namibian territory.

South African domination of Namibia's transport networks

Firstly, the state-controlled South African Transport Services (SATS) manages Namibia's road and rail transport system on a contract basis, and administers the ports.

Secondly, although Namibia's communications infrastructure is well

developed in comparison with many other SADCC states, it was established
to serve the military, economic, and administrative interests of South Africa
as the occupying power, rather than to serve the goals for which SADCC was
formed.   As a result, Namibia's transport links with its other neighbouring
states — Angola, Zambia, Zimbabwe, and Botswana — are very restricted.

Taking these two factors together with South Africa's occupation of
Walvis Bay, it is clear that South Africa could, if it wanted, impose a trade
blockade on Namibia, in much the same way as it did on Lesotho in 1985.

South African domination of Namibia's production and trade

Namibia inherits a distorted production system, shaped for the most part by
colonial interests, but also by a small population and a very particular
ecology. [57]   85 per cent of goods produced in Namibia are exported, and 80
per cent of goods consumed are imported — mostly from South Africa, from
where 75 per cent of Namibian imports originate.[58]   Half of the food
consumed in Namibia is imported from South Africa. [59]

Although, for the time being, most exports must be routed either through
South Africa or through South African-held territory (Walvis Bay), there is

*Judging cattle at the Otjiwarongo Agricultural Show for commercial farmers,
Namibia, 1985. Most of Namibia's viable farmland is owned by commercial farmers.
Peasant farmers subsist in the poor, overcrowded, 'homelands'.*   (Susanna Smith / Oxfam)

real international demand for Namibian raw materials (in particular for its uranium, base metals, diamonds, beef, and fisheries products). And, for as long as this demand continues, there will not be total trade dependence on South Africa, which presently accounts for only 25 per cent of all Namibia's exports by destination.[60]

Uranium, diamonds, and copper account for a third of Namibia's GDP, and 85 per cent of export earnings.[61] In the long term, Namibia's dependence on mining earnings leaves it vulnerable to external demand and price shocks, although the outlook is good for the time being.

Most of Namibia's population depend on agriculture (although in many of Namibia's impoverished rural areas it is not possible to speak even of 'subsistence' agriculture), but the development of small-scale agriculture has been ignored. The colonial authorities concentrated resources on the white-owned commercial farming sector[62] (mostly ranching), while black Namibian farmers were actively discouraged from the commercial production of fruit, cereals, and vegetables in order to give South African producers a captive market for their own food surplus.[63] Some 48 per cent of the 6,000 cattle and karakul ranches are owned by foreign (mostly South African) absentee landlords. who either live in town and make occasional visits to their farms,

A resident of Otjimbingwe, central Namibia. Many of the households in this area are headed by women caring for their grandchildren, while their sons and daughters are looking for work in the towns.   (Susanna Smith / Oxfam)

or who live abroad (mostly in South Africa).[64]

All of Namibia's oil and coal supplies are shipped in through Walvis Bay, or brought in by rail from South Africa. However, Namibia has significant energy resources of its own — gas and oil — which remain to be fully exploited.

South African state and private corporations

Namibia's mining industry is totally dominated by foreign investors, mainly by British and South African TNCs.[65] In the overall context of this foreign ownership pattern, South African corporations — especially Consolidated Diamond Mines, Gencor, and the parastatal Iscor — play an important role.

In particular, the diamond industry (which generated US$271 m. in export earnings in 1986) is dominated by Consolidated Diamond Mines (CDM), a wholly owned subsidiary of de Beers, itself controlled by (and a major shareholder of) the giant Anglo American Corporation.

Namibia's offshore fish resources are among the richest in the world, but have been almost entirely exhausted by foreign interests (principally, South African[66] and Soviet[67]). On independence, the Namibian government will be able to do much to secure these resources for the national benefit.

Debt

South Africa claims that Namibia stands to inherit a national external debt of some R500 m., over 10 per cent of its GDP (1989 figures),[68] a 'debt' which has accrued because of South Africa's occupation.

From the early 1980s onwards, the South African-appointed administration financed the country's budget deficit by transfers from the South African government, and by commercial loans from South African banks guaranteed by the South African government. During the 1980s, the South African government cut back its funding of the territory (from 21.6 per cent of GDP in 1983 to 3 per cent of GDP in 1989[69]), with the result that the deficit became increasingly financed by commercial loans, and by greater domestic tax revenue. In effect, payment for South Africa's illegal occupation was being deferred — until the establishment of an independent nation.

Namibia will also inherit a budget deficit of R382 m.,[70] partly as a result of South Africa withdrawing budgetary support during the transition period. The South African government was unwilling to underwrite fresh loans to cover this. According to the South African-appointed Administrator General, Louis Pienaar, "The question is the incoming government's approach to the country's debt obligations".[71] Implicit in this statement is a clear warning to the independent government not to refuse responsibility for its inherited debt.

Katatura, Namibia, 4 May 1989: the anniversary of the Kassinga massacre in 1978, when South African troops killed 700 SWAPO refugees in southern Angola. The crowd is also celebrating Namibia's forthcoming independence.

(Kelvin Jenkins / Oxfam)

During the politically crucial first few years of independence, when the popular expectations which fuelled the struggle for independence will run high, the new nation will need to raise loans to finance development projects. Independent Namibia's economic and development challenges will be difficult enough as it is; an inherited debt burden will be a serious additional handicap. Under international law, a strong case can be made to the effect that the independent nation should not be held liable.[72] Coordinated international action is needed to relieve newly-independent Namibia of this burden.

Rand Monetary Area and Southern African Customs Union

Two key decisions for the independent government of Namibia to tackle are Namibia's membership of the Rand Monetary Area (RMA),[73] and the Southern African Customs Union (SACU).[74] In both cases, Namibia has been involved involuntarily as if it were a part of South African territory. These structures have done much to knit Namibia's economy into South Africa's.

Among other things, membership of the RMA has meant that all financial transactions are made in rand, and that South African regulations apply to all international movements of capital in and out of Namibia. Separation from the RMA would therefore involve the establishment of a Namibian Central Bank, a national currency, and a policy on exchange rates. The independent strength of a new currency would mostly depend on the origins and destination of Namibia's trade, its main foreign-exchange earner. If Namibia manages to develop and diversify its trading relationships successfully, then there will be less pressure on the independent government to re-enter SACU. However, in the short term, the 'cash in hand' incentive of SACU customs pool receipts[75] will put the new government under considerable pressure to negotiate entry into SACU as a separate state.

The reintegration of Walvis Bay and the construction of more regional transport networks are crucial, not only to Namibia's future independence from South Africa, but also to its independence, if so desired, from SACU. Although more than 70 per cent of the value of Namibia's exports could be transported directly to international markets by air, more than 90 per cent of all imports come directly from, or via, South Africa by sea, road or rail.[76] South Africa is well placed to exert leverage and ensure Namibia's continued trading dependence.

But there would be long-term disadvantages of SACU membership for the economy. In particular, the development of local industry and therefore Namibia's future capacity to play a full role in SADCC's 'Investment in Production programme (for strengthening regional production and trade) would be hampered by tariff-free imports from South Africa, where there is a relatively efficient, high-volume production capacity. Furthermore, it has been calculated that some 80 per cent of Namibia's imports would be cheaper if bought from elsewhere.[77] On the other hand, if it is to develop a viable, indigenous industrial/manufacturing base, Namibia will have to produce goods for overseas export which either compete with, or cannot be produced by, other countries in the region.

Although Namibia will join SADCC on independence, all the signs are that Namibia's economic independence will continue to be compromised by South Africa. The process of delinking will have to be gradual (and will in all probability never be absolute). Even so, it will require substantial international pressure to reintegrate Walvis Bay, and to increase Namibia's foreign trade. It is to be hoped that the future relationship between Namibia and post-apartheid, democratic South Africa will show that the many 'natural' economic linkages between them need not be manipulated as political levers.

South Africa's dependence on the region

Much attention is paid to the economic vulnerabilities of the SADCC states in relation to South Africa, but this is not the whole picture. The South African economy has itself become significantly dependent on the SADCC region, despite its greater size and its unrivalled dominance.[78] This dependency has been enhanced by international trade and financial sanctions, and by trade protectionism in the West.

South Africa is looking to expand exports throughout Africa. Reportedly, in 1989, South African exporters were doing business in 47 African countries.[79] In spite of sanctions, foreign exchange shortages and other technical snags, South African government and business leaders believe that increasing the export of finished and semi-finished goods to African markets is vital for further growth in the economy. It is also thought that new export opportunities have been created in Africa for South Africa to take advantage of, because of the general downturn in international aid (much of which was tied to the purchase of imports from the donor countries).[80]

By the mid-1980s (South African trade statistics have been classified as strategic information since 1986, and later data are therefore unavailable[81]), the SADCC states were purchasing 10 per cent of all South Africa's exports and 20 per cent of its non-gold exports. At the same time, South Africa's exports to SADCC were valued at $1.7 bn., $135 m. more than South Africa's total exports to the EC of all food, agricultural, and coal products. With substantially fewer SADCC imports moving the other way, South Africa had a net trade surplus with the SADCC states of $1.3 bn., an amount which was equivalent to 44 per cent of its world-wide surplus.[82] (See table 5.2.)

South Africa's balance of payments surplus with the region is further increased by other major flows, including revenue from transport services, and the profits and dividends on South African investment in the region. The Overseas Development Institute estimates that on top of the visible trade surplus given above, South Africa was running an overall invisible surplus as high as $150 m. The most important element of this surplus is the revenue earned by South African Transport Services (the state-owned rail and port authority) for carrying SADCC's extra-regional trade, which brings in an estimated income of between $200 m. and $300 m. a year. (As we have seen, a substantial part of these earnings derives from South Africa's destabilisation of the alternative SADCC transport corridors.) The main reverse payment flows from South Africa to the region were derived from migrant workers' remittances, and from SACU dues to Botswana, Lesotho and Swaziland.[83]

Table 5.2: South Africa's net current account surplus with SADCC countries * ($ m.)

	Net receipts	Net payments
Visible trade	1,300-1,500	
Invisibles		
Transport	200-300	
Other non-factor services	100-200	
Labour remittances, pensions, etc		
from South Africa		200-350
from SADCC	50-100	
Profits & dividends	100-150	
Customs union **		300
Total	1,750-2,250	500-650
Overall balance	1,250-1,600	

*   Summary estimate, mid-1980s

**   These represent gross payments from the common customs pool. Taxes paid by Botswana, Lesotho and Swaziland (BLS) to the pool are partially included in the cif value of their imports from South Africa. Payments into the pool (a) for excise duties paid on excisable production in BLS, and (b) for import duties or import surcharges on goods imported from outside the customs area by BLS, are not available, but represent flows to South Africa from the BLS.

(Source: "SADCC in the 1990s: Development on the Front Line", op.cit., p.134)

Thus, the extensive economic links between South Africa and much of the region are part of a complex web of interdependence. This circumscribes the SADCC states' political independence and scope for economic development, but it also limits South Africa's economic responses to international pressure.

SADCC is working to reduce dependence on South Africa to levels which remove some of these constraints.[84] It also aims to promote intra-SADCC economic linkages, thus correcting the over-reliance on trade with South Africa created by history. Much hinges on this process and its outcome, and two key issues arise: first, the vexed question of the effect which increased international sanctions against South Africa might have on the SADCC states; and second, the prospects for future regional cooperation with South Africa.

Sanctions and South Africa's neighbours[85]

It is often argued that imposing or extending sanctions against South Africa will increase the poverty and suffering of people living in the SADCC region. The argument is two-fold. One strand is that the harm done to South Africa's own economy will have adverse knock-on effects on the rest of the region. The second strand is that South Africa will respond to increased international sanctions against it by imposing its own sanctions against its neighbours, possibly severing links altogether, thus causing additional poverty and hardship.

In direct contrast to this view, SADCC,[86] the Commonwealth, the UN, and the FLS alliance repeatedly call on the international community to step up their sanctions pressure on the South African government, and many countries have complied.[87]

However, towards the end of the 1980s, as the human and economic costs of destabilisation mounted beyond all expectations, as the South African economy has become increasingly dependent on the SADCC region, and as cumulative pressures on apartheid are seen to bring results, the equation has altered. It is now increasingly held that, on balance and in the long run, effective measures to hasten the end of apartheid, even including sanctions, would enhance the region's economic prospects. A number of factors have to be assessed.

The risk of retaliation

Of course, in the volatile political atmosphere of South Africa's politics and its relationship with the SADCC region, it is impossible to predict with accuracy what political pressures might bear on the future decisions of the South African government. However, if the growing influence of the 'verligte' outlook in government continues, South Africa seems unlikely to take extreme retaliatory measures, because such actions would further reduce the government's international standing.

As far as the economy is concerned, there are compelling reasons of self-interest why South Africa should not completely sever its links with the region. The economic interdependency factor means that it would be in neither side's interest.[88] However, targeted economic retaliatory measures might well be adopted in the future to cause economic damage, just as they have been frequently in the past.

If South Africa did not comprehensively sever its economic links with the SADCC region, and regardless of whether or not it adopted targeted retaliatory measures, there would nevertheless be various inevitable consequences.

The knock-on effects of sanctions against South Africa

The knock-on effects on the SADCC region have been assessed as likely to be a mixture of negative and positive.

On the negative side, the weakness of the SADCC economies and the range of their economic dependence on South Africa mean that, to the extent that sanctions against South Africa lead to lower growth rates in its economy, the demand for SADCC's imports and labour may be reduced. In turn, this will tend to reduce domestic demand within the SADCC economies, which will decrease their demand for South African exports, and thus stimulate a regional deflationary spiral — a run-down of trade and economic activity.[89]

On the positive side, the SADCC region's export trade may get a boost. Firstly, although South Africa is a major supplier of SADCC's imports (and it must be noted that many of these are crucial to export production), it accounts for less than 10 per cent of SADCC's export markets, with the important exceptions of Lesotho and Swaziland. The most important influences on SADCC's export trade are the price and demand for their products outside the region (see Chapter 8).

Furthermore, one of the effects of already existing sanctions against South Africa has been to depress the value of the Rand, which has in turn reduced the price of South Africa's exports and services to the SADCC region,[90] on which there is considerable dependence.[91]

On balance, the difficulties created by the complex pattern of interdependency — whether increased sanctions provoke increased retaliatory action or not — should not be underestimated. However, it is thought that the adverse knock-on effects will be gradual enough in nature to permit a step-by-step programme of adjustment. In particular, there is a strong case for the international community to consider international aid to 'cushion' the SADCC region against adverse shocks, and ease the adjustment process.[92] Lesotho — the 'hostage state' — would need to be treated as a special case.[93] Britain, however, is set against the idea of compensating the SADCC region for losses incurred through sanctions against South Africa.

The wider context

It is, however, a partial view to consider the arguments for and against sanctions as if the regional context was otherwise 'normal'. As this report aims to show, the people of the SADCC region are already paying a very high price for the way in which history has made South Africa the dominant economic and military power.

To the incalculable human costs of South Africa's regional policy must be added the gigantic economic costs. The most important issue therefore is to tackle the root causes of poverty and underdevelopment in the region, among which apartheid in South Africa is prominent. As Peter Msumi, the Chairman of SADCC's Council of Ministers and Vice-President of Botswana, said when he opened the SADCC annual conference in Harare on 30.1.86,

> When we join the international campaign for effective measures to end apartheid, we do so in the full knowledge that some of the effects of such measures will impose hardships on ourselves. But we accept these hardships, like a woman in labour, in the hopes that they will usher in a new era of peace, stability and security for the region.
>
> When an exasperated international community calls for effective measures to incapacitate South Africa's economic motor, which drives the aggressive machine, our dependency relationship is invoked as rationale and justification for resisting such action ... How much more suffering can be saved by world inaction and acquiescence to apartheid?

Southern African economic cooperation after apartheid

In a post-apartheid southern Africa, the potential for increased economic cooperation throughout the region will be substantial. However, for as long as apartheid and minority rule persist in South Africa, a triple economic brake is applied to the region.

Firstly, South Africa's destabilisation has cost the SADCC region an estimated US$62,450 m. between 1980 and 1988. [94] As Chapters 4 and 6 point out, conflict in Angola and Mozambique still ravages local subsistence, the national economies, and neighbouring economies. Moreover, South Africa's aggressive economic actions have compounded these costs.

Secondly, economic development in South Africa itself is limited by apartheid in a number of important ways. The majority of South Africans have no democratic political rights and therefore no say in how the country's economy should be run to reflect their economic interests. Black education and training have been neglected, to the point where the industrial sector now faces a skills shortage.[95] Apartheid legislation restricting where people may live and work affects their economic options.[96] The huge inequalities in wealth and public service provision severely limit the development of human potential. Internal markets are restricted not only by the size of the population, but also by the vastly lower living standards of black people. The bureaucratic and security apparatus in place to police and administer apartheid is extremely costly and inefficient.[97] Disinvestment and sanctions are having an effect,[98] stimulated by political instability, a narrowing economic future, and public opprobrium.

Collecting water in the Transkei 'homeland'. Massive resources will be needed to redress the extreme inequalities created by apartheid.

(Monique Blanchet / Oxfam)

As is often pointed out, some economic developments inside the country are beginning to undermine many of the state's apartheid constructs, but it cannot be claimed that they will, alone, be able to demolish the system. The relaxation of some apartheid restrictions has facilitated the emergence of black entrepreneurs, but this alone cannot change the poor economic prospects of the majority — especially the millions of people living in the 'homelands'.

This debate was given a thorough airing in mid-1988. In a speech to the Royal Commonwealth Society, Sir Geoffrey Howe, then Foreign Secretary, said,

I believe that industrial interdependence in the modern South African economy, combined with demographic trends, will make apartheid increasingly unworkable ... On a reasonable birthrate projection the ratio of black to white in ten years' time will be eight to one. The means of life, and basic economic and social rights, cannot be provided for numbers like these within the straitjacket of apartheid.[99]

Some three weeks later, Oliver Tambo, President of the ANC, replied, in a speech given on his behalf to a conference in London,

Once more it is being argued that economic development within South Africa and population growth will, in themselves, lead to the destruction of the apartheid system. Yet the point has been demonstrated over and over again that it was during the period of the strongest growth of the South African economy, during the sixties and the seventies, that the apartheid regime and the racist system were at their strongest and most vicious.

To take care of the rapid growth of the African population, even at that time, the apartheid regime carried out a vast programme of forced removals of the African people into the Bantustans and resettlement camps ...

At this point, we would like to advise, in all humility, that it does not contribute to the ending of the South African tragedy to have senior British politicians take on board and reiterate the false images of South African reality which the Pretoria regime propagates in its attempt to justify the existence of the apartheid system. One of these is the notion that the substance of the politics of our country is determined by the jostling of various tribes for a place in the sun.

A funeral gathering in Alexandra Township, South Africa, 1986. In the background is a casspir — the armoured vehicle used by the police and the SADF.   (IDAF)

What defines the substance of the turmoil in our country is the confrontation between the forces of democracy on the one hand and those of racism on the other ... [100]

Over the last decade, it has become increasingly clear that apartheid is serving business interests poorly. In the view of the British Industry Committee on South Africa, "A healthy economy is impossible without political change and continued reform."[101] And in a speech to The Urban Foundation in Johannesburg, Sir Robin Renwick, Britain's Ambassador to South Africa, said,

It is unfortunately a myth that capitalism guides the key decisions of the State in South Africa. I only wish it did. In fact the principles of free enterprise and of racial segregation are totally incompatible ... By modern standards this is a hopelessly over-regulated society, with one of the world's more cumbersome bureaucracies. And many if not most of those regulations, for instance the restrictions on land use, as well as a high proportion of those bureaucratic jobs, stem from the continued enforcement of aspects of the apartheid system. [102]

Apartheid and minority rule in South Africa act as an economic brake on the region in a third way, in that they inhibit the realisation of full regional economic cooperation. Because of apartheid and South Africa's regional destabilisation, economic cooperation projects remain limited to those requiring the minimum of political cooperation. Yet the potential of full regional cooperation is immense, as was long ago realised by colonial Britain, and has since been recognised by South Africa and the SADCC states themselves.

What then are the prospects for future regional cooperation involving South Africa once democratic majority rule is established? There has not been a great deal of research into this question. Two different issues need to be separated in this highly speculative realm.

One is the market-led effects of South Africa on the region, which could cut both ways. For example, if South Africa's economic growth proves to be more rapid, one result of a higher rate of growth on the region is likely to be an increase in regional exports to South Africa. But at the same time, market forces alone may well, due to the dominance of South Africa's economy, continue to suck in resources from the region without promoting a more equitable form of regional development.

The other issue is the need for positive economic cooperation of the sort which requires a fair degree of political commonality. In this regard, there is ground for belief that the future holds greater, mutually advantageous, economic cooperation. For example, a great deal more could be done on a wholly regional basis to improve the region's transport system.[103] Repair and maintenance facilities could be better (and more economically) pooled, ensuring access to all partners. And South Africa could greatly help the SADCC regional food security programme.

As SADCC spokespeople have pointed out, even after the advent of majority rule in South Africa, future economic cooperation must tackle the distorted economic relationships which have been built up over the years.[104]

It has been argued that the establishment of majority rule in South Africa may not work in the interests of regional economic advancement.[105] This point of view holds that the sheer dominance of South Africa's economy, together with the need for the future government to give priority to the pressing domestic economic concerns which apartheid has created for the future, could combine to undermine equitable regional development.

Another point of view holds that SADCC programmes are wasting resources which should rather go towards developing the productive capacity of the separate countries of the region and towards the liberation of South Africa: "The most telling questioning of SADCC comes from the South African liberation movements. They point out that the underlying assumption of SADCC is that South Africa will be no nearer liberation in twenty or more years. If this is not the case, then surely the huge investment in this project is a catastrophic waste?"[106]

SADCC's view, however, is that South Africa will be a great asset to the rest of the region, provided that a more balanced relationship is built. As Simba Makoni, SADCC's Executive Secretary, explained,

> Economic cooperation on southern Africa is not based on our abhorrence of apartheid. It is firmly rooted in the realisation of the inadequacies of small, under-developed and truncated national economies, unable separately and individually to sustain a viable modern industrial base. It also recognises the benefits to be derived from an equitable, balanced regional integration based on the natural resource endowments of the different countries. It is based on the acceptance of collective self-reliance, inter-dependence and equity, rather than dependence and domination.

> On this basis, SADCC and its member states have stated right from the beginning that an independent Namibia and a democratic South Africa will automatically be admitted into the organisation. A democratic South Africa, conducting its affairs according to the will of the people, and in accordance with regional and international norms, and accepting the rules of cooperation and equitable interdependence, holds enormous potential for the development of our region.[107]

The key point is that the region's full economic potential cannot be discovered until the whole region can actively cooperate politically. Forward-looking collaborative ventures based on extensive inter-governmental cooperation, such as prevails within Europe, for instance, require basic political common denominators. Although some joint initiatives are already being undertaken, for example, the Highlands Water Scheme in Lesotho and the Cabora Bassa Dam project in Mozambique, there is unlikely to be full cooperation for as long as apartheid and minority rule exist in South Africa.

6

The economic costs of destabilisation

The economic costs arising from South African-backed conflict in the region have been massive. The greatest losses have been directly due to conflict in Angola and Mozambique, intensified and prolonged by South African support to the rebel movements. The war-torn countries themselves are the worst affected, but the costs to the other countries in the region have also been high.

The economic consequences of this situation will be long-lasting. 'Recovery' is an elusive concept while war continues to ravage vital transport routes and economic infrastructure. It is the poor who are most vulnerable to the sharp economic decline which war has so greatly aggravated throughout the region.[1] (Chapter 8 describes the other economic pressures affecting southern Africa.)

The economic instruments of destabilisation

The southern African transport network is the key to the region's economic vulnerability. Systematic rebel sabotage of Mozambique's transport routes has seriously affected the economies of Zimbabwe, Zambia, Malawi, and Mozambique, and it has also increased the region's dependence on South Africa. This is because much of their trade has to be re-routed (at increased cost) to South African ports, using South African transport systems. Mozambique has lost the revenue which it could have earned from the trade traffic. Zambia and Zimbabwe have also suffered from deliberate, costly delays on routes through South Africa. (Lesotho, landlocked, and surrounded

Guarding the Beira line. Enormous resources have been diverted to defence. Zimbabwe spent an estimated US$ 3 bn. between 1980 and 1988 to protect its trade routes through Mozambique.   (Keith Bernstein / Oxfam)

by South Africa, is especially vulnerable to South African interference with its trade routes: a blockade mounted in December 1985 brought about the fall of the anti-apartheid government in January 1986.)

In addition, direct attacks on production units, especially those earning foreign exchange such as tea estates, mines, and petroleum installations (as has happened in Mozambique, Angola, and Zimbabwe), cause loss of output and therefore revenue.

Widespread terror campaigns in the rural areas of Mozambique and Angola have not only destroyed peasant agricultural production and government services, but they have also created the need for massive relief programmes to cater for millions of displaced and destitute people.

As the years roll on, these factors have had a cumulative effect on national economic performance.

The economic costs

Many factors must be assessed when computing the economic costs of conflict and South Africa's regional policy.[2] The main elements are the destruction directly caused to infrastructure, services, and property; the extra defence costs, which represent a diversion away from development and

Table 6.1:   Gross Domestic Product (GDP) loss in the SADCC region, 1980-1988

($ m. in 1988 prices)

Country	1988		1980-1988	
	Loss	% of actual GDP	Loss	% of 1988 actual GDP
Angola	4,500	90	30,000	600
Mozambique	3,000	110	15,000	550
Zimbabwe	1,350	25	8,000	145
Malawi	550	30	2,150	133
Zambia	500	20	5,000	200
Tanzania	500	10	1,300	26
Botswana	125	10	500	40
Lesotho	50	7	300	42
Swaziland	30	5	200	33
All SADCC	10,605	43	62,450	210

(Source: National data and preliminary GDP estimates)

productive investment;[3] the loss of economic output; higher transport costs; and the costs of providing relief and survival assistance to the victims of war.

The total economic cost of conflict and South Africa's regional policy to the SAADCC states between 1980 and 1988 has been estimated by the UN's Economic Commission for Africa at $62,450 m. (on a GDP loss basis, at 1988 prices, see table 6.1[4]). This is equivalent to over twice the combined annual Gross Domestic Product (GDP) for 1988 of the SADCC states, and three times as much as the gross inflow of external resources into the region (aid grants, 'soft' loans, export credit, and commercial loans) for 1988.[5]

Each of the SADCC national economies is differently affected by conflict and South Africa's regional policy, according to their different economic, geographic, and political positions within the region and in relation to South Africa. The following case study of Malawi illustrates how just one of the economic consequences of conflict listed above — the transport factor — has hobbled a national economy and worsened the (already narrowing) economic survival options for the poorest. Between 1980 and 1988, the disruption of transport routes alone cost Malawi approximately $500 m.[6]

Displaced young people in Quelimane, Mozambique, crowded into the local school in December 1986. The war has done incalculable damage to the education and training of this generation.   (Jenny Matthews / Oxfam)

Case-study: How conflict in Mozambique affects the economy of Malawi

Sometimes described in tourist brochures as the "Switzerland of Africa", landlocked Malawi has lakes, mountains, and beautiful scenery. But the picturesque analogy is limited. Malawi, along with Mozambique, is one of Africa's poorest countries. In terms of Gross National Product (GNP) per capita, it is the sixth poorest country in the world, according to World Bank data, which recorded a figure of $160 in 1987.[7] The national economy faces very serious problems due to the combined effects of land shortage, international debt service obligations, unstable commodity prices, and rising import costs. Furthermore, since independence in 1964, the government's harsh economic development policies have eroded the livelihoods of the poor. (See Chapter 8.)

This is the context in which the effects of the war in Mozambique should be seen. Although Malawi is the only southern African state which has formally established diplomatic relations with South Africa, it has suffered a great deal from the consequences of South Africa's support to the MNR.

The peculiar political geography resulting from the colonial division of southern Africa has made Malawi vulnerable to the effects of the war in Mozambique for two main reasons. Firstly, because of its long, rural border with Mozambique, an estimated 790,000 Mozambican refugees have fled to Malawi. They impose an unprecedented burden on local host communities and state services. Secondly, because it is landlocked, Malawi's economy, dependent on the export of primary commodities, has been strangled by MNR sabotage of the two 'natural' rail routes to the coast — the lines through Mozambique to the ports of Nacala and Beira.

The disruption of Malawi's rail routes out to the sea through Mozambique began in 1982.[8] It has exacerbated the structural weaknesses of Malawi's economy — its high degree of dependence on imported manufactured goods and on its overseas export crops (which contribute over 90 per cent of national foreign exchange earnings),[9] a high level of external debt, and a very poor rural population, extremely dependent on employment in the export crop sector.

A landlocked agricultural economy

Hundreds of thousands of poor families depend, wholly or in part, on the wages of unskilled workers in the commercial agriculture sector. This has arisen because (in the absence of any other developed natural resource) agriculture for export is the chief productive sector of the economy, and (ironically) because of land shortage which has undermined subsistence agriculture, especially in the Southern Region. British investment still plays a key role in Malawi's export crop industry. (British companies involved include Lonrho plc, Eastern Produce (Holdings) plc, the Africa Lakes Corporation plc, Standard Commercial Tobacco Co. (UK) Ltd., Allied Lyons plc, and Unilever plc.)

Malawi's export trade involves the freight of high-bulk, low-value cargo, principally tobacco, sugar, and tea. According to the way in which local transit and transport systems are priced, the direct rail routes through Mozambique have been the only cost-effective means of exporting this produce.

The disruption of these routes means not only that exports have to be rerouted overland, at extra expense, to South African and Tanzanian ports, but also that commodities must be stockpiled, waiting for transport. For example, in June 1987, a British tea estate manager explained that transport hold-ups were affecting the 70-75 per cent of the estate's crop which was destined for overseas markets, and meant that "34 weeks of tea is sitting around in stores. It hasn't been economic to sell a lot of last year's crop and the next season's

Tea pickers on a commercial estate in Mulanje District, south eastern Malawi, July 1988 — earning the equivalent of 15 pence for a 10-hour day.   (Jeanne Fitzsimmons)

crop is coming up. The only thing which may save us is the nasty war in Sri Lanka which is upping our price."

These factors, together with the fundamental economic insecurity caused by falling and unstable commodity prices (see Chapters 8 and 9), have squeezed the foreign exchange cash flows of the commercial agricultural sector and the national economy, aggravated the decline in the profitability of the export crops sector, and so further weakened Malawi's international terms of trade. This, in turn, has adversely affected the other productive sectors of the economy, and their employment potential. This is particularly serious for the poorest in Malawi because, unlike many other African countries, land shortage means that many do not have the 'last resort' option of returning to the land and subsistence agriculture.

Because Malawi is landlocked, the profitability of its export crops and industrial sector is acutely sensitive to freight and insurance costs, as well as to timing. Until 1982, some 95 per cent of Malawi's trade went by rail through the Mozambican ports of Beira and Nacala (which handled approximately 65 per cent and 30 per cent of the total respectively). By 1987, however, over 95 per cent of external trade was passing through South Africa, either via the Tete corridor to Zimbabwe and thence to South Africa, or to Zambia for onward transportation to South Africa via either Zimbabwe or Botswana. The distances involved are more than four times greater.

A further costly complication arises from the fact that the Tete road route through Mozambique's Zambezia Province (Malawi's shortest overland link with Zimbabwe and therefore with the South African ports), is kept open by a substantial presence of Zimbabwean soldiers, who escort all convoys, Malawi's included. During 1987, Zimbabwe complained to Malawi about the cost of this security cover.[10]

In addition to the long road haul to South Africa, a northern trade route of sorts has been in operation since 1985, leading to the Tanzanian port of Dar es Salaam. In its present state it involves several time-consuming and costly trans-shipments, and many stretches of the route are in bad repair. It has been able to handle only a small amount of Malawi's external trade (3.5 per cent in 1986).[11] Now a SADCC project, the plan to upgrade Malawi's access to the Tanzania/Zambia 'northern corridor', has attracted substantial pledges from donors, in order to ease Malawi's transport problems. 1988 estimates projected that the upgraded northern corridor will be operational in 1991/2. However, reports caution that even when the newly upgraded corridor is fully functional, it will not be able to handle more than 25 per cent of Malawi's external trade, because of the anticipated rise in pressure on the handling capacity at Dar es Salaam's port, which is expected also to have to cater for an increased amount of the trade of landlocked Zambia. Much therefore depends on upgrading the handling capacity of Dar es Salaam. This raises, in turn, problems for Tanzania's own cargo handling and domestic transport facilities. Tanzania could switch to using Mtwara or Tanga ports, but only at the cost of considerable investment.

Malawi's external trade transport costs were estimated to have wiped a fifth off the value of annual exports in 1987.[12] CIF/FOB margins (the difference between the value of imported goods, priced to include Cost Insurance and Freight, and the value of exports, priced as Free on Board — the most sensitive economic indicator of the transport factor) went up from 22 per cent in 1980 to around 40 per cent in 1985, much of which is a direct foreign exchange cost, since Malawian-owned road transport facilities have not had the time to develop in compensation.[13]

The extra foreign exchange transport costs which Malawi has had to pay since 1982, taken together with its debt-service obligations, have resulted in an unmanageable burden on the country's foreign exchange reserves. Consequently, Malawi approached its major Western donors (the UK, France,

Italy, Japan, the USA, and West Germany — also the main trading partners of South Africa — together with the World Bank and the IMF) in June 1988 for funds to meet a two-year external financing gap of $555 m. According to reports of the 1988 meeting, the donors agreed "by and large" to Malawi's request.[14] Although some policy measures are likely to have been made conditional on this aid package, it was none the less clear that it mainly served as an interim rescue measure to alleviate pressure on the country's foreign exchange crisis. The donors accepted that Malawi's Mozambican trade routes cannot open up in the foreseeable future. They also hoped that the upgraded 'northern corridor' (together with improved economic performance to facilitate debt servicing) will make future rescue packages of this sort unnecessary. However, given the bleak outlook for peace in Mozambique, and reservations about the future handling capacity of the 'northern corridor', it was unlikely that any dramatic improvement in Malawi's transport and economic performance problems would take place during the two-year grace period permitted by the agreement.

Further, whether Malawi can make progress in managing its external debt repayment obligations depends, in part, on investors' confidence in the agricultural export sector, and the little-developed, import-dependent industrial sector. For the reasons outlined above, there is little room for optimism. Interviews with members of the expatriate business community in Malawi revealed that fresh private investment in Malawi's agricultural sector had tailed off in the 1980s (reflecting the trend throughout Africa in the 1980s). With transport constraints set to continue, the task of riding the world commodity market fluctuations is made all the harder. As one expatriate businessman explained, "Only those companies which already have substantial investment here in the form of estates, processing plants etc., can keep hanging on, for the time being. At the moment, many of our concerns are operating at a loss, but we have a big stake in Malawi and so we keep going in the hope that the coming years will see improvements."[15]

In 1986, due to the combination of the low world sugar price and war-related transport costs, one foreign transnational corporation decided that transporting the proportion of its sugar crop destined for the world market out through Harare and then on to Beira was decidedly uneconomic. So the company decided to start burning its stocks. However, this proved difficult, because the sugar turned into a sticky toffee-like substance, difficult to handle and dispose of. So they turned to a fermentation process, converting the sugar into alcohol, which was easier to burn than the raw sugar. Although the world sugar price has since recovered, the transport constraints remain. It is a cruel irony that so much ingenuity had to be used to find crop disposal measures in a country where thousands of people cannot grow enough to eat.

In mid-1989, the situation improved when the MNR stopped attacking the Nacala line. Reportedly, this was part of a deal between the Malawian government and Afonso Dhlakama, the MNR leader: in return for halting MNR sabotage of the Nacala line, Mr Dhlakama and his entourage were allowed to travel through Malawi to Kenya, to attend the Nairobi peace talks. Although this has partly relieved Malawi's transport problem, it is obviously not a long-term solution.[16]

Tanzanian communities have collected money to support the Mozambican government's defence effort against the MNR. Ako Gidabung'ed-Daremng'ajeg, a Barabaig man from northern Tanzania, gave the sale proceeds of a bull in 1987. "It is a Barabaig tradition to respond to such calls: you never know when you might need help yourself."

(Charles Lane)

South Africa's regional policy: recent developments and future prospects

Changing regional strategy

During 1988 and 1989, a rapid succession of developments, together with an accumulation of pressures over time, combined to alter South Africa's regional policy and bring it into a new state of flux.

With the South African government now adopting a much more defensive posture, the consistently aggressive phase of its regional policy has been adapted. It is not yet clear whether a fully consistent forward-looking alternative has emerged, or whether its strategy is more a matter of *ad hoc* responses to developments.

However, certain features are clear. Firstly, as stated in the National Party's 1989 election manifesto Five Year Plan, the government's key national objective is the establishment of a policy of 'group rights' of some kind. It follows that regional policy will be fashioned according to the view of the governments on how such a dispensation can best be pursued.

The evidence suggests that pressure is causing South Africa's policy to be reshaped in the following ways:[1] firstly, South Africa's international isolation (a result of apartheid) is forcing it to seek relationships with other nations and communities of nations. Secondly, the shift (from the mid-1980s onwards) in US policy away from 'constructive engagement'[2] prompted South Africa to seek to repair this and other international linkages by means of efforts to extend its 'formative' relationships within Africa. This involves an important shift away from its former emphasis on being part of 'the West'. As South

Africa's Director-General of Foreign Affairs (widely regarded as part of the 'verligte', or progressive, element of government) said of South Africa's regional relations in early 1989,

> South Africa — we have to be honest — has also tended to allow relations with its neighbours to become polarised. Certain events over the last five years have added to the polarisation, to the animosity. We hope the time has now come where we can use the positive climate created by the Angolan/Namibian agreement to try to re-enter a period of talking and stretching out of hands across borders, and looking at the positive things we have in common.[3]

South Africa, it is argued, will pursue its perceived role as the regional 'leader' — a role based on its economic and military dominance. It will seek greater 'formative' political integration with the region through diplomatic contacts, economic linkages, and military protection'.[4] At the same time, it will aim to use its integration into Africa as one way of extending its wider international diplomatic contacts, as has already happened to a significant extent during the Angola/Namibia negotiations.

Significant developments during 1988 and 1989

Actual events in the region during 1988 and 1989 demonstrate that South Africa is having to respond to increasing pressures, now seemingly beyond

South African children, detained during widespread school boycotts, being returned to their Soweto homes. The boycotts were organised after the clampdown on opposition groups (including five youth organisations) in February 1988. (IDAF)

its control. Some of these developments have strengthened the influence of the 'verligte' viewpoint, commonly associated with Foreign Affairs personnel, somewhat tempering the 'verkrampte' (conservative) outlook, commonly associated with the Defence establishment.

South Africa's Director-General of Foreign Affairs, for example, explained his view of how international censure affects the balance of policy-forming views within government. When asked in 1989 how his government intended to deal with the issue of the detention of children, he said,

> Yes; that is a very good example of the issues that have caused us a great deal of concern abroad. If you look at the last year in the US, the so-called detention of children was just about the number one issue on which people focused their attention in Congress. We see it as a very important task in Foreign Affairs to continually sensitise our domestic constituency on these issues. Hopefully, in that way, we will also be able to make a positive contribution to domestic policy formation.[5]

However, it is equally important to stress that the hawkish element in the formulation of policy on regional relations still has significant influence. For example, in February 1989, Commonwealth Foreign Ministers meeting in Harare learned that South Africa had recently finished building a number of 'Cheetah' military aircraft, which had been especially modified to increase their range northwards into Africa.[6] Two days later, South Africa threatened Zimbabwe (which, it held, had been investigating the possibility of purchasing British Harrier jump jets). South Africa's Deputy Defence Minister said,

> If we at any time feel that it is going to threaten our way of life or the stability of South Africa and the region, we will take whatever necessary steps seem fit at that moment. The only reason they want aircraft like that is to do something about the situation in South Africa.[7]

Angola and Namibia

Following a negotiated settlement (sponsored by the USA) between South Africa, Angola, and Cuba, South Africa and Cuba agreed to withdraw their forces from Angola, and South Africa agreed to implement the long-delayed UN Plan for Namibia's independence. These positive developments illustrate the extent to which South Africa's regional behaviour is adapting under pressure.

A number of key factors combined to unblock South Africa's intransigence in this area of the region. This intransigence, together with the escalating superpower rivalry over Angola, has had incalculable adverse effects on the people of Namibia and Angola. In Namibia, it prolonged conflict and caused widespread suffering and underdevelopment.[8] In Angola, it certainly

Namibians waiting to vote in Ovamboland, in their country's first free and fair general election, November 1989.

(Hugo Dixon)

intensified and has probably prolonged the civil conflict. The SADF invasions into Angola and the related presence of Cuban troops meant that all possibilities of finding a political solution to the civil conflict between the MPLA and UNITA were blocked. In turn, this has probably made the conflict all the harder to resolve.

Chief among the reasons why South Africa changed its strategy on Namibia and Angola were the following four factors.

Firstly, South Africa suffered military defeat on a grand scale in Angola during 1988. The military balance in the war between Angola and South Africa began to shift in Angola's favour from September/October 1987 onwards. Angola had achieved air superiority over South Africa, and military advances on the ground forced South Africa to negotiate, rather than risk widespread white casualties.[9]

Secondly, there were powerful economic factors at play, both in South

Africa and Angola. South Africa was experiencing long-term economic difficulties, on top of which the massive costs of its war in Angola, and its occupation of Namibia, were becoming unsustainable.

Meanwhile, the Angolan government's efforts to restructure the country's economy needed the resources of western governments and institutions such as the World Bank and the IMF. At the same time as the USA was blocking Angola's access to the IMF, the world oil price fell, thus undermining Angola's economic lifeline, its oil revenues.

Thirdly, the superpower dimension was important. The foreign policy implications of *perestroika* in the Soviet Union were being felt worldwide. In Angola, the Soviet Union began to see that it was in its domestic interests to seek a political solution to this long-running and expensive military stalemate. Moreover, the new relationship between the USA and the USSR, which involved cooperation over regional conflicts, based on what has been called 'a convergence of interests', helped reduce the superpower rivalry which had been a further block to progress for so long.

And fourthly, the failure of South Africa's long-standing attempts to foster an 'internal settlement' in occupied Namibia, in place of independence and majority rule in accordance with the UN Plan, had culminated in the handing back of power to the South African-appointed Administrator General for Namibia. This move ended years of South Africa's costly plans for an 'internal settlement', and highlighted the futility of its Namibia strategy. Although this was reported not to be a decisive factor, combined with other factors, it prompted Pretoria to reassess its Namibia policy. Nevertheless, the complex transition process in Namibia has shown that the strategy of South Africa is to maximise its political leverage over the independent nation. (The foundations for its economic leverage have been laid over the last century.) The tragic events of April 1989, when over 300 SWAPO guerrillas were killed by Koevoet forces at the official start of the transition process to independence, served to reinforce South Africa's influence over the transition process.[10]

In Angola, although the agreement to withdraw Cuban and South African troops largely unblocked the international obstacles to peace, the internal ones remained to be resolved.

In June 1989 it was widely reported that President Mobuto of Zaire had sponsored a ceasefire and the start of peace talks, in a deal apparently sealed by President dos Santos and Jonas Savimbi, the leader of UNITA.[11] However, it soon became clear that the seven-point peace plan which the Angolan government had proposed had not in fact been accepted by Savimbi, mainly because of the government's condition that he should be removed from the scene for a period of 'exile', and its insistence that UNITA should be integrated into the MPLA.[12] Continued US support for UNITA, reportedly to pressurise the Angolan government into abandoning one-party rule, has undoubtedly prolonged and further complicated the prospects for peace.

Tragically, fighting has intensified since the failure of Mobutu's initiative. Despite the efforts of other African governments to resuscitate peace talks, the political differences between the government and UNITA are being fought out on the battlefield. The civilian casualties continue to mount. Oxfam field reports towards the end of 1989 stressed a marked increase in conflict.

Mozambique and Zimbabwe

Despite the developments in Angola and Namibia in 1988/89, there was no sign of any let-up in the conflict in Mozambique. In fact, MNR brutality in Mozambique and eastern Zimbabwe persisted. Towards the end of 1988, for example, as the Angola/Namibia peace talks were nearing conclusion on the other side of the region, an Oxfam worker reported from eastern Zimbabwe,

> On 23 October (1988), there was an MNR raid some 40 km from one of the Primary Health Care centres Oxfam supports. They killed a chief, his wife and four others. One Zimbabwean soldier was killed.

> On 16 November, in an MNR raid just 10 km away, 20 people were abducted, and two Zimbabwean soldiers killed by a landmine.

> On 30 November, the MNR burnt down 20 houses along the border in the Rusitu valley. Nobody was killed, because the people there have been sleeping out in the bush for fear of night- time attacks.

> An immaculately typed letter, purportedly from the MNR, ordered the Rusitu religious mission (a United Baptist Mission station, which includes a secondary school) to shut down by 29 December, or be attacked.[13]

It was not until well into 1989 that it started to become accepted that the South African government, partly because of diplomatic pressure and led by international opinion, was probably no longer supporting the MNR. South Africa claims that improving relations with Mozambique is now high on its foreign policy agenda.[14] But, as most observers agree, little can be done to bring about lasting solutions in Mozambique — with rural development as a key element — until MNR aggression ceases. Whether the South African government can prevent the private support for the MNR emanating from South Africa remains to be seen. MNR atrocities in Mozambique and eastern Zimbabwe continue, emphasising the urgent need for a resolution of conflict. In October 1989, for example, an Oxfam field worker reported on a visit to eastern Zimbabwe where one of the Oxfam-supported doctors had just carried out *post mortem* examinations on seven MNR victims. All were Zimbabwean villagers, and all but one were children.

Prospects for peace in Mozambique

In June 1989, months of behind-the-scenes diplomatic work by the Catholic and Anglican churches in Mozambique culminated in the public announcement that both the Mozambican government and the MNR were prepared to agree to a ceasefire, and negotiate an end to 14 years of bitter war. This move was backed by the USA, the Soviet Union, the UK, and South Africa. President Moi of Kenya and President Mugabe of Zimbabwe emerged as mediators.

Two rounds of talks were held in Nairobi in August and October 1989. However, in spite of the earlier intention to agree to a ceasefire, the fighting intensified during these months. At the end of 1989, the peace talks appeared deadlocked, largely over the issue of mutual recognition. The MNR insisted that the FRELIMO government should recognise them as a genuine political party; FRELIMO insisted that the MNR must accept the "established order" in the country. But with so much at stake, not only for Mozambique, but also for other Front Line States, and for western interests in southern Africa, there is substantial pressure for the peace talks to resume.

Judging from what is understood about the nature of conflict in Mozambique, it is probable that a range of measures will be needed to establish peace. The war is unlikely to be won by military means.

First, international support for the MNR must be stopped. This would require a coordinated international effort.

Second, as FRELIMO's fifth Congress in July 1989 agreed, a number of far-reaching political and economic policy reforms must be implemented, alongside the amnesty for MNR guerrillas and the government's commitment to peace talks. In particular, it was agreed that broadening democracy and thus establishing a more stable society was a national priority. However, the MNR's claims to recognition as a political party are likely to be a key obstacle to the emergence of a multi-party basis for democracy in the foreseeable future.

Thirdly, it is also clear that massive reconstruction and rural development programmes are needed to re-establish a degree of social, economic, and therefore political normality within the country. This presents an enormous national, regional, and international challenge. As the catalogue of destroyed aid projects and government services shows, continued MNR sabotage means that reconstruction and economic development cannot progress in the midst of armed conflict.

Thus, although a peace agreement between the government and the MNR is an essential first step, it is unlikely that lasting stability can come as a result of this alone, even if the MNR leadership is able to order all its regional commanders to obey a ceasefire. This is largely due to the rural banditry which has become a way of life for groups outside MNR control (or minimally within it);[15] it is also due to the inability of civil administration structures to prevent the MNR's feudal, coercive control over large numbers of rural people. It is therefore likely that a major programme of rural development (to counteract the breakdown in rural life which encourages conflict and banditry) will be needed, alongside the development of structures to guarantee civil law and order. Yet both these options are blocked by the very conflict they could help to resolve, and it is not yet clear how this vicious circle can be broken.

At the beginning of the 1990s, the prospects for peace are mixed, and much depends on the pressure which can be brought to bear on the MNR. As one writer put it,

> RENAMO demands political recognition on a par with FRELIMO. Perhaps the degree to which it is accorded any such respect should be contingent on a reversal of its strategy of destruction and terror, within the context of some structured system of workable democratic institutions which link civil society to a responsible and accountable Mozambican state. This would allow RENAMO, by contributing through a grassroots democracy to the remaking of a country it has done so much to destroy, the opportunity to earn credit as a genuine political force. Nevertheless on present evidence it would have a very long way to go to attain credibility as a political party.[16]

Meanwhile, the fighting continues, and a number of MNR massacres in southern Mozambique were reported during the last few months of 1989. During her visit to Africa in March 1989, Mrs Thatcher expressed a view identical to Oxfam's when she said,

> No country can develop peacefully and constructively while it is riven by terrorism, and terrorism of a particularly brutal and cruel kind.[17]

Inside South Africa

There were also significant developments in South Africa over this period. In particular, there was movement towards unity among the anti-apartheid organisations.[18] A gulf remained, however, between Inkatha on the one hand and COSATU, the UDF, and the ANC on the other, with Inkatha unwilling to agree to a third round of proposed peace talks in 1989. There also remains a gulf between the organisations allied to the ANC, and the 'Black Consciousness' organisations allied to the Pan-Africanist Congress (PAC). Nevertheless, as developments in the late 1980s have confirmed, the ANC has clearly emerged as the political party with the largest following.

In the aftermath of the popular uprising, which was at its height between 1984 and 1986, the internal anti-apartheid movement reassessed its strategy.

It had sustained serious organisational setbacks due to state repression. Leaders also identified a key tactical error in some of their actions, especially the prolonged consumer boycott actions — and strategy was changed accordingly.[19]

The Mass Democratic Movement emerged in 1989, partly to fill the political vacuum which followed the 1988 restriction orders on the UDF,[20] and partly as a deliberate attempt to frustrate state repression by forming an outwardly amorphous movement, whose leadership structures are deliberately obscure. From mid-1989, leading up to the September 'general' elections, the MDM started up a successful and imaginative 'defiance campaign' which attracted much international media coverage. Restricted organisations 'unbanned' themselves, black people demanded treatment at 'whites only' hospitals and rides on 'whites only' buses, and some 'whites only' beaches were declared non-racial. This period of intense organisational activity culminated on election day in a mass stayaway from work organised by the Congress of South African Trade Unions (COSATU) and the National Confederation of Trade Unions (NACTU). Some three million workers stayed away in protest at the 'apartheid elections'. This was the largest demonstration of trade union organisational effectiveness ever seen in South Africa.

The years 1988 and 1989 also spanned a crucial period in the development

Members of the Mass Democratic Movement Defiance Campaign protesting against apartheid on Cape Town's beaches in August 1989.   (IDAF)

of ANC diplomacy. Negotiations and consultations inside South Africa have produced major pressures on the South African government, with significant international support.

In 1988, the ANC produced its "Constitutional Guidelines for a Democratic South Africa", which developed the vision of the 1955 Freedom Charter.

In June 1989, representatives from the ANC, COSATU, and the UDF held a consultative meeting to discuss a common position on negotiations, as a basis for widespread consultation within South Africa. Arising from this meeting, the ANC drew up a comprehensive policy on negotiations (which included their constitutional guidelines and the measures needed to establish a climate for negotiations). This has become known as the "Harare Declaration" (see Appendix 2), following its complete approval by the OAU summit which took place in Harare in August 1989.

The Declaration was subsequently approved by the Non-Aligned Movement, and was then put forward as the basis for a common UN General Assembly position, adopted on 14 December 1989 (see Chapter 10). Inside South Africa, the Harare Declaration was the centrepiece for debate at a mass consultative conference held from 9 to 11 December 1989. This Conference for a Democratic Future was attended by an estimated 4,600 delegates from anti-apartheid organisations throughout South Africa, including many of the organisations which Oxfam supports. Although the conference failed to bridge the political rift between the mainstream MDM/ANC alliance and the (much smaller) Black Consciousness/PAC group by as much as had been hoped, it demonstrated widespread democratic support for the Harare Declaration.

Future prospects

The key to South Africa's changing role in the region in the late 1980s lies in the nature of the remarkable pressures which have come to bear on apartheid and white minority rule.

Pressure from the people of South Africa has come about in two key, related, ways: firstly, through mass, organised, political resistance to apartheid, and secondly through what are sometimes called 'demographic' and 'socio-economic' pressures.

On the organised political front, the ANC's dominance of the South African political scene is becoming increasingly accepted, even by the National Party. And the remarkable growth of the trade union movement has significantly increased the capacity for internal mass organisation and for black people to use their economic power.

The MDM Defiance Campaign, Cape Town, 13 September 1989. This mass, peaceful march against apartheid defied all the repressive legislation and the Emergency powers of the South African government.   (IDAF)

The demographic and socio-economic pressures stem from the structural weaknesses of an industrialised society in which a white minority, constituting 13 per cent of the population, rules over a black majority.[21] The political and economic effects of mass urbanisation have helped to erode apartheid legislation through sheer pressure of numbers. Similarly, the growing consumer strength and entrepreneurial power of black people must now be taken into account. This has happened against a backdrop of organised resistance to apartheid legislation and practice.

South Africa is also undergoing considerable economic difficulties. These have been largely caused by the costly need to restructure the economy (in the face of falling terms of trade and rising debt-servicing obligations), against the background of falling confidence among foreign investors. The slowdown in economic growth is due primarily to political instability; the economic 'braking effect' of apartheid;[22] substantial capital flight;[23] the cumulative effect of sanctions; and recession. The economic situation has increased the impact of international sanctions and made the government more receptive to international pressure.[24]

The international dimension has also been important, both Soviet and western. Largely led by public reaction to developments inside South Africa and within the region, the international community became markedly more vocal during the 1980s in its criticism of South Africa. Most importantly, the USA, the Commonwealth, and the European Community adopted targetted economic sanctions against South Africa.

In the USA public pressure, largely from the powerful black lobby, led Congress to approve the first sanctions legislation in 1986. The Bush administration believes sanctions are a useful tool to back up its policy. This is in direct contrast with the view of the British government.

The Commonwealth put South Africa high on its agenda again when it adopted the Nassau Accord sanctions in October 1985. These specific, limited, and mostly voluntary measures were followed in 1986 by the Commonwealth's much-publicised Eminent Persons Mission to South Africa in 1986. A key issue has been Britain's reluctance to agree to a Commonwealth package of increased sanctions. In response, the other 48 Commonwealth leaders have opted for a strategy of collective action without Britain on this issue.

The European Community adopted its Common Policy on South Africa in 1985, which introduced the 'dual-track' approach. As originally stated, the dual track combined sanctions (specific, limited, mostly voluntary) with 'positive measures' (including aid to black South Africans and increased aid to SADCC). (Chapter 11 deals in more detail with EC policy.)

Finally, SADCC has achieved considerable progress, especially in the rehabilitation of Mozambique's transport routes, and in attracting international political and financial backing.

All this has caused the South African government to reassess its position. Realising that the status quo cannot survive under such pressures, the National Party has chosen to reform the apartheid system in South Africa so that it becomes more streamlined, adaptable, and, ultimately, defensible. As the September 1989 elections results indicate, the National Party accepts that much of the apparatus of apartheid which has grown up over the years will have to go, so that the essential feature — some form of institutionalised white supremacy — survives.[25] The key issue for the international community, therefore, is whether enough coordinated pressure can be brought to bear to ensure that the political leadership of the disenfranchised majority have the backing they need to see that apartheid is fully negotiated away, and replaced by democracy.

The first steps are to create an acceptable climate for negotiations. The MDM/ANC's demands of the South African government have been clearly

In December 1989, 4,600 delegates from anti-apartheid organisations all over South Africa attended a conference to discuss negotiations for democracy. The conference gave full backing to the 'Harare Declaration'.

(IDAF)

laid out in the Harare Declaration, and all these demands were ratified by the UN General Assembly in December 1989.

By the end of 1989, the South African government had taken some initial steps in response to this agenda. Eight political prisoners had been released, the government had effectively authorised a number of mass anti-apartheid demonstrations (including an ANC rally of some 80,000 people in Soweto to welcome the released prisoners), as if testing the water for lifting the State of Emergency. Some apartheid practice was abolished, notably the particularly 'visible' racial restrictions on beaches, buses, parks, and libraries; and President de Klerk announced his intention to repeal the Separate Amenities Act.

As the wealth of international comment has made clear, these advances are encouraging, and further demonstrate the central role which pressure is playing. But those who have suffered under apartheid are at pains to point out the immensity of the task ahead, and the continuing need for strong international support for democracy. At the end of 1989, some 98 organisations remained banned or restricted,[26] with their members liable to prosecution for "furthering their aims". There were over 700 political prisoners, including an estimated 60 on 'Death Row', and over 600 individuals remained restricted (i.e. prevented from taking part in political activity, with many subject to twelve-hour house arrest). The rights of assembly, free speech, and a free press were denied under the State of Emergency.

However, even if these conditions are lifted, the hardest task will undoubtedly be the abolition of apartheid in all its forms, the establishment of a non-racial democracy, and the transformation of the distorted economic structures which have been created by apartheid.

Thus, the key issue for the 1990s is that of maintaining pressure on the South African government. As Allan Boesak, a prominent South African church leader, said of President de Klerk on the eve of the October 1989 Commonwealth Conference,

> He is a man who responds to pressure. He had not even thought of the possibility of a black government: now he thinks about it, but does not yet do anything. We must go on concentrating his mind.[27]

Section II
Global and national constraints on development

8

Trade, debt and problems of national policy

What poor countries and poor groups need is the type of development that is not modelled on that of the richer countries and regions. Indeed, a major element in the real development of the poor is that the rich should be stopped from imposing misdevelopment on the world. The notion of liberation through development needs then to be complemented by that of development through liberation.

(Excerpt from the Gilbert Murray Memorial Lecture, given by Father Smangaliso Mkhatshwa, Oxford 1985[1])

As we have seen, South Africa's regional policy has had devastating effects on the people and economies of southern Africa. However, it would be misleading to suggest that all the SADCC region's development problems relate to South Africa. There are many other factors which have undermined equitable development in the region. The enduring effects of colonial economic policies, distorted North/South economic relations, external debt, and post-independence failures of development policy have also come together to make development in the interests of the poorest an elusive goal. This chapter examines some of these other structural and policy issues, and the way they combine with South Africa's regional policy to frustrate equitable development in the interests of the poorest.

The SADCC region bears a double burden: not only does it suffer from the range of economic pressures currently affecting most of sub-Saharan Africa, but it also shoulders the consequences of South Africa's regional policy. It follows that the advent of majority rule in South Africa will be a necessary

An adult literacy class in Katatura, Namibia. Widespread illiteracy has been one of the most damaging legacies of colonialism throughout southern Africa.

(Chris Johnson / Oxfam)

but not a sufficient condition for equitable development in the SADCC region. While it is essential to establish peace and a more fairly structured regional economy (which would include a majority-ruled South Africa), other development constraints must also be addressed.

An effective response to suffering, poverty, and underdevelopment in the region must tackle a whole range of factors. North/South economic relations and inappropriate domestic policies in the SADCC states must also be challenged, alongside apartheid and minority rule in South Africa, if real progress is to be achieved.

Colonial legacies

Southern Africa's colonial history is especially well documented, and there are many detailed studies which examine the links between poverty and colonial development policies.[2]

Many of today's development problems stem from colonial factors: inherited inequalities and the neglect of basic services for the majority of the population; severe economic dislocation on independence; reconstruction needs following liberation wars; and the inheritance of distorted production structures and external trading relationships.

It should be stressed from the outset that colonial history in the SADCC

*A pottery workshop in Lichinga, northern Mozambique, set up to re-establish
artisanal skills, which had been largely destroyed by the colonial system.*

region is not part of the distant past. Tanzania, the oldest SADCC state, came
to independence in 1961, while Namibia's independence has been delayed
until 1990. Nor was colonial experience uniform throughout the region.
However, all the SADCC states have grappled with some or other of these
issues, in different proportions, and in relation to the different colonial powers
involved in the region (Britain, Portugal, Germany, and South Africa). To
avoid misleading generalisations, it is important that each country's set of
circumstances is examined individually.

In Zambia and Malawi, for example, independence in 1964 not only meant
majority rule and self-government, but it also meant coping with the
consequences of breaking away from the Central African Federation (1953-
1963), which had been created by Britain. Under the Federation, these two
territories had been used to develop Southern Rhodesia. Zambia's labour and
mineral wealth, and Malawi's labour, had been exploited and extracted for
this purpose. Moreover, as many as possible of the Federation's services and
institutions were located in Southern Rhodesia, home of the Federation's
government. As a result, on independence, Zambia and Malawi lacked such
things as parliament buildings, a university, a Central Bank, and a national
teaching hospital. Even Zambian psychiatric patients needing hospital
treatment had to be referred south. But, most critically for the decades to
come, Zambia and Malawi inherited economies which were heavily

Storeroom worker at Xai-Xai cashew factory, southern Mozambique. Most SADCC states depend heavily on the export of primary commodities for foreign exchange earnings. Cashew nuts are Mozambique's single most important export crop.

(Ron Giling / Panos Pictures)

dependent on the export of primary commodities and migrant labour.

In Zimbabwe, the massive social and economic inequalities left by colonial rule still act as a major brake on development. The costs of repairing the damage done by a century of discrimination have been massive, and are proving increasingly hard to sustain. In Angola and Mozambique, inherited inequalities were coupled with the severe dislocation of commerce and government caused by the mass exodus of the Portuguese settler community around the time of independence. (The development problems of Zimbabwe, Malawi, and Angola are illustrated in case-studies in Chapter 9.)

However, the most topical case in point is Namibia. Over the next decade, the independent nation will have to begin confronting the complex set of development constraints it has inherited from its colonial past.[3] Although nobody expects Namibia to be able to tackle all its inherited problems quickly, nevertheless the nature and pace of change during the 1990s will be crucial for the impoverished majority. Namibia's post-independence development options are particularly constrained by its economic dependence on South Africa.

Commodity trade

At the root of the deep economic crisis affecting most developing countries is the collapse in the prices of many commodities during the 1980s. Between 1981 and 1985, for example, the cumulative loss in the commodity export earnings (excluding oil) of developing countries was $57 bn., nearly double the total value of those countries' commodity export earnings in 1980. In 1986, average real commodity prices (excluding oil) were at their lowest level ever recorded, with the possible exception of 1932.[4] The southern African region is no exception.

SADCC's trade with the industrialised North

Chapter 5 looked at the SADCC region's trading relationships with South Africa, but it should be noted that overall the region's trade with the industrialised countries of the North is also important (see table 8.1).

The injurious trading relationship which has grown up between Africa and the industrialised world has its roots in the slave trade. Southern Africa was affected by the trade both to the East and to the West. A leading historian had this to say about the 'Atlantic trade' (from Africa's western seaboard to the plantations in the Americas), which particularly ravaged Angola:

> Essentially, the Atlantic trade was a large and long-enduring exchange of cheap industrial goods, mainly cottons and metalware and firearms, for the 'raw' material of African labour. (The inverted commas are ... necessary because the labour was in fact often skilled in those very techniques most required in the Americas: tropical farming and metal working.) Every question of humanity apart, this trade struck at Africa in two ways, both of which spelt impoverishment. By providing Africa with cheap substitutes, it undermined the local production of cotton goods and metalware; against this partial benefit, it discouraged expansion from the handicraft stage.[5]

The overseas slave trade could be regarded as an early type of colonial economy, of the exchange of European goods for African 'raw material'.

Today, the SADCC region trades extensively with the OECD countries,[6] of which the European Community forms an important part (see table 8.1).

Dependence and diversification

> In our analysis, the agenda for southern Africa is patently clear. The challenge is to eliminate the senseless dichotomy which makes us wholesale exporters of raw materials, and wholesale importers of finished goods, under terms determined entirely by the industrialised countries, terms that compel us to increasingly produce and sell more of our raw materials in order to afford less of their products.

(Dr Simba Makoni, Executive Secretary of SADCC, October 1989)

Table 8.1: SADCC's main trading partners (latest available year) (% of total)

DESTINATION OF EXPORTS

	1	2	3	4
Angola (1988) *	USA (13)	FRG (13)	Brazil (12)	Bahamas (12)
Botswana (1987)	Rest of Europe ** (90)	SACU *** (4)	Other Africa (4)	UK (1)
Lesotho (1983)	S. Africa (85)	Other Africa (5)	FRG (3)	USA (3)
Malawi (1987)	UK (23)	USA (11)	S. Africa (11)	Netherlands (10)
Mozambique (1987)	USA (17)	Japan (15)	GDR (9)	Spain (7)
Namibia (1988) ****	UK ***** (30)	S. Africa (20)	FRG (15)	Japan (10)
Swaziland (1986)	EC (34)	S. Africa (33)	Canada (8)	S. Korea (5)
Tanzania (1986)	FRG (17)	UK (12)	Japan (7)	Italy (6)
Zambia (1985)	Japan (26)	China (11)	UK (7)	USA (7)
Zimbabwe (1987)	FRG (16)	UK (13)	S. Africa (10)	USA (7)

*	Angola figures from EIU report, based on IMF Direction of Trade Statistics; figures exclude trade with Eastern bloc and should be treated with caution.
**	Mainly diamond exports via Switzerland.
***	Southern African Customs Union, i.e. the SACU members' trading links have not been differentiated, but it can be assumed that the major partner is South Africa.

In common with other African countries, the SADCC region's[7] dependence on the export of primary commodities (see table 8.2) to the North for foreign exchange earnings with which to buy imports is a major structural vulnerability. It is a key factor which has led to the external debt trap of the 1980s. It has its origins in the way that colonial economies were deliberately fashioned to create wealth for the imperial powers and the European settler minorities. Post-independence policies in most SADCC states have exacerbated the problem. The sharp drop in the prices of many primary commodities experienced during the 1980s, together with the steadily rising

ORIGIN OF IMPORTS

	1	2	3	4
Angola (1988) *	Brazil (15)	France (12)	Portugal (9)	Netherlands (9)
Botswana (1987)	SACU *** (97)	Other Africa (8)	Rest Europe (7)	UK (2)
Lesotho (1983)	SACU *** (79)	UK (1)	Rest EC (1)	-
Malawi (1987)	S. Africa (35)	UK (20)	PTA countries ****** (10)	Japan (6)
Mozambique (1987)	Italy (14)	S. Africa (12)	USA (10)	USSR (9)
Namibia (1988) ****	S. Africa (75)	FRG (10)	USA (5)	Switzerland (5)
Swaziland (1986)	S. Africa (90)	UK (4)	Australia (1)	Japan (1)
Tanzania (1988)	UK (15)	Japan (9)	FRG (9)	Italy (7)
Zambia (1985)	USA (21)	S. Africa (12)	FRG (12)	UK (7)
Zimbabwe (1987)	S. Africa (21)	UK (12)	USA (9)	FRG (9)

**** Estimates - no breakdown is published in official data (EIU).

***** Mainly diamonds exported via Switzerland for sale in London.

****** Preferential Trade Agreement Members (Southern and East Africa).

(Source: EIU Country Profiles 1989-90)

prices of the North's manufactured exports and services, have meant that Africa's terms of trade (the purchasing power of its exports) have declined significantly (see table 8.3).

SADCC's terms of trade have likewise deteriorated (see table 8.4). This in turn has slowed down development progress (and in many cases reversed it), as national earnings dwindle and as countries have fallen into debt.

The loss to poor countries represents a transfer to their richer trading partners in the form of cheaper imports and profits from exports. Between

Table 8.2: *Primary-commodity dependency in SADCC countries*

Country	Commodity	% of national export earnings	% of national export earnings derived from primary commodities
Angola (1985)	oil products	95.6	100.0
Zambia (1987)	copper	84.0	100.0
Malawi (1987)	tobacco tea	60.4 10.4	92.9
Mozambique (1986)	prawns cashews	38.0 17.0	95.0 *
Zimbabwe (1987)	tobacco gold cotton nickel	18.0 17.0 5.0 4.0	82.0
Tanzania (1985)	coffee cotton cloves	40.0 8.0 5.0	92.9
Namibia (1987)	diamonds uranium base metals cattle fish products	40.0 24.0 18.0 7.0 4.0	95.0 **
Botswana (1987)	diamonds copper-nickel matte meat	85.0 5.0 4.0	95.0
Lesotho (1984)	mohair	24.0	46.2 ***
Swaziland (1986)	sugar woodpulp	42.0 17.0	95.0 (est.)

*   However, migrant labour remittances and transport revenue are key foreign-exchange earners for Mozambique.

**   1986

***   However, only 6% of Lesotho's foreign exchange earnings comes from trade.

(Source: Economist Intelligence Unit reports, latest data available)

Table 8.3: Changes in terms of trade for sub-Saharan Africa 1965-1988 (average annual % change)

1965-73	1973-80	1980-85	1986	1987*	1988**
- 8.5	5.0	- 2.3	- 23.2	3.3	- 5.3

* estimated

** projected

(Source: World Bank, *World Development Report, 1989,* p.151)

Table 8.4: Terms of trade in the SADCC countries (1980 = 100)

	1982	1983	1984	1985	1986	1987
Malawi	107	113	137	101	88	67*
Tanzania	88	91	94	90	104	90
Mozambique	84	...	104	...	...	...
Zambia	72	78	74	72	69	79
Zimbabwe	...	...	96	84	86	84
Angola	106	...	102	...	...	...
SACU**	87	86	86	85	64	71*

*   estimates

**   Southern African Customs Union (comprising South Africa, Namibia, Botswana, Lesotho and Swaziland).

(Source: World Bank, *World Development Report*, tables for Growth in Merchandise Trade, 1986, 1987, 1988 and 1989 editions.)

Daodi Paulo (left) with his brother, preparing land for cotton, the only cash crop which grows well in Tanzania's Meatu District. But the costs of fertiliser and insecticide are rising faster than the producer price for cotton.   (Geoff Sayer / Oxfam)

1981 and 1986, the transfer on the trade account through the deterioration in the Third World's terms of trade amounted to more than $90 bn.[8]

Despite efforts to industrialise and diversify their economies,[9] most SADCC countries are heavily dependent on the export of primary commodities, as table 8.2 illustrates. While the SADCC states share a considerable degree of dependence, clearly some are far more vulnerable than others to depressed world prices.

In comparison with the other SADCC economies, Zimbabwe is the most developed in terms of a diversified economic base. Zimbabwe has well-functioning manufacturing industries and a developed agricultural export sector, and it exports minerals.

War-torn Mozambique, on the other hand, no longer has an adequately functioning industrial base; its mineral resources are not exploited (apart from coal), and it depends on the export of agricultural and fish products as well as on its transport revenue and migrant workers' remittances.

Before independence, Angola stood to inherit a well-diversified economy, comprising the production of a wide range of primary products, with a comparatively well-developed industrial sector. However, the economic chaos and the skills vacuum caused by the mass exodus of settlers around the time of independence, weak economic management after independence, and war have reduced Angola's economic base to the lucrative oil sector, and a handful of foreign-dominated enclave enterprises in mining and construction.

Zambia did not inherit a diverse economic base on independence. On the contrary, copper was and still is its only developed export asset.

Malawi is another case in point. It relies on agricultural commodities for over 90 per cent of its export earnings;[10] it has an import-dependent and underdeveloped industrial sector;[11] and its mineral deposits remain unexploited (except for coal). Although Malawi has a wider range of main export commodities than, for instance, Zambia or Angola, nevertheless it largely relies on three commodities, all of which have experienced falling and fluctuating prices on the world market during the 1980s..

The costs of dependence
Such a high degree of dependence on the North, and on a narrow economic base has direct implications for people. A recent example occurred among the workers on the tobacco estates in Malawi, where tobacco is the single most important export. (In 1988, it accounted for 64 per cent of the value of agricultural exports.)

There were high hopes for Malawi's 1989 tobacco earnings. The previous year had seen record prices and production levels for the Burley variety, in which Malawi specialises. (This variety alone accounted for over a third of Malawi's total foreign earnings in 1988.) As a result, 1989 production levels were increased by a further 10 m. kg, equivalent to double the 1986 crop. But expectations were dashed on the auction floors as the bumper crop attracted hopelessly low prices. The problem was that mould, caused by the particularly heavy rains during the 1988/1989 growing season, had spoiled the crop's quality.[12]

This was bad news for the rural poor. Although peasant production of Burley, normally a high-quality tobacco type, has been largely restricted to enhance the earnings of the large commercial estate owners, nevertheless thousands of families are dependent on the wages of labourers on the Burley-producing commercial estates.[13]

Towards the end of 1989, as the social consequences of the slump in Malawi's Burley prices were expected, initial reports of the effects on workers and their families indicated that Mozambican migrant workers employed on some of the tobacco estates may have been the first to be laid off. UNHCR personnel in Malawi believe that this was a contributory factor behind the sudden increase in the population of the country's settlements for Mozambican refugees. The settlements' population suddenly shot up towards the end of 1989.[14]

What makes this structural dependence a problem is the fact that the market prices of many primary commodities are not only falling (though the trend is often a long-term one), but some also fluctuate wildly. In spite of international efforts to stabilise prices and provide cushioning finance, uneven commodity earnings continue to make systematic economic planning very difficult.

Zambia's copper (on which it heavily depends) is a good example not only of a commodity whose price in the long term has been falling, but also of a commodity whose price can fluctuate wildly. During the first decade of independence (1964-1974), the price of copper was buoyant, but between 1975 and 1986 it fell sharply.[15] Then, in 1987 and 1988, the world price rose significantly, to over $1 per pound (although this is widely regarded as a 'blip', rather than a long-term trend). During 1989, although still high, the price of copper again fluctuated considerably from one month to another.[16]

In Zambia, it is the urban and rural poor who bear the brunt of rising unemployment, spiralling prices, and cut-backs in basic public services.[17] Zambia's fatal dependency on copper, and its deep structural economic distortions are largely to blame.

Angola's oil is another example. Since 1973, oil has been the country's chief export (though it does not yet export oil to other SADCC states). By 1985, when the oil sector had been successfully built up, Angola's oil earnings accounted for 96 per cent of its total exports,[18] and enabled it to maintain a trade surplus, although the 1985/86 drop in oil earnings suddenly and seriously upset the government's debt-management strategy. Even though oil is undeniably a great asset, Angola has become over-dependent on its oil revenue following the decline in its diamond and coffee exports, and the ending of its iron ore exports in 1975.

Although the massive costs of war overshadow life for its people, and are a key reason why Angola's oil earnings are not invested in development, the fluctuations of the world oil market since late 1985 have also seriously affected Angola's economic stability.

Up until 1980, Angola's oil export receipts grew rapidly, because of the steep rise in world prices. The country's oil earnings then stabilised in 1981, declined in 1982, resumed an upward trend in 1983/4 (due to increased production as world prices were weakening), came to a halt in 1985, and dropped precipitously in 1986, despite another large increase in production. In 1987, Angola sustained a dramatic recovery, with its exports doubling in value. Behind this lay a recovery of oil and diamond prices, and an increase in oil production.[19]

The reasons for the fall in commodity prices

Like all prices, those of commodities are determined by the laws of supply and demand. Changes in both sides of the equation during the 1980s have resulted in an unstable and generally depressed commodities market.

A number of influences have affected the prices of major commodities produced in the SADCC region.[20] The level of economic activity in the major industrialised countries of the world has played a key role in determining commodity prices. The growth rate of industrial output in the OECD countries has exerted a strong influence. Apart from year-to-year fluctuations, OECD growth over the 1980s slowed down from an average of 3.4 per cent between 1970 and 1979 to 1.8 per cent between 1980 and 1986. An UNCTAD study of 19 commodities experiencing declining growth in demand in recent years showed that this accounted for three quarters of the decline.[21]

Agricultural protectionism among the countries to which the SADCC states export has also had an impact. Most northern industrialised countries protect their agricultural sectors from competition with internationally traded products, such as sugar, beef, and vegetable oils. The result is frequently a reduction in imports and, as in the case of sugar, an increase in exports. By paying farmers a guaranteed price of between 18 and 22 US cents per pound from 1980 to 1988, the European Community's sugar regime was designed to protect the income of EC farmers and processors and ensure a steady flow of home-produced beet sugar on to the market. The net result was a tremendous increase in European production. In 1986 the EC produced a surplus of 5 million tonnes.[22] All the surplus sugar is disposed of by exporting it on to the free, world market.

Another form which protectionism has taken is an escalation in tariffs. In order to protect their own processing industries, industrialised countries erect tariff walls around a commodity, which increase at each step of the processing operation. This makes it harder for the poorer Third World producer nations to develop their own processing industries to 'add value' to their primary products. Coffee is a case in point. While processing industries have nevertheless been established in many countries of Latin America and Asia, in general African countries have been adversely affected by this trend.[23]

The use to which biotechnological developments in the industrialised world are put is also affecting primary commodity prices. The world price of sugar, for example, has been greatly affected. Developments in the USA made it possible to convert maize to a sweetener known as High Fructose Corn Sugar (HFCS) in western factories. By 1984, a number of major soft drinks manufacturers had switched from using sugar to HFCS. This meant that the USA, the world's largest single market, no longer needed to import vast quantities of Third World cane sugar. It slashed its import quotas accordingly.[24] Other crops traditionally grown in the Third World are likely to be affected by biotechnological developments, including tobacco and vegetable oils.

Technological changes in the industrialised world have also had an impact on commodity prices. One aspect is material substitution. Many traditional materials are being replaced or made obsolete as First World technology becomes increasingly sophisticated. Copper, for example, was largely replaced by modern alloys in armaments manufacture, and is now being replaced by optical fibres in telecommunications. A 45 kg length of fibre cable can transmit as much as a tonne of copper wire.[25] Partly as a result of this, copper prices went through a period of depression from 1982 to 1986. This had a profound effect on copper-dependent Zambia.

Technological advances in the North have also enabled the phenomenal development of the micro-chip. To be involved in this trade requires sophisticated component and assembly industries and an appropriately skilled workforce. In the present climate of instability and economic uncertainty, it is unlikely that the SADCC region could attract the investment and provide the skilled people necessary for this form of industry.[26]

The shift to service industries in the North has meant a reduction in the overall share of world trade for those countries in the South which depend on exporting primary commodities. The comparatively underdeveloped nature of the SADCC economies means that they are also failing to benefit from the growing share of world trade represented by the service sector.

The fierce competition between the world's two most powerful trading nations, the USA and Japan, has meant that the world's trade has increasingly become a matter of transactions between developed, industrial economies. This trend has been reinforced by the increasing power of northern trans-national companies (TNCs). As Europe moves towards 1992, its sights are on its position in relation to these giants. Improving North/South trading relations is not the EC's priority.

Future prospects for the SADCC region

As we have seen, economic trends in the industrialised North are increasingly jeopardising the economies of those Third World countries, including most SADCC states, which depend on exporting primary commodities.

Trends in primary commodity prices leave little room for optimism. Some experts believe that the world's primary-products economy has become uncoupled from its industrial economy. The IMF, while not so pessimistic, believes that there will not be a major recovery in the foreseeable future, expecting commodity prices to remain roughly unchanged into the early 1990s.[27]

The prospects of effective international action to reverse the decline in North/South terms of trade are also bleak. Four major internationally commissioned reports[28] on North/South economic relations over the last 30 years have highlighted the disastrous consequences of allowing distorted global trading structures and relations to continue unchecked. Nevertheless, despite the fact that it is not in the industrialised countries' interest to starve the Third World of adequate foreign exchange with which to buy their exports, the North has effectively failed to implement the recommendations of these commissions, and it is unlikely that concerted measures will be taken to reverse the decline in commodity prices.

Furthermore, the SADCC region faces immense problems of low production levels and undeveloped local markets. (In 1987 only 4.4 per cent of SADCC's total trade was conducted between member states, and within this small proportion, Zimbabwe's trade was dominant.[29]) As SADCC's Executive Secretary, Dr S.H.S. Makoni, has explained,

> (A key) constraint arises from our small and truncated national markets, with very low buying power, which have resulted in the establishment of small and non-competitive production structures with limited capacity to respond to changing market trends. For this reason our products have great difficulty breaking into the highly competitive international markets. To crown it all, because of the small size of our economies, we are unable to provide the necessary institutional support at an affordable cost necessary for structural transformation to take place. It is in this context that regional cooperation and integration provide a potent force for development.[30]

Dr Makoni has further argued:

> Our approach to trade in the region is not based on the orthodox trade liberalisation strategies. We believe — in fact, we have observed — that reduction or even elimination of tariffs and other barriers to trade does not always yield increased trade, in the absence of tradeable goods. How can tariffs inhibit trade when there is nothing to trade? In our view, the greatest single barrier to trade is lack of production. Hence our motto is "Let production push trade, rather than trade pull production".[31]

Southern Africa's future is indeed gloomy, when viewed from the perspective of the trading relationships of individual underdeveloped nations with the industrialised countries of the North. At the regional level, there is at least greater room for improvement.

Firstly, as has been argued in Chapter 5, when majority rule comes to South Africa, the region as a whole stands to benefit economically — both from a reduction in tension and from the results of wider economic cooperation.

Secondly, SADCC's recently approved economic strategy ("Investment in Production"), which stresses the need for regional cooperation and integration, could go a long way to building a stronger regional economy. With its accent on improving skills training, on balancing out structural economic distortions (both nationally and regionally), and on expanding markets by promoting intra-regional trade, this programme could help in two main ways. It could reduce unnecessary North/South trading dependency; and it could enable SADCC, as a comparatively strong economic bloc in place of several, individually weak, nations, to participate in global trade on more advantageous terms.

It is clearly acknowledged, however, that the SADCC region's trade with the North is necessary to finance regional development — in particular its Investment in Production programme — and also desirable in an interdependent world. To this end, a number of measures are planned to improve the SADCC region's overseas trade.

SADCC intends to establish revolving export funds in each of the member states, to help overcome the foreign exchange shortage which constrains industrial production. An Export Credit Fund is also under study which would allow exporters in the region to offer trade credits competitive with those offered to South African and European companies.

SADCC is also seeking easier access to overseas markets for its exports. Like other developing countries, the SADCC states face increasing levels of protectionism in the industrialised North. Tariff and non-tariff barriers inhibit trade expansion and economic diversification, especially in sectors like textiles and processed agricultural products, where the SADCC states have good potential.

Although the preferential access to markets afforded by the European Community's Lomé Convention is valuable, increased access is needed. One example is provided by the Nordic countries, which as part of the special 'Nordic-SADCC initiative' have agreed to treat the SADCC region as a special case on political grounds, with possible preferential reductions in non-tariff barriers. The Swedish government has funded a special import-promotion drive to encourage the purchase of SADCC products.

Countertrade — exporting goods in return for essential imports — is also thought to have potential for overcoming the lack of foreign exchange which partly constrains the development of the SADCC region's foreign trade. Joint marketing arrangements between SADCC states could cut costs.

SADCC's donors, especially since they are also among its key trading partners, could do more to help build up the region's trading strength and economic sustainability. Aid alone is not enough: other ways must be found to translate the North's economic growth into development resources for the South. Apart from increased levels of aid to the vital sectors of transport and production, greater efforts should be made to provide untied aid where this would help to stimulate local production and employment. Following the Nordic countries' example, other donor countries could adopt more enlightened trading and purchasing policies. There needs to be a reversal of Northern protectionist measures which adversely affect the SADCC region's efforts at trade and economic diversification.

Given that the South will remain dependent on primary commodities for the foreseeable future, it is also necessary to develop ways whereby the substantial resources devoted to research and development in the interests of the industrialised countries and their TNCs can equally benefit Southern producers. More research must be financed to develop new uses for primary commodities, rather than looking for ways to do without them.

Finally, in line with UNCTAD's "Common Fund" proposals, ways must be found for Third World countries to participate far more fully in the processing, marketing, and distribution of commodities — a domain currently dominated by Northern TNCs.

Packing tea for export on a commercial estate in the Honde Valley, eastern Zimbabwe, 1986. The labour force of over 3,000 people is supplemented by a further 1,000 women, working on a casual basis.

(Chris Johnson / Oxfam)

However, although SADCC's programme aims to tackle the major constraints on the region's economic development, it remains to be seen whether the position of the poor within the SADCC states will be improved as a result. One great danger is that yet more national resources will be concentrated in the large urban centres, at the expense of rural people and their production. Another danger is that land reform in the interests of the poor will be neglected in favour of land usage for export-led growth.

Debt and arrested development

The South is tired of being the world's Taker — whether of import and export prices; of interest rates and political conditionality for financial and commercial transactions; of technology; of ideology; and of self-interested advice; and even of charity and benevolence.

(Julius K. Nyerere, speaking as Chairman of the South Commission[32])

According to UNICEF, 400,000 children in Africa die each year as a result of the debt-induced economic crisis. In per capita terms, the income of sub-Saharan Africa fell by a quarter between 1982 and 1987, and per capita investment levels were lower in 1987 than in the mid-1960s.[33]

As an analysis of the principal causes of the 'debt crisis' shows, the Third World's debt is a responsibility shared between the debtor and creditor countries alike. However, the debtor countries, and in particular the poorest

Children scavenging on a Maputo rubbish dump. Urban poverty in Mozambique has been made far worse by war, and the urban poor are particularly vulnerable to structural adjustment measures.   (Ron Giling / Panos Pictures)

people within them, shoulder a wholly disproportionate amount of the burden. Furthermore, it is a burden which grows heavier with time, as indebted economies deteriorate and as the outstanding loans, even those made on concessional terms, stretch away into the future, accumulating compound interest.

Debt in the SADCC region

The 1990s bring the chance of real movement towards an end to apartheid and, therefore, the chance for the SADCC region to recover from the enormous economic damage which South Africa's regional policy has wrought. After a decade of disruption, the SADCC region's prospects for recovery are finally brighter. However, the cumulative impact of the SADCC states' external debt undermines their prospects for economic recovery. (See table 8.5.)

The World Bank believes that sustained economic growth at the minimum rate of 4—5 per cent is necessary "if Africa is to avert hunger and provide its growing population with productive jobs and rising incomes".[34] The massive economic costs of destabilisation mean that this target level of growth is well

Table 8.5: The SADCC region's external debt (1987)

Country	Total external debt ($m.)	Total debt per capita ($)	GNP per capita ($)	Total long-term debt as a % of GNP	Total long-term debt service as % of: GNP	exports of goods and services
Angola*	1,849	208	1,020***	13***	2.6***	13.1****
Botswana	518	470	1,050	38	5.2	3.7
Lesotho	241	150	370	37	2.3	4.4
Malawi	1,363	172	160	98	6.0	23.3
Mozambique*	2,001	137	170	129	11.4	135.2****
Swaziland	293	418	700	46	5.2	6.1
Tanzania	4,335	181	180	144	2.9**	18.5**
Zambia	6,400	888	250	228	6.7**	13.5**
Zimbabwe	2,512	279	580	37	6.8**	23.2**
Total	19,512					

**   Relates to external public debt service only.

***   Using 1986 GNP data (latest available from OECD).

****   To OECD countries, CIF (Cost, Insurance, Freight).

(Source: World Bank, except for those countries marked *, where OECD data are used)

Table 8.6: Average rates of real change in GDP, 1980-1988	
Angola*	2.4
Botswana	11.3
Lesotho	2.5
Malawi	1.8
Mozambique**	-2.1
Namibia	-0.2
South Africa	2.2
Swaziland	4.1
Tanzania	1.6
Zambia	0.8
Zimbabwe	3.9

*   no data available for 1987, 1988

**   no data available for 1980, 1981

(Source, EIU Quarterly Review 1/1986, EIU Country Profiles, 1986-87, 1987-88, 1989-90)

below the minimum needed for reconstruction and essential development in the SADCC region, especially if a more open and responsive style of government is to emerge. Yet the rate of economic growth in key SADCC states between 1980 and 1988 fell consistently below the required level (see table 8.6), although in 1987 and 1988 there was some improvement[35].

In 1987, the total external debt of the SADCC countries ($19.5 bn.) was only a small proportion of sub-Saharan Africa's debt of $128.8 bn.,[36] and only a tiny proportion of the total debt of the world's heavily indebted countries ($472 bn.[37]). Nevertheless, under current conditions, honouring the debt-servicing obligations of the debt-distressed SADCC countries and meeting the terms of debt-management strategies have proved particularly difficult, especially for Mozambique, Malawi, Tanzania, Zambia, and Angola.

Furthermore, some aspects of the economic adjustment programmes which key SADCC states have had to adopt have caused direct harm to the poor. Without an immediate, radical reduction of its debts, leading to outright cancellation, the region is unlikely to make the economic progress its people so badly need.

The leader of Khuzana Village Women's Cooperative, eastern Zambia, 1987.

"We took out a loan to grow maize for sale, so that we could have some extra money to spend on our families. But then the price of fertiliser shot up, and the things we wanted to buy became too expensive."

(Susanna Smith / Oxfam)

The causes of debt distress in the SADCC region

A number of underlying causes have led to debt distress among key SADCC states. The extent to which they have affected each of the SADCC countries varies considerably. Hence, each country needs a separate 'diagnosis' and 'treatment' according to its particular circumstances. By the same token, however, where there are common underlying causes, whether regional or global in nature and origin, these also need to be taken into account when national debt-management and internationally supported structural adjustment policies are being drawn up.

There are three broad reasons for the SADCC region's debt crisis: the effects of political and military conflict in the region; the effects of North/South economic relations; and the effects of national economic policies (see the final section of this chapter).

The effects of conflict in the region

As already discussed in Chapter 6, conflict has most seriously affected the war-torn economies of Mozambique and Angola, but the knock-on effects for their SADCC neighbours — especially for Zimbabwe, Malawi and Zambia — have also been significant.

The enormous defence costs arising from foreign-backed conflict and direct South African aggression have been a particular drain, not least because they absorb a large amount of foreign exchange. In 1986, for example, Mozambique was spending 41.9 per cent of its national revenue on defence, and Angola 40.4 per cent.[38] The Economist Intelligence Unit reports that about half of Angola's debt has been borrowed for defence purposes from the Soviet Union.[39]

The conflict in Mozambique also lies behind Zimbabwe's substantial defence expenditure. Zimbabwe's defence costs are roughly equivalent to its current account deficit, or approximately 10 per cent of the gross national product.

Moreover, in Mozambique and Angola especially, the barely calculable damage which war has done to production, and therefore to national earnings and prospects for economic recovery, creates a spiral of decline. This makes continuing defence expenditure and debt servicing — neither of them productive in nature — increasingly burdensome.[40]

It is also important to look briefly at the economic impact of the war in Rhodesia during the 1970s. Zambia and Mozambique paid a high economic price for the war and the decolonisation process in Rhodesia. Alongside other factors, the economic consequences of this turbulent period of history live on in those countries' external debt burdens.

Like Malawi's, Zambia's economy was closely linked to Rhodesia's. During the late colonial period this was because the Central African Federation was designed with Southern Rhodesia as the economic centre of gravity. By the time of its independence in 1964, Zambia depended on Rhodesia Railways for most of its import and export trade.

Zambia was therefore very vulnerable to the imposition of international sanctions against Rhodesia, and had to make urgent and costly contingency arrangements. In 1968, when UN oil sanctions against Rhodesia were adopted, Zambia's oil supplies were also cut off. The consequent stream of heavy tankers plying between Dar es Salaam port and the Zambian copperbelt and capital caused the linking road to be called the 'hell run'. Even so, expensive airlifts of oil supplies were also necessary. An oil pipeline had to be quickly built, linking Zambia to the Indian Ocean port of Dar es Salaam in independent Tanzania.

In 1973, Zambia closed its border with Rhodesia in compliance with UN sanctions against the Smith regime. This meant that all Zambia's trade had to travel by road to Dar es Salaam, a costly necessity. In 1976, the Great Uhuru Railway, linking Zambia to Dar es Salaam, was completed. After being turned down by Britain, the USA, the UN, and the World Bank, Zambia received an interest-free loan for construction of the line from China, and Chinese workers and equipment were imported to build it. Repayments were initially deferred until 1983, but by that time Zambia was already in deep economic crisis.

In 1976, at the time when Zambia's copper earnings had started to drop (see below), UN officials estimated that the closing of Zambia's border with Rhodesia had cost it $450 m.[41] However, during the 1980s, despite the many difficulties of maintenance and joint management (with Tanzania), Zambia was to benefit from having the rail link and the oil pipeline to Dar.

The diversion of the government's attention and the economic price Zambia paid for the decolonisation process in Zimbabwe were major factors which contributed to its failure to diversify and strengthen its economic base during the years immediately after independence. At the same time the government was undertaking costly infrastructural projects to break away from its economic dependence on Rhodesia. Therefore, regional factors have played a role in sustaining the country's structural economic vulnerability, and its current economic crisis, of which debt is an important part.

However, Mozambique paid and was later to pay an even greater price. Not only did compliance with international sanctions against the Smith regime cost independent Mozambique some $556 m. in lost transport revenue (transport and port revenue is Mozambique's main source of foreign exchange earnings),[42] but this came at a time when the newly independent country was trying to redress the colonial neglect of infrastructure and services. Worse, the MNR and the economic destruction it has wrought are a direct legacy from the Rhodesian regime.

The effects of North/South economic relations
Many of the SADCC countries came to independence inheriting an external debt from their colonial governments. Thereafter, loan finance was needed to begin the massive task of 'nation building', that is transforming a colony into a modern, self-governing state. Finance was needed to develop basic infrastructure and services; to increase energy supplies; to build improved

transport links; and to invest in economic development. The rights and wrongs of each SADCC country's early economic development model have been vigorously disputed ever since, often with the benefit of hindsight and without analysing the limitations of the available options. Nevertheless, the fact remains that each of the newly independent governments faced massive development and infrastructural needs which required very considerable investment. During the 1960s and the early 1970s, when the South African economy was receiving large amounts of direct private investment, the emerging independent nations of the wider region had to seek loan finance for their development needs.[43]

A study of the way in which Zambia's debt has accumulated shows that during the last few years of the country's comparatively prosperous period (1964—1974) when copper prices were high (on average), there was an increase in loan procurement in order to finance costly infrastructural projects, mainly in the transport, energy, and industrial sectors.

Examples from the early 1970s include a World Bank loan of Kwacha 29 m. towards the costs of building a hydroelectric power station on the north bank of the Kariba Dam, and a loan from China of K287 m. towards the construction of the rail link to the Tanzanian coast. In 1973, the government decided to redeem the bonds it had issued in order to get majority participation (51 per cent) in the copper mining industry formerly controlled by the South African company Anglo American, through a loan raised on the Euro dollar market — a market which was later to be vulnerable to increases in interest rates.[44]

From the mid-1970s onwards, however, major economic factors came into play which entirely disrupted the economies of non-oil-producing nations, hitting the developing countries particularly hard. The debt trap was set. Poor countries had first to borrow to stay afloat, and thereafter were sunk not only by the continuing hostile global economic environment, but also by their external debt burden.

The two oil shocks of the 1970s caused the price of oil to rise from $1.30 per barrel in 1970 to $32.50 in 1981. During the 1970s, this factor alone accounted for 70 per cent of the increase in Third World debt.

The two periods of global recession, in 1973-75 and 1980-83, which originated in the industrial North, upset the world's trading and financial systems. The recessions contributed to the depression of primary commodity prices, price increases for manufactured goods, and falling levels of net capital flows to the Third World.[45] In spite of the North's subsequent economic recovery, OECD economic activity has been at a lower level, and most primary commodity markets have not recovered. This has left those countries dependent on primary commodity exports with worsening terms of trade, and therefore less earning power.

External debt repayments are normally payable in foreign exchange. Debtor countries worldwide — particularly those with declining terms of trade — which are attempting to honour their debt-servicing obligations have experienced serious shortages of foreign exchange. This has reduced their ability to pay for essential inputs to maintain their export sectors' productivity. Unless they borrow the foreign exchange necessary to secure these inputs, their foreign exchange earnings will fall all the faster, and so on.

Thus the structural deformities in the South's economic and political relationships with the North have been aggravated by the debt crisis. Naturally, the impact of all these global factors has been felt in the SADCC region.

In Zambia's case, for example, 1975 was the turning point in its fortunes. It was the year in which copper prices collapsed after two years of oil price rises. As a result, independent Zambia registered its first trade deficit, of K76.5 m. By the end of 1976, Zambia's foreign reserves had dropped to register an all-time low of -$42 m.[46] These reserves were principally needed for importing essential inputs for the mining industry. As foreign exchange became scarcer, so the productivity of the mining industry, Zambia's main foreign exchange earning sector, was affected. Zambia increasingly resorted to borrowing to cover its balance of payments deficits, getting deeper into debt all the time. The problems of falling national earnings and rising debt obligations, together with seriously deficient economic management policies, have hobbled this highly distorted economy ever since. Zambia is now the most debt-distressed country in the SADCC region.

For Malawi, the danger point came at the end of the 1970s, when the country began to experience balance of payments deficits. Falling concessional flows from Malawi's industrialised donors, and declining agricultural export earnings meant that the country could no longer finance the rising prices of the imports needed for industrial and infrastructural development. The government resorted to external borrowing as a way of both financing projects and balancing its books (see the case study in Chapter 9).[47]

The failure of international debt-crisis management

To date, the creditor countries, those with the power to help the debtor nations escape the debt trap, have failed to tackle the problem effectively. A number of crisis management plans have been unveiled, each one a cautious extension of the former (see box)

International debt-crisis management

For bilateral debt

Unilateral initiatives have cancelled some aid debt owed by low-income Africa. The UK, Canada, West Germany, and the Scandinavian Group have adopted aid debt cancellation schemes. The 1987 'Lawson Initiative' makes debt relief conditional on acceptance of IMF-approved economic reform programmes, and a good debt-servicing record.

There have been two agreements for rescheduling official non-concessional bilateral credits through the Paris Club (the group of western creditor nations), the first following the 1987 Venice economic summit, and the second following the 1988 Toronto summit. The 'Toronto Plan', which finally convinced the USA and West Germany that relief should be provided for non-aid debt, broke new ground in creating a major exception to a key rule that had previously governed all Paris Club reschedulings. An 'option' was agreed which would permit the rescheduling of non-concessional bilateral loans at concessional interest rates. A 'menu' of options was agreed:

a. cancellation of 33 per cent of debt service covered by the agreement, and rescheduling of the rest, with an eight-year grace period and 14-year maturity; or

b. reduction of interest rates by either 3.5 percentage points or by 50 per cent, whichever is less, and rescheduling of debts over 14 years with eight years' grace; or

c. extension of grace periods to 14 years and maturity to 25 years.

As development agencies have pointed out, option (c) (introduced at the insistence of the USA) provides no real debt relief, as few countries could ever repay principal; so it should be cancelled. Moreover, the Toronto Plan is available only for some 18 countries which are both classified by the World Bank as debt-distressed and undertaking IMF/World Bank structural adjustment programmes.

However, as a policy of debt reduction, the Toronto Plan is a useful first step towards the longer-term necessity of debt cancellation, and it recognises that creditors should share the burden of Third World non-concessional debt. Malawi, Mozambique, and Tanzania (as officially classified 'low-income' countries following approved adjustment programmes) have benefitted from the Toronto Plan. Zambia has yet to conclude a new IMF-backed economic reform programme, while Zimbabwe and Angola are not classified as 'low-income'.

For multilateral debt

Far less has been achieved on this front. In 1986, the IMF's Structural Adjustment Facility was created, and in 1987 its Enhanced Structural

Adjustment Facility was established, both offering softer terms than former IMF loans to low-income countries. The main drawbacks to these facilities are that the recipient has to undertake an official IMF stabilisation programme; that the drawings on this facility have been disappointingly low; and that these new facilities, although useful, have added a new rescheduling horizon to recipients' debt-servicing commitments, falling due in the mid-1990s. The problem is therefore merely postponed until a later round of rescheduling.

Some concessional finance has been made available to refinance non-concessional World Bank loans. In 1988, the World Bank announced interest payment relief for 13 low-income African nations on Bank loans they had received in previous years. The Bank also pledged $400 m. a year of additional loans from the International Development Association (IDA — established by the Bank in 1960 to provide soft loans to poor countries), to be cofinanced by $950 m. yearly of new bilateral aid. An initiative has been launched by the Nordic countries to subsidise World Bank debt.

For private, commercial debt

The Baker Plan and other commercial debt initiatives were aimed at the Highly Indebted Countries, because the possibility of default posed a threat to the western financial system. Commercial creditors have taken no policy initiatives towards low-income Africa, although several middle-income African countries have had their commercial debts rescheduled by the London Club (the group of private western creditors).

The notable lack of initiatives from the international banks also constrains progress on official debt reduction. The governments of the 'Group of Seven' (the USA, UK, West Germany, France, Japan, Canada, and Australia), anxious not to 'bail out' the banks any further, are opposed to putting more money into debt reduction until they see the commercial banks making parallel moves.

The cumulative failure to address the problem has brought serious problems in its wake. It has made world trade more unstable because of the shrinking import and export capacities of the debt-distressed world. Former debt strategies, based on the notion that the Third World's main problem was liquidity and that the solution was therefore to provide more loans and extend repayment periods, have succeeded only in increasing indebtedness in the low-income countries. Worst of all, the failure to tackle the debt crisis has seriously undermined poor countries' economic fabric and prospects of recovery.[48]

Martha Lamek (right), a community health worker in Isunga village, part of a programme supported by the District Hospital at Sumve, Tanzania. The doctor in charge, Dr van der Feltz, says the country's structural adjustment policy is undermining health care: "The supply of drugs is deteriorating. We can't even get iron tablets or injectable penicillin — or tetanus vaccine, at present. Government Zonal Stores can provide us with less and less since their expenditure was cut again this year (1988)."

Geoff Sayer / Oxfam

In general terms, international debt management policies have slowly moved from rescheduling to reduction. However, none to date has been sufficiently far-reaching to achieve the two essential concurrent targets which Oxfam believes must be met: sustainable and sustained national economic growth, together with a flexible level of debt servicing which ensures that debt payments do not take precedence over provision for people's basic needs.

For the SADCC states, with all the additional economic problems they shoulder, nothing short of radical measures aimed in the first instance at substantial reduction, and thereafter at cancellation, could achieve these two development-orientated requirements.

More debt measures needed[4]

Because of the tremendous economic stresses and challenges facing the SADCC states as a group, debt relief should be an integral part of a comprehensive international policy to tackle underdevelopment in the region. If there is to be real economic progress as a result of the advantage of 'economy of scale' which the SADCC region could enjoy over and above its separate members, then the policies of the region's main creditors must take account of the SADCC regional identity.

In conventional debt analysis, there is no scope for such regional economic groupings. Rather, indebted countries are separately categorised according to their economic status only. For example, the World Bank makes a distinction between sub-Saharan African countries of 'low income' and 'middle income'. Among the SADCC states, the World Bank classifies Lesotho, Malawi, Mozambique, Tanzania, and Zambia as 'low income', whereas Angola, Botswana, Swaziland, and Zimbabwe are categorised as 'middle income'.

It is widely acknowledged that these distinctions are somewhat arbitrary, in the sense that the 'middle income' category frequently fails to reflect the poverty in which large numbers of a given country's population live. Angola and Zimbabwe are good examples of this. Consequently, in looking at the nature of debt and the types of debt-management policies needed for the SADCC region, it is the working assumption here that all the economically destabilised SADCC countries should be regarded as having a 'low income available for development'. Likewise, the World Bank's inclusion of Malawi, Mozambique, Tanzania, and Zambia in its 'debt-distressed' category is wholly correct. However, largely due to the costs of conflict, Zimbabwe and Angola should also be considered 'debt-distressed'.

As far as the SADCC region is concerned, Angola, Malawi, Mozambique, Tanzania, Zambia, and Zimbabwe should all be regarded as debt-distressed. As SADCC's regional economic identity develops, the state of each national economy will have increasing consequences for the others.

On this issue, the first step must come from the SADCC states themselves. By the end of 1989, SADCC had not produced a debt policy statement, although it is understood that this matter is under consideration.

On bilateral debt

Creditor governments are the major potential source of debt reduction for Africa as a whole, including the SADCC region (see table 8.7). A step-by-step approach is needed in the first instance, and should be internationally coordinated so that all the OECD, OPEC, and CMEA[50] creditor countries are working in harness.

All outstanding concessional (aid) credits should be cancelled outright. Britain took a lead in this respect in 1978, and is well placed to coordinate an international programme. Some donors, notably the USA and the Soviet Union, have not cancelled any aid debt.[51] Angola, Malawi, Mozambique, Tanzania, and Zambia in particular would benefit — jointly their official bilateral aid debts owed to OECD creditors totalled $3.2 bn. in 1987.[52] Any

Table 8.7: SADCC external debt profile (1987), % of total debt by category

Country	Long-term debt — Debt owed to OECD countries — Bilateral: Aid	Bilateral: Non-concessional bank and export credits*	Private commercial	Multilateral: Conc./Non-conc.	Debt owed to non-OECD countries, OPEC, CMEA, + others	Short-term debt: Banks	Trade credits	IMF	Total debt on concessional terms	Total debt on non-concessional terms
Angola	10.8	49.9	3.1	2.3 / 1.6 0.7	3.0	18.8	11.7	0.0	15.5	84.5
Botswana	6.4	37.4	1.2	44.8 / 9.0 35.8	4.0	3.7	0.8	0.0	19.5	79.0 **
Lesotho	1.2	6.8	1.2	81.9 / 70.3 11.6	0.4	2.0	0.4	0.0	75.5	20.8 **
Malawi	14.0	7.0	4.1	60.6 / 49.3 11.3	2.0	1.9	1.1	8.2	63.9	27.0 **
Mozambique	25.6	26.5	4.4	11.8 / 9.6 2.2	11.7	5.8	12.7	0.8	48.0	52.0
Swaziland	28.6	11.4	2.9	51.7 / 14.3 37.4	2.9	1.3	0.0	0.9	44.0	55.0
Tanzania	13.7	21.2	1.1	28.2 / 21.5 6.7	22.0	3.9	7.7	1.9	48.4	49.6
Zambia	17.7	17.4	1.5	20.4 / 8.4 12.0	12.0	11.4	3.7	15.4	31.5	52.7
Zimbabwe	20.3	22.6	13.1	19.5 / 3.8 15.7	5.9	9.9	1.1	5.8	26.8	66.0

conc. = concessional   non-conc. = non-concessional

* Officially supported

** Other unidentified liabilities account for the fact that totals for concessional and non-concessional debt do not add up to 100%

(Source: OECD world debt tables)

even-handed cancellation of aid debt should involve dropping the insistence of some creditors on adherence by debtors to a rigid, orthodox, IMF-approved stabilisation programme in order to be eligible for aid debt cancellation. While it is of the greatest importance that structural economic deformities are urgently addressed, the standard IMF approach to correcting balance of payments deficits incurs unacceptable social costs.

Non-concessional bilateral loans (largely medium-term project export credits) are a major burden on debt-distressed countries, because they lead to excessive build-up of interest and penalty charges which accrue on rescheduled obligations and arrears. In the SADCC region, Zambia, Tanzania, Angola, Zimbabwe, and Mozambique in particular would benefit from a substantial reduction in this category of debt. For these countries, the total debt burden of this type was $4,195 m. in 1987.

It has been calculated that the world's low-income debtor nations need to have some two-thirds of this category of debt cancelled simply in order to return to 1982 levels.[53]

On multilateral debt

Multilateral debt is a key component of the SADCC region's debt, accounting for an average of 35.6 per cent of the region's total debt.

Experience has shown that establishing effective measures for tackling multilateral debt in sub-Saharan Africa is far more politically awkward than it is for bilateral debt. This is because a large measure of international political cooperation is needed, and also because the IMF and the World Bank in particular cannot finance substantial debt reduction without extra resources being supplied by their OECD member states.

To help promote the right pre-conditions for sustainable economic growth and development, the creditor multilateral institutions must provide net inflows of resources, on softer terms than before, so that development is possible alongside multilateral debt-servicing obligations. They must also seek to reduce future servicing burdens.

The SADCC states owe money to a number of multilateral organisations, including the IMF, the World Bank, the African Development Bank and Arab/OPEC multilateral creditors. (Table 8.8[54] shows SADCC's debts to the World Bank and the IMF.)

The September 1989 annual IMF and World Bank meetings in Washington were particularly disappointing for those countries which were lobbying for substantial, additional measures on multilateral debt reduction. Although there was general support for a proposal to increase the funds of the World Bank's International Development Association, the USA and Britain, in particular, rejected the 100 per cent increase in the IMF's Enhanced Structural

---

Table 8.8: Total outstanding disbursed debt owed by SADCC countries to the IMF and World Bank (concessional and non-concessional), as at end of 1987 ($ m.)

Country	World Bank	IDA	IMF	Total
Angola	0	0	0	0
Botswana	180.4	14.4	0	194.8
Lesotho	0	81.4	0	81.4
Malawi	104.0	509.0	110.0	723.0
Mozambique	0	87.0	17.0	104.0
Swaziland	68.5	7.3	3.0	78.8
Tanzania	325.0	801.0	95.0	1,221.0
Zambia	555.0	260.0	957.0	1,772.0
Zimbabwe	373.0	58.0	156.0	587.0
TOTAL	1,605.9	1,818.1	1,338.0	4,762.0

(Sources: for concessional and non-concessional World Bank debt, World Bank debt tables 1989/90; for IMF debt, OECD data)

Adjustment Facility (ESAF), called for by the 'G24', the group of developing countries representing the indebted Third World.[55] Bernard Chidzero, Zimbabwe's Minister of Finance and the Chairman of the World Bank's Development Committee, explained that the G7 countries perceive multilateral debt reduction and debt-service reduction as issues which are already being tackled

> ... within the context of structural adjustment programmes. These are being used by the G7 as an instrument to influence the policies of developing countries which conflict with the expectations of the industrialised countries. The industrialised countries are pre-occupied with inflation and the need to harmonise their industrial policies.[56]

In 1987, the SADCC countries owed the IMF a total of $1,338 m., with by far the largest share owed by Zambia ($957 m.). However, in view of subsequent adjustment agreements reached with the IMF by Tanzania and Mozambique, the total figure will since have risen.

The IMF's ESAF should be strengthened, on condition that the IMF relaxes harsh conditionality, and ensures that there is a net inflow of resources to the debt-distressed countries. In the longer term, however, far more durable solutions need to be found to the underlying causes of debt crisis in Africa's low-income countries, and in this regard the OECD creditor countries should seek ways to write off outstanding IMF debt.

Likewise, for a number of SADCC states, the key issue is how to cancel outstanding balances owed to the World Bank (listed in table 8.8), rather than simply receiving concessional credit to subsidise interest payments on them. A concerted effort by the OECD community is needed to put up sufficient resources to write off debt-distressed countries' debts to the World Bank.

On commercial debt

In line with most of sub-Saharan Africa, private commercial debt is not a large proportion of the SADCC region's total debt, accounting for some $2,428 m. altogether in 1987. In terms of the percentage of total long-term and short-term debt, commercial debt was most significant for Angola, Zimbabwe, Zambia, and Mozambique respectively in 1987.

Nevertheless, it is important to achieve substantial commercial debt reduction, because commercial interest rates are a significant proportion of total debt-service obligations, and because progress made on reducing official debt risks being consumed by commercial debt servicing.

European commercial banks have a high exposure in sub-Saharan Africa, and should be urged to take substantial debt reduction initiatives in the SADCC region.

The SADCC region's short-term, trade-credit debt totalled $1.1 bn. in 1987, and was almost totally composed of debts owed by Tanzania, Mozambique, Zambia, and Angola. Trade credits accounted for 7.7 per cent, 12.7 per cent, 3.7 per cent, and 11.7 per cent respectively of those countries' total debt in 1987.

With commercial interest rates attached to it, trade-credit debt accounts for a higher proportion of debt service than concessional debts. Furthermore, failure to pay up often means future credit is blocked and, in the case of essential imports, economic growth and efforts to meet basic needs are affected accordingly.

These are the key debt-reduction and cancellation initiatives which the poor in the SADCC region, and indeed most of low-income Africa, need. However, it must be stressed that debt-service reduction is not an end in itself. It is a critical step to restore the flow of resources from the North to the South. As such, it is a necessary, although not a sufficient, condition for the resumption of economic development and the rise in per capita incomes in indebted countries.

Managing indebted economies: adjustment or transformation?

Throughout the 1980s, more and more debt-distressed Third World countries have had to turn to economic adjustment measures (that is, the restructuring of their economies to reduce balance of payments deficits) in order to try and cope with debt and structural economic problems.

As we have seen, following the first oil shock at the end of 1973, and the subsequent world economic slump, many developing countries faced financial disaster, and borrowing was one temporary way out. However, many of these debts then fell due in the late 1970s, at the same time as oil prices quadrupled for a second time, and as interest rates began to rise.

The IMF negotiated the rescheduling of many loans at this time, on condition that debtor nations adjusted their economies according to plans drawn up by the Fund. By February 1989, 28 African countries had outstanding agreements with the IMF under the categories of Stand-By, Extended Stand-By, Structural Adjustment Facility, and Enhanced Structural Adjustment Facility arrangements, and in June 1988, 19 African countries had structural adjustment agreements with the World Bank.

Although it is unclear to what extent the effects of recession are implicated,[57] there is now substantial evidence[58] to show that some aspects of economic adjustment, particularly where the IMF has insisted on rapid change, have caused considerable hardship to vulnerable sections of society, particularly the urban poor and the landless or near-landless rural poor. Linked to this, in Tanzania, Zambia, Zimbabwe and Malawi, it has been Oxfam's experience that the immediate effects of economic adjustment programmes on basic social services and the economic survival options of vulnerable groups have made local-level development work all the harder.[59] Moreover, in the long term, as far as the countries dependent on primary commodities are concerned, it is also questionable whether the type of adjustment programmes financed by the IMF and the World Bank will eventually lead to sustainable economic and social development in the interests of the poor. Within the SADCC region, some countries (Angola and Zimbabwe, for example) have followed their own economic adjustment programmes independent of the IMF, while others (Malawi, Mozambique, Tanzania, Lesotho, and Zambia) have turned to the IMF and the World Bank for finance conditional on their adopting 'structural adjustment' programmes. However, the special economic context of the southern African region, in particular the costs of South Africa's regional destabilisation, has not been adequately allowed for in the Fund's and Bank's 'prescriptions' for adjustment and economic recovery.

Mrs Jere lives in Jack Compound, one of Lusaka's shanty areas. She supplements her family's income by breaking stones for the building industry, and by growing vegetables on wasteland near her home. Her husband, a driver in government service, has seen the value of his earnings sharply eroded by economic adjustment measures.

(John Clark / Oxfam)

Adjustment and conditionality

What do economic adjustment programmes consist of? There are two basic policy packages available to countries attempting to adjust to adverse external economic developments. These are not mutually exclusive options.

Stabilisation programmes, normally pursued by countries not undertaking IMF-supported adjustment programmes, are those which attempt to reduce domestic demand (in order to meet a reduced level of external resources) through a range of austerity measures. Zimbabwe and Angola and, formerly, Zambia and Tanzania, have adopted their own stabilisation programmes.

Structural adjustment programmes are normally supported by the IMF and the World Bank, and seek to reduce the current account deficit through a number of measures. These include reducing public expenditure levels; increasing domestic savings levels; liberalising the economy to remove state controls on imports, prices, and distribution; promoting private foreign investment; and promoting exports, especially in sectors where the country is considered to have a 'comparative advantage'.

The concept of 'conditionality' is now central to adjustment planning. Loan finance from the IMF and the World Bank is tied to the recipient country's acceptance of a programme of structural adjustment approved by these financial institutions, whose decision-making structures are dominated by the Northern industrialised states. But the introduction of conditionality in 1971 (it was not codified until 1979) marked a major departure for both the Fund and the Bank, and caused considerable controversy. Some criticisms challenged the notion of conditionality, while others centred on the substance of the conditions.

Once again, a new generation of 'conditionality' is provoking controversy as more bilateral and multilateral donors are insisting that their aid should itself be tied to recipient governments' acceptance of IMF stabilisation programmes. For example, in the negotiations running up to the Lomé IV Agreement to define the terms of European Community trade, aid and cooperation with the 66 African, Caribbean and Pacific signatory states during the 1990s, some EC states, Britain and West Germany in particular, pressed the view that some EC aid should be made conditional on a country's adoption of IMF-approved economic reform programmes.

The IMF and the World Bank

The World Bank (International Bank for Reconstruction and Development) and the IMF (International Monetary Fund), known as the 'Bretton Woods' institutions, date back to a 1944 conference held in a US village of that name. They were conceived by the western powers as twin intergovernmental pillars supporting the structure of a new global financial and economic order after the depression of the 1930s and the reconstruction needs arising from World War 2, especially in Europe. These organisations were not originally set up to cope with the economic problems facing Third World nations, and many believe they are ill-suited to that purpose.

Although they have separate functions, there are also many similarities between them which create confusion. The key difference between them is that the World Bank intends to be primarily a development institution with a long-term outlook, whereas the IMF seeks primarily to maintain an orderly system of receipts and payments between nations and has a short-term outlook. Underlying both is the western economic philosophy of promoting the free movement of capital and goods throughout the Fund's and Bank's member countries (virtually all the world's nations apart from the

Soviet Union and some of its allies).

IMF adjustment loans

Stand-By Arrangement Facility: allows a member country to draw a stated amount of foreign currency from the IMF — valid for a limited period of time. These resources are supposed to help restore confidence in a member's currency when it has a deficit and/or is under pressure from speculators. Disbursements are tied to specific performance criteria.

Structural Adjustment Facility, and Enhanced Structural Adjustment Facility: designed to provide medium-term assistance to those members of the IMF who find themselves in greater balance-of-payments difficulties than can be solved by an ordinary tranche drawing on the Fund. This facility is meant to correct major structural imbalances.

World Bank adjustment loans

Structural Adjustment Loan: an injection of untied credit which can be used for almost any type of import, or for the repayment of foreign debts falling due. It is a comprehensive tool for promoting policy change, reaching into almost all sectors of the economy, and focusing on both macro-economic and sectoral reforms. The World Bank defines the purpose of SALs as "to support the implementation of policies and institutional changes necessary to modify the structure of an economy so that it can maintain its growth rate and the viability of its balance of payments in the medium term". Defined by one leading critic of the World Bank as "An attempt to combine large quantities of untied aid ... with an unprecedented degree of meddling in the formulation of ... policy."[60]

Sector Adjustment Loan: Like Structural Adjustment Loans, these are designed to support adjustment programmes, but are quicker to disburse, and are focused on particular sectors of a nation's economy — agriculture, for example.

Power and influence in the Bretton Woods institutions

> The leaders of developing countries are abdicating responsibility for improving the lives of their populations because the centres of decision-making are outside their countries; economic policy depends on outside developments more than internal ones.
>
> *(A.M. Osman, Minister of Finance, Mozambique[61])*

Although, by definition, all countries which have World Bank and/or IMF programmes are paid-up members of those organisations, nevertheless the World Bank and the IMF are widely seen as representing the interests of the First World, rather than those of the Third World.

In the case of the World Bank, the poor member nations have slightly more voting power than in the Fund.[62] Nevertheless, greater power is given to those nations which make the largest contributions to the Bank's capital. This is because voting power in both institutions is proportionate to each nation's financial contributions, which in turn is determined by a country's wealth.

In 1989, the World Bank's votes were divided up as follows: USA (16.33 per cent), Japan (9.43 per cent), West Germany (7.29 per cent), UK (6.99 per cent), France (4.76 per cent), Canada (2.78 per cent), and Australia (2.10 per cent). In the same year, the countries with the biggest share of the votes in the IMF were: USA (19.91 per cent), UK (6.88 per cent), West Germany (6 per cent), France (4.98 per cent), and Japan (4.69 per cent). Canada and Australia, the other members of the 'G7' group, controlled 3.27 per cent and 1.80 per cent of the votes respectively.[63]

This voting power, together with the way in which the decision-making structures are formed, means that the main western industrialised nations dominated 49.6 per cent of the Bank's vote and 47.5 per cent of the Fund's vote in 1989. It is not, therefore, surprising that many developing countries question whether there really is a commonality of interests between all the members of the Bretton Woods institutions. However, as the turbulent relationships between the Fund on the one hand and Tanzania and Zambia on the other have shown, the lack of alternative sources of international finance for debt-distressed countries leaves those nations with little choice but to accept the IMF's terms.

A key reason is that other sources of vital western aid and investment, concessional and commercial, tend to dry up if an indebted country has not accepted the IMF 'medicine'. In mid-1987, Kebby Musokatwane, Zambia's then Prime Minister and former Minister of Finance explained, "The main reasons why countries go to the IMF is not to get money, it's to get credibility to satisfy the donor community."[64]

At the time (May 1987), Zambia had just prematurely terminated its IMF agreement because of the high political costs of the strict austerity measures it had been forced to impose. Street riots broke out in the copperbelt, where strong trade unions have long been in a position to challenge the government. In response to Zambia's unilateral decision to break off relations with the IMF, the British Government announced it was cutting its programme aid to Zambia, aid worth some £30 m. for that year.[65]

Adjusting the world's economy to development: the need for structural transformation

This section is mainly concerned with the effects on the poor of the internationally-sponsored structural adjustment approach towards the economic difficulties of poor, indebted states in the SADCC region, as promoted by the IMF and the World Bank. However, 'home-grown' economic adjustment programmes have also caused hardship, not least because they do not benefit from external funding on soft terms to ease the process.

Adjustment programmes should be assessed both in terms of the short-term effects on the poor, and in terms of the long-term prospects for development. Although the World Bank and the IMF have increasingly come to acknowledge that poverty may be exacerbated by the short-term effects of adjustment, nevertheless, it is argued, adjustment necessarily involves undergoing a period of hardship before the benefits of growth can be realised. As the World Bank puts it,

> ... one clear lesson from experience with adjustment programmes has been that failure to adjust is likely to hurt the poor and that an orderly adjustment process is indispensable to improve the long-term position of the poor.[66]

Furthermore, just as the economic structures of adjusting countries are not homogenous, so the effects of interventions will differ from one country to another.

Oxfam is particularly concerned with the effects on two particularly vulnerable groups: the urban poor, and the rural landless and land-hungry.

The social effects of adjustment measures also depend on the degree to which the poor are integrated into a country's 'money' economy. Of the SADCC states undergoing adjustment programmes, Malawi, Tanzania, Zambia and Zimbabwe are (comparatively speaking) highly monetised economies. By contrast, Angola and Mozambique have been reduced, mainly by war, to economies typified by very limited surplus agricultural production. Barter is the main means of trade in rural areas; widespread destitution has replaced economic production; and in a few urban centres the black market economy dominates what remains of the monetary economy. For adjustment programmes to deliver benefits to the rural poor in these countries, basic economic structures must first be revived, and an essential pre-condition for this is peace. A major drawback to the far-reaching structural adjustment programme being undertaken in Mozambique is that war continues to prevent the effective re-establishment of rural/urban trade.

An important background factor affecting the way in which some adjustment measures have harmed the poor is the pace at which they have been implemented. Where structural adjustment programmes are concerned, this is largely dictated by the limited amount of finance available to the IMF and the World Bank to support adjustment programmes. If adjustment measures are to be more gradual, the industrialised North must make more resources available. However, most bilateral donors have indicated that they are unwilling to expand support for adjustment in the poorest countries.[67]

The immediate effects of economic adjustment on the poor

A key aim of structural adjustment policies for sub-Saharan African countries has been to redirect the economic focus away from the urban, consumer-led economy towards a rural, producer-led one, building on the so-called 'comparative advantage' of primary-commodity producing economies which are locked into exporting to the North.

As a result, many rural producers, especially those well served by rural infrastructure and with sufficient land for surplus production, have benefitted in terms of their net earnings from the rise in producer prices and improved rural/urban terms of trade. But without special compensatory measures, this has proved to be a blunt instrument. Unintentionally, it has harmed both the urban poor who depend on wages, and rural people who are either landless or have insufficient land on which to satisfy their subsistence needs and produce cash crops.

There are three main elements of adjustment programmes which are of general concern to development agencies, and which are causing hardship in the SADCC states undergoing rapid economic adjustment.

Firstly, stabilisation measures aimed at reducing domestic economic demand (in order to help quickly restore external balance of payments equilibrium) have seriously affected some people's real incomes — either through changes in wages and employment or through price changes which alter producers' net earnings. In Zimbabwe, for example, the government's own stabilisation measures included wage freezes which, together with rising prices, hit the low-paid urban workers and their dependants particularly hard. In Malawi, although the better-off rural producers have benefitted directly from the increase in maize prices, the hundreds of thousands of land-hungry rural people have not (see the case-studies in Chapter 9).

Secondly, consumer price increases introduced to benefit agricultural producers have harmed the urban poor and those rural households who are net food purchasers. In Zambia, for example, the price of maize meal, the staple food, was raised by 50 per cent overnight in 1985. This was the first stage of removing the long-standing state subsidy on mealie meal, one of the few

An overcrowded class at Mwabuzo Primary School in Tanzania's Shinyanga Region, 1988. The head teacher commented: "We have very few reading books; Standards 1 and 2 have none. The children have to buy most of their own exercise books."

(Geoff Sayer / Oxfam)

'safety nets' the government had consistently provided for the poor since independence. Its removal caused particular hardship for the urban poor, who have no land on which to grow their own food, and for whom there is no cheaper alternative than mealie meal.[68] In Mozambique, as a result of its structural adjustment programme, basic commodities are at least now available in the shops of Maputo and some provincial towns, but priced way out of the reach of the poor. And in Malawi, the price of maize, also the staple, rose steeply in 1987, partly as a result of the structural adjustment programme's liberalisation of internal trade. In some cases, Zambia and Malawi for example, a rise in the price of fertiliser, fuel, and transport has partially offset the benefits of increased maize producer prices.

Thirdly, in support of financial stringency, adjusting governments have to choose which expenditure items to cut. Where social programmes are affected, the poor are likely to suffer disproportionately. Cuts in health and education expenditure are compounded by the generally deteriorating levels of maintenance in infrastructure and services.

In Zimbabwe, for example, government restraint in health spending during the 1983 to 1985 period was reflected in a loss of momentum in the spectacular improvements in child nutritional status and welfare which were taking place (although real health spending levels have since been restored). In Zambia, where universal access to health and primary education was a key achievement of post-independence development, government expenditure has been cut back.[69] As a result, services have deteriorated, and fees have been introduced for state schools and health services. Mozambique and Tanzania are now managing to reverse the former declining trends.

Furthermore, this precipitous run-down in a nation's investment in its 'human capital' has serious consequences for its future development. SADCC's development emphasis during the 1990s is to be centred on 'enterprise, skills, and productivity'. Simba Makoni, SADCC's Executive Secretary, explained why the SADCC states themselves must make greater efforts to maximise the skills and training of their people. It follows that the next generation must not be held back.

> In my five years with SADCC, I am now convinced that the most immediate constraint on development is not the shortage of funds, but our capacity to foster the necessary conceptual framework for development, to identify, design, and implement projects and to operate and maintain them efficiently thereafter. At this point in time, in our region, the human factor remains the weakest link in the development chain. This factor does not only manifest itself in the shortage of professional and skilled personnel *per se*, but more so in the under-utilisation and even misallocation of the limited and skilled professional people we have.[70]

In its November 1989 report on sub-Saharan Africa, the World Bank acknowledges the central importance of people in the development process, and calls for higher rates of investment by governments and donors in education and health. While this is a welcome development in the Bank's outlook, it fails to acknowledge the role of the Bretton Woods institutions in pressing for substantial budgetary cutbacks. Further, it is unclear how the Bank envisages that higher rates of social spending can be achieved when there is a continued emphasis from donor governments on the need for poor countries to cut public spending.

In the short term, it is clear that in order to protect and compensate those sections of society vulnerable to the process of adjustment, special measures are required. A number of initiatives are needed in the SADCC region.

For the urban poor, it is vital to increase employment, and introduce targeted food subsidies (which are being implemented in Zambia and Mozambique). In Malawi it is essential that land reform be undertaken to alleviate the plight of the landless and near-landless, and that more is done to ensure that food prices are pegged within the reach of the poor. Likewise, in

Zimbabwe, the slow-down in the land resettlement programme must be reversed.

Government spending on essential social services must not be cut back: on the contrary, support is needed to help these services develop and to deliver services more appropriate to the needs of the poor, particularly children.

The full impact of the special economic consequences of conflict in Mozambique and Angola must be recognised and allowed for when international approval is sought for adjustment programmes. Not only should especially concessional terms be available for adjustment loans (as has happened in the case of Mozambique), but also the disruption which war causes to commerce, internal trade, and production must be allowed for. Further, the substantial humanitarian costs and responsibilities borne by the governments of the war-torn economies should be more fully recognised. While they are actively pursuing a resolution to conflict, the governments of Mozambique and Angola (if and when Angola reaches adjustment agreements with the IMF and the World Bank) must have special adjustment agreements for as long as millions of their people are destitute and largely dependent on handouts.

The long-term development prospects of economic adjustment policies

Some aspects of adjustment programmes have been useful in addressing internal structural constraints on development in the SADCC countries. In Malawi, for example, adjustment measures have gone some way to redirect government's economic development focus away from the privately owned agricultural estates towards the peasant sector. In Zambia, the need for economic adjustment has caused the government to redirect income away from the urban sector to the rural producers.

However, in two major respects the IMF/World Bank structural adjustment model (the only one with substantial resources behind it) has failed to address key development constraints for the South in general, and the SADCC region in particular.

Sharing the burden

The poor countries of the South have had to carry a wholly disproportionate share of an economic crisis which largely originated in the North, and for which North/South responsibility should be actively shared. Increasingly, the North's chief answer to poverty and underdevelopment in the South is to press for structural adjustment. The most powerful actors on the stage, the IMF and the World Bank, have approached what is fundamentally a global economic problem[71] from the supposition that remedial work on the economies of the South alone would be sufficient to resolve matters.

Furthermore, it has been the poor within the adjusting countries who have suffered most. This is not only because they are more vulnerable to rapid economic change, but also because of poor government. In key SADCC states, the institutional checks and balances necessary for democratic government have been eroded; in others they were never in place. This has meant that development in the interests of the poorest has often not been a political priority. Vulnerable sections of society, lacking political influence, do not figure in the government's political power base. So when it comes to the hard political choices forced on governments by the need for economic stringency, effective poverty-alleviation and sustainable development are often the casualties of other political priorities.

In Malawi, for example, the World Bank's modest suggestions for land reform have not been taken up, as is also the case in Kenya. In Zambia, another society with an extremely uneven distribution of wealth,[72] comparable to Kenya and Brazil, government cut-backs in expenditure on health and education in response to the IMF's demands for financial stringency have hurt the poor in two main ways. Firstly, it is the poor who need the state health services most; there is a well-established private sector available for those who can pay. And secondly, along with subsidies on basic foodstuffs, state investment in health and education was the main element in the otherwise limited post-independence efforts to create an egalitarian society. Zambia's own economic reform programme, instituted after its 1987 break with the IMF, maintained cut-backs in social spending.

Investing in decline and dependency?
In the indebted countries which are dependent on exporting primary commodities, structural adjustment programmes have failed to stimulate the major structural changes needed to help these countries survive the long-term decline in commodity prices.[73] This is demonstrated through the resulting increased dependence on external financial flows, and greater emphasis on production for the export market. The World Bank's policy of encouraging exports has sometimes contradicted the view taken by the Bank's commodities specialists.[74]

As the World Bank now agrees, there needs to be a commitment to an industrialisation strategy providing greater equity between rural and urban producers.[75] Linked to this is the need to diversify the range of the South's trading partners. For as long as the South is locked into producing primary products, there will be limited trading complementarity between Southern countries. However, since the developing world is recognised as a major market for manufactures, the potential exists for increased South/South trade.

But hitherto, structural adjustment programmes have tended in practice towards improving the existing model of commodity dependence. As UNICEF has put it,

> Adjustment is designed to remove the wedge driven between farmers and world markets by governments to finance their rather unproductive investment and consumption. Due to excessive margins, farmers in Africa throughout the 1970s suffered progressive immiseration [sic] — it took longer and harder work to produce the same return. The problem is that by removing one set of constraints, one may simply replace one kind of problem for another. Adjustment may produce a more externally oriented agriculture, but if it remains simply that, the immiseration process will continue, as well as removing land and labour from domestic food production.[76]

These considerations underline the urgent need for diversification of commodity-dependent economies, either into more processing of agricultural exports to 'add value', or into exporting manufactures, or into import substitution. Regardless of which mix of adaptations is considered, certain vulnerable sections of society stand to suffer in the transition process unless more resources are available to help ensure gradual, orderly change.

Prospects for change

As far as regional economic groupings like SADCC are concerned, the international financial institutions and donors may need to adapt their conventional procedure of negotiating with each recipient country individually.

As more has become known about the effects of rapid economic adjustment on the poor (and due in part to the pressure brought to bear by research initiatives and development agencies like UNICEF, Oxfam and its sister non-governmental agencies), the World Bank and the IMF have become increasingly concerned about the social consequences of adjustment. The governments of adjusting countries have also come under pressure to ensure adjustment with equity. This brightens the prospects for growth with equity in the 1990s.

However, much depends on increasing the level of cooperation from the OECD countries, and present indications are gloomy. The industrialised North is preoccupied with avoiding another period of recession, and with sizing up the enormous economic opportunities presented by rapid political change in Eastern Europe. There is marked 'aid fatigue', and a reluctance to review the structural adjustment model, the pace at which it is applied, the resources behind it, and the need for the North to share more of the South's burdens.

Policy failures in the SADCC states

Pressures from South Africa and from the industrialised North have been mostly responsible for the SADCC region's current economic difficulties which are undermining development. Nevertheless, government policy errors and failures have also played an important part, and must also be addressed if development in the interests of the poorest is to become a reality.

In Zambia, poverty is on the increase as a result of a complex set of factors.[77] National policy errors must be highlighted among the catalogue of causes. The government failed to diversify the country's economic base when it could have afforded to do so during the first decade of independence (1964 — 1974), at a time when copper prices were high and before its international terms of trade had begun to falter.[78] Instead of investing in a sustainable programme of economic diversification, particularly in agriculture and rural industries, a number of inconsistent and flawed economic development programmes were attempted. [79]

The pressing political imperatives of the time resulted in Zambia taking a different economic and political path. With no other readily available source of income, and a great deal of local and foreign (including South African) vested interests in the copper industry, Zambia continued to let the mining sector dominate the economy, thus perpetuating its fatal dependence. Rural development, which all along has clearly been the most neglected development sector, was compromised in favour of the powerful demands of the urban population, particularly of the growing middle class. The needs of the rural poor did not match the political leverage of the urban elite, nor even that of the urban poor.

A comprehensive 'welfare state' structure of public services — itself ultimately dependent on copper earnings — was established, and through it the 'fruits of independence' were delivered. In many senses, Zambia's emphasis on providing services to the poor, such as health, education, and subsidies on staple foods, brought great rewards, but they were not enough to offset the shortcomings in government policy on rural production and the increasingly inequitable distribution of the country's wealth. The underlying malaise of declining rural/urban terms of trade, which had first grown up in the colonial era, was not reversed by government policy. Instead, a wealthy urban elite came to dominate national political priorities, and their interests did not lie in rural development.[80]

During the 1980s, much of Oxfam's long-term anti-poverty work throughout the region has focused on helping poor people to organise for a greater say in the decisions that affect them. The key issue here is the process

Vusisizwe Rural Development Centre, Zimbabwe, built to facilitate local people's meetings and discussions. Here a group of rural pre-school workers are attending a training course.   (Chris Johnson / Oxfam)

of democratisation — in the sense of widening people's participation in decisions about their own development. For example, in Zambia's copperbelt, where the social impact of the country's economic decline is most apparent, township youth have organised to identify the causes of their poverty. In addition to criticising the vested interests in the IMF, they have also recognised how the wealthy elite of their own country act against the interests of the poor.

In Malawi there is an urgent need for greater popular participation in identifying and addressing poverty and development issues. Long-term strategies to cope with the consequences of land hunger, for example, cannot begin to be addressed in a society where it cannot be officially considered or openly discussed as a major development constraint.

Injudicious government policy has also contributed towards Malawi's economic problems and to the country's substantial debt. Detailed research has demonstrated that many aspects of government development policy during the 1970s created new dimensions of economic vulnerability for the poorest in the interests of boosting Malawi's export-crop earnings. Now that

Malawi's period of macro-economic prosperity is over, the results are laid bare.

The following specific aspects of the export-led drive for economic growth have had a particularly damaging impact on the poor:[81] the taxation of peasant farming to subsidise the commercial estate sector; the use of direct controls on production to discriminate against small farmers, for example largely restricting the growing of Burley tobacco to the commercial estate sector;[82] a low-wage policy aimed at assisting agricultural estate development; and the government's direction to commercial banks to support estate agriculture beyond the limits of commercial prudence. Furthermore, because government policy favoured the large company estates at the expense of smaller family holdings, whatever potential the smallholder sector once had to provide an employment safety net capable of meeting the growing needs of the poor has been consistently eroded (see the case-study in Chapter 9).

In Zimbabwe, where there is much greater scope for land redistribution than in Malawi, in practice the government has not sided unequivocally with the land-hungry poor. Even allowing for all the constitutional, technical, and economic constraints which have impeded the land programme, nevertheless it also appears that government's decisions have further delayed implementation (see Chapter 9), with harmful consequences for the poorest.

The democratisation of economic management and planning, so that the poor have a greater say in national agricultural and other development policy, especially in Mozambique and Angola, are also vital. In Mozambique, heavy-handed attempts at collectivisation in the rural areas shortly after independence, and over-centralised organisation of agricultural production during the early years, alienated people from the government in some areas, and depressed rural production. This dissatisfaction is widely thought to be one of the factors which work in the MNR's favour.[83]. FRELIMO's 1989 Congress recognised the need for important policy changes to facilitate a greater degree of democracy at local level.

In Angola, the independent government's nationalisation of the commercial agricultural sector and the country's internal trading structures had disastrous effects on export production and national food security, mainly because of the country's particularly disruptive colonial legacy.

Another weakness in economic management has been profligate spending. In some SADCC states, scarce resources have been spent on prestige projects which were neither productive in nature nor relevant to the needs of the poor. In Malawi, for example, during the late 1970s, the government undertook a series of major investments, mainly of a non-productive kind. An expert on the economy of Malawi has cited the examples of President Banda's personal 'palaces', military aviation facilities, and a new international airport.[84]

Another example occurred in Zambia in 1984, when it was already quite clear that Zambia's economic problems were deep and long-term. It was announced that contractors had been commissioned to build new Lusaka headquarters for the nation's only political party, UNIP (United National Independence Party). Conservative estimates at the time put the cost at £20 m.[85] Meanwhile, Oxfam reports were highlighting the poor condition of rural services: clinics were short of essential drugs, village schools could not be staffed for lack of Ministry resources, and crops from many areas could not be collected, because trucks and rural roads had not been maintained.

Furthermore, during the 1980s, international credit encouraged the widespread trend in sub-Saharan Africa towards consumption at the expense of production.[86] Zambia is just one example of a government allowing the importation of luxury goods to satisfy wealthy urban consumers. As the Guardian noted in 1988,[87] the IMF-inspired 'kwacha auction' distributed precious foreign exchange to the highest bidder, when even the most essential commodities were in very short supply. At that time, South Africa was the source of many of the luxury imports which became noticeably more available in Lusaka's shops.

On the central issue of the need for regional integration towards a brighter economic future, as SADCC spokespeople have pointed out, there is an urgent need for greater practical commitment among the member states to regional integration and cooperation, if SADCC is to help the region face up to the massive economic demands of the 1990s.

The following chapter looks at the issues raised here in the context of three very different SADCC states: Zimbabwe, Malawi, and Angola.

9

Three case-studies: Zimbabwe, Malawi, and Angola

Case-study 1: Zimbabwe

Development after independence

The first decade of independent Zimbabwe's development has been shaped by three main elements. Firstly, by its inheritance of deep inequality, together with a major degree of dependence on foreign interests and the skills of the white minority. Secondly, by various pressures on the economy beyond the government's control — destabilisation by South Africa, drought, and falling commodity prices. And thirdly, by internal political conflict which seriously affected development in Matabeleland during the mid-1980s.

Inherited inequality and dependence

In 1980, when the long struggle for majority rule and independence was over, the poor of Zimbabwe were left with a legacy of unequal access to land, employment, and basic services such as health, education, and agricultural support.

A daunting task confronted the independent government: how to balance the development of an outward-looking modern economy with a major redistributive programme to build up basic services and overcome inherited inequality.

Zimbabwe also inherited an economy which was heavily dependent on foreign investment, particularly South African and British,[1] and on the capital and skills of the settler community. Nevertheless, in comparison with the less-

Photographed in 1981 when it was back in use, this school in the Matabeleland Mzola Communal Area was destroyed during the war. A huge reconstruction programme was undertaken immediately after independence. (Oxfam)

favoured colonial economies of the region, Zimbabwe also came to independence with a comparatively well-diversified and developed modern economic sector and infrastructure.

The terms of the Lancaster House constitution (on which significant Western aid and investment flows were made contingent) ensured that foreign and minority interests would be protected for the first years of independence. The most important provisions concerned property rights. No matter how land or mineral rights had originally been obtained, they could only change hands on a 'willing-seller, willing-buyer' basis. The protection thus afforded to settler and foreign investors meant that they would continue owning more than half of the economy, most of the productive land, nearly all the mines, and nearly all of the manufacturing industry and other businesses.

With investment in the productive sectors of the modern economy dominated by foreign interests, the imperative of profit maximisation in the interests of shareholders has naturally taken precedence over wider considerations of development in the interests of the poor. The government has expressed its desire to increase local control in the private sector, and measures have been adopted to reduce some forms of dominance of foreign investment. [2] Nevertheless, national development plans have sought to rely on the inflow of foreign investment, because it is acknowledged that domestic resources are insufficient to finance the desired rate of economic growth. Little new investment has come in, however.

Together with the new government's policy of reconciliation, which added the vital political ingredient, the protection of foreign interests also meant that independent Zimbabwe was able to make the transition to majority rule without a head-on confrontation with international investors, and without losing all the skills and managerial experience of the white minority. Many settlers did leave around the time of independence, taking with them whatever assets they could, but enough remained to prevent dislocation on the scale which had been recently experienced in Mozambique and Angola.

Zimbabwe's political and legal independence was clearly constrained by its economic inheritance of inequality and dependence. The new government's scope of action to redress inequality was tempered by the vested interests which stood to lose. Nevertheless, the independent nation did inherit an economy which made its substantial programme of social investment possible, in spite of the generally adverse economic pressures of the 1980s. Much remains to be done, however, particularly in the area of land redistribution.

Development strategy — growth with equity
The Zimbabwean government has been faced with a complex set of dilemmas in the formulation and implementation of national development policies. On the one hand, the sheer scale of the inequalities still to be redressed nearly ten years after independence is daunting. On the other hand, the means of implementing the necessary changes have been fraught with a wide array of obstacles. By and large, therefore, the national development strategy — widely known as "Growth with Equity"[3] — has been a delicate balancing act.

To meet popular expectations, the most important elements of the 'equity' side of the equation have been plans for large-scale investment in land, health, and education. Progress in transforming the health and education sectors has been substantial. However, this has not been matched in the complex area of land redistribution.

The 'growth' side of the equation has been necessary to finance the 'equity' dimension. Accordingly, the government has attempted to maximise productivity within the economic structure it inherited on independence, in order to create the resources necessary for a gradual transformation of inequality, as well as for reinvestment in the economy, especially the key export sector.

There continues to be vigorous debate about the "Growth with Equity" strategy. Some argue that the very maintenance of pre-independence patterns

The Hippo Valley Sugar Estate at Chiredzi, in which the South African company Anglo American has a large stake, is an important earner of foreign exchange for Zimbabwe. The air around the plant is filled with a sweet sickly smell, and the ground is covered with black ash ('Chiredzi snow'), as the dense clouds caused by cane burning gradually settle. "Hard is not the word for my work," commented this worker.

(Julian Quan / Oxfam)

of ownership and control is a betrayal of the expectations of the majority, and the terms on which the poor joined the independence struggle. Others argue that Zimbabwe's priority must be to consolidate and expand its modern economy, taking advantage of its comparatively well-developed manufacturing sector and diversified basket of export commodities. They argue that if Zimbabwe is to survive and pay for internal development in a hostile world economic climate, then it must promote, rather than alienate, international and local business interests. In 1989, government policy shifted further over towards the latter position as a new investors' code was unveiled prior to a large and prestigious London conference, organised by the Confederation of British Industry, the Confederation of Zimbabwe Industries, and the Southern Africa Association, aimed at reassuring the World Bank and foreign investors.

Obstacles to "Growth with Equity"

During the 1980s, much has been achieved in often difficult circumstances. But there have also been a number of key factors which have impeded progress towards the national "Growth with Equity" goal.

Table 9.1: Zimbabwe's percentage economic growth rate, GDP 1980-88								
1980	1981	1982	1983	1984	1985	1986	1987	1988
10.7	9.7	1.5	-3.6	2.3	7.3	2.0	-0.7	5.3

National economic performance, although good in comparison with other countries of the region, has not consistently met the annual economic growth targets of eight per cent originally envisaged as necessary for adequate investment in equitable development programmes and services (see table 9.1).

The country experienced grave problems after the economic boom of 1980/1. Agriculture has been hit by two serious spells of drought, mining by falling world prices, and manufacturing by the consequent shortages of foreign exchange and the contraction in domestic demand. Zimbabwe's rising defence costs (incurred because the army is deployed in Mozambique to help defend the country's trade arteries) have been a major factor inhibiting economic progress.

Rising external debt-servicing obligations have also had an impact. This has been mainly due to external borrowing for the financing of parastatal and infrastructural development.[4] Debt-servicing rose from 2.2 per cent of export earnings at independence to a peak of 32.3 per cent in 1983 (declining to 19.8 per cent in 1984). Shortage of foreign exchange has severely constrained economic growth, by limiting the capacity to import necessary inputs not just for reconstruction and development, but even for the maintenance of the existing economic structure.

Economic growth needs fresh international investment, and by and large this has not been forthcoming. One key inhibiting factor is the budget deficit, running at about 10 per cent of GNP in 1989. This has arisen mainly because of the massive costs of South Africa's regional policy. The government has pledged to reduce the deficit, but — since Zimbabwe's defence expenditure is necessary to keep its trade arteries open — the savings are likely to come from development investment.

Zimbabwe's budget deficit has been at the root of a prolonged dispute about economic development policy between the government and the IMF. Because of the costs of defending its trade routes through Mozambique, the government has had to run a deficit. The IMF could not agree to this strategy, concerned as it was only with Zimbabwe's balance of payments equilibrium and not with the consequences of South Africa's regional policy, nor with the need to implement large-scale development programmes.[5] Since March 1984, when the government broke with the IMF, it has therefore pursued its own economic reforms, without IMF assistance.

Finally, old political tensions between the ruling party, ZANU, and the main opposition party, ZAPU, led to serious civil conflict and state repression in Matabeleland during the mid-1980s.[6] The government pursued a brutal military and political campaign to suppress armed dissidents in Matabeleland. Civilians and their development organisational structures suffered enormously. Oxfam partner organisations were directly affected, and the government's development investment and activities in the area were markedly curtailed. Even urgent relief operations were hampered by the emergency regulations and the army.

At the expense of democratic pluralism, the Unity agreement between ZANU and ZAPU of December 1987 was none the less welcomed. It was the much-needed political solution to this conflict, and it also removed the political barriers to Matabeleland receiving its fair share of development investment.

Progress in land, health, and rural development

Oxfam's programme in Zimbabwe since 1980 has spanned a critical period, in which our partners and field workers have seen enormous reconstruction and development achievements, especially in the provision of essential services such as health, education, and agricultural support to people in the poor Communal Areas (known before independence as the Tribal Trust Lands).

But it has also been a time in which the early momentum for change in the interests of the poor has been slowed down by external and internal pressures. This has been particularly evident in the land redistribution programme, in the factors affecting health status, and in the narrowing of options facing self-help organisations committed to rural development.

Problems of land reform

A curious feature of post-independence Zimbabwe has been the lack of significant land reform. For decades the iniquitous nature of land distribution has been widely recognised. Black protests over land, including appeals to the British government, were first voiced over 70 years ago. During the nationalist struggles of the 1960s and the guerrilla war of the 1970s, both main political parties, ZANU and ZAPU, committed themselves to radical land reform on achieving political power. They attracted massive popular support from rural peasants because of this promise. So there was high expectation of rapid change in 1980.

Yet, after a decade of independence under a ZANU-led government, the

Cynthia Nhongo is the manager of Mutzarara Cooperative, established on a fruit farm formerly owned by settlers, near Harare. Like many other co-ops, this one lacks sufficient resources. (Chris Johnson / Oxfam)

land issue remains strikingly unresolved, and the position of the white commercial farmers appears more secure in 1990 than at any time previously. Resettlement has not begun to reach the modest targets set in 1980/1. Numerous and often conflicting plans to reform the Communal Areas have remained for the most part on the drawing board. Blacks who have moved on to abandoned 'white' farm land have been dubbed 'squatters' and evicted with the full force of law, even in the most politically sensitive parts of the country. Lydia Sinimana, aged 62, complained,

> We thought the liberation war was fought to give us back our land. My grandfather was born on that land (in Chimanimani), my husband died there, and now they throw us off.[7]

ZANU's promise "to re-establish justice and equity in the ownership of land" has manifestly not been fulfilled. Why?

In Kenya, where there was a comparable land problem and a guerrilla war fuelled by land grievance, the British government sought to defuse the situation by offering to buy out white farmers who were reluctant to continue living in the country after independence. This was duly done, and there were hopes at one time that a similar solution would be adopted at the time when Rhodesia became Zimbabwe.

The British government did recognise the political need for land reform and, to some extent, its own responsibility for purchasing land and compensating white farmers who wanted to leave. This was because the majority of companies and individuals who owned land in Rhodesia were of British origin.

In the mid-1970s, during the constant round of diplomatic manoeuvres, the notion of an Anglo-American development fund, to which Britain agreed to contribute at least £75 million, was put on the table. The fund was to help buy out white farmers and so, hopefully, end the war more quickly. The idea attracted broad support, not least from the ZANU/ZAPU 'Patriotic Front'. By 1979, however, when the contending parties sat down at Lancaster House to hammer out an independence constitution, there had been a change of government in Britain. The earlier proposal was dangled before participants as a bait to reach agreement, but it was ultimately put back on the shelf, not without Zimbabwean complaints of British chicanery. In its place was put the compromise — some would say capitulation — that land could change hands only on a 'willing-seller, willing-buyer' basis. In other words, whites who wished to keep their farms were free to do so; there would be no expropriation of land. Only 'under-utilised' land required for resettlement or other public purposes could be compulsorily acquired by the new government, but this would also have to be paid for immediately and at the full market price. In a last-minute amendment, it was agreed that compensation in such cases also had to be remittable in foreign exchange..

So the hands of the new Zimbabwean government were to a large extent tied by the Lancaster House agreement, which was to last until April 1990. They were tied also by the immediate need for reconstruction. The last few years of the war had devastated the countryside. One-fifth of the rural population had fled. Nearly half a million had flocked into the towns to escape the conflict; a quarter of a million had fled the country; and some three-quarters of a million had been rounded up into 'protected villages' by the Smith regime. Various disease-control programmes had broken down. The result was a severe dislocation of peasant production.

Historically, there had always been bitter competition between black and white farmers in Rhodesia, with the state providing extensive and crucial support to white agriculture. But, in some more favoured areas at least, peasant farmers had remained resilient. They were encouraged to produce maize for the home market during periods when white farmers were concentrating on export crops, such as tobacco. But after Prime Minister Ian Smith unilaterally declared independence in 1965, the subsequent sanctions imposed against his regime made it harder to export agricultural commodities, so settler farmers switched back to domestic markets — at the expense of the peasants. This factor, combined with the severe rural dislocation caused by the war, meant that at the time of independence in 1980 the white commercial farmers were producing nearly 90 per cent of the country's marketed food requirements (and an even higher proportion of agricultural exports). At that precise moment, they seemed crucial to Zimbabwe's survival.

This view was endorsed by the strong advice which the new Zimbabwean government received from its staunchest wartime ally, Mozambique. When Mozambique finally became independent in 1974/5, there followed a mass exodus of Portuguese settlers. FRELIMO, which had done nothing to discourage this exodus at the time, soon came to regret it, and the very firm advice given to Robert Mugabe's new government in 1980 was that it should strive to retain white expertise and skills, notably on the land. The recent experience of famine in the Sahel further underlined the need for food self-sufficiency, and indeed the need to earn foreign exchange by exporting food, rather than spending it on food imports. All this combined to produce a policy of national reconciliation, which Robert Mugabe unveiled to the nation on the day of his electoral victory. The white farmers, who only a few months earlier had been the targets of guerrilla attacks because of their secondary role as part and parcel of the regime's security forces, had suddenly become a protected species.

At independence, some 42 per cent of the country's land was taken up by large commercial farms, then exclusively white-owned. As a result of past land policies and wholesale evictions of blacks, population densities were three times higher in the Communal Areas than in the commercial farming areas. As a matter of both social justice and ecological equilibrium, something had to be done.

The new government offered to resettle people living in the artificially overcrowded Communal Areas on land which it bought from white farmers, within the framework of the Lancaster House agreement. Ambitiously, it hoped to resettle some 162,000 families by 1984. Two schemes were adopted: Model A, where individual farmers received 5-6 hectare plots of arable land plus access to common grazing, the size varying according to region; and Model B, in which abandoned farms were taken over by producer cooperatives.

The costs of resettlement involved both buying land and developing the necessary infrastructure. The British government agreed to meet half the costs, provided the Zimbabwean Government matched them pound for pound. If the Zimbabweans should falter, Britain would not step into the breach. Britain pledged an initial £20 million, with more promised by Mrs Thatcher

Members of the Svimuri Cooperative in eastern Zimbabwe, established on a settler farm abandoned during the war. Many of the co-op members are ex-combatants, who have had to learn the necessary farming skills. (Chris Johnson / Oxfam)

during her visit to Zimbabwe in March 1989.

From 1980 to 1988, progress on land purchase was extremely uneven. By 30 June 1989 the total hectarage bought for resettlement had risen to 2,713,725, or about 16 per cent of the area owned by commercial farmers in 1980. But only 52,000 families had been resettled, about 416,000 people, or 32 per cent of the 1984 target of 162,000 families.[8] A number of factors lie behind this pattern and explain why there has always been more land on the market than the Zimbabwean Government has taken up, and why there is a great deal of spare capacity on the land which has been bought for resettlement.

The initial burst of buying comprised virtually all the farms abandoned during the war, mostly in the war zones of the north-east, or land belonging to farmers who decided to sell up and leave after independence. Thereafter, few large blocks of land became available, making advance planning more difficult. The land which was on offer was not necessarily situated in areas where people wanted to live, and land prices started to rise, especially in the more favoured regions.

From 1983 Zimbabwe's domestic budget came under increasing pressure, with the government being told to reduce its budget deficit by the World Bank, by the British government, and by other western governments. It was much easier for it to shut down a resettlement programme still at the planning stage[9] than to starve the newly established schools and clinics of funds.

The severe droughts of the mid-1980s also impeded progress, with some people who had moved to resettlement areas returning to the Communal Areas in search, literally, of greener pastures. Moreover, the droughts affected national economic performance, and entailed costly relief expenditure. The droughts may also have reinforced the Zimbabwe government's initial response of treating the commercial farmers with kid gloves.

There was a strong tendency for white farmers who stayed on to offer for sale only the marginal remnants of their farms, which they wanted to get rid of, and to retain the much more productive core. This meant that the land offered for resettlement was unsuitable, while at the same time property values stabilised. The Commercial Farmers' Union (CFU) lobbied hard and successfully in favour of slowing down the whole process of resettlement.

The government tended, for ideological reasons, to support and push Model B, while the majority of the people hoping to resettle favoured Model A, or even more individualised settlement options. Incentives for people to move were also not great; they received only conditional, annual permits of occupancy, while disincentives included losing the right of access to land in the Communal Areas.

The post-independence boom[10] in peasant production misled the government into thinking that a sustainable increase in Communal Area production, capable of meeting welfare needs, was possible without extensive resettlement. In fact, on closer investigation of the aggregate figures, it became clear that the bumper yields had been achieved by the better-off peasants, in the better-watered Communal Areas (particularly in Mashonaland). These farmers were in a position to respond to the improved price incentives on offer from the new government.[11] Many agricultural extension workers tended, having been brought up under the old regime, to be distrustful and contemptuous of peasant capacities and initiatives. There was also rivalry between ministries over control of the resettlement programme, and the planning ministries lacked the staff to support the programme.

A major problem was that of paying for resettlement infrastructure. The Zimbabwean government claimed that while the British government was prepared to put up money for the purchase of land, the conditions it laid down — in terms of detailed planning and surveying before resettlement could take place — were far too strict. Zimbabwe simply did not have sufficient surveyors to meet such restrictions. There were those too who argued that

British conditions were particularly onerous in the case of the Model B areas, because of their disapproval of the socialist ethic embodied in the cooperative movement. The British in turn argued that the Zimbabweans had always been slow in matching the money which Britain had provided. Zimbabweans countered that because they had created political stability, land prices had risen. This meant that far too much of the money allocated to the land programme had been spent on buying land, rather than on the 'follow-through' costs of resettling people.

The statistics do not of course reveal the complete picture. Any white farmer wishing to sell land had first to offer it to the government, which could then decide to inspect the land. If it did not want it, it issued a certificate stating 'no present interest', which left the owner free to sell on the private market. Literally hundreds of farms changed hands in this way, many to senior members of the government and the new ruling elite. In the late 1980s, as the government slowly deliberated over land reform, the debate was certainly complicated by the fact that for some of its members land redistribution meant grabbing land for themselves. At least ten government ministers were known to be members of the Commercial Farmers' Union.[12]

Land reform in the 1990s?
The lack of adequate resources and organisational capacity has hampered the resettlement programme, but the political constraints are perhaps the biggest threat to land redistribution in the 1990s. Powerful commercial vested interests are pitted against the basic needs of the poorest.

The government has been tentatively considering a new resettlement phase for implementation during the 1990s, when the Lancaster House conditions expire.[13] But so far, all that has happened is the emergence of a powerful counter-lobby composed mainly of the CFU, the British government, and the World Bank.

In August 1989, Joshua Nkomo, by then a senior Minister in the President's office, himself reported to be a landowner on an extensive scale, told the CFU's annual congress that the situation was "morally unacceptable, economically unjustifiable and politically untenable".[14] He also told them that white commercial farmers would be "persuaded" to sell their unused land to the government after 1990.[15] The commercial farmers were alarmed to the point where high-level shuttle diplomacy was privately undertaken to reassure them that in spite of politicians' speeches, there would be no dramatic change in government policy over the next year.[16]

Also in 1989, the new British High Commissioner to Zimbabwe did not endear himself to Robert Mugabe when he advised him of Britain's concern at the prospect of land being seized from commercial farmers after 1990.[17] And the World Bank, which has been making loans to Zimbabwe since 1980, and since 1987 has led a powerful lobby to liberalise Zimbabwe's trade,[18] also stresses the view that export farming efficiency will be compromised by land redistribution to the poor.

The main argument of those opposed to substantial redistribution of land centres on the issue of 'efficiency'. It is held that the government's 1982 resettlement target (of 162,000 families) would require an estimated 60 per cent of the Large Scale Commercial Farming sector's land, and that this in turn would lead to a 'proportionate drop' in production and employment, only partially compensated for by the benefits to the resettled families. Within this body of opinion, an 'environmentalist' lobby has emerged, taking up a theme familiar from colonial times. Its proponents (mainly western governments, white commercial farmers, and black technocrats) argue that resettlement would simply extend environmental mismanagement, and therefore low productivity, and that land degradation would be exported from the Communal Areas to commercially-farmed land. An article in the *Economist*[19] summed up the conflict as seen by this lobby, which believes that investment in the Communal Areas is a preferable option to land redistribution:

> ... the commercial farmers like their scrublands and their water catchment areas. In the communal lands, by contrast, the soil is losing fertility and eroding. That is where most voters live and where most of Zimbabwe's population growth — of 3 per cent a year — takes place. The return on new investment would be even greater there, mainly because the high cost of buying land from the white farmers would be avoided.

> ... Land redistribution may win votes next year. But if it scared away foreign investors ... it would lose many votes in 1995.

Yet the anti-poverty lobby in Zimbabwe argues[20] that there need not be a 'trade off' between equity and efficiency, and that those with vested interests have deliberately masked important facts:

First, that the 'proportionate drop' (between land given over, and agricultural production plus employment) would in fact be far less because the land given for resettlement is, and has always been, underutilised.

Second, the process of resettlement to date demonstrates that in more marginal, semi-arid areas (half of the resettled areas to date have fallen into this category) the number of resettled people outnumbers those formerly employed in commercial agriculture by factors ranging from five to ten.[21]

Third, that production on resettlement farms is already surpassing the long-term targets, and in some cases rivalling the yields of comparable commercial farms, thus leading to greater agricultural productivity.

And lastly, detailed research shows that indigenous conservation methods are far more sustainable and ecologically sound than much commercial farming technology.[22] The major cause of declining soil fertility in the Communal Areas is overuse. Until substantial land redistribution takes place, the majority of rural Zimbabweans will have no other land.

Indications at the end of 1989 were that the government appears to have accepted the CFU's argument — bolstered by the second-best tobacco crop in the country's history[23] — that serious land reform would undermine white confidence, reduce exports and employment opportunities, threaten the business community and the new drive for foreign investment, and lead to a white urban exodus. At which point the tap of Western and multilateral aid would be turned off.

Immediately after Zimbabwe's independence in 1980, an Oxfam consultant toured the country to ask rural people for their views of development and reconstruction priorities. She wrote:

> Land is the major country-wide issue. People claim that they primarily fought for a fair distribution of land and economic opportunities. Most people would like to move back to their original land or be given better land elsewhere. This is a sore point in most rural circles, especially among those who live very close to large, private farms. They see their land deteriorate every day, their area getting more crowded as their children grow up and share the little land there is with their parents, their cattle thin and dying because of inadequate grass and water, and yet next door to them is vast, under-used, private land.[24]

The commercial farmers now have more powerful local allies than ten years earlier. So peasants may have to wait much longer for land reform.

Workers' housing on a commercial farm near Harare, 1989.   (Chris Johnson / Oxfam)

Inequality in health: the background to today's challenge

The link between poverty and poor health was dramatically evident in the year of independence, when the ratio of infant mortality rates between whites, urban blacks, and rural blacks was 1:3.5:10, corresponding to a 39:5:1 ratio in income.[25]

Despite the inadequate nature of health status data collected during the colonial period, research demonstrates that the disease pattern prevalent in colonial Zimbabwe was rooted in the distorted economic system. Hence much of the pre-independence pattern of ill health persists, and it is widely thought that it will continue until the process of equitable economic distribution is taken much further.

While the affluent minority showed disease patterns similar to those of the better-off people in industrialised western economies, the majority of the population of Rhodesia — the black urban workers and rural subsistence farmers — suffered the nutritional deficiencies, communicable diseases, and problems of pregnancy and childbirth which are all characteristically associated with poverty. Undernutrition, which from historical accounts appears to have increased after colonisation, was particularly prevalent in the Tribal Trust Lands (now called Communal Areas), and among the children of workers on the commercial farms. As is now well documented throughout the developing world, poor nutrition increases susceptibility to infection, especially among small children.

War and poor health

The liberation war created new dimensions of poverty and ill health, as well as conflict-related civilian casualties.

People in the rural areas suffered most. The widespread undernutrition long established in the rural areas turned into mass hunger.[26] Thousands of able-bodied people left rural production, either to join the guerrilla armies or to seek the relative safety of the towns. This, combined with widespread insecurity, affected the ability of those remaining on the land to produce food. In many rural areas, the local administrations collapsed, and transport (of essential agricultural supplies and everything else) was curtailed.

Furthermore, in an attempt to prevent the rural population from assisting the nationalist guerrillas, the government introduced a number of policies which severely disrupted the lives of the rural poor, and increased their poverty. Chief among these was the forced removal of people into 'protected' and 'consolidated' villages, especially in the east and south of the country. By early 1978, an estimated 750,000 people had moved into 'PVs' (protected villages), so that their movements could be better monitored and curtailed by the security forces.

During the war, 'Protected Villages' were established in an attempt to prevent civilian support for the nationalist guerrillas. Here a member of the Rhodesian security forces searches people on return from their fields before curfew. (Camera Press)

Life in the PVs involved not only severe restrictions on people's subsistence livelihoods, but also the widespread destruction by the security forces of their water sources, homes, property, foodstores, standing crops, animals and poultry, which the villagers were forced to leave behind.

Towards the end of the war, according to the International Red Cross, two million rural people (conservatively estimated) were dependent on emergency relief. By the time of independence, the long-standing pattern of chronic poor health among the black majority had given way to suffering of crisis proportions.

Health services

The provision of health services during the colonial era began with a network of hospitals concentrated in the urban areas to serve the settlers. Thereafter, mine hospitals and infectious diseases hospitals were established for certain sections of the black population. This was done both to minimise the risk of epidemic diseases spreading to the whites, and because the economic prospects of the colony depended on a healthy workforce, particularly in the mines, where dangerous underground working conditions and appalling living conditions in the mine-labour compounds had become the subject even of official controversy.

From 1909 onwards, rural dispensaries and hospitals began to be established by missionaries and government, and in 1931 the government divided the country into large areas, providing each with a rural hospital and several dispensaries. Preventive services began in 1948, but always received a minute proportion of state health expenditure.

Reflecting the way in which the Rhodesian colonial process created and sustained the division between rich and poor, health service trends up to the time of independence created a gap between white and black, urban and rural, curative and preventive, private and public. Medical training was orientated towards hospital-based curative care, while the educational system limited the entry of black students into medical studies.

Government facilities in the Tribal Trust Lands (TTLs) were rudimentary, and most of the health services on offer to the black majority were provided by mission hospitals and staff. Not only did the missions provide a much-needed service, albeit with a bias towards curative care, but, until independence, they were responsible for the training of most black Medical Assistants. For many years, because of an acute shortage of doctors in the TTLs, it was the mission-trained Medical Assistants who provided most of the simple curative care at the primary level for the rural poor. The missions also provided an important preventive medical service, particularly in the areas of ante-natal care, child-growth monitoring, and immunisation.

During the war, these rural health services were severely affected. By the end of the war in 1979, many hospitals and clinics had been destroyed or shut down, while those that remained open were only partly functioning. From a former total of 50, only four mission doctors were still working in the TTLs.[27]

Although people's need for health services had become more acute, the widespread insecurity meant that hospital staff, health outreach staff, and patients alike were afraid to travel. The introduction of martial law, covering most of the TTL areas, further restricted travel. Beds lay empty, clinic attendances dropped, sick people did not get treated, women went without ante-natal and post-natal care, and children were not vaccinated.

The establishment of a National Health Programme[28]

When the independent government came to power in 1980, its health policy faced a two-fold challenge. The first priority was the rehabilitation and restoration of the war-torn health infrastructure. Oxfam was asked to help by recruiting doctors and nurses to be placed in a number of government-supported mission hospitals in the Communal Areas. Their job was to help rebuild the service offered by rural hospitals, and to help develop a national Primary Health Care programme relevant to the needs of the poor. Because of the widespread social and economic dislocation experienced during and

A simulation exercise under way as part of a training course for community health workers at Kunaka Hospital, in Zimbabwe's Seke Communal Area. (Chris Johnson / Oxfam)

directly after the war, when rural food production had to be reestablished, and when hundreds of thousands of uprooted people were returning to their homes with little or no foodstocks or cattle, the Oxfam health workers were also involved in a country-wide supplementary feeding programme for those most at risk.[29] As sufficient numbers of Zimbabwean health personnel have become qualified, Oxfam has gradually reduced its staffing programme.

The government's second, longer-term, task was to transform the inherited health services from their former racial, urban, curative bias into a service relevant to the needs of the poor majority.[30] The government planned for a health service accessible to all. Oxfam-supported health workers were also involved in this longer-term work. In September 1980, health care was made free to anyone earning less than Z$150 per month, the majority of the population.[31]

The new health service was to be integrated with other development services, and the introduction of a national Primary Health Care programme was an important innovation, aimed at directing resources and appropriate services to the most impoverished areas of the country.[32]

Achievements since independence
Dramatic achievements in health provision in the early years of independence, together with improvements in agricultural and other development services undertaken shortly after independence, resulted in a

significant reduction in the national Infant Mortality Rates. These fell from the pre-independence estimate published in the late 1970s as between 120 to 220 per thousand live births[33] to an estimated 83 per thousand in 1982.[34]

In 1981, a national Expanded Programme of Immunisation was introduced to combat the six major childhood infectious diseases, and perinatal tetanus. Coverage studies showed that the proportion of rural children immunised grew from 25 per cent in 1982, to 42 per cent in 1984, and up to 69 per cent in 1986.[35] Other appropriate health services were introduced — including programmes to combat childhood diarrhoeal disease and malnutrition, and to improve hygiene. Expenditure on preventive services rose to 15 per cent of the (greatly expanded) total health budget in 1984/85.[36] Provincial and district hospitals were upgraded, and by January 1987, 224 rural health centres had been completed.[37]

Poverty, health, and the economy
However, since widespread poverty is the root cause of ill health, Oxfam's health workers agree that the health improvements brought about by improved services cannot, of themselves, create and maintain overall good health among people living in poverty. The key factors which determine good health are economic security, educational atttainment, and adequate and appropriate health services.

In response to the large deficits first experienced in 1980/81, the government adopted its own programme of economic stabilisation and restraint, before reaching an agreement with the IMF, which it broke off in 1984. These stabilisation measures have had a direct impact on the rate of development investment, the pace of land reform, and the cost of living — all of which are key factors affecting the health status of poor people.

Investment in health
The real value of state expenditure allocated to the Ministry of Health soared after independence as government began to implement its commitment to a rapid expansion of health services in a buoyant economic climate. However, it then dropped in 1983 as economic stabilisation measures were introduced to reduce the impact of external economic pressures on the country's balance of payments deficit.[38] Fortunately it has since recovered, and is on a slow growth trend, with a rising proportion being spent on primary health care.

Other stabilisation measures such as wage freezes and the removal of subsidies on basic food commodities have also adversely affected the poorest, both urban and rural. For example, in 1982/83 prices rose by some 100 per cent for the staple mealie meal, 50 per cent for milk, and 25-30 per cent for bread.[39] The urban poor are dependent on wages and bought food, and in the rural areas the families who cannot grow enough for their own subsistence requirements need to supplement their own production with bought food.[40]

Oxfam fears that the adverse effects on the national economy of an unfavourable world economic climate, together with the costs of conflict in Mozambique, risk reversing the government's substantial achievements in the health sector, and increasing the cost of living for the poor. Persistent and widespread poor health will be one of the most visible consequences.

Oxfam's experience

The experience of Oxfam's health work in Zimbabwe is that the huge task of establishing and running accessible and appropriate health services for the rural majority involves sustained, long-term investment if the achievements already made in health care since independence are to be maintained and built on. The following extracts from Oxfam field reports illustrate the day-to-day problems faced by rural health teams.

One of Oxfam's medical team reported in 1988 that, in spite of a well-coordinated national system for the rationalisation of essential drugs, and a decentralised drugs supply structure, serious shortages of essential drugs in remote rural areas have been a persistent problem.

> National economic problems have caused shortages of essential drugs ... recently, the clinics in our area have only received 11 per cent of the drugs they have ordered from the Provincial medical stores. The situation is so serious that most of the clinics are without essential items like procaine penicillin, paracetamol, aspirin, and gauze.

Reporting on his work during 1988, one of the Oxfam-recruited doctors employed by the government in a remote area of Manicaland, bordering on to Mozambique, decided to illustrate his working life with a diary extract. Typical of health workers' problems in poor countries, his diary notes illustrate the way in which the overall shortage of resources acts to the detriment of curative care.

> 2.00 a.m. I receive a phone message from the clinic: "Doctor, we have admitted a patient with suspected poisoning. She is unconscious and gasping. The oxygen cylinder is empty as the District Council had no money to pay for oxygen. A second patient was brought in on a wheelbarrow and her blood pressure is difficult to record because our equipment isn't working properly. She delivered a baby yesterday at home, retained the placenta and is bleeding heavily."
>
> 2.10 a.m. Arrive at the clinic. Suction machine not working, no oxygen. Assist the only trained nurse on duty and one voluntary nurse to resuscitate the patient.
>
> 2.45 a.m. A car from Rusitu arrives with two patients. One is a woman in labour with her eighth child, and the position of the baby is obstructing labour. The other is a young man who has been wounded by MNR shooting

on the border. Two of these new patients need to be taken immediately to hospital in Mutare, but the car which brought them here has run out of petrol and the petrol station doesn't open until 6.30 a.m.

3.00 a.m. The clinic does not have its own transport, so I phone the District Administrator for help, after suturing the MNR victim.

4.00 a.m. Transport not yet here, the only District truck has gone to deliver food relief and is stuck with a puncture 100 km away.

4.15 a.m. A child is admitted with convulsions, presumed to be caused by malaria; resuscitated.

4.30 a.m. Put the critical patients on the open truck for Mutare.

4.40 a.m. Home for a cup of tea.

5.10 a.m. Call from a local white farmer: "I've had a cough for the last five days and I saw my private doctor in Mutare who gave me some medicine, but I am not yet OK. Can I come and see you, Doctor?"

7.45 a.m. In office to chair District Health Executive Meeting.

10.00 a.m. Attend full District Council meeting.

1.20 p.m. Telephone message from the hospital: "Doctor, we have a long queue here and the patients are complaining. Are you coming to see them?"

2.00 p.m. Hospital work until 8.00 p.m., then home.[41]

Rural development — fighting marginalisation

Underdevelopment is a process in which poverty and powerlessness are increased in people and their nation. It is to control nothing of your own, to have no say and no role in matters and actions that may improve your life.

(Excerpt from a development education seminar of rural people in Zimbabwe who have formed their own development organisation, The Organisation of Rural Associations for Progress (ORAP)[42])

Another major part of Oxfam's Zimbabwe programme has been support for community-based rural development through ORAP, a Zimbabwean non-governmental development network, founded in 1981. ORAP links together some 300 village groups in Matabeleland and the Midlands, and has a small staff of development advisers.[43] ORAP reports illustrate the way in which rural people analyse and act on the development issues facing them. Their experience offers invaluable insights into the way that national pressures combine with local ones to affect rural people.

A vital part of ORAP's work has been its programme of 'development education', the process of facilitating meetings and seminars in which rural people can meet to discuss and analyse their problems, and plan their own strategies to deal with them.[44] Through this process, ORAP groups have formed clear perceptions of the development constraints faced by rural people. As one ORAP development worker explains,

Delegates from ORAP groups meet regularly so that information can be shared and decisions reached democratically.   (Julian Quan / Oxfam)

What's interesting is that ORAP groups are clear that dependency cripples, that it opens the way for manipulation, exploitation, and control from those who give resources. ORAP members' consciousness for self-reliance is very strong.

Now, as part of the process of planning a development project or activity, we discuss all the implications. As far as resources are concerned, we first discuss whether the necessary resources are available within the village itself. If not, then we try to secure resources from our government, either at local or national level. Only in the last resort do we turn to foreign funding sources. Our groups want to take full advantage of the Zimbabwean resources available to them. ORAP believes that development is about integrating rural people into mainstream national life, empowering them to have bargaining muscle within our economy. We believe that this process of integration, of 'citizenship', begins with the way you run your own life and village development affairs. So, in this way, ORAP groups want to play a full part in national life, but not on terms which tie them up with exploitative structures.

For example, three ORAP groups in Matabeleland have started up their own beef production schemes, with the aim of empowering the groups so that they have control and bargaining power over their economic assets.

Keeping cattle has long been a strong economic tradition in Matabeleland, but people have come to believe that the increase in beef exports to Europe under the Lomé Convention threatens their self-reliance. Taking advantage of the beef trade, commercial farmers have been buying villagers' cattle at low prices, fattening them, often using bought feed, and then selling them on to the Cold Storage Board for a profit. This is a typical example of how our village economy is being exploited.

The groups have studied our traditional resources, they have rediscovered which grasses, roots and tree pods are good for fattening indigenous cattle, and have agreed that by using our own resources in an organised way, they can fatten cattle and sell direct to the Cold Storage Board without needing the middlemen.

This activity started in 1987, and it's really working well. It has removed dependency on imported feed, and by using local feedstuffs, we feel that the programme relates directly to our ecology. People are protecting their grassland and trees: they see the economic importance of doing so. The villagers are also benefitting directly in cash terms: whereas they would have been selling an animal to a commercial farmer for between Z$50 and Z$150, now they can get between Z$400 and Z$1,000. They have to pay for veterinary supplies, and during the drought they had to pay for some fodder, but they still came out on top. We hope that other groups will take this idea up, and earn resources which can then be circulated in their local economies.[45]

In this way, rural people are engaging more profitably in a mainstream economic activity - the beef trade. They have at least removed one layer in the handling process from producer to consumer.

Zimbabwe's European Community beef quota, first agreed in 1985, is a significant foreign-exchange earner. Most of Zimbabwe's beef exports go to the EC. Zimbabwe's EC market quota was raised from slightly over 8,000 tons to 9,850 tons in 1988, but reports in mid-1989 indicated that supply cannot keep up with demand.[46] In 1987, Zimbabwe earned Z$478.4 m. from its meat exports, although the high costs of protecting its trade routes through Mozambique have affected its net export earnings.

Through the ORAP 'development education' process, member groups have become well aware of the factors outside their control, and outside their government's control, which limit the scope of rural people's development — as the following extracts from ORAP reports make clear:

The economic system and the investment pattern have perpetuated minority control of the nation's resources, leaving the vast majority, who are based in the rural areas, poor and with little chance to break out of the system.[47]

... it is important for us to note that the poor are not developing in isolation. The fact that they are late-comers in this game of development puts them at a very big disadvantage in that, unlike the developed sectors, they are having to struggle against domination, manipulation, poverty and powerlessness.

Therefore, all those who support us in our work have to be clear whose side they are on. They have to understand the local as well as the global structures under which we live, in which developed countries are directly involved in our local politics and development strategies, for the most part to ensure that their interests are not threatened.

Rural people want to develop. For them, development is a process in which (the factors causing) underdevelopment are stopped and reversed ... there is no neutral partner in development. If we are all to be on one side, some local and international interests will have to give up some of their power and control over village people and the resources they need for development.[48]

Describing the ways in which popular participation in development is limited by forces beyond village people's control, ORAP's coordinator wrote,

Zimbabwe has, over the last few years since Independence, recognised the need for people to participate. But it inherited economic structures which inhibit popular participation. Like all Third World countries, although not to the same extent as many, Zimbabwe is often forced to pay its external debt first, before it responds to some of its most needy rural sectors. This ... is partly responsible for government's cut back in national subsidies on basic foods and other commodities, as well as foreign currency allocations necessary for importing some of the materials and machinery and materials which may be needed to boost rural development efforts. These are some of the obstacles which are not only beyond rural people but also beyond government. They are international problems ... [49]

Development and destabilisation

Landlocked, with minority and foreign interests dominating its national economic affairs, and tied by its export orientation to a global trading system which favours developed economies, Zimbabwe is vulnerable both to South Africa's regional policy and to the precarious world of international trade.

It is against this background that the adverse effects of South Africa's regional policy should be seen. The whole process of "Growth with Equity" has been directly affected by the war in Mozambique and by South Africa's hostile economic and military actions against Zimbabwe. Destabilisation has cost Zimbabwe an estimated $8,000 m. between 1980 and 1988.[50] It has been estimated[51] that without war in Mozambique, and with the same rate of foreign resource inflows as have come into the country, Zimbabwe would have averaged an economic growth rate higher by some 2.5—3.0 per cent during the 1980s. This would have enabled the government to have sustained its investment in health and education, and it would also have been possible to settle many thousands more families on the land which the government has bought for resettlement. Lynda Chalker, then Minister responsible for southern African affairs at the Foreign and Commonwealth Office, said in May 1989,

It is ... undeniable that Zimbabwe and its landlocked neighbours remain vulnerable to South African economic pressure. These are very real problems, and they should not be glossed over.[52]

Case-study 2: Malawi

Malawi has always been a very poor country, with one of the highest mortality rates among children under five in the world.[53] Without any exploited mineral resources (except coal), it relies on its agricultural potential and on its other principal resource — labour.

A number of factors lie behind the poverty in Malawi. By far the most important is the growing problem of land hunger in the 'customary land' areas where 80 per cent of the population live, dependent on small scale-agriculture.

Malawi has long been densely-settled, but successive national economic development strategies, both before and after independence in 1964, have exacerbated poverty. This is because the country's land and labour resources have been exploited in the interests of the ruling authorities, rather than in the interests of the poor.

Drying pounded cassava at Mponda Village in central Malawi. Many of the poorest households in Malawi are headed by women.

(Jeanne Fitzsimmons)

Tea pickers weighing their baskets at a tea estate in Mulanje District, Malawi. Working on the commercial agricultural estates has long been an important way of surviving land hunger.

(Jeanne Fitzsimmons)

From the late 1970s onwards new pressures on the poor have emerged. Falling world commodity prices have undermined the Malawian economy (Malawi depends on the export of agricultural commodities for over 90 per cent of its foreign earnings). This has been a key factor leading the country into debt. In order to meet its debt-servicing obligations, Malawi has embarked on a structural adjustment programme supported by the IMF and World Bank. Although this did not involve major shifts in existing government economic policy, nevertheless the poor have been adversely affected by some of the structural adjustment measures, and it is still far from clear whether Malawi's economic health will ever recover. All this has coincided with the enormous social and economic costs which Malawians are paying for the conflict in Mozambique.

Land hunger, migrant labour, and export-crop dependency

Land hunger, affecting the poorest people, has reached alarming proportions in much of southern and central Malawi. About a quarter of rural households are nearly landless,[54] and about two-thirds of the population live on land holdings which are too small to provide a full year's food requirements.[55]

Esme Justin's story

Esme Justin is a woman living in Mulanje District of southern Malawi. She is one of the many people involved in an Oxfam-funded action research programme aimed at helping rural people to identify the development obstacles that confront them. Her story illustrates the complex barriers to development which countless poor Malawians face: problems which are getting worse with time.

Esme is in her mid-twenties. She is the head of her household and has four children. Her husband works in Blantyre, but Esme has not heard from him for seven months and now believes that he has simply "run out" on her. Esme worries that if her husband does not return soon, his relatives may ask her and the children to leave their home, because the land belongs to them. She does not know where she will go if this happens, because her own family have left the area and she does not know where they have gone. Even if she did know, she would find it difficult to afford the transport costs to go very far.

Three of Esme's children are of school age, but none of them attends school, because she cannot afford the fees. Last year, they ran out of food two months after their annual harvest. Esme has a small 'garden' (landholding) of approximately one quarter of an acre, in which she cultivates maize and beans. In addition to the small size of her garden, another factor which affected her harvest was drought during the previous growing season. Worse still, Esme was reaching the end of her most recent pregnancy during last year's cultivation season, when all the heavy work had to be done. As a result, she was unable to look after her garden as well as she had hoped.

For nine or ten months of each year, Esme relies on 'ganyu', the informal means whereby better-off peasant farmers employ the labour of the poor in need of 'off-farm' incomes, normally on a seasonal, piecework basis. But because of the drought, ganyu has been scarce; and this year, as a result, Esme's family has had to go without food, often for two days at a time. This coming harvest is likely to be worse than last year's, because Esme and her children have begun to eat the maize cobs from their garden even before they were ripe.

Esme says that land shortage is her main problem. She stresses that the drought and her pregnancy last year worsened their situation, but that the core of her problem is lack of access to sufficient land. Esme cannot afford fertiliser, which could give her higher yields, and she is too poor to be eligible for government credit with which to buy fertiliser.[54]

At the same time, about 14 per cent of cultivated land is thought to be in the commercial estate sector.[57] Even in the very unlikely event of this land being redistributed to peasant farmers, it has been estimated that this would only alleviate land hunger for ten to fifteen years, unless sustainable methods for improving smallholder agricultural productivity can be found.

There is a long-standing tradition of labour migrancy. Driven by rural poverty, most migrant workers stay within Malawi, working on the large commercial agricultural estates which produce mainly for export. This is one way in which the poorest rely directly on the country's commodity trade. Others rely on the commodity trade via the local system of informal rural employment — known as 'ganyu' — whereby the poor do casual piecework on richer peasants' land, some of which is used for growing export crops.

A historical overview will illustrate how Malawi's modern political economy retains many essential features from the past.

The colonial era, 1891—1964

The British Protectorate of Nyasaland was established in 1891. Under colonial rule, three economic categories were deliberately fashioned to help the colony pay its way: the commercial plantation sector; the peasant sector, which included cash-crop as well as subsistence production; and the migratory labour revenue sector. Poverty was woven into all three of these interlinked sub-economies.

The plantation sub-economy was the first to develop, and it helped to create both land hunger and the highly disruptive institution of migrant labour. The plantation economy was encouraged by the early colonial authorities, who wanted to make the colony self-sufficient, and believed that African agricultural practice, based on shifting cultivation techniques (which are now widely acknowledged to be environmentally sustainable, where there is sufficient land), were primitive and wasteful. Accordingly, the colonial government facilitated the transfer of large areas of 'customary land' from the peasant population to European settlers.[58]

But even then, world commodity prices were unstable, and the territory's landlocked position meant that the costs of transporting produce to the coast were high. The colonial government saw that the future of its enclave, export-oriented, plantation economy depended on plentiful supplies of very cheap labour. Accordingly, it pursued a number of policies to force men away from traditional production cycles and into the export crop sector. Much of the land given over to the European settlers was not expected to come under plantation cultivation. Rather it was appropriated so that the colonial state could exact rent from the large numbers of people living on it. The rent thus 'owed' was payable in labour. This much-hated system of labour recruitment was, and is still, known as 'thangata'.

Wherever Africans occupied good land which the settler farmers wanted to bring under cultivation, they were moved either to less productive parts of the plantation or to 'Crown Land'. People living on Crown Land were subject to a 'hut tax'.

Given that selling one's labour was virtually the only way to earn cash, the end result was the same, whichever category of land people happened to be living on. African males were forced to seek waged employment in the European economy. However, even then Nyasaland was a weak state compared with others in the region, and this was to give rise to an ironic conflict of interests..

The demand for labour from Nyasaland's own plantation economy was substantial: by 1895, for example, some 17,000 acres were under coffee.[59] However, the very measures which the state had taken to force people to work on the plantations were so exacting that many men chose to earn their cash in neighbouring colonial economies instead. The high level of peasant taxation, the state's heavy-handed methods of tax collection (which amounted to forced labour in many instances), and its low-wage policy created enormous stresses on the rural poor. They made the recruitment offers from the mining and commercial agriculture sectors in South Africa and Rhodesia seem attractive alternatives.

Thus, from the early 1900s, a tradition of 'out-migration' from Nyasaland (which had already started even before the imposition of colonial taxation) was firmly established. It was to remain a key feature of Malawi's political economy up until the mid-1970s: by 1972, approximately 30 per cent of the adult male population was working outside the country.[60]

The tradition of out-migration began with the colonised people exercising rational choice between the limited options open to them. However, the colonial government was to capitalise on it, as the revenue from migratory labour became an important sector of the economy.

Rising out-migration, from 1903 onwards (when the Witwatersrand Native Labour Association first began to recruit labourers in Nyasaland), led the white settlers in Nyasaland to complain afresh that they were short of labour; but the colonial government saw advantages to it. The local coffee industry had collapsed in 1902, due to drought, plant disease, and competition from Brazil, and having largely destroyed the cohesion of the local African agricultural systems, the colonial government had a labour glut on its hands.

Although the government made some attempts to control out-migration (under pressure from the settler community, who were turning from coffee to cotton, tobacco and tea), over the next four decades its policy was to prove inconsistent. For economic and political reasons, it was impossible to reconcile the contrary pressures of labour needs for the plantation sector and the benefits to government revenue from migrants' remittances.

On the economic front, Nyasaland's plantation sector was dogged by cost inefficiency, unstable commodity prices (cotton and tobacco prices collapsed in the early 1930s), and by the high transport costs created by the territory's landlocked position. On the political front, Nyasaland was always a low priority for Britain in a region where it had much more important stakes —in labour-hungry South Africa and Rhodesia.

As a result of land theft and the damage done by colonial interests to the traditionally evolving peasant agricultural economies, particularly those in the southern and central areas of the territory, a deep crisis of social dislocation and poverty had been engineered. Village households were suffering from man-made shortages of labour, land, and food. From the early 1900s, as the plantation sector declined, the government abandoned its previous policies towards smallholder production, and began to encourage peasant production for export. For those peasants still living in the well-watered areas of the country, this became a preferable alternative to migrant labour as a way of paying taxes. However, in most of the country it meant a reduction in the quantity of subsistence crops which could be grown

Thus, the colonial government's attempts to foster economic development by finally turning to the African farming households for the production of export crops came too late to be an unqualified success. Largely as a result of the excesses of former strategies, and inadequate extension resources, the policy of building up the peasant export-crop sector was unevenly implemented. A disaster brought home the point that economic development based on such extreme levels of exploitation cannot be sustained.

In 1949, a famine, probably the worst in the region's history, laid bare the extent to which African society had been undermined by colonial policies, and forced a reappraisal of sorts. Although the official famine relief measures were seriously inadequate and misconceived,[61] the colonial authorities were at least forced to realise that food security must be assured as a precondition for further development of the plantation- and peasant-sector export trade. Also, the 1950s saw an improvement in world commodity markets.

In the late colonial period, when Nyasaland was part of the Central African Federation (1953-1963), along with Northern and Southern Rhodesia, it was seen as the 'poor cousin' — not much more than a picturesque labour reserve. Although the peasant cash-crop sector had become established (and 'thangata' was officially abolished), nevertheless it was difficult for the poorest to benefit from it, and migrant labour remained an important option.

Post-independence, 1964 — 1980

When Malawi came to independence in 1964, it had a highly distorted economy oriented to the export of crops and labour, and based on deep, structural poverty. Yet Malawi's fast economic growth during the 1970s earned it a reputation as an African 'economic miracle'. This reputation, which lived on longer than it deserved to, was achieved by effectively reversing the policies of the later colonial period. Beginning in the late 1960s, the plantation (estate) sector was boosted at the expense of the peasant smallholder sector.[62] Tobacco, tea, and sugar were identified as the export crops most suitable for production.

Investment during the 1970s in the large export-crop estates was made possible by changing the pattern of labour migrancy, and was funded by taxing peasant agricultural production, as well as by raising big loans from the country's two commercial banks. Malawi's 'economic miracle' was therefore achieved at the expense of not investing in sustainable economic development and food security for the poor on their own land.[63]

During the 1970s, labour migration trends altered dramatically, as out-migration largely became replaced by internal migration. Out-migration peaked in the early 1970s, and the consequent reduction in numbers has been due to a number of factors. Key among them were changes in South Africa's Chamber of Mines employment policy; the long liberation war in Zimbabwe, which deterred migrants from Malawi; a plane crash in the mid-1970s in which a number of migrants returning from South Africa lost their lives; and supply constraints imposed by the Malawian government so as to redirect labour back to the estate sector.

The expansion of the estate sector successfully absorbed the thousands of migrant workers returning from abroad, and during the boom years it also managed to absorb labour from the land-hungry areas.

Peasant crop production was taxed through the operations of ADMARC (the Agricultural and Development Marketing Corporation), the parastatal company which then had sole responsibility for the marketing of cash crops and the provision of credit and inputs to the peasant sector.[64] During the 1970s, the considerable profits which ADMARC had accumulated through its taxation of peasant produce were mainly invested in the estate sector,[65] thus further undermining the viability of peasant production.

Government economic development policy in the 1970s: effects on the poor

The rapid development of the estate sector during the 1970s deepened Malawi's structural poverty in three main ways. Firstly, by paying deliberately low prices for peasant agricultural produce, and by granting private individuals and companies the ownership of leases on 'customary' land, the economic development strategy of the 1970s undermined the peasant agricultural sector, which had begun to get established during the late colonial period. In turn, this reduced rural people's economic options and security. Overall, national *per capita* food production declined between 1960 and 1980, and recurrent localised food shortages became commonplace.

Secondly, the economic development policy pursued during the 1970s increased dependence on waged labour in the estate sector. During the 1980s, this proved to be a liability for the poor. Peasants (men and women) moved into estate employment because of the state's deliberate manipulation of pricing structures in the peasant sector (making most cash-crop production on limited land holdings uneconomic), and because of land hunger.

But Malawi's post-independence 'export boom' was short-lived, lasting only from 1964 to 1978. Following the second 'oil shock', the country's terms of trade declined by a third during 1979 and 1980. A financial crisis was immediately precipitated in the tobacco commercial estate sector, and the country's two commercial banks were found to be particularly exposed — with over 40 per cent of their portfolio out on loan to the tobacco estates. It rapidly became clear that this strategy offered little more sustainable security for the land-hungry poor than the emphasis on the plantation sector had done nearly a century before.

And thirdly, the development strategy of the 1970s wasted scarce resources which could otherwise have been invested in diversifying the economy, and in the development of crops and cultivation methods which could help overcome the principal development constraint facing the poor — land hunger.

Official development aid fails the poorest

Alongside the deliberate expansion of the commercial estate sector ran a parallel programme for the peasant sector, largely paid for by foreign aid. Based on the mistaken assumption that a separate rural development programme for the poor could compensate for the massive emphasis on the estate sector in national economic policy which effectively squeezed them, this approach could not yield the hoped-for results.

Although moderate improvements resulted for the better-off peasant families, little was achieved for the poorest. The World Bank was to reach much the same conclusion when it reviewed its Malawi aid policy towards the end of the 1980s.[66]

Initially, from 1968 to 1977, there were four large Integrated Rural Development Projects (IRDPs) in the country, three of which were financed by the World Bank, and the fourth by the West German government. The main IRDP, in the Lilongwe area, was the first-ever IRDP to be supported by the World Bank, and was an important testing ground for future World Bank policy.[67] The idea behind these programmes was to raise the living standards of the poor by simultaneous investment in various rural sectors, mainly agricultural production. In all four of the IRDPs, the two key areas of emphasis were investment in agricultural services (in which credit was an important component) and training, as well as infrastructure — such things as roads and crop-storage facilities.

By and large, the IRDPs failed to meet their own objectives. The Lilongwe scheme, however, at least fared better than the Lower Shire Valley scheme, which attempted to increase cotton and food production. In this scheme, the better-off farmers benefitted at the expense of the poorest. The poorer households, those which lacked enough land on which to grow both their year-round food needs and cotton, were forced to withdraw from the scheme: it presented them with unacceptably high risks.

Those who decided to give over some of their land to cotton then had to rely on their cotton earnings to buy food. Because of a declining national food surplus, food prices were rising higher than cotton prices. Furthermore, the Lower Shire area is drought-prone, and for those who could not afford any form .

The better-off farmers benefitted for two main reasons: firstly because they could afford the risks without compromising their household food supply; and secondly because, overnight, the poorer farmers who had withdrawn became cheap agricultural labourers. Overall, the IRDP phase of Malawi's development aid history was found to be unsatisfactory by the donors, principally because it was too costly for the proportion of the population that it managed to cover (about one-fifth). In its place a cheaper model was planned, and extended to the rest of the country. The key components of the new model continued to be infrastructure development, extension and credit.

Thus, the National Rural Development Plan (NRDP) was launched in 1978. It too failed according to its own objectives (and in the judgement of World Bank evaluation reports of the late 1980s), because much stronger forces were pulling in the opposite direction from a consistent national emphasis on investing in sustainable development for the poor. The country's need to adjust to the deteriorating macro-economic trends of the 1980s conflicted directly with the long-term development needs of the poor.

Debt

By the end of the 1970s, Malawi had started to get into debt. By 1987 Malawi's total external debt was $1,363 m., a figure greater than the country's

GDP for the same year ($1,110 m.).

The country's debt-servicing problem dates back to its economic crisis of 1979/80, when it became obvious that the government's economic development policy of the 1970s was unsustainable. The main elements of the 1979/80 economic crisis were the country's extreme vulnerability to falling tobacco prices; the generally declining international terms of trade; financial mismanagement in the estate sector; a series of major investments in non-productive prestige projects during the late 1970s; and a failure of the rains in the 1979/80 season. Malawi's 1979/80 economic crisis could not have come at a worse time. Just after the government had started to borrow heavily on commercial terms,[68] international interest rates spiralled upwards in response to recession in the North and the growing US budget deficit.

As a consequence, Malawi's debt burden grew particularly sharply from 1979. Debt service had climbed to $89 m., equal to 27 per cent of the export of goods and services by 1981. Recognising that this level was unsustainable, the government negotiated the first rescheduling of its debt repayments through the London and Paris Clubs[69] for 1982 and 1983, and entered into structural adjustment agreements with the World Bank and the IMF. Since then, the external forces affecting the national economy have also worsened the debt burden. The 1980s brought a further deterioration in the country's international terms of trade (due in part to the grave economic consequences of conflict in Mozambique), together with a cyclone, earthquake, drought, and floods.

It is increasingly hard to see how Malawi will ever be able to achieve sustainable growth and equitable development while attempting to manage its foreign debt. Despite a number of substantial rescheduling agreements with its creditors, and favourable concessional flows, current projections are that a substantial proportion of the country's revenue will continue to go on servicing obligations over the next decade. [70]

National economic policy 1980 — 1990: adjusting to a hostile economic climate

National economic development policy during the 1980s was mostly concerned with trying to cope with the effects of worsening terms of trade, debt, and destabilisation on an unsustainable economic structure. Malawi has embarked on a long-term structural adjustment programme with the IMF and the World Bank, in return for sizeable loans.[71]

This programme has been complex and diverse in nature, as indeed are the macro-economic shocks it is designed to help Malawi to adjust to. The structural adjustment prescription, aimed at enabling the economy to meet balance of payments targets, has involved a number of measures.[72] Some have been singled out for their adverse effects on the poorest.

In order to make Malawi's traded commodities more competitive on the world market, there have been currency devaluations. In an attempt to enhance production from the smallholder sector, the nominal producer price for maize has risen. In order to reflect the 'real costs' of agricultural production, and 'liberalise' government involvement in the economy, the subsidy on fertiliser has been removed and the prices of some basic household essentials, such as cooking oil, have been decontrolled. Further, the local marketing operations of ADMARC (the parastatal organisation responsible for the inputs and marketing of hybrid maize in the smallholder sector) have been curtailed. In the hope of promoting efficiency in the internal marketing of maize, the staple food, ADMARC's monopoly over outlets was broken, so as to legalise and increase private traders' share of the internal maize market.

However, from the point of view of helping the poorest now and in the future, there are three serious problems in Malawi's economic situation which have not been addressed.

Firstly, as is the case with all structural adjustment programmes, debt-distressed Malawi has undergone far-reaching economic reforms, yet many of the underlying reasons for its indebtedness are the product of the global economic and trading system dominated by the industrialised North.

Secondly, as has been the case with most of the structural adjustment prescriptions experienced in the SADCC region, insufficient account was taken of the economic realities of the regional situation after 1983, when MNR sabotage of Malawi's trade arteries started to take effect. Malawi's structural adjustment policies were not modified with an eye to the costs of conflict in Mozambique, nor with an eye to SADCC's development priorities — both of which have profound implications for Malawi's economy.

And thirdly, insufficient consideration was given to the nature of poverty in Malawi, least of all by government. The importance of land hunger was not taken into account, particularly how it limits people's ability to respond to agricultural production incentives, and makes them vulnerable to some liberalisation measures, such as the removal of subsidies.[73]

The effect of adjustment on the poor: Oxfam's experience

Some of the policy changes led by the structural adjustment programme were welcomed by the development community. For example, pressure was brought to bear on the operations of Press Holdings, the large holding company owned by the President, which had controlling interests in numerous agricultural estates, businesses and services. Also, the focus of

A polio rehabilitation programme in Malawi which, alongside a mass immunisation scheme, concentrates on children.

(John Clark / Oxfam)

government economic policy has been redirected towards giving greater priority to the smallholder sector.

However, as has happened in other poor African countries, a conflict has emerged between the need to adjust to macro-economic pressures and the need to transform the country's economic structures in favour of the poor. Furthermore, it is Oxfam's experience that the process of adjusting to the macro-economic factors has had adverse effects on the poorest.

Currency devaluations

Currency devaluations, together with the decontrolling of prices on basic commodities, have led to a marked fall in the real value of officially controlled wages (since Malawi's local manufacturing base is heavily import-dependent). For example, by June 1987 the cost of soap had risen by 25 per cent against the previous year; the price of cooking oil — now well beyond the reach of the rural poor — went up by over 100 per cent over the same period.

At that time, the government's low-wage policy meant that the official minimum wage was pegged at the rate of 77t (21 pence) per day for rural workers, and MK 1.05 (28 pence) per day for urban workers. Thus, to keep a family in maize meal for a month was costing rural people up to more than four times their total monthly earnings (assuming that they could find full-time work, which many could not).

The government announced a rise in the minimum daily wage, effective from May 1989, to help compensate for the high increases in the cost of living over the previous three years.[74] However, over the same period, there were three major devaluations of the kwacha, and the rate of inflation rose from around 15 per cent to almost 32 per cent.[75]

Price incentives for the smallholder sector

The raising of the producer price for maize will indeed have brought some benefits to the better-off smallholders. By and large, those who have enough land for both subsistence and cash cropping, who can afford a margin of risk in undertaking cash-crop production, and can attract the credit necessary for the inputs to produce hybrid maize have been able to take advantage of this price incentive measure. In so far as these better-off smallholders will be in a position to supply 'ganyu' work to poorer people, these measures will have had some 'trickle down' effect.

However, the rise in fertiliser prices (caused by destabilisation sending up import prices, the removal of the fertiliser subsidy, and the effects of devaluation — all of Malawi's fertiliser is imported) has meant that the rising cost of the inputs necessary for the production of hybrid maize has offset the incentive to a considerable extent. In October 1989, for example, the government announced sharp increases in the prices of fertiliser and maize seed which outstripped the modest rise in the maize-producer price (even though world prices for fertiliser fell by over 50 per cent in the 1980s).[76]

Liberalising agricultural markets

The 1987 cutbacks in ADMARC's maize-selling operations have also had adverse consequences for the poor. World Bank experts were correct to conclude that ADMARC's poor financial performance during the early 1980s needed attention. The root of the problem lay in the fact that ADMARC had been obliged to add a number of commercial agricultural production operations, including the management of some estates, to its former role of providing inputs, taxing, and marketing output from the smallholder production sector. But there was no corresponding change in its budget and management structures..

Oxfam's experience of ADMARC's rural maize-marketing operations, the aspect which is most relevant to the needs of the poor, was that it provided a comparatively efficient service. ADMARC depots, located throughout the rural areas, sold maize to all comers at the official fixed price. Oxfam fieldworkers felt that the rapid cutting back of ADMARC's role as an outlet for maize in the rural areas, especially during the 'hungry season' when the poorest need to buy food, was a serious error which affected food security.[77]

Partly as a result, the price of maize rocketed in 1987.[78] The price of a bag of maize, sufficient to feed one family for a month, rose as high as four times the official price in the last few months of 1987.[79] Oxfam's local assessments of the factors governing maize sale prices during the 1987/88 season indicated that, in spite of nominal controls on pricing, private traders selling maize for consumption had taken full advantage of scarcity in some areas.

Oxfam's overall conclusion is that the results of the adjustment programme, while mixed, have not yielded the breakthrough needed to address the structural nature of poverty in Malawi.

Although the government's track record in supporting poverty-focused development strategies has not been good, the development needs of the land-hungry poorest have also been a casualty of the macro-economic adjustment which Malawi is having to undertake in a hostile external environment.

It is also thought that land hunger has been worsened by the structural adjustment programme during the 1980s. This is because increased export-crop production in the commercial sector, as a spontaneous response to the IMF-designed currency devaluations, has resulted in further erosion of customary land tenure. However, according to a 1989 study,[80] the most recent structural adjustment programme recognises the role of land hunger as a constraint on economic growth, and a freeze on estate expansion in densely populated areas has been proposed. Also, in 1989 Oxfam received the welcome news that the World Bank, in its dealing with the Malawian government, is "emphasising the need to halt further land transfers to the Estate Sector, intensify land use by estates, and return underutilised estate land to the smallholder sector".[81] But it is quite possible that this is too little, too late. It is most unlikely to be made a conditional issue, because of the vested political interests in the commercial estate sector, and because it conflicts with the export-led growth model which is at the centre of the adjustment prescription for Malawi.

What choices are left for the poor? — Oxfam's experience

In 1987, Oxfam decided to undertake an action research project[82] in six villages in Mulanje District, an area in south eastern Malawi which is particularly affected by land hunger. The findings illustrate the very limited range of survival options available to the poorest. With land hunger expressed as the principal economic constraint facing poor villagers, the survey found that local people's analysis of their economic survival options were limited to two — both of which present great difficulties for the poorest.

People identified the need to maximise their crop yields on what land is available to them. And they pointed to the need to find sustainable 'off-farm' income-earning opportunities which did not require them to divert scarce labour resources away from their own farming activities during the peak cultivation season. Migrant labour and 'ganyu', on which so many of the poorest rely for their survival, normally has this distinct disadvantage.

Problems of boosting crop yields

Concerning the potential to maximise yields on small land holdings, various techniques have been tried. These include increased intercropping of nutritious legume crops with the staple crops, and the application of fertiliser and of organic composted materials.

Given the pressure on customary land holdings, Oxfam fieldworkers were not surprised to learn through the community survey that many villagers believe the fertility of their land is declining. One fieldworker reported,

> We came across many instances where people, particularly elderly people, informed us that up to fifteen years ago land was more readily available in the area. Hence farmers generally used to be able to leave certain sections of their land fallow each year, and by rotating their cultivation the problem of soil depletion was minimised. With increasing population pressure, whereby land holdings are sub-divided with each new generation, farmers are forced to cultivate their land more intensively, and to over-use marginal lands. Many elderly people informed us that the result of this had been increased pressure on traditional community mechanisms for coping with social stress. They pointed to the increasing number of land disputes brought before the village courts in recent years, and more theft of people's fieldcrops ...

> In addition we noted a few cases where, because of land shortage, the traditional system of husbands moving to the wife's village on marriage had broken down, and some women had instead had to move to their husband's village. This, of course, implies a change in gender power relations.[83]

Intensive intercropping of local varieties of beans and peas with staple crops (principally maize, but also cassava, sorghum, and millet) is practised, and is an important food-security strategy for those with small land holdings. However, Oxfam found that poverty is undermining even this practice.

> Many people do extra ganyu after the first rains have started, often for seeds or as a means of earning enough to buy seeds. But people often have to eat the seeds they were saving for planting, and we estimate about 30 per cent of the households in our survey were in this situation. In some places we found that seeds for haricot beans, kidney beans, pigeon peas, and sweet potatoes were particularly difficult to find locally, and this meant people were not able to intercrop and thus lessen their dependence on maize.[84]

Malawi imports all its fertiliser, and this is one of the major imported commodities whose cost has risen as a result of the war in Mozambique and as a result of structural adjustment, wiping out much of the value to producers of the rise in maize prices. The application of chemical fertiliser could have useful results for the poor. This has been recognised by the World Bank's

International Fund for Agricultural Development which, in 1988, funded external costs of $12.8 m. for a new fertiliser drive aimed at reaching smallholders on government seasonal credit. The fertiliser is sold in packages as small as 10 kg, with the two-fold aim of improving its availability to the poorer smallholders, and of raising the number of smallholders using official credit from the 1988 level of about 200,000 to 400,000.[85]

Although this initiative is welcome, some of the detailed findings of Oxfam's village survey indicate that even this measure will not, of itself, help the poorest. Oxfam reports,

> Almost all the farmers in our survey felt that the application of fertiliser on their land would improve yields, but most were unable to purchase chemical fertilisers or to obtain credit to purchase it ... Recently, as a result of the new fertiliser programme, smaller credit packages have been offered, together with 10 kg fertiliser packs (costing MK 14.75, equal to £3.90). But this represents the equivalent of three months' total household income for many people, and is therefore a substantial risk. Many of the farmers felt that the fertiliser pack should come as small as 5 kg, as this would bring the financial risk down to more manageable proportions.

> We also found that government credit was often not available for poorer farmers wishing to buy the 10 kg fertiliser packs. The reason for this is that, although in theory credit is available to all, in practice the system used to disburse credit only benefits the better-off villagers — those with holdings of 1.5 hectares or more ... This is because government credit for agricultural inputs is disbursed through a network of Farmers' Clubs, to which only about 10 per cent of farmers belong, because the Clubs are self-limiting. They operate by making each member responsible for indirectly guaranteeing the seasonal loans taken out by other members. As a result, only those with some degree of land security receive credit. Existing Club members consider that poorer people are too risky. The argument given is that if people cannot afford to buy the new size of pack outright, then they would probably have difficulty in paying back the credit.[86]

Problems with 'off- farm' employment

As far as opportunities for 'off-farm' income generation are concerned, the general outlook for the poorest is also bleak. The underlying economic trends have already undermined the commercial agricultural estate sector, which, as the largest employer of labourers from land-hungry or landless families, was at least capable of acting as a 'safety net' for the poor during the more profitable years of the 1970s. Nowadays, however, those lucky enough to earn the minimum rural wage paid on the agricultural estates are no longer working in a boom industry. The former growth in employment opportunities has tailed off, and so the 'safety net' can no longer be expected to catch the new generation of work seekers.

Ganyu labour, on richer peasants' land, is one option open to the poorest. Although ganyu labour means that all but the absolutely landless have to divert their labour away from their own land holdings at critical periods in the cultivation season, nevertheless it is becoming an increasingly important survival option for the poorest. But, because it is an informal mechanism, ganyu is acutely sensitive to local conditions of supply and demand, and is therefore an insecure form of employment. A season of poor rains can mean less ganyu employment when it is most needed. And, as the cumulative effects of national economic decline and population growth result in more work-seekers coming on to the market, ganyu rates of pay may decline because of an oversupply of labour.

Oxfam's survey found that land-hungry people are desperate to find alternative and sustainable 'off-farm' activities to generate income as a supplement to ganyu.   However, the very lack of purchasing power in the rural areas makes most forms of local artisanal production precarious.

Longer-term family strategies include making sacrifices to put children through school, in the hope that this will increase their adult earning-power. But this course of action requires cash in hand, and is out of the reach of people in Esme Justin's position. Further, it requires expanding white-collar employment opportunities, and sustained state investment in education — neither of which is happening at present.

International action needed

A number of factors have combined to thwart the hoped-for results of the IMF/World Bank structural adjustment programme in Malawi. The effects of destabilisation (worsened by Malawi's former support of the MNR), land hunger, geographical limitations, low wages, and insufficient secure employment have combined to show that poverty in Malawi has more roots than can be tackled by the IMF/World Bank prescription.

What the poor in Malawi need is structural adjustment in the interests of sustainable development for the poorest. Immediate measures are needed. These should include debt cancellation; land redistribution and a halt to further estate expansion in the most populated areas; economic adjustment programmes which fully take into account the political and economic realities of the southern African region; and a thoroughgoing commitment by the government to widen the survival options facing land-hungry people, and to invest in basic services for the poor.

Case-study 3: Angola

Food, agriculture, and hunger

Agricultural production in Angola has long been affected by upheavals in the country's history. In particular, the devastating consequences of the Atlantic slave trade and of the colonial forced-labour policy caused major disruption to production and economic survival patterns.[87] Yet Angola has the natural resources to be one of Africa's largest net exporters of food. Indeed, during the 1960s and 1970s, under colonial rule, Angola was exporting sizeable volumes of agricultural produce.[88]

However, during the 1980s, food production in Angola has been declining (see table 9.2). The reasons for this decline can be traced to three interlinking issues: the colonial legacy, policy errors made since independence, and war.

By 1985, household food security had dropped to the point where Angola's Under-5 Mortality Rate was one of the highest in the world, along with Mozambique's and Afghanistan's.[89]

The complex social and economic relationships between food production levels and people's food security require research of a sort which is not possible in war-torn Angola. However, some links are clear. As the UN African Emergency Task Force pointed out in 1988, "The nutritional status of children is overwhelmingly poor, because of insecurity and the agricultural and economic deterioration that causes food scarcity, not only in the war-torn areas, but throughout the country."[90]

The colonial legacy

During the Portuguese colonial era,[91] a dual system of agricultural production was created, consisting of commercial and subsistence sectors. The country's productive land was divided between large, commercial estates, run and

---

Table 9.2: Angola: indices of food and agricultural production (1979/1981 = 100)

	1982	1983	1984	1985	1986	1987
Agricultural production per head	94.31	91.95	89.99	87.49	86.29	85.84
Food production per head	95.81	94.22	91.44	89.77	88.34	87.34

(Source: EIU Country Profile, 1988-89, p.15, compiled from FAO monthly bulletins, broad estimates only)

controlled by settlers; smaller commercial settler farms; and peasant holdings. The commercial farms grew most of the export crops (coffee, cotton, palm oil, sugar, bananas, citrus fruits, sisal, maize, and tobacco). They also grew much of the cities' food requirements. The peasant producers grew mainly for their subsistence needs, but from the mid-1950s to the early 1980s, as the market economy developed, the peasant sector also marketed food and export crops.

Various colonial policies had ensured that both sectors grew to be heavily dependent on the skills and resources of the settler community. The commercial sector was deliberately developed by the Portuguese colonial authorities to encourage white settlement, and to make the colony pay its way through agricultural exports. Substantial measures were taken to build up the export sector. In many reported cases, peasant communities were forcibly moved from their traditional land holdings to make way for commercial farming enterprises. Economic incentives included investment in land grants, large irrigation schemes, infrastructural development, agricultural research and extension facilities, and various loans and subsidies, most of which were available to settlers only. Cheap and, in many cases, free African labour was also guaranteed by the colonial authorities, to the detriment of peasant production. Furthermore, the policy of job reservation ensured that much of the semi-skilled work on the commercial farms went to illiterate and unskilled settlers, thus blocking any opportunity for African farm workers to gain managerial and technical expertise. Lastly, preferential credit and marketing facilities policies ensured that settler farmers were generally paid a higher rate for their produce than African farmers were.

The peasant sector was also dependent on the settler community, because the rural marketing system was entirely run and controlled by Portuguese 'bush traders'. These traders travelled the country to buy up surplus produce around harvest time. They knew what crops were ready when, and where they were grown. They also traded in basic consumer goods from their village stores. Using a barter system, which sometimes involved extending credit to be redeemed at harvest time, the traders exchanged crops for goods such as cloth, lamps, blankets, seeds, fertiliser, and agricultural tools, and essential commodities such as salt and sugar. Like other settlers, the traders also left in a hurry. They took with them their knowledge of the crop cycles and marketing circuits, and whatever capital and assets they could. Thus the rural market economy was thrown into confusion. Peasant producers were suddenly left with little or no incentive to produce surplus crops.

As a result of the way in which the commercial sector had been developed, it collapsed when the settler farmers left after independence in 1975. Tens of

Pounding maize at a resettlement centre for war-displaced people in Angola's Huila Province, 1987. (Akwe Amosu)

thousands of farm labourers were suddenly without work, farm machinery lay idle, and large herds of livestock were unmanaged.

Against this background, war could only make disaster a certainty. Since the liberation struggle began in the early 1960s, the only peaceful period Angola has known were the years between 1976 and 1980. It is therefore hard to separate one set of causes from another when apportioning weight to the various factors involved. However, as successive development and relief assessments have recently pointed out,[92] not only has warfare directly affected agricultural production, but it also presented enormous obstacles to the implementation of any new policy measures to improve production.

Post-independence policy failures

The independent government's early policies to rehabilitate the large estates and the rural trading network, through state enterprises, failed disastrously. The massive economic dislocation of the immediate post-independence period, combined with the acute shortage of appropriately skilled people, compounded policy errors and undermined agricultural production for years to come.

The commercial farms became registered state companies, but the state could not provide the experienced and skilled personnel necessary to manage them, and to maintain the mechanised equipment. Productivity rapidly dwindled, as did national earnings from export crops. By the early 1980s, it was clear that the few remaining commercial farms had only survived because of costly state subsidies.[93] Independent Angola had not had the opportunity to invest in training and education to the required level.

The nationalised marketing system has been dogged by inefficiency and lack of resources. Transport was inadequate, and the state could not maintain sufficient supplies of consumer goods in the rural areas. When a private trading system of sorts resurfaced, often providing goods which were not available within the state marketing system, government responded at first with unpopular attempts to force peasants to sell surplus produce only to the state. Later the black market became more widely tolerated.

As the supply of consumer goods for barter became more erratic, the state tried unsuccessfully to monetise the rural economy. Immediately after independence, the producers, used to the economic security of the barter system, and aware that cash earnings were of limited value when there was so little to buy, responded by opting out of surplus production. Occasionally, when consumer goods became available, farmers offered limited quantities of produce for barter. Between 1976 and 1980, the years of comparative peace, surplus market production rose again, only to vanish after 1980 as a result of war. The government had to start importing large quantities of food to feed the cities. On top of this, the government's war-induced economic austerity measures of 1985 further curtailed the importation of both essential consumer goods and staple food for the growing urban and uprooted rural population.[94]

Drought

Given the extent of economic breakdown and population displacement in Angola, the regularly occurring periods of drought are of special concern. Moreover, given the dominance of the black market and the barter trading system over any more conventional means of internal marketing and trade, grain has become an important currency in many areas as well as a subsistence food crop — so a poor harvest is a double blow.

In late 1989, several provinces in the south began their fourth consecutive year of drought, and the situation was described by many relief agencies as a potential disaster of major proportions. The 1988/89 drought affected many areas which normally produce a surplus to feed the southern towns. The crop loss was estimated at 60 per cent. Insecurity in the whole area has made it extremely difficult to assess this disaster adequately. Conflict has also hampered the effective distribution of relief supplies. In 1989 Oxfam approved over £40,000 to help with the warehousing and transport of food aid, and to strengthen the government's emergency coordination service.

Economic reform

In August 1987, prompted by the 1986 fall in oil prices on which Angola depends for 95.6 per cent[95] of its foreign earnings, and following on from a 1985 reform package, the government announced a new programme of economic reform. The Saneamento Economico e Financeiro, the "SEF", which acknowledges many of the past policy errors.

The economic reform plan was reported to have been welcomed in Angola, not least because people hope it will help to eradicate the powerful black market economy which feeds off the lack of effective internal marketing and trading structures. It is intended that the huge and 'invisible' private sector should be legalised, permitting private interests to offer goods and services which were previously heavily restricted by the centrally planned, rigid economic structure. It has also been welcomed by Britain.

In order to gain access to the international financial backing necessary to implement its reforms, the government also applied for membership of the IMF and the World Bank.

For the following couple of years, however, the implementation of the SEF was constrained. There were two reasons for this, both of which would have been virtually sufficient on their own. In combination, they paralysed progress.

Firstly, continuing conflict has not only destroyed food production, but also ensured that the country's skilled personnel, resources, and transport facilities are consumed by the defence effort. If there were an end to the war, trained personnel, vehicles, fuel, foreign exchange, and — most important of all — government priority could all be redirected to national reconstruction and development.

The second reason for the delay in implementing the economic reforms was that, using its power within the IMF's decision-making structures, the US administration blocked Angola's accession, despite being Angola's major trading partner. It is widely thought that the USA used its position of dominance in the IMF, together with its support for UNITA[96] and its refusal to recognise the Angolan government, as a bargaining chip to exert pressure on the pro-Soviet Angolan government to accommodate UNITA, which it sees as a pro-Western party.

According to Ministerial statements, Britain took a different view, but was

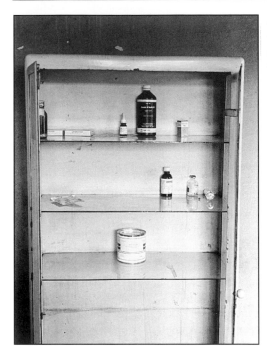

Angola is a country of great economic potential, but government services have broken down because of war and economic policy failures. This is the entire drug supply at a village clinic near the northern town of Uige.

(Jenny Matthews / Oxfam)

not prepared to criticise the US Administration openly. In February 1989, when asked whether the UK government would press the US Administration to recognise the Angolan government and to cease opposition to Angola's membership of the IMF and the World Bank, Lynda Chalker, then Foreign Office Minister responsible for southern African affairs, replied,

> United States policy must be a matter for the new President and his team, who are well aware of our position. We see that Angola is looking for sensible ways of becoming financially more robust. We are sure that in the longer term it will need help to do that. We have provided some aid for a number of years, but it is nothing like what will be needed for the change that it will have to undertake. I do not believe that any country will stand in the way of Angola when the right time comes.[97]

Angola's IMF membership application was finally approved in September 1989. The USA was outvoted on the IMF's executive board; the UK voted for Angola's membership.

Peace and effective emergency assistance first

Although the 1987 economic reform programme has been welcomed by many, nevertheless its implementation rests on further reinforcing the government's stabilisation measures. This is at a time when over three million people within Angola are highly dependent on government and international relief assistance. Many of them would otherwise be producing food in the rural areas.

An end to the war is needed before economic recovery and development for the rural poor can be realised. Rural production in large areas of the country cannot be revived until the transport routes are secure, and people feel safe to return to their land and farm. Even those who have been resettled on land in more secure areas are not able to make a full economic contribution. Research shows that among the displaced people who have been resettled, few are capable of meeting even their subsistence needs. The most fertile central highlands have been the areas most affected by war. In the generally less fertile resettlement areas, land holdings (which rarely exceed one hectare per family) are insufficient for year-round subsistence, and conflict continues to affect the supply of agricultural inputs. [98]

Despite the country's economic potential, the millions of people who have been impoverished by war badly need more relief and reconstruction assistance before long-term economic adjustment programmes can benefit them. They also need the government to give much greater priority to small-scale peasant producers. Current government policy focuses on large production units and industrial workers.

Until there is peace, and a chance for reconstruction and development to make progress, it is important that appropriate international emergency aid is given to help the people most in need. In the long term, however, Angola's vast economic potential should obviate the need for large amounts of development aid.

In the short term, Angola's particular circumstances make even the effective use of relief aid difficult. As various assessments have pointed out, over the last few years the needs for relief, let alone reconstruction and development, have been so great that they could not be properly met by the existing government structures.

Again, the combined effects of colonial history, conflict, and domestic policy have a direct bearing. Still struggling with the enormous handicap left by the colonial authorities' neglect of education and other basic services, the government diverted many of its best-skilled people and organisational resources into defence and the oil industry. In spite of the UN's special focus on the need for resources and personnel to strengthen government relief structures, [99] inadequate attention is paid to this critical constraint by the Angolan government. This was one of the key reasons why the 1988 UN Emergency Appeal for Angola failed to fulfil expectations on the ground.

Whether the conflict in Angola is ended soon or not, the planners of relief

A clinic run by the national women's organisation in Angola. There was an acute shortage of trained people when the country gained independence. (Jenny Matthews / Oxfam)

aid programmes must seek more constructive ways of ensuring that their assistance reaches those who need it most. In particular, much greater priority must be given, firstly by the Angolan government, to building up the institutions, skills, and management capacity of the relief and development structures. This urgently needed aid should not be seen as a short-term measure. Investment now in strengthening these institutions will be of great help in the enormous longer-term task of reconstruction and development facing the people of Angola, once peace is finally achieved.

Section III
The roles of Britain and the European Community

10

The role and responsibilities of Britain

Britain plays a particularly significant role in the affairs of southern Africa, because of its colonial past, its present-day links, and its membership of key international groupings. Besides belonging to the European Community, the Commonwealth, and the 'G7' grouping, Britain is an ally of the USA, a permanent member of the UN Security Council, and an influential member of the IMF and World Bank. Moreover, when the Reagan Administration came to an end in 1988, British diplomacy on southern Africa assumed even greater significance, marked by the Prime Minister's visit to the region in March 1989, and the emergence of a new phase of British diplomatic activity on South Africa.

No other country has stronger links with the southern African region than Britain. Given the consequences of South Africa's regional policy, Britain's especially strong links with South Africa heighten its responsibilities towards the whole region, to help resolve the interlinked issues of apartheid, conflict, and economic decline.

Historical links with South Africa

As the colonial power in South Africa, Botswana, Lesotho, Swaziland, Malawi, Zambia, Zimbabwe, Tanzania, and Namibia,[1] Britain bears responsibility for creating those aspects of today's structural development problems which are rooted in the colonial past.[2] British economic interests were also involved in colonial Angola and Mozambique, both directly and indirectly (through British investments and political leverage over Portugal[3]).

British interests in Mozambique were particularly strong.

Of all the elements of Britain's long and complex colonial history in southern Africa, its history in South Africa, especially its role in laying the foundations for apartheid, is perhaps of greatest significance to present-day southern African affairs. Although apartheid was introduced by the National Party after it first came to power in 1948, nevertheless the foundations of disenfranchisement and institutionalised racial discrimination at all levels of society had already been laid.

British colonial rule in South Africa, 1806-1910

When Britain took the Cape Colony by armed force from the Dutch in 1806, it was in order to guarantee the security of the sea route around the Cape, on which its lucrative oriental trade, mainly with India, depended. The white settler farmers of Dutch origin (known as 'Afrikaners', or 'Boers' — 'farmers' in Dutch) stayed on, and in the late 1830s they moved northwards en masse to settle land away from British control. They wanted to maintain their accustomed mode of agricultural production, which depended on the labour of slaves imported from overseas Dutch possessions, and from Mozambique. After the Great Trek, the Afrikaners founded the Transvaal and the Orange River Boer Republics (now the Transvaal and the Orange Free State Provinces of the Republic of South Africa) in the 1850s. Britain recognised the status of the Boer Republics, although future conflict over economic spoils was to follow.

The British colonial plan was to relax Afrikaner control over the labour market, and encourage the development of a wage-labour system, in order to fuel industrial expansion at home. Britain wanted to create more overseas markets to buy the goods produced by its booming industrial sector, and it wanted to develop commercial plantation-style farming in its colonies in order to provide its industrial economy with cheap raw materials and to make the colonies self-financing. Hence, slave trading by British subjects was outlawed in 1807 when the moral arguments dovetailed with the economic requirements of the newly industrialised imperial state. In the British Cape Colony, however, slavery was not finally ended until 1838.

Anglo-Boer political relations were already poor when gold was discovered in 1886. As far as the British colonial outlook was concerned, the discovery transformed South Africa from an unpromising outpost necessary for the oriental trade to a key colonial possession of great economic significance. However, the gold-bearing reef was in the Transvaal, and although substantial British investments were pouring into the gold industry, nevertheless political control rested with the Afrikaner government, which was regulating and taxing British mining interests in pursuit of its own

SOUTH AFRICA AS IT WAS IN 1896

Salisbury

BRITISH SOUTH AFRICA
(CHARTERED)
COMPANY TERRITORY

Beira

GERMAN
SOUTH-WEST
AFRICA

BECHUANALAND
PROTECTORATE

Bulawayo

MOZAMBIQUE

Gaborone

TRANSVAAL

Pretoria

Lourenço
Marques

Johannesburg

**ORANGE
FREE STATE**

SWAZILAND

Kimberley

NATAL

BASUTOLAND

Durban

CAPE

COLONY

East London

Cape
Town

Port Elizabeth

| Main railways | ········ |
| Projected railways | ·-·-·- |

political goals. Britain's chief aim in prosecuting the Anglo-Boer War (1899-1902) was therefore to secure full control over the gold mines in the Transvaal.

The terrible brutality of the war was one of the key factors which reinforced the anti-British strands of Afrikaner nationalism. Harsh tactics were used against the civilian Afrikaner population. In particular, the British army attempted to break the Afrikaners' support system and fighting morale by interning thousands of women and children. Over 20,000 people died of starvation and disease while in captivity.

The terms on which the war was settled laid the foundations for present-day apartheid and white minority rule. The 1902 Vereeniging Peace Treaty enabled Britain to consolidate its influence over the mineral-rich Afrikaner

Boer delegates arriving at the peace conference camp at Vereeniging. Photographed in May 1902 from inside a British soldier's tent.   (Leslie Pryce)

territories. But the Boer leaders bargained hard with the British, determined to secure the greatest possible degree of independence, and one of the concessions which the British granted was that of postponing the question of franchise for black people.

In spite of the British crusade against slavery, and British criticism of the Afrikaners' abuse of black people, Britain negotiated a peace treaty which betrayed the interests of the black population of the Boer Republics, and effectively prepared the ground for lasting white-minority rule in the most economically powerful nation of the region.

Many of the black people in the Boer Republics and Natal had assisted the British war effort on the understanding that their political position would improve as a result. (The British had already introduced limited franchise for black people in the Cape Colony — later to be abolished in 1936.) But contrary to their expectations, the relevant clause in the peace treaty read,

> The question of granting the franchise to natives (in the former Boer Republics, Transvaal and Orange River Colony) will not be decided until after the introduction of self-government.[4]

Having won the Boer War, Britain gained control of the Boer Republics, and thus extended its rule to cover all of the territory now known as South Africa, which was incorporated into four British colonies. In 1908, a National Convention of white representatives from the four colonies (Cape Colony, Transvaal, Orange River, and Natal) was established to plan the details of a united South Africa.

The all-white Inter-Colonial Conference at Pretoria, 1908.   (The Hulton-Deutsch Collection)

A major issue on which the white Convention could not reach agreement was that of the franchise. Delegates therefore agreed to let the existing systems in the various colonies continue under the Union. Only whites were to be members of the new parliament.

In 1909, the South African Native (National) Convention was called by some prominent black South Africans to counter the conclusions of the white National Convention. They demanded a colour-blind franchise, to include all adult males, and an end to racial discrimination. A delegation of the African People's Organisation (formed in 1902, the first nation-wide political organisation to demand full equality for all South Africans) went to Britain to press their case, but found that few British politicians would support them.

In 1909, the South Africa Act was passed by the British Parliament in preparation for the granting of white self-rule, and became effective as the constitution of the new Union of South Africa in 1910. It closely followed the white Convention's recommendations, except that it maintained the limited franchise for non-white males in Cape Province. Together, the terms of the Boer War peace treaty and those of the Act of Union meant that black South Africans' political rights were given away, for reasons of economic self-interest, by the British colonial administration to the white settlers.

The South African Native National Congress (SANNC) was founded by black South Africans in January 1912, changing its name in 1923 to the African National Congress. Its main goal at the outset was the maintenance of the Cape African franchise and its extension to other provinces, as well as an end to racial discrimination. In 1914 it sent a delegation to Britain to protest against theNatives Land Act of the previous year, which destroyed the independence of African peasant farmers.

In 1931 British legislation conceded full sovereignty to the Dominions, among them the Union of South Africa, in which white minority rule had become firmly, institutionally, entrenched. When the National Party came to power in 1948, the foundations for their policy of apartheid were already laid.

In 1986, the report of the Select Committee on Foreign Affairs on South Africa summarised the responsibility stemming from Britain's part in the evolution of white minority rule and apartheid as follows:

> Despite the United Kingdom's subsequent good record in the process of granting independence, the means by which the white minority in South Africa obtained exclusive control over the government and economy of what is now the Republic of South Africa were largely facilitated by the inadequacy of the legislation adopted by our own Parliament, and the development of apartheid as a legal system was made possible by the British Parliament's release of its responsibilities for the non-white population in 1909.

> The re-establishment of the rights of the non-white majority in South Africa must therefore remain a primary concern of the British Government and Parliament. Although the United Kingdom Government has no residual legal powers in the matter, one cannot deny our continuing responsibility to try to ensure that this post-colonial aberration is resolved according to the moral and political criteria to which all the main political parties in the United Kingdom subscribe.[5]

Economic links

Because of its colonial history, Britain has extensive economic links with most countries of southern Africa, especially with South Africa. From the nineteenth-century discovery of diamonds and gold onwards to the present day, Britain's policy towards the wider region has been largely determined with reference to its interests in South Africa.

Although Britain's trade and investment in southern Africa are diminishing in relation to its economic interests in other parts of the world, nevertheless British economic links continue to rank highly as far as most of the southern African countries are concerned. Southern Africa, especially South Africa, continues to be a high-priority foreign policy issue for Britain.

Trade

As we have already seen, the SADCC states and Namibia are highly dependent on international trade. The same is true for South Africa, which

Table 10.1: UK trade with southern Africa (1986-88)

Country	Exports to (£m.)			Imports from (£m.)			Rank by value of 1988 UK exports to Africa
	1986	1987	1988	1986	1987	1988	
South Africa	850.0	949.0	1,075.0 (1,065.0)	829.0	658.0	808.0 (4,632.0)	1
Namibia	3.0 *	4.0 *	4.0 *#	7.0 *	8.0 *	3.0 *#	
Angola	31.0	30.0	26.0	43.0	2.0	10.0	20
Botswana	9.0	10.0	27.0	17.0	12.0	8.0	18
Lesotho	2.0	1.0	1.0	0.2	0.5	1.0	49
Malawi	29.0	18.0	28.0	57.0	44.0	30.0	17
Mozambique	13.0	21.0	24.0	1.0	7.0	6.0	21
Swaziland	4.0	2.0	2.0	48.0	37.0	33.0	48
Tanzania	63.0	92.0	88.0	40.0	26.0	26.0	7
Zambia	78.0	75.0	85.0	28.0	30.0	25.0	10
Zimbabwe	62.0	63.0	58.0	81.0	80.0	86.0	11
SADCC total	291.0	312.0	339.0	315.2	238.5	225.0	
TOTAL	1,144.0	1,265.0	1,418.0	1,151.2	904.5	1,036.0	

* Data unreliable because DTI statistics do not properly differentiate between South Africa and Namibia.

\# Estimated

(Source: UK Overseas Trade Statistics, DTI. Eurostat data given in brackets.)

has the general trade profile of an exceptionally well-developed exporter of primary products. Table 10.1 illustrates the level of UK trade with southern Africa between 1986 and 1988.[6]

South Africa's foreign trade (visibles)

South Africa's economy is highly dependent on international trade. Although it has a developed manufacturing sector, this is not geared up to export on a scale which challenges the country's reliance on the export of its raw and processed primary products and the import of capital goods Foreign trade accounts for some 60 per cent of the country's gross domestic product (GDP),[7] and because new sources of investment in the economy are drying up (see below), South Africa has come to rely increasingly on generating a trade surplus to earn foreign exchange.

South African citrus fruit being loaded for export at Durban docks. (GideonMendel/Reflex)

Seventy per cent of South Africa's exports are mining products, with gold contributing over 40 per cent of export earnings (1987 figures). Coal, iron, steel, and uncut diamonds account for a further 5 – 7 per cent of export earnings each.

The profile of South Africa's imports shows that it is highly dependent on the import of high-technology products, capital equipment, and components for assembly operations. Machinery is the largest import category, followed by transport equipment and chemicals. Oil imports are also vital.

Six industrialised countries (Japan, West Germany, the UK, the USA, Italy, and France) account for some two-thirds of South Africa's visible foreign trade. During the 1980s, however, the ranking of South Africa's main trading partners changed,[8] as the level of some countries' trade increased, and that of others decreased. According to the UN, comparing 1987 with the 1983-85 average, Japan, Taiwan, West Germany, Italy, Spain and Turkey significantly increased their level of trade with South Africa. Over the same period, South Africa's trade with the UK, Denmark, and the USA decreased.[9]

In 1987, Japan replaced the USA as South Africa's largest export market and first trading partner. In third, fourth, and fifth places were West

Germany, the UK, and France.[10]. According to 1988 data given by the statistical office of the European Community, which differ significantly from those of the British Department of Trade (see below), the UK was South Africa's first trading partner, with West Germany in second place.[11]

Britain's trade with South Africa

Despite Britain's sanctions against South Africa, which were stepped up in 1985 and 1986, and despite decreasing levels of British trade with South Africa from 1985 to 1987, British trade increased in 1988. According to Department of Trade figures, exports rose by 13 per cent, and imports rose (for the first time since 1985) by 19 per cent. However, according to the statistical office of the European Community (Eurostat), the value of Britain's imports from South Africa in 1988 was revealed to be over five times the total value reported in official British statistics for the same year,[12] and seven times the value (as given by official British statistics) of imports for the previous year. The difference is thought to be due to the way in which transit trade in gold and diamonds is accounted for.[13] In August 1989 the US General Accounting Office, which monitors the Government and the Administration, issued a report which found that South African gold bullion was being imported into the USA, in contravention of US sanctions legislation passed in 1986, via the UK and Switzerland.[14]

According to the Eurostat figures, the UK was South Africa's foremost trading partner in 1988. According to Commonwealth statistics for the first nine months of 1988 (based on Department of Trade data), the UK is South Africa's third largest trading partner after West Germany and Japan.[15] Again according to Eurostat data, in 1988 South Africa was the seventh largest source of imports to the UK, and the eighteenth largest destination of exports.

Britain's trade with the SADCC states

The nine SADCC states and Namibia are dependent on South African and Northern trading partners, and do not have large enough economies and populations to provide markets capable of sustaining even the present level of industrial production. Grouped together, they form a bloc capable of sustaining enhanced growth and economic development, and better able to adjust to the changing global environment. SADCC's trading links with the industrialised world remain vital, both now as an essential source of earnings to boost regional integration and national development, and later once the region has been able to develop on an integrated basis.

UK trade with South Africa alone is about nine times greater than its trade with the entire SADCC region (excluding Namibia). However, the UK is also an important trading partner of the SADCC states. Overall, it is a major source of imports for the region, and a key destination of exports from Malawi, Tanzania, and Zimbabwe (see table 8.1).

Trade credit insurance

UK exports to (and investment in) southern Africa are helped by the insurance facilities extended by the Export Credit Guarantee Department (ECGD). Although it is run on commercial lines, this is a governmental department responsible to the Secretary of State for Trade and Industry. Its chief aim is "helping British exporters to overcome many of the risks in selling overseas", and with an annual turnover of £15 billion, it covers some 20 per cent of the UK's visible, non-oil exports worldwide each year.[16] ECGD insurance covers suppliers' and purchasers' credits taken out by British firms, as normally extended by banks and other finance houses, and can guarantee short, medium, and long-term credit. It fixes its rates of cover for each country according to the commercial risk it judges to be entailed. This is evident in the disparity of ratings given for southern Africa (see table 10.2).

Although the UK government does not provide direct export credits for trade with South Africa, it does, through the ECGD, provide export credit guarantees for privately extended credit. Outstanding export credit debt owed to Britain by the SADCC states totalled £493 m. in 1989.[17] In 1988, the

---

Table 10.2: ECGD credit insurance ratings for southern Africa

Country	ECGD insurance surcharge (£)
South Africa:	0.37
Namibia:	0.37
Angola:	4.59
Botswana:	0.37
Malawi:	1.24
Mozambique:	Credit insurance unavailable
Swaziland:	0.37
Tanzania:	Confirmed Irrevocable Letter of Credit
Zambia:	Credit insurance available
Zimbabwe:	0.37

(Source: *Africa Analysis*, 1989)

officially guaranteed portion of UK-based banks' South Africa trade credit exposure stood at well over half a billion pounds sterling.[18] While Japan supplies South Africa with the largest amounts of insured non-bank credits, the UK (through the ECGD) supplies the highest level of insured bank credits.[19]

Investment and loans

For the last century, South Africa has been the magnet for foreign investment in the region, with Zimbabwe in second place. Most of the private investment which has gone into the SADCC region has come either from Northern-based transnational companies (TNCs), often via their regional headquarters in South Africa, or from South African companies. During the 1980s, there has been a marked disinvestment trend throughout sub-Saharan Africa as Northern-based TNCs have changed their method of operating and their geographic areas of focus.

While the SADCC region has had to rely increasingly on concessional, official sources of finance (see Chapter 8), South Africa has attracted substantial commercial financial flows. However, although South Africa's debt is far less burdensome than that of most SADCC economies, nevertheless it too has reduced the government's room for manoeuvre and is widely thought to be a key factor behind recent political shifts in National Party outlook.

Investment in South Africa

The high international exposure of the South African economy is as strong in the 'invisible' spheres of investment and loan finance as it is in trade.

Foreign direct investment plays a major, although diminishing, role in four of South Africa's key economic sectors. In 1980, foreign ownership in the mining, manufacturing, and trade sectors accounted in each case for about a third, while in finance it was about a fifth. Between 1978 and 1984, long-term foreign investment contributed a third of Gross Domestic Fixed Investment in each of mining, manufacturing, and trade, and just over half in finance.[20] However, changes in the world's financial and trading institutions and structures, and the disinvestment trend of the 1980s are altering the nature of foreign involvement in South Africa's economy. This has been helped by the growing levels of indirect (loan) investment coming from abroad.

Since the discovery of gold a century ago, when the technical and financial requirements of the mining industry enabled large foreign-owned companies to flourish and dominate the economy, foreign TNCs have played an especially important role in South Africa's political economy. They facilitate financial flows to South Africa (through transnational banks), and they are especially active in the production, distribution, and external trade operations of mining and manufacturing. In September 1989, after a marked spate of disinvestment, the UN Commission on TNCs reported there to be 535 TNCs with equity interests of more than ten per cent in a company or companies in South Africa.[21]

Foreign TNCs have sustained and strengthened the South African economy, and therefore the country's ruling structures, in a number of ways. They have been instrumental in the process of capital formation and in many other areas: facilitating capital inflow to the private sector; mobilising domestic capital; financing import substitution; introducing advanced technology; introducing technical and managerial skills; providing capital intensive investment; making international trade links; funding, through their taxes and purchase of government bonds, apartheid and state repression (including military expenditure); and helping the government to protect the economy against sanctions.[22]

Disinvestment from South Africa

Foreign direct investment started to tail off after the Soweto uprising of 1976, which meant that South Africa then had to increase its international borrowing. During the 1980s, there has been a growing and complex 'disinvestment' trend, particularly marked among US companies. The International Chamber of Commerce estimates that over 500 foreign companies sold their South African holdings between 1985 and 1989.[23]

The UN Commission on TNCs finds that there are a number of reasons for

From The Guardian, June 1986   (Peter Clarke/The Guardian)

TNC disinvestment from South Africa. Key among them have been the deteriorating economic situation in South Africa, and public pressure, especially where this has been translated into actions against companies with South African links. In the USA, for example, the anti-apartheid selective purchasing and contracting policies adopted by a number of cities, counties, and states have been effective in causing companies to disinvest. The disinvesting TNCs are concerned to project a more positive public image; to maximise foreign-currency returns on investment, and to keep enough control over their former subsidiaries to allow re-entry into South Africa at a later date. [24]

According to each disinvesting company's mix of motives, objectives, and opportunities for altering its operations, a number of different modes of disinvestment have been adopted. The most common modes of disinvestment have included selling up to a local South African company, selling to local management or employees, closing down, and selling to another foreign company.[25]

A substantial proportion of disinvesting companies (about 50 per cent of disinvesting US companies) have retained non-equity ties with their former subsidiaries. So, for example, foreign companies have maintained franchising and licensing arrangements in South Africa after ending their direct investment. This generally permits continued profits at a reduced level of risk.[26]

A 1989 report prepared for the Commonwealth Committee of Foreign Ministers on Southern Africa found that the impact of foreign disinvestment on financial flows out of South Africa was mitigated by the financial rand system, whereby money leaving South Africa is valued at a far lower rate of exchange than money entering the country. It found that the most significant effect was the undermining of prospects for new direct foreign investment, which is a key reason why loan finance has, during the 1980s, become increasingly important to the South African economy.

Britain's investment profile in South Africa

Detailed official data for the level of British investment in South Africa are not available,[27] but estimates based on various sources[28] give Britain's total investment (direct and indirect[29]) as £8,586 m. in 1986, £7,924 m. in 1987, and £6,400 m. in 1988.[30] Britain is the largest foreign investor in South Africa, providing around 40 per cent of all overseas investment (80 per cent of the European Community's total investment) in 1986.[31]

UK-based TNCs are the most prominent of all foreign TNCs investing in South Africa. According to the UN Commission on TNCs, of the 535 foreign TNCs with equity interests of more than ten per cent in South African companies in 1989, 216 were UK-based.[32] Furthermore, of the largest (in terms of numbers of employees) ten TNCs operating in South Africa, eight are UK-based. They are Lonrho Plc, BTR Plc, Unilever Plc, BET Plc, BOC Plc, British Petroleum, Northern Engineering Industries Plc, and Royal Dutch/Shell (UK/Netherlands).[33]

British companies have been slower than those in the USA to disinvest. In the opinion of the UN Commission on TNCs, this is mainly because South African business represents a larger proportion of the global operations of UK companies than that of US companies. According to a spokesperson from the US Investor Responsibility Research Center, it was also due to three other factors. Firstly that US companies had been exposed for a longer period to shareholders' campaigns; secondly that there was a higher level of adoption, at local level, of selective purchasing and contracting measures targetted against companies with South African interests; and thirdly that US sanctions legislation was more advanced, particularly in respect of the 'Rangel Amendment', which eliminated tax credits for taxes paid on earnings to the South African government.

Nevertheless, some 132 UK-based TNCs disposed of their equity interests in South Africa between 1985 and mid-1989, a further 16 reduced their equity interests, and a further seven were reported to be in the process of disposing of their equity interests.[34] The sale of the South African subsidiaries of Barclays and Standard Chartered alone resulted in a 10 per cent reduction in the book value of UK investments in South Africa.

South African investment in the UK

For many of the same reasons that have caused the international trend towards disinvestment from South Africa, South African-based companies have also been investing abroad, although the momentum of the early 1980s has been curbed by the financial rand control on the export of capital. South African investment has gone particularly to Brazil, West Germany, the UK, and the USA. The International Confederation of Free Trade Unions has identified 88 South African-based companies which control 437 companies in 44 countries.[35]

Loan finance and debt

South Africa's economy is now particularly constrained by the shrinking level of international finance coming into the country. The economy cannot sustain the rate of growth necessary even to keep pace with population growth and its debt-servicing obligations, without substantial new sources of foreign exchange. Moreover, the government's room for manoeuvre in restructuring the economy to meet the demands of an increasingly hostile external environment is similarly constrained.

According to the Commonwealth Committee of Foreign Ministers on southern Africa,[36] the squeeze on loan finance arises for several reasons. Foreign banks are uninterested in new lending to non-OECD countries; foreign trade credits provide only a short-term and one-off increase in borrowing; and major capital-exporting economies have banned new investment in South Africa. Potential foreign investors are discouraged by the political uncertainties caused by apartheid, the associated poor economic outlook, and the economic uncertainties stemming from disinvestment pressures, and trade and financial sanctions. Gold, the country's key export, faces fluctuating and uncertain price prospects; and there are limited opportunities to increase non-gold exports.

Unable to use any but very short-term foreign borrowing to finance economic growth, the country has been required to run a substantial trade surplus to meet both interest payments and capital repayment on foreign debt.

During 1985 and 1986 a number of countries, including the USA, Japan, the Nordic states, and the Commonwealth (with the exception of the UK) introduced bans on new loans to South Africa, and some stopped export credit guarantees. In 1989, all Commonwealth Heads of Government (except the UK) called for a 90-day limit to trade credits, which it is estimated would halve total outstanding trade credits and be equivalent to obliging South Africa to pay an extra $2 bn.[37] Although these governmental decisions were prompted by rising international public outrage against the South African government's brutal repression of extra-parliamentary opposition, they were also following the lead of the transnational banks, which had already begun to regard South Africa as a bad commercial risk.

At a time of falling commodity prices, substantial foreign disinvestment, and capital export by domestic companies, South Africa was thus unable to secure access to long-term finance, including official multilateral loans. Short-term borrowing, especially trade credits, is therefore even more important.

South Africa's debt crisis

South Africa's debt profile (see table 10.3[38]) is quite different from that of the SADCC region. South Africa has no debt to multilateral organisations (its IMF loan was paid off in 1987), and no bilateral debt apart from what it owes to foreign government export-credit banks. Its debt is owed principally to foreign-based transnational banks, and its rescheduling agreements have therefore been conducted between the government and the creditor banks.

Table 10.3: Foreign creditors of South Africa by type of creditor (US$ bn.)

Foreign creditor	12/85	6/86	12/86	6/87	12/87	6/88
Bank	17.459	16.725	16.145	16.324	16.876	16.052
Gov't-insured portion	1.996	1.776	1.802	1.796	2.232	1.787
Non-bank	2.0	...	2.5	...	2.1	...
Gov't-insured portion	1.076	1.113	1.353	1.294	1.618	1.475
IMF	0.851	...	0.468	...	0.0	...
Bonds	3.2	...	3.5	..	3.7	...
TOTAL	23.473		22.593		22.618	

(Source: United Nations Commission on TNCs, Public Hearings of September 1989, op. cit., E/C. 10/AC.4/1989/6, p.7)

Over 80 per cent of South Africa's debt to transnational banks is held by UK, US, French, West German, and Swiss banks in descending order of exposure (see table 10.4[39]). As is the case with trade, there have also been marked changes in the levels of exposure of the banks of each of the five major countries. Between 1985 and 1988, the UK and Swiss levels of exposure have increased, while the US, French, and West German levels have decreased.[40]

Although it became severe in 1985, South Africa's debt crisis dates back to the late 1970s, when foreign borrowing — undertaken, among other things, to invest in large projects to circumvent the UN oil and arms embargoes — was stepped up during a period when commodity prices had started to decline and

Table 10.4: Money owed to banks by South Africa at the beginning of 1989

Country	US$ bn.
UK	4.1
USA	2.5
France	2.0
West Germany	2.0
Switzerland	1.7
Japan	1.2
Italy	0.5
Netherlands	0.2
Belgium	0.1
Others	0.3

when the South African government, despite its centralised control over the economy, was not adjusting effectively to the country's deteriorating terms of trade. Its foreign debt rose from $6 bn. to $24 bn. between 1980 and 1985. A substantial proportion of the borrowing was in the form of short-term loans, and South Africa was dependent on the creditor banks agreeing to 'roll over' the loans — that is, lending new money as these loans fell due, to help service them.

In 1985, the imposition of the State of Emergency in South Africa led US banks, followed by European banks, to refuse to 'roll over' their loans. South Africa was suddenly faced with repayment obligations that it could not meet, and announced a moratorium on repayments of commercial bank loans.[41] The crisis has been temporarily resolved by three rounds of negotiations between the government and its major creditors.

In the first round of negotiations, in 1986, the creditor banks' demand for political reform featured strongly in the negotiations. However, by the time of the second round, in 1987, political issues had apparently dropped off the banks' agenda. The 1987 agreement allowed the South African government to draw on part of the funds it was to hold for loan repayment. The Pretoria government used its access to this finance to fund military and other state expenditure.[42]

The third round of rescheduling occurred in 1989 and gave the South African economy significant breathing space. It also drew widespread criticism, because it directly contravened the demands of a large international campaign which included the OAU, the ANC, the Mass Democratic Movement, the South African Council of Churches, the World Council of Churches, and the UK-based Southern Africa Coalition.

Instead of rescheduling one year at a time, as requested by the Commonwealth Committee of Foreign Ministers on Southern Africa and other organisations, the banks agreed to a period of three and a half years (up until December 1993). For the time being at least, South Africa's debt crisis has slipped again from international public view.

South Africa's debt: Britain's profile
British banks have been the largest lenders to South Africa, followed by the US, West German, and Swiss banks. At the end of 1987, the exposure of UK-based monetary sector institutions amounted to 26 per cent of the total bank exposure, and 23 per cent of South Africa's total foreign debt.[43]

There has also been substantial lending to South Africa by UK branches of foreign banks, such as Swiss and Japanese banks, significantly increasing the value of British exposure in South Africa. For example, in June 1988 there was $4,557 m. in outstanding loans made by UK-based banks to South

Africa, and $3,024 m. in outstanding loans made by UK branches of non-UK based banks.[44]

UK-based banks hold the majority of the South African public sector (state and parastatal) bank debt, while US-based banks hold most of South Africa's bank-to-bank debt.[45]

The level of UK exposure is reported to be increasing, mainly in the form of export credit guarantees. The UN Commission on TNCs reports that the British government's Export Credit Guarantee Department is insuring a general-purpose line of credit for £70 m. to cover an eight-and-a-half-year period for UK credits. This will help British exporters to profit from the large Mossel Bay 'oil from gas' project in South Africa, an import substitution project which will help circumvent the UN oil embargo.[46]

The leading British banks with outstanding South African loans are Barclays, Standard Chartered, and National Westminster.[47] Barclays and Standard Chartered have both sold their local banks in South Africa, but, as a legacy of their direct involvement, they have retained the largest exposures of any creditor banks. All three of these banks sit on the Technical Committee which negotiates rescheduling with the South African government..

Investment and finance in the SADCC region

Although foreign TNCs (particularly those operating from a regional base in South Africa) have played an important role in shaping the economic structures of the region, it has generally been the case that while private investment flowed into South Africa, the other southern African countries were starved of sufficient productive investment on which to generate resources for their development plans. Instead they had to borrow, and beg for aid.[48] More recently, during the 1980s, when all the SADCC member states have agreed they want foreign investment, net transfers of private investment have been falling. SADCC's crucial Investment in Production programme depends on foreign investment and concessional flows, among other things, for its success.

Investment in the SADCC region: Britain's profile

In 1984, direct private investment by British companies in the SADCC region totalled over £100 m.,[49] about 3.6 per cent of the value of British direct investment in South Africa for the same year,[50] and it has fallen sharply since then as economic instability has undermined business confidence.[51]

In most of the SADCC region, British investment has been prominent alongside investment from South Africa (see table 10.5[52]). After South Africa, Zimbabwe has been the second destination of British private investment in the region.[53]

Table 10.5: Key private foreign investments in SADCC states, by country of investing company

Angola

Oil: USA, Belgium, Brazil, Italy, France, Spain, UK, FRG
Mining: South Africa, Belgium, Austria, Yugoslavia
Transport: Belgium
Import/Export: Nigeria

Botswana

Mining: South Africa, USA, UK
Agribusiness: South Africa, UK (CDC')
Other manufacturing: South Africa, Zimbabwe
Construction: South Africa, UK
Freight: South Africa
Wholesale and retail: South Africa, UK
Hotels: South Africa, UK
Banking: UK
Insurance: South Africa and UK

Lesotho

South African investment dominates all sectors

Malawi

Agribusiness: UK, USA, South Africa
Manufacturing: UK
Freight and forwarding: South Africa
Construction: South Africa

Mozambique

Freight and forwarding: South Africa, Belgium, Portugal
Industry: Portugal, USA, South Africa, UK
Energy: Portugal (state and private), UK
Agriculture: UK, Norway, Algeria, Portugal

Swaziland

Sugar: UK (private and CDC), Nigeria (state), USA, Japan
Timber: UK (private and CDC), South Africa
Mining: UK, South Africa
Industry: South Africa, UK (private and CDC)
Banking: UK, South Africa
Wholesale and retail: South Africa
Road transport: South Africa

Tanzania

Agriculture: UK (private and CDC)
Manufacturing: UK, USA
Mining: South Africa

continued overleaf....

Zambia

Mining: South Africa
Engineering: South Africa, UK
Other industry: UK (private and CDC), South Africa, Italy
Breweries: South Africa, UK
Freight and forwarding: South Africa, Belgium, UK
Hotels: South Africa, UK
Energy: Italy, UK
Banking: UK
Agriculture: UK (private and CDC), South Africa

Zimbabwe

Agriculture: UK, South Africa, USA
Manufacturing: South Africa, UK
Mining: UK, South Africa
Distribution: South Africa, UK
Transport: UK, South Africa
Finance: UK

*   Commonwealth Development Corporation

Table 10.6: Total gross bilateral aid from the UK to the SADCC region and Namibia

	1988 (£000)	Aid per capita (£) 1988	Total aid 1980-88 (£000)
Angola	505	0.05	1,624
Botswana	8,251	7.20	100,152
Lesotho	4,898	3.01	40,156
Malawi	46,494	6.09	186,166
Mozambique	30,512	2.09	87,019
Swaziland	5,058	7.09	46,716
Tanzania	33,502	1.40	245,877
Zambia	16,683	2.32	209,371
Zimbabwe	24,127	2.68	182,280
Namibia	2,033	1.67	5,483
Total aid to SADCC region	170,030		1,099,361

(Sources: "British Aid Statistics 1980-84", "British Aid Statistics 1984-88" (Overseas Development Administration))

Aid

Because Britain's aid programme has traditionally been focused on its Commonwealth partners, substantial amounts of aid have gone over the years to its ex-colonies in southern Africa. (See table 10.6 for details of Britain's gross bilateral aid to the SADCC region and Namibia.) In 1988, five SADCC countries ranked among the top 20 recipients of UK bilateral aid: Malawi ranked third, Tanzania fifth, Mozambique seventh, Zimbabwe eleventh, and Zambia nineteenth. British aid contributions to SADCC totalled £60 m. from 1980 to 1988.

In 1987 and 1988, official British bilateral assistance to refugees and displaced people in southern Africa totalled £8.67 m.[54]

Table 10.7 gives details of British multilateral aid to SADCC countries. Britain has contributed to the IMF and World Bank's facilities for assisting the structural adjustment programmes of low-income African countries, with a pledge of £327 m. over 14 years to the IMF's Enhanced Structural

Table 10.7: UK share of multilateral aid to SADCC countries, 1980-87 (latest year available)

	1987 (£000)	Aid per capita (£) 1987	Total aid 1980-87 (£000)
Angola	1,660	1.03	9,230
Botswana	1,370	7.21	7,930
Lesotho	1,630	8.28	13,240
Malawi	5,830	4.75	37,490
Mozambique	5,790	1.97	28,730
Swaziland	840	9.01	6,310
Tanzania	8,680	3.06	73,190
Zambia	4,780	5.35	38,510
Zimbabwe	1,690	2.09	18,830
Total aid to SADCC countries	32,270		233,460

(Source: Statistics Division, Overseas Development Administration)

Adjustment Facility, and £250 m. over three years to the World Bank's Special Programme of Action for Sub-Saharan African Countries.[55] Britain's contribution to the World Bank's concessional facility — the International Development Association (IDA) — totalled £485.5 m. over the period 1986-1988. An increasing proportion of British bilateral aid is conditional on the recipient country undertaking an IMF/World Bank-approved adjustment programme, and Britain has been pressing for more EC aid to be made conditional on this factor.

In line with government policy, some of Britain's aid to the SADCC region has boosted British business. Between 1984 and 1988, elements of 'Aid and Trade Provisions' (whereby UK companies are entitled to apply for contracts involved in the development programme supported) have featured in UK bilateral aid pledged to Botswana, Malawi, Mozambique, and Zimbabwe.[56]

UK aid to South Africans

Britain also provides aid resources to individuals and non-governmental organisations in South Africa. In 1988 total UK bilateral aid to South Africans was £4,288,000, of which £3,351,000 was for South African students and trainees;[57] total UK aid to the European Community's 'Special Programme' (see Chapter 11) was £3.5 m.; and total UK multilateral aid to the UN and Commonwealth scholarship schemes for South Africans was £125,000. [58]

The British Council has been working in South Africa since 1958, and the Overseas Development Administration's programme of support started in 1979. However, the level of Britain's aid programme to South Africans was significantly stepped up in 1987, following the EC's adoption of 'positive measures' as part of its South Africa policy, formulated in 1985 and 1986.[59]

Diplomatic links

Britain maintains direct diplomatic links with all the nations of southern Africa.[60] These direct diplomatic links are reinforced, and sometimes strained, by shared membership of the Commonwealth, in which Mozambique has been granted informal observer status, and to which Namibia is widely expected to accede. South Africa and Angola remain the only nations in the region quite outside the Commonwealth. (South Africa resigned in 1961, in the face of mounting pressure from the other members for its expulsion.)

Another important link is through the European Community. The principal instrument which links the EC and the SADCC states is the Lomé Convention. All the SADCC states are signatories, which entitles them to benefit from a range of trade and aid measures. (See Chapter 11.)

In response to calls for Britain to withdraw its diplomatic representation from South Africa, British government officials argue that it is the depth of Britain's engagement in South Africa which, combined with its senior diplomatic representation, places it in a unique position to influence the South African government. It is also argued that Britain's diplomatic presence in South Africa permits wide-ranging contacts with the diverse sectors of South African society. Lynda Chalker, as the Foreign Office Minister then charged with southern African affairs, argued in February 1988, "You do not convert a country to Christianity by withdrawing the missionaries."[61]

British interests and policy considerations

As we have seen, the key to British interests in the region is South Africa. A policy perspective in which South Africa figures as the epicentre of the region has long dominated the formulation of British policy towards the other countries. But Britain also has interests at stake in each of the SADCC states, which determine policy at a lower level.

Britain's interests in South Africa

The key 'British interests' which shape the UK government's South Africa policy are the protection of British trade, investment and loan finance interests in South Africa as well as in the wider region; the desire to maintain access to strategic minerals; and a determination to ensure that there is not a mass exodus of whites to Britain.[62]

According to a 1985 Foreign Office statement, the broad aim of British policy towards South Africa is "... to promote early and peaceful transition to a genuinely non-racial democracy and to further the considerable British interests in South Africa".[63] When asked why Britain's relations with South Africa remain important, Sir Robin Renwick, the British Ambassador, explained,

> Primarily because what happens here is the key to future prospects for the whole region. Of course, we have quite important economic interests here, but to put those in perspective, our trade here constitutes about one per cent of our exports world-wide. The same goes for our investments here. If we believed that sacrificing that one per cent would end apartheid, then we would do it tomorrow. But we know that it wouldn't have that effect. Another very important link is the fact that there are at least 350,000 British passport holders here, and at least another half a million probably entitled to them.[64]

In 1986, a delegation from the British Council of Churches stated their view that Britain's South Africa policy " ... reflects much too clearly the views of the English-speaking business community with whom British business has close ties based on self-interest ... (but which) politically constitutes a small minority, whose motives are distrusted by urban blacks.'[65]

Britain's 'special relationship' with South Africa adds to British responsibilities for the whole region, not only because of Britain's role in laying the foundations for apartheid, but also because the extensive and long-standing British economic links were instrumental in building up South Africa's economic power. This has enabled South Africa to dominate the region economically and militarily, and to use both these levers in pursuit of its narrow national interests. South Africa's economic power has also paid for the complex apparatus of internal political repression and brutality.

British interests and relationships in the SADCC region[66]

Britain and Zimbabwe

After South Africa, Zimbabwe is the most important country in the region as far as British interests are concerned. As well as looking after the interests of the estimated 30,000 British passport holders who live there,[67] and honouring its commitment to the post-independence training and reorganisation of the Zimbabwe National Army (which arose from the need to integrate the opposing factional armies after independence), British policy also seeks to protect and further its investment and trade interests. In her speech to the Zimbabwe Investment Conference in London in May 1989, Lynda Chalker, then Foreign Office Minister with responsibility for southern Africa, said,

> Overseas investment, and in particular British investment, can make a major contribution to Zimbabwe's future economic development. We believe that new investment will follow if the conditions are right.

Britain's aid programme to Zimbabwe has focused on the land redistribution and resettlement programme which has come to a virtual standstill, due to a variety of pressures. Although Britain is the major foreign donor to the resettlement programme, it also has significant interests in the commercial agriculture sector. As discussed in the Zimbabwe case study in Chapter 9, there is a sharp conflict between the commercial farming sector and the pro-resettlement lobby. According to governmental sources in Harare, Britain is urging that land in the most agriculturally productive areas of the country, where commercial farms dominate, should not be allocated as part of the resettlement programme to small-scale farmers.[68]

Britain's relations with Mozambique and Zambia were greatly enhanced by the support these two states gave to the Lancaster House negotiations in 1979. They helped to resolve one of Britain's major foreign affairs problems of the time. Using their substantial influence with ZANU (PF) and (PF) ZAPU respectively, Presidents Machel and Kaunda were able to mediate with the Patriotic Front.

Britain and Mozambique

For this reason, and because the conflict raging in Mozambique undermines the international trade of Zimbabwe, Malawi, and Zambia (where Britain has trade and investment interests), British aid to Mozambique has been greatly increased as the conflict in Mozambique, backed by South Africa, has escalated.

British aid to Mozambique rose from £6.3 m. in 1979 to £30.5 m. in 1988. In 1987, at the height of Mozambique's emergency needs, Britain was Mozambique's sixth largest bilateral aid donor,[69] and in the same year Mozambique ranked fourth among the SADCC states as a recipient of British bilateral assistance. Britain's programme of military assistance to Mozambique is also significant, not least because it was approved at a time when other western nations were reluctant to provide defence for their aid investments. Now, a number of other countries have followed Britain's lead.

Britain also supports Mozambique's structural adjustment programme. By 1988, 44 per cent of the UK's total bilateral aid to Mozambique was allocated under ODA's 'programme aid' category, which is approved expressly to support structural adjustment programmes approved by the IMF and World Bank.

However, Britain's trade with Mozambique is negligible in comparison with other of its trading partners, such as the USA, Italy, the Soviet Union, and Japan. If Mozambique joins the Commonwealth, as it reportedly hopes to do, and if stability and therefore business confidence can be restored, this situation may alter.

Britain and Malawi

British trade and investment is significant from Malawi's point of view (see table 8.1), although not from Britain's. Since Zimbabwe's independence, Malawi's importance as a diplomatic post has fallen away.

However, Britain is one of Malawi's main aid donors, and bases its Southern Africa Aid Division in Lilongwe. Official statements have often expressed Britain's commitment to helping Malawi overcome its critical trade disruption problems, caused by conflict in Mozambique, and Britain has funded SADCC projects designed to overcome this crippling constraint.[70]

Britain and Zambia

Britain is of crucial importance to Zambia, not least because the world's copper trade is managed by the London Metal Exchange. Since its precipitous economic decline, Zambia's main value to Britain is its political role as a key Front Line State.

Substantial links were built up during the liberation war in Zimbabwe, when the British Embassy in Zambia was upgraded because of the country's strategic importance. The 1979 Commonwealth Conference was held in Lusaka, shortly after Mrs Thatcher became Prime Minister. At this conference, President Kaunda facilitated significant progress towards setting up the Lancaster House negotiations. However, two factors have combined recently to cool bilateral relations.

Firstly, in May 1987, Zambia unilaterally terminated its structural adjustment programme with the IMF. In response, Britain cancelled 'programme aid' worth £30 m. for the year, and was unsympathetic to the Zambian government's subsequent requests for help with its own economic reform programme.[71]

Secondly, President Kaunda's publicly hostile reception of Sir Geoffrey Howe in 1986, during his controversial[72] and largely fruitless mission to the Front Line States (in his capacity as President of the EC Council of Ministers) has apparently had lasting adverse effects on bilateral relations. It has been cited as the main reason why Mrs Thatcher did not wish to visit Zambia during her trip to southern Africa in March 1989.

In 1989, as Zambia reopened discussions with the IMF, there were indications that Britain was beginning to increase its aid to Zambia. Britain also offered to cancel Zambia's outstanding aid debt, totalling £56 m.,[73] if the Zambian government reaches agreement with the IMF.[74]

Britain and Angola

Despite British trade and investment in colonial Angola, and the responsibility for post-independence reconstruction conferred on all the member states of the NATO alliance (which gave military support to Portugal during the long and brutal liberation war), British bilateral links with Angola have been minimal since its independence in 1975.

This is mainly due to independent Angola's alliance with the Soviet Union and Cuba, and the Marxist development pathway which it adopted; but it is also due to the dominance of US, French, and Italian interests in the oil sector, and the fact that, unlike Mozambique, neither Angola's geographic position nor its political position is central to other British interests in the region.

Although there are growing British trade links with Angola (mainly due to the opportunities for British exports to the oil and military sectors), official government statements remain cool. For example, in late 1987, Lynda Chalker was challenged in the House of Commons to explain why Britain was sending aid to a close ally of Cuba and the Soviet Union. Mrs Chalker, then speaking for the Foreign Office, replied, "I assure my hon. Friend that in no way are we assisting Angola, other than in a humanitarian sense."[75]

Underlying British diplomacy is the fact that it has largely been influenced by the USA's highly antagonistic policy towards Angola. For example, during the 1980s, although Britain dismissed as irrelevant the US concept of 'linkage' (whereby international cooperation over Namibia's independence was made conditional on the withdrawal of Cuban troops from Angola), nevertheless Britain allowed its Namibia policy to be stalled by this factor.

British policy on South Africa

On ending apartheid and minority rule in South Africa

A lasting solution to the region's complex problems depends essentially on the establishment of majority rule in South Africa. The enormous pressures and tensions generated by the political and economic dispensation in South Africa are a continuing source of instability. As Margaret Thatcher has said, "I do not see how, in the modern world, it is possible to achieve political stability except on a basis where all adults have the vote."[76]

A post-apartheid South Africa could greatly enhance southern Africa's economic development. Much depends on how, how soon, and at what cost

Candlelit vigil held on the steps of a church near the South African embassy in London's Trafalgar Square to protest against detentions, December 1986

(Camilla Garrett-Jones,/ Oxfam)

the end of apartheid is achieved. However, positive economic cooperation between all the states of the region could contribute greatly to a lasting resolution of political tensions and economic decline. In as far as the economic breakdown in Mozambique gives oxygen to the banditry and terrorism spawned by the MNR, economic development in that country is doubly needed.

The 1990s bring an unprecedented opportunity for international pressure to make a major contribution to the eradication of apartheid, and the establishment of full democracy in South Africa. However, in its strategy for helping to defeat apartheid, the UK government has so far failed to give full support to the mass popular movement for democracy, and has unilaterally opposed the idea of maintaining targetted economic pressure, at a time when maximum international cooperation is needed.

British response to popular demands for democracy

In the words of Sir Robin Renwick, Britain's Ambassador to South Africa, Britain is committed to an active role in South Africa's affairs:

> So far as Britain is concerned, we do not believe in disengagement. We do not intend to walk off the pitch. .... We are determined to help defeat apartheid. And we intend to demonstrate that we too do not lack staying power.[77]

Official statements have also stressed the view that the potential for international pressure is limited, but that Britain has a key role to play in facilitating internal movement towards democracy. As Sir Geoffrey Howe, then Foreign Secretary, explained in 1988:

> The power of outsiders to influence events in South Africa is limited. They have to find courses of action which will be effective. ... The lead for change must come from inside South Africa. We can only give advice and encouragement. And the best form our help can take is pressure and persuasion, doing all we can to bring South Africans to start a genuine dialogue between the communities.[78]

Much has been said and written about British influence on the South African government.[79] Because of the extensive historical and present-day links between the two countries, Britain is indeed in a strong position of influence. However, as developments in South Africa rapidly unfold, it is important to examine what British policy means to the wide-ranging and politically vital alliance between the Mass Democratic Movement and the African National Congress which, despite the many divisions and rifts in South African society, has clearly emerged as the central mass movement for full democracy. Although the Foreign Office claimed in a policy statement in 1988 that "The Government are pursuing policies designed to promote internal forces for change which will have a positive, practical influence", nevertheless, UK policy is widely interpreted, most importantly by the MDM/ANC alliance itself, as negative.

There have been some positive signals. For example, although Britain insists on making representations to the South African government over political trials on a case-by-case basis only, where protests have been made, they have been greatly welcomed. The last-minute reprieve of the 'Sharpeville Six' in 1987, for example, is widely thought to have been helped by Margaret Thatcher's intervention. [80]

However, in overall terms, Britain has consistently refused to heed the MDM/ANC call for tougher pressure on the South African government. This reluctance to lend full backing to the mass movement for democracy was most recently illustrated in December 1989, at a special session of the UN General Assembly, where the ANC sought support for the Harare Declaration (which embodies the MDM/ANC political strategy on negotiations, and their constitutional guidelines — see Appendix 2). A key tactical aim of the exercise at this critical point was to secure consensus agreement, since yet another UN anti-apartheid resolution backed only by a majority would not, in the words of one observer, "be worth the paper it was written on". Britain and the USA, however, declared in advance that they could not agree with crucial aspects of the Harare Declaration.

In the diplomatic negotiations between the ANC and key Security Council members preceding the special session, a draft declaration was drawn up for submission to the General Assembly. It differed from the Harare Declaration on major issues, but was unanimously adopted at the General Assembly. Perhaps the most important omission, at the insistence of the British government,[81] was the Harare Declaration's concept of an interim government to rule South Africa during the transition period from white minority rule to full democracy.[82]

Recent experience over the negotiations of the terms of Namibia's independence, and afterwards of Namibia's transition period, was thought to be a key factor in the ANC's inclusion of the concept of an interim government in its strategy. The 1988 tripartite agreement, which removed the obstacles to the implementation of UN Security Council Resolution 435 on Namibia's independence, was agreed between Angola, South Africa, and Cuba; it was therefore a deal made over the head of SWAPO (the South West Africa People's Organisation).[83] Although it was, by then, in South Africa's wider international interests to promote Namibia's independence, events have shown that South Africa's actions were not consistent with the provisions of the UN Plan, and that South Africa's effective political control greatly contributed to military tension, and frustrated the complex legal procedures during the transition process.[84]

In South Africa itself, where the UN has no special authority as it did in Namibia, a situation permitting the government to remain in full control during the period of negotiations and transition could be detrimental to prospects for a peaceful move to full democracy. For its part, the National Party has made clear in its Five Year Plan its intention to remain in control of the pace and nature of any negotiating process. Its views on the nature of negotiations are quite different from those expressed in the Harare Declaration.

Nevertheless, British policy is being shaped, to some extent, by pressure from the democratic movement. One key respect in which British policy has been refined concerns the future constitution of South Africa. The view of the Foreign and Commonwealth Office, repeatedly stressed, had been as follows:

> We seek the abolition of apartheid. We want to see it replaced by a non-racial, representative system of government. It is not for the British Government or any outsiders to prescribe details.[85]

And, as Margaret Thatcher has explained,

> At every stage I have made it clear that future constitutional arrangements for South Africa must be worked out by South Africans. They cannot be laid down by outsiders.[86]

However, in voting for the UN General Assembly's "Declaration on Apartheid and its Destructive Consequences in Southern Africa" of December 1989 (see Appendix 3), the UK signalled its support for all the main elements of the ANC's constitutional guidelines for a future South Africa, including the following vital clause:

> All its people shall have the right to participate in the Government and administration of the country on the basis of universal, equal suffrage, under a non-racial voters' roll, and by secret ballot, in a united and non-fragmented South Africa.[87]

It remains to be seen whether the UK's support for the UN Declaration — a non-binding statement — will be carried through in terms of practical diplomacy and action.

Britain claims to be acting as a force for mediation between the opposing political forces in South Africa. As Lynda Chalker, then FCO Minister, explained in February 1989, "Britain is engaged in South Africa at all levels and with all sides. We cannot be otherwise if we hope to seek to influence those in power in that country."[88]

However, as a consequence of British policy over the years, the MDM/ANC alliance doubts whether Britain would act as honest broker in the process of ending apartheid. Rather, Britain is seen as having its own agenda, because of its substantial economic interests in South Africa and the wider region.

In May 1988, Sir Geoffrey Howe, then Foreign Secretary, said,

> No one's good faith should be questioned because they disagree with the advocates of punitive sanctions. There is nothing intrinsically moral about punitive sanctions: nothing intrinsically moral about disinvestment. Opposition to sanctions does not mean support for apartheid.[89]

However, as an ANC spokesperson explained to Mrs Chalker (when she was Foreign Office Minister) in a public meeting, it has to be understood that Britain's international anti-sanctions crusade is widely viewed in South Africa, by people of all political persuasions, as a policy which protects the South African government and undermines the right of the disenfranchised South African people to determine their own future.[90]

Key Oxfam partners in South Africa have consistently expressed a critical view of British policy — Church, UDF, and COSATU leaders in particular. For example, in January 1989, the only two UDF leaders not restricted at the time visited London and met Mrs Chalker at the Foreign Office. Afterwards they said that it was "... still early days to think of policy changes. More meetings will be needed for the British government to change their position."[91]

In May 1989, a senior South African church delegation (Archbishop Tutu, the Reverend Allan Boesak, the Reverend Frank Chikane, and the Reverend Beyers Naude) asked President Bush to take back the lead role in western diplomacy, on the grounds that British policy lacked credibility with the democratic movement.[92]   In June 1989, on the occasion of F.W. de Klerk's visit to Britain, COSATU and the UDF criticised the visit, saying that it reduced the likelihood of Britain's becoming the "honest broker".

In January 1989, a World Council of Churches delegation led by Frank Chikane — the General Secretary of the South African Council of Churches — met Sir Geoffrey Howe, then Foreign Secretary, to press their view that Britain should step up its sanctions against apartheid. After the meeting, Sir Geoffrey Howe told the House of Commons,

> ... no voice arguing the case for change in South Africa is heard with more attention than that of the Prime Minister of this country. There are two simple reasons for that - our opposition to apartheid is unqualified, but our opposition to sanctions is equally unqualified. In our judgement the imposition of sanctions would make the matter a great deal worse, not better.[93]

Frank Chikane was reported as saying that he had wasted his time.[94]

Aid and diplomacy

The British government points to its aid programme as evidence that it is engaged with the victims of apartheid. In early 1989, Lynda Chalker (as Foreign Officer Minister) explained, "We see our programme of aid to black South Africans as an important way of promoting the internal forces for change in South Africa."[95]   Indeed, it is Oxfam's experience that support is much needed in a country where poverty and vast inequalities are deeply rooted, and where organisational support and training are important tools for change.   However, there are a number of objections to this aspect of the British government's position.

People in South Africa are well aware that the British aid programme was rapidly stepped up as part of the concept of 'positive measures', designed expressly as an alternative to sanctions.   Moreover, Britain has tried to change the focus of the European Community's Common Programme away from its original 'dual-track' approach (which prescribed both positive and restrictive measures) towards its 'positive measures' element, in a way which has strengthened the MDM's view that their political legitimacy is not properly supported by the British government.   (See Chapter 11 for more details of the EC special programme.)

Public diplomacy gives strong signals.   In 1984, Mrs Thatcher received President Botha, and in June 1989 she received Mr de Klerk (then leader of the ruling Nationalist Party and widely expected to become President of South Africa), considerably boosting his chances in the forthcoming 'general' election.   However, although official statements have acknowledged that the ANC is an important political organisation,[96] and although Mrs Thatcher has frequently called for the release of Nelson Mandela, and the unbanning of political parties in South Africa, at the end of 1989 the British government had still not officially met the ANC at Secretary of State or Prime Ministerial level.[97]   In this way, the ANC leadership is prevented from having direct political access to the foremost decision makers at a critical period in South Africa's history, and the view is conveyed that the British government does not accept the ANC's position as the focal point for extra-parliamentary opposition.

Developments indicate that this stance may be softening, however.   A high-level delegation from the United Democratic Front (UDF) (a key organisation in the MDM, and one strongly linked to the ANC), including Albertina Sisulu (Co-President of the UDF) was received by Mrs Thatcher in July 1989.   Following their meeting, the UDF delegation issued a statement saying,

The delegation regards the meetings with both President Bush and Mrs

The ANC's 'Freedom Charter', demanding equal rights for all in South Africa, was first ratified by a Congress of almost 3,000 delegates from across the country, meeting in Kliptown in 1955.   (Eli Weinberg/IDAF)

Thatcher as significant as it is the first time that an Anti-Apartheid organisation from inside South Africa has been received at this level in both the White House and Downing Street. Both meetings constitute acknowledgements by these governments that the future course of South Africa cannot be determined by the white minority alone.[98]

The need for international coordination

As Sir Geoffrey Howe, speaking as Foreign Secretary, has urged,

... the sooner white South Africans accept the need for negotiation and change, the greater the odds that change will be peaceful and democratic ... The South African Government have to take the lead. Dialogue cannot take place against a backcloth of violence and repression.[99]

However, in spite of the growing evidence that external economic pressure has contributed to the National Party's recognition that it must adapt its strategy,[100] Britain remained opposed to applying further economic pressure. As a result, UK policy on South Africa has been widely criticised for undermining other international and internal strategies to hasten the South

African government to the negotiating table.

Britain and West Germany have weakened the European Community's Common Policy on South Africa (explained in detail in Chapter 11). Further, in the two Commonwealth Heads of State summits since the Nassau summit in October 1985, when Britain agreed to specific, limited, and mostly voluntary sanctions, Britain has refused to cooperate with other member states on proposals to increase sanctions. Britain's limited programme of economic pressure has also lagged behind other states', including the USA and the Nordic countries.

The 1989 Commonwealth Heads of Government summit at Kuala Lumpur, when Britain issued its own unilateral communiqué after signing the official consensus communiqué, provided another forceful illustration of British unilateralism on the question of South Africa.[101]

International differences over what levels of economic pressure to apply to South Africa mean that those who apply least measures undermine the efforts of those who apply more.[102]

The 1990s — a key opportunity for coordinated international diplomacy

The rapid developments which have taken place in South Africa and the wider region since 1988 have, as the Harare Declaration notes, given rise to the real possibility of a negotiated end to apartheid.

In particular the change in the Soviet Union's foreign policies permitted improved international cooperation on southern African issues. The regional log-jam started to break up around the edges, with agreement over Namibia and Angola and a perceptible reduction in South African aggression. There was a change of leadership in South Africa, with clear signs that the pressures on the political and economic structures of apartheid had stimulated the beginnings of a change in outlook in the National Party.

The outcome of this period of flux is not possible to determine at this stage. Whether a refined form of apartheid or full democracy emerges is impossible to predict, and much depends on international reaction to events.

Following the change of leadership in South Africa in the summer of 1989, international expectations of the South African government were raised to new heights. The UK and USA stressed to Mr de Klerk that his government must quickly make significant move towards negotiations. Most political commentators agreed that the South African government had no more than 18 months in which to meet western expectations. This grace-period was sharply defined in October 1989, when the US Administration announced that it wanted to see significant developments by the start of the February 1990 session of the South African parliament. It was therefore widely understood that the potential for international influence and leverage over the pace of developments in South Africa had greatly increased.

By the end of 1989, as if testing the water, the South African government had taken some initial steps towards satisfying the first set of demands outlined in the Harare Declaration (and presaged by the Commonwealth Eminent Persons' 'negotiating concept' of 1986): that of creating the democratic space necessary to begin the central political process of negotiations (see Chapter 7). These initial shifts were seen as important evidence of progress. But they also brought into sharper focus the most crucial task: that of negotiating full democracy in place of the deeply-entrenched system of apartheid.

Minority rule, a fragmented state, and a complex edifice of apartheid legislation (including the 'cornerstone' laws — the Population Registration Act, the Natives Lands Act, and the Group Areas Act) are the most obvious, immediate targets. But the destructive legacy of apartheid will take years to overcome. The challenge of removing the deep inequalities in wealth, education, housing, health provision, and employment opportunities will be immense.

A democratic system of government, which enables all South Africa's people to shape their future, is clearly essential for equitable development and regional stability. The daunting scale of the tasks which lie ahead — of establishing political democracy and balancing out the enormous inequalities of South African society — require full international support.

A more enlightened British policy could make an immediate concrete contribution to the struggle for democracy. If increased pressure were brought to bear in support of the ANC/MDM's specific demands for the creation of a climate conducive to negotiations (in accordance with section III of the Harare Declaration), the chances for the establishment of lasting democracy would be enhanced. High on its list of priorities, the MDM stresses the need for a free political environment if it is to maximise its potential as a force for democracy. As Jay Naidoo, COSATU's General Secretary, has explained,

> ... the (condition) we stress is freedom of association and freedom of speech. In order for us to have negotiations, organisations will have to put their programmes to the people, to canvass the people and get mandates. That implies that any negotiations have to be open.[103]

In the longer term, full British support for the democratic movement would greatly enhance the prospects for a transition to the stable form of democracy needed to redress three centuries of exploitation.

British policy on southern Africa

On destabilisation and dependency

Britain's policy towards the consequences of South Africa's regional policy has been a two-pronged strategy. On the one hand is British policy to end apartheid (as discussed above), and the application of diplomatic pressure to persuade the South African government to stop destabilisation. And, on the other hand, Britain has provided 'positive measures' aid to the SADCC states and SADCC projects. In the words of a statement issued by the Foreign and Commonwealth Office shortly before the 1987 Vancouver Commonwealth Heads of Government summit,

> Southern Africa is one of the major challenges facing the international community today.
>
> Instability and economic difficulties in the region are largely attributable to the unjust and immoral apartheid system, and the tension this has engendered between South Africa and her neighbours.
>
> The British Government is determined to do all it can to alleviate these problems. We intend:
>
> — to work for peaceful dialogue in South Africa leading to the elimination of apartheid and its replacement by a non-racial representative system of government;
>
> — to help promote the peaceful, stable and prosperous development of all States in the region.
>
> These two aims are inextricably linked — only through the abolition of apartheid will South Africa be able to forge stable, friendly relations with her neighbours.[104]

British policy has been helpful in some important respects which deserve recognition. British aid for the transport sector of SADCC's dependency-reduction programme has made a much-needed contribution. And key aspects of British policy towards Mozambique, in particular, have been welcomed. For example, Margaret Thatcher has used the tool of public diplomacy to maximum advantage in condemning the brutality of the MNR. Britain also took the lead in supplying military training and non-lethal military aid to the Mozambican government, which has helped to protect the convoys carrying relief aid. British defence support to counter destabilisation has also been given to Zimbabwe, Tanzania, and Malawi. And, despite the markedly circumspect nature of official comment on the issue of South African support for the MNR[105] until late 1988,[106] private British diplomatic pressure has been directed towards persuading the South African government to change its policy. As Robin Renwick explained in an interview published in May 1989,

Children with toy instruments and microphones which they have made at a Resources Centre established in Lichinga, in Mozambique's war-torn Niassa Province.

(Keith Bernstein / Oxfam)

We have worked very hard over the past year to contribute to the Namibia agreement, and to encourage and contribute to improved relations between South Africa and Mozambique. As far as South Africa's initiatives in the region are concerned, some are consistent with what I have described. These initiatives show what positive results can be achieved by negotiation.[107]

Nevertheless, the weaknesses of British policy on ending apartheid have undermined the effectiveness of its policy to mitigate the effects of destabilisation and dependency. British relief and dependency-reduction aid, alongside other donors' assistance, has been attacked and destroyed by the MNR, and destabilisation has prevented relief aid from reaching many of those in most need.

The reduction of dependency is a necessary but not a sufficient condition for sustained economic growth and equitable development. It is a first and necessary step, but other factors need to be addressed alongside it. Most importantly, for as long as foreign support fuels the war in Mozambique and Angola, and political instability in South Africa threatens the region, "stable and prosperous development" will be an elusive objective.

On the issue of the SADCC region's economic domination by South Africa, it is fitting that British aid should be going to the SADCC programme of dependency reduction, given that Britain helped to oil the wheels of the lopsided regional economic integration with South Africa in the first place.

But although British aid to SADCC's transport sector programmes has been extremely useful, much more could be done to support SADCC's priority focus for the 1990s: Investment in Production. As we have seen, the economic independence of the SADCC states depends on transport routes. But it also depends on a halt to the economic decline which has affected most of the region, and the promotion of sustainable economic growth in its place. This, in turn, hinges on a widening of the region's productive, industrial, and market base, for which peace in the region, and economic cooperation with a majority-ruled South Africa are needed.

The weaknesses of Britain's South Africa policy have, likewise, undermined other elements of policy towards the rest of the region, especially policy in respect of economic adjustment, trade, and investment.

On debt relief and structural adjustment

As we have seen, key SADCC states are facing unprecedented levels of economic dislocation as a result of destabilisation, on top of which they are also suffering from a crippling debt burden which inhibits economic growth and starves those countries of the resources necessary to relieve poverty and promote development.   From 1978, at a time when Britain was increasingly giving aid on grant or concessional terms, most of Britain's outstanding aid credits were written off under the 'Retrospective Terms Adjustment' agreement.   The southern African countries which then benefitted from Britain's aid debt forgiveness were Botswana (by £20.7 m.), Lesotho (by £0.4 m.), Malawi (£30.7 m.), Mozambique (£22.5 m.), and Tanzania (£3.4 m.).[108]

Nearly a decade later, the British government's 'Lawson initiative' on the official bilateral debt burden of Africa's most debt-distressed countries stimulated the 'Toronto agreement' of 1988, which focused on the needs of low-income African countries.   Chancellor Lawson proposed a three-point debt relief strategy at the April 1987 IMF meeting.   The package was on offer to low-income countries undertaking internationally acceptable economic adjustment programmes. It consisted of the conversion of all aid loans into grants; the extension of repayment periods for non-concessional official debt; and the cutting of interest rates on official debt to below commercial levels.[109]

However, Britain was not prepared to act alone. The British Treasury argued that if the UK operated independently of the other G7 nations, then the debtor nations would simply use the savings to repay their other creditors. By the time of the Toronto G7 summit of June 1988, although some other G7 members backed the British plan, US intransigence (mainly because of the strict Congressional controls on government spending aimed at reducing the national budget deficit) effectively reduced the scope of Britain's initiative.

In order to present a common programme which would include the USA, the G7's Toronto Plan ended up as a compromise. At the insistence of the USA, a third 'option' was added, which simply provided for the extension of the grace and maturity periods on non-concessional bilateral debt, without providing any real debt reduction.

Britain's lead in cancelling aid debt and in forging the Toronto Plan puts it in a good position to work for more bilateral debt reduction. A good start would be to press for G7 agreement to cancel the 'third option' of the Toronto Plan. Thereafter, a continued programme of debt reduction must urgently be pursued. The debt-distressed SADCC countries need special consideration. The SADCC region's trade-credit debt to Britain alone is £493 m.[110]

On the relief of multilateral debt, since Britain primarily views its contribution to the IMF and World Bank facilities for low-income countries (facilities which are tied to the recipients' acceptance of structural adjustment measures) as an important part of its policy to extend structural adjustment,[111] it is therefore unlikely to press for across-the-board cancellation of multilateral debt.

The internationally sponsored structural adjustment measures which have been undertaken to manage indebted economies have created additional hardship for some vulnerable groups. Further, in determining the economic targets to be achieved by the structurally adjusting countries, there has been insufficient regard for the particular economic stresses created by destabilisation in the region, and they are not designed to stimulate long-term solutions for nations dependent on exporting primary commodities.

However, British policy on structural adjustment is firmly committed to encouraging the form of economic adjustment favoured by the Bretton Woods institutions throughout the debt-distressed countries of Africa.[112] An increasing proportion of Britain's aid to debt-distressed countries is offered on condition that the recipient country undertakes such a structural adjustment programme.

On trade and investment

The major forum for direct measures to improve SADCC's foreign trade potential is the European Community's Lomé Convention (discussed in Chapter 11).

British statements argue that SADCC's long-term aims for integrated economic development depend on the adoption of the economic reforms promoted by structural adjustment, which will stimulate increased investment and trade.   As Chris Patten, then the Minister for Overseas Development, explained to SADCC's 1989 Annual Consultative Conference,

> Let me now turn to production — the well-chosen conference theme. This region, with its large market and vast natural resources, must aim at economic advance through development of production for both consumption and export. Aid donors have an important role to play in fostering what can be called the "enabling environment". We can help provide the necessary infrastructure; we can help provide resources for structural adjustment and for institutional reforms.
>
> But ultimately private investment will only be attracted if the economic climate is right. And this is something that only SADCC member states themselves can foster — with investment codes and protection agreements, and freedom for the remittance of profits.
>
> When conditions are right, both domestic and foreign private sectors will respond ... there is no doubt that private sector decisions are influenced by their perception of the national and regional investment climate.[113]

While it is unquestionably true that the SADCC states must adjust their economies to the changing external environment, and address the structural weaknesses which block equitable development, more is needed from the industrialised world. Far higher levels of concessional finance are needed, greater 'burden-sharing' on debt and economic adjustment, and a coordinated international programme to enhance the commodity-dependent nations' prospects of economic diversification.

Further, as we have seen, the region's best hope of achieving a sustainable and attractive investment climate requires, among other things, an early end to political instability in South Africa, so that a majority-ruled South Africa can fully participate in the regional economy. In this respect, the flaws in Britain's South Africa policy undermine the logic and long-term progress of its policy towards development in the SADCC region.

The role and responsibilities of the European Community

Britain is not the only country in the European Community which is linked historically with southern Africa. The Netherlands was the original colonial power in South Africa; Germany originally colonised Tanzania and Namibia; and, until relatively recently, Angola and Mozambique were Portuguese territories.

In contemporary terms, the relationship between the European Community (the EC[1]) can be considered on three main levels. Firstly, the twelve individual EC states have their own, national ties with and policies towards southern Africa. Secondly, at Community level, the EC has direct (bilateral) links to each SADCC country, and its own (multilateral) relations with SADCC. The EC's special relationship with the 66 African, Caribbean, and Pacific states which have historical ties with its members is governed by the terms of the 'Lomé Convention', an international treaty first incorporated in 1975, which is mainly concerned with preferential aid and technical cooperation, and trade, and was designed to promote a 'New International Economic Order'. All the SADCC states are signatories to the Lomé Convention and Namibia is expected to accede on independence. (The fourth Lomé Agreement was ratified in December 1989.) Thirdly, at Community level, the EC has adopted a Common Policy intended to abolish apartheid.

Separately and together, the nations of the European Community have an important role to play in contributing to stability and development in southern Africa.

Economic links with southern Africa

EC trade with the SADCC region

South Africa's importance to the EC in comparison with other states of the region is reflected in the pattern and levels of EC trade (see table 11.l). In 1988, the value of exports from the whole SADCC region to the EC totalled only some 20 per cent of the value of South Africa's exports to the EC, while for imports the figure was about 35 per cent.[2]

The economic crisis which the SADCC region experienced during the 1980s is reflected in the substantial decline in EC exports to the SADCC region. It has been estimated that Europe has lost some 1.2 bn. ECUs in export orders.[3]

Nevertheless the twelve member states of the EC form an extremely important trading region for the SADCC countries (see table 8.1), and the future development of EC trade policies under the Lomé Convention — particularly when the Single European Market comes into operation — is

---

Table 11.1: EC trade with southern Africa (1988)

a. Exports from EC countries* to southern Africa, 1988: percentages of total exports

	SA**	Ang.	Bot.	Les.	Mal.	Moz.	Swa.	Tan.	Zam.	Zim.	Total
West Germany	33.93	0.69	0.08	0.02	0.23	0.28	0.05	0.91	0.71	1.05	37.95
UK	19.19	0.46	0.48	0.02	0.50	0.44	0.03	1.57	1.51	1.04	25.24
France	6.64	1.52	0.25	0.05	0.08	0.46	0	0.20	0.35	0.39	9.95
Italy	6.34	0.65	0.03	0.01	0.08	0.98	0.06	0.72	0.35	0.23	9.44
Netherlands	3.49	1.07	0.01	0.01	0.06	0.20	0.02	0.42	0.18	0.32	5.78
Belgium	3.74	0.34	0.08	0	0.02	0.05	0	0.15	0.11	0.12	4.61
Portugal	0.32	1.86	0	0	0.01	0.30	0	0.03	0	0.02	2.53
Spain	1.47	0.57	0.13	0	0	0.07	0.01	0.09	0.01	0.04	2.39
Denmark	0.15	0.08	0.06	0.03	0.04	0.05	0.02	0.40	0.08	0.15	1.06
Ireland	0.88	0.04	0	0	0.01	0	0.02	0.02	0.05	0.03	1.05
Total	76.15	7.26	1.14	0.15	1.02	2.83	0.22	4.52	3.33	3.39	100.00

*   excluding Greece (no data available)

**   including Namibia

important to the development of SADCC's strategy of investment in production.

EC trade with South Africa

Europe is a key trading bloc for South Africa. In 1987 Western Europe accounted for 55 per cent of South Africa's total trade.[4] There have been changes in the pattern of trade in recent years, primarily as a result of sanctions measures. Comparing 1987 levels with an average for 1983-85, we see that West Germany, Italy, and Spain were among the countries which increased the value of their trade with South Africa, while the UK, Denmark, and Ireland reduced theirs.[5]

In 1987, Japan was South Africa's foremost trading partner, while the data published by the European Community Statistical Office for 1988 put the UK in first position as South Africa's main export market. An important factor behind both British and West German trade with South Africa is those countries' importance as a source of investment. According to UN data on the major sources (by home country) of foreign direct investment in South

b.   Imports to EC countries* from southern Africa, 1988: percentages of total imports

	SA**	Ang.	Bot.	Les.	Mal.	Moz.	Swa.	Tan.	Zam.	Zim.	Total
UK	47.58	0.10	0.08	0.01	0.39	0.05	0.34	0.25	0.27	1.08	50.14
Italy	12.53	0.24	0.03	0	0	0	0.02	0.15	0.65	0.65	14.27
West Germany	9.59	1.45	0.13	0.01	0.13	0.03	0.03	0.40	0.11	1.19	13.07
Belgium	6.93	0.95	0.02	0.01	0.04	0	0.05	0.08	0.29	0.28	8.64
France	4.29	0.48	0	0.08	0.07	0.07	0.23	0.05	0.54	0.14	5.95
Netherlands	1.71	0.98	0.01	0	0.20	0.01	0.03	0.14	0.02	0.38	3.49
Spain	1.96	0.50	0.03	0.03	0.01	0.20	0.01	0.04	0.01	0.12	2.91
Portugal	0.65	0.18	0	0	0.02	0.04	0.08	0.11	0.01	0.19	1.29
Ireland	0.07	0	0	0	0	0	0.01	0	0	0.02	0.11
Total	85.34	4.87	0.30	0.14	0.89	0.41	0.80	1.24	1.90	4.10	100.00

*   excluding Greece (no data available)

**   including Namibia

(Source: "External Trade", Eurostat, 1989)

Africa between 1981 and 1986, the UK and West Germany came in first and third places respectively. Further, the UK and West Germany are among the countries which received foreign investment from South African TNCs during the 1980s.[6]

EC loans to South Africa

EC member states' banks are heavily exposed in South Africa, especially those based in the UK, France, West Germany, Italy, the Netherlands, and Belgium (as ranked in descending order of importance according to early 1989 data), with a total of $8.9 bn exposed.[7]

EC aid to southern Africa

EC aid to southern Africa is a major source of the region's total aid flows. There are three main types.

On an individual, national level, member states have their own aid programmes. At Community level, they contribute to the EC's aid programme, most of which is channelled through the National Indicative Programmes, negotiated with each recipient country (see table 11.2[8]). In addition, the EC has other aid budgets which benefit the SADCC region,

---

Table 11.2: Lomé III: EC aid allocated to SADCC states under National Indicative Programmes, 1985-1990 (ECU m.)

Angola	109
Botswana	35
Lesotho	51
Malawi	139
Mozambique	205
Swaziland	31
Tanzania	218
Zambia	90
Zimbabwe	81
Total	959

Note: Figures include extra allocations made during the mid-term review. In addition, 141 m. ECU was allocated under Lomé III to SADCC's Programme of Action.

Table 11.3: EC aid to its Special Programme in South Africa and Namibia
1986	ECU 10 m.
1987	ECU 20 m.
1988	ECU 30 m.
1989	ECU 25 m. (proposed)

including a special multilateral facility for funding SADCC;[9] emergency relief; aid to refugees and returnees; food aid; the STABEX and SYSMIN facilities (which partly compensate countries in the South for loss of export earnings due to circumstances beyond their control); and a special aid fund to support countries undertaking structural adjustment programmes.

And lastly, at Community level, as part of its policy to hasten the end of apartheid in South Africa, the EC has provided financial support to some South African and Namibian organisations. (See table 11.3,[10] and the section on the EC Special Programme for the Victims of Apartheid below.)

EC policy towards southern Africa

EC policy on SADCC

During the late 1970s, the EC was a major backer of the SADCC idea. It gave useful support, both political and material, to the southern African states trying to establish their own regional economic cooperation body. EC assistance to correct the SADCC region's structural economic deformities (in its relationship with South Africa, and with the North) is seen as especially important. At Community level it represented a shift of emphasis away from Europe's traditional preoccupation with trade and investment in South Africa.

During the early 1980s, EC bilateral and multilateral aid to SADCC was disappointing, largely due to the prevailing lack of British and West German support for SADCC's goal of reducing its dependency on South Africa. However, EC funding for SADCC was markedly stepped in response to increasing pressure for sanctions

EC aid to SADCC states

EC bilateral and multilateral aid to the SADCC region has increased in volume since the mid-1980s, and has been a valuable source of support. However, there are two key conditions affecting EC bilateral aid which hinder growth with equity in the SADCC region.

One condition is an increasing insistence on structural adjustment programmes. The EC — in common with other major bilateral and multilateral aid donors — is increasingly making aid conditional on the recipient country implementing structural adjustment measures as approved by the World Bank and the IMF.[11]

As we have seen, although some aspects of this structural adjustment model are beneficial, it has also proved to have special disadvantages for some social groups, and for the long-term prospects of commodity-dependent countries. Moreover, there needs to be a special practical emphasis on helping the destabilised SADCC states to adjust with equity.

The other condition is the provision of tied aid. There has been a marked trend among EC member states towards linking their bilateral aid to export opportunities. Given the SADCC region's need to develop its own integrated production and market base, such restrictions are not normally helpful: they reinforce the South's trading dependence on the North for manufactures and capital equipment. An important feature of the EC's aid funding is that its aid is tied to the use of goods from EC or ACP (African, Caribbean and Pacific) countries. Where possible, therefore, all EC and member states' bilateral aid to SADCC should encourage the purchase of inputs from the SADCC region.

Britain has taken a lead here, for example, in purchasing food aid from within the region.

Trade policy

The European Community is a major trading partner of the SADCC region. Furthermore, special measures have been introduced under Lomé agreements to cushion the effects on southern Africa of the sharp decline and fluctuations of the commodity markets. These include the STABEX and SYSMIN programmes for agricultural commodities and minerals respectively, and special protocol agreements.

When these measures were first introduced,[12] it was thought that they would be an important preliminary step to balancing out North/South inequalities and creating a 'New International Economic Order'. But these facilities were no match for the extent of the decline in commodity prices experienced during the 1980s. Although they have become heavily overdrawn by commodity-dependent ACP states, their net effect has been only marginal.

Nevertheless, the SADCC region has benefitted to some extent from EC trade measures. Zambia, for example, has benefitted from the SYSMIN scheme, having received some 90 million ECUs in loans to help stabilise the fluctuating copper prices during the 1980s.[13] Zimbabwe and Botswana benefit from the Beef Protocol. Independent Namibia should benefit from the Beef Protocol and Fisheries agreements. Malawi, Swaziland, Zimbabwe, and Tanzania have been cushioned from falling world sugar prices[14] by the Sugar Protocol of the Lomé Convention, which allows a number of the member ACP countries to export sugar to the EC at guaranteed prices.   Malawi, for example, exports some 13 per cent[15] of its crop to the EC at about double world prices, while only 8 per cent is sold at world market rates.[16]

As Europe moves towards the Single European Market in 1992, the fear among many of the African, Caribbean, and Pacific nations who are signatories to the Lomé Convention is that the EC may raise trade barriers against their exports in 1992, rather than reduce protectionism. However, until more details are negotiated, it is far from clear what the net impact of 1992 will be on the trading relationship between the EC and the ACP in general, and the SADCC states in particular. The Single European Market is designed to benefit Europe, and increase its power as a trading bloc in a climate of fierce international competition. The main world players are the USA and Japan. The world's poor, commodity-dependent, nations are becoming rapidly marginalised except for their value as markets.[17]

Within the multilateral negotiations under the General Agreement on Trade and Tariffs (GATT), the EC has offered to liberalise its import regime on tropical products. Since the value to the ACP states of the Lomé trade preferences depends on their being accorded more preferential terms of access than other third-party suppliers to the EC market, any such generalised liberalisation is potentially of concern to them. However, the EC offer on tropical products has been tailored to minimise its direct impact on ACP preferences.[18]

Debt relief

In spite of a growing level of EC aid being made conditional on recipient countries' acceptance of structural adjustment programmes to manage their debt-distressed economies, debt relief has not, as yet, been accepted into mainstream Community-level policy, on the basis that it is a matter of member states' sovereign economic policy.[19]

Instead, the bilateral debt relief measures most relevant to the SADCC region's debt profile have been implemented at 'G7' level (the common members are the UK, France, and West Germany), and were considerably weakened by the position of the USA. On multilateral debt, although the EC votes as a bloc at meetings of the General Agreement on Trade and Tariffs, the member states vote separately on the boards of the IMF and World Bank.[20]

Nevertheless, in 1989 the EC member states together commanded more votes in the IMF and the World Bank than the USA and Japan combined.[21] On non-concessional debt, the lack of a coherent EC response means that the USA has been allowed to determine the development of creditor government strategy, and mainstream US strategy on private commercial debt is not concerned with the low-income countries of Africa.

Although more could be done, Europe gives valuable aid and trade support to the SADCC programme and member states. But neither Europe's trade nor its aid has been able to compensate for the particular combination of economic stresses faced by the SADCC states. The economic loss which the SADCC region has sustained as a result of destabilisation, falling investment and production levels, plunging commodity prices, and debt presents a continuing challenge to EC policy.

Most crucially, the effectiveness of the EC's support to the SADCC region is undermined by the weak and uneven implementation of EC policy on South Africa.

EC policy on South Africa

In 1985 events in South Africa were high on the international agenda. Images of escalating violence and the government's ruthless crackdown on anti-apartheid organisations were seen around the world. Throughout the European Community, there were increasing public calls for action, echoed in the European Parliament. The Community's leaders were universal in their condemnation of apartheid, but divided about the most effective action to take. A delegation of three Foreign Ministers and the Commissioner for External Relations visited South Africa at the end of August. The Troika Mission, as it became known, confirmed the need for Europe to "keep up pressure on South Africa".

Following their report, the EC Foreign Ministers agreed a Common Policy on South Africa in September 1985, which was enlarged by the European Council in 1986. The clearly stated objective of EC policy is "the complete abolition of apartheid as a whole, and not just of certain components of the system". The official communiqué pledged that the EC states "will therefore pursue their efforts until this has been achieved".[22] The EC Ministers made clear their view that a negotiated settlement should be pursued, and that this would be possible only if the South African government engaged in genuine dialogue with the representatives of the disenfranchised black population. They called on the South African government to implement certain specific measures immediately, in order to make negotiations possible. These were:

— the lifting of the State of Emergency;

— the immediate and unconditional release of Nelson Mandela and other political prisoners;

— the end of detentions without trial and forced relocations;

— a firm commitment to end apartheid and to dismantle discriminatory legislation, particularly the pass laws and the Group Areas Act.

In June 1986, an extra condition was added to this list: the unbanning of the ANC, the Pan-Africanist Congress (PAC), and other political parties.[23]

The EC sought to push the South African government towards its objectives by adopting a 'dual-track' approach. A limited range of restrictive measures was coupled with a number of 'positive measures' including the Special Programme for the Victims of Apartheid.

The restrictive measures adopted were:

— a rigorous imposition of the UN arms embargo;

— a refusal to cooperate in the military sphere, the withdrawal of military attachés from South Africa, and the refusal to grant accreditation to military attachés from South Africa;

— the discouragement of cultural, scientific and sporting links;

— a ban on oil exports to South Africa;

— a ban on exports of security equipment;

— a ban on any new collaboration in the nuclear sector.

In September 1986 further restrictive measures were agreed, imposing a ban on imports of iron and steel products and gold coins, and a ban on new investment in South Africa. However, no agreement was reached on banning imports of South African coal.[24]

The positive measures were:

— a programme of assistance to non-violent anti-apartheid organisations, particularly the churches;

— increased EC support for 'non-white' education;

— more contacts with the 'non-white' community in the political, trade union, business and other sectors;

— a strengthening of the 'code of conduct' for European firms operating in South Africa;

— a programme to increase awareness among the citizens of member States resident in South Africa;

— increased aid to SADCC and the Front Line States.

The EC presented the restrictive and positive measures as a combined package, accepting the view of anti-apartheid organisations inside South Africa. The churches, trade unions and other organisations, backed by

European voluntary agencies working in South Africa, have consistently reinforced this position during the lifetime of the Common Policy. As the Reverend Frank Chikane, General Secretary of the South African Council of Churches, told the SACC conference in 1989,

> For us ... there is a difference between helping us to be prepared for the future and assisting us to eliminate the system. The positive measures therefore cannot be used as an alternative to the restrictive measures. The restrictive measures in fact are of vital importance to force the regime to abandon apartheid and to participate in a process of negotiation to establish a new, non-racial, democratic South Africa. [25]

The EC has made it clear that the Common Policy will be reviewed in the light of developments inside South Africa. According to the September 1985 policy statement,

> The question of other measures, including sanctions, remains. As the Ten, together with Spain and Portugal, stated on 22 July this year, they may have to reexamine their attitude in the absence of significant progress within a reasonable period, and they will assess the situation regularly.[26]

Implementation of the dual-track policy

Thus the EC's policy on South Africa has a clearly stated goal (the end of apartheid), a clear vision of the fact that negotiations are the best strategy towards that goal, and a set of clearly defined measures geared to promoting movement towards its goal. Since by the end of 1989 there had been no policy statement from the European Council of Ministers to supersede those made in 1985 and 1986, formal policy remained unaltered, with its goal of the "complete abolition of apartheid as a whole".

However, although positive measures have since been increased, there has been no agreement to adopt increased restrictive measures between September 1986 and December 1989, despite the subsequent intensification of state repression, and despite the fact that some of the "immediate steps" which the EC laid down in 1985 to hasten negotiations had not been taken.

The effective freeze on EC restrictive measures reflected the central disagreement between EC members on the issue. Regardless of developments, the UK, West Germany, and Portugal remained firmly opposed to any additional restrictive measures. Their position paralysed common agreement within the Community on the issue of increased pressure, and undermined the terms on which the Special Programme was agreed with the South African partner organisations. As the key conclusion of the European Parliament's 1987 'Report on the Implementation of EC Restrictive Measures against South Africa' stated:

> Closer scrutiny of the sanctions announced by the Foreign Ministers of the

Twelve and of the legislation and administrative measures the member states have used to implement them reveals the symbolic nature of the measures, which are designed to placate a broad body of public opinion without actually satisfying its demands. The number of gaps and loopholes described gives rise to the suspicion that either effective sanctions were never the intention or the Foreign Ministers could not agree on them.[27]

As a result of differences between the member states, positive measures were effectively uncoupled from restrictive measures. In spite of the freeze on restrictive measures, positive measures were increased both in terms of the resources allocated to them, and in the way that official statements frequently highlighted them and diminished the role of restrictive measures.[28] The differences in the EC Development Commission's statements at three successive annual SADCC conferences illustrate the prominence which positive measures have been given. In 1987, the EC's Commissioner for Development had this to say about South Africa:

> Since 1985, the South African government cannot have doubted for one moment that the Community would adopt further restrictive measures if no progress was made towards dialogue at national level. And indeed such measures were adopted in September last year.[29]

In 1988, however, a very different interpretation of the Community's policy was given by the Director General for Development in the Commission:

> The restrictive measures against South Africa introduced in 1986 are mainly to be implemented by the EEC member states on a bilateral basis. The Community has concentrated instead on the implementation of a series of positive measures directed towards the situation in South Africa and towards the situation in the southern African region.[30]

And, in 1989, the new Development Commissioner made no reference whatever to restrictive measures in his statement. He said:

> I take this occasion to repeat that the European Community condemns both the apartheid system and South Africa's policy of destabilisation. The European Community has not confined itself to verbal condemnation. For some time now, it has been running a Special Programme of Assistance for the victims of apartheid in South Africa and Namibia, which today covers 222 projects. The special programmes which are fully supported by the EEC member states and the European Parliament will continue.[31]

This emerging emphasis on positive measures as the preferable alternative to restrictive measures runs counter to the grounds on which the EC's South African partner organisations accepted the Special Programme.

In mid-1988 a senior delegation of South African church leaders travelled to Europe in a bid to persuade EC member states that developments inside South Africa had deteriorated to the point where increased EC restrictive measures should be adopted, but they were unsuccessful.

In July 1989, at a conference of the South African Council of Churches, Frank Chikane urged the EC to return to the dual-track policy by strengthening its restrictive measures. He explained:

> Our major concern is that the European Community seems to be using the Special Programme as an excuse for not taking action at a level of economic pressure.[32]

The EC is in the uncomfortable position of having, as a central plank of its policy on southern Africa, an aid programme for partners who are highly critical of their uneven policy implementation. The South African partners face the dilemma of whether to refuse much-needed funds because they believe the Special Programme offers European governments a cheap means of protecting their economic interests from increased sanctions.

The political value of the EC Special Programme is particularly significant to Britain. While the British contribution to the EC Special Programme (£3 m. from 1986 to January 1989[33]) is smaller in monetary terms than Britain's own bilateral aid programme to South Africans (which totalled £13.5 m. over the same period[34]), it none the less assumes great political importance, because it is part of a common European political position on South Africa — an area of policy in which the UK is otherwise internationally isolated.

The EC Special Programme for the Victims of Apartheid

Since its inception in 1986, the European Special Programme for the Victims of Apartheid has disbursed a total of nearly 95 m. ECU (£60.8 m.) to educational, community, and health projects in South Africa.[35] In 1988 more than 100 projects received funding from the Special Programme. Many of these projects are the same as those which Oxfam and other non-governmental agencies have supported in South Africa for many years, and others are very similar. The funds involved are substantial, and they support vital work; for instance, there has been less call on Oxfam's hard-pressed resources to support legal advice offices in recent years, because many now receive EC funds.

But the Special Programme has assumed much wider significance than this, because it is perceived by some EC states as an alternative policy instrument to sanctions. Consequently, it is the parties most closely involved — the partner organisations in South Africa and the voluntary agencies in Europe who channel the funds — who have tried to balance the prominence given to the Special Programme, and place it once more in the context of the

EC's Common Policy, aimed at the complete abolition of apartheid.

How the Special Programme works

There are four channels in South Africa which can propose projects for funding: the South African Council of Churches (SACC), the Southern Africa Catholic Bishops' Conference (SACBC), the trades unions, and the Kagiso Trust (KT). While for the first three, channelling Special Programme grants is only a small part of their everyday work, the KT was established specifically as an umbrella body for secular projects supported by the Special Programme. In 1989 nearly 65 per cent of the Special Programme's funds were channelled through the KT, which has become a central pillar of the Special Programme.

The SACC, the SACBC, and the KT each have a partner body in Europe, made up respectively of Protestant, Catholic, and secular agencies which, because of their experience of working in South Africa, are well placed to act as the link between their South African partners and the European Commission.

The partner organisation to the Kagiso Trust is the South Africa and Namibia Association (SANAM), of which Oxfam is a founder member.[36] Within the European Commission, the Special Programme is the responsibility of the Development Commissioner, who has appointed a 'Committee of Experts' to oversee project allocations.

The Special Programme prescribes strict criteria governing how EC funds may be used. Firstly, funds for South Africa must go through one of the three designated South African organisations, or the trade unions. Secondly, no funds are to go to the South African government's programmes, or to activities which government should be expected to pay for, such as formal schooling and hospital services. No funds are to go to institutions formally associated with the 'homelands', and no funds should be made available to political parties. Thirdly, projects must meet the following criteria:

— they should promote non-racialism, and seek to unite people of different cultural, racial and ethnic backgrounds;

— they should enjoy the support of the communities in which they are based;

— they should be run democratically, with the fullest possible participation of the beneficiaries;

— they should educate and raise awareness in ways which contribute to the process of liberation.

In short, the Special Programme's working principles mean that it is not a charity for passive victims. Its aim is not to make life under apartheid more

Queues for water at Onvervacht, South Africa, an impoverished `dumping ground' set aside for people forcibly removed from their homes under the apartheid system. Oxfam supports a range of communities and organisations fighting forced removals.

(Nancy Durrell-McKenna/Oxfam)

bearable; rather it is one level of support to those working to abolish apartheid and replace it with a unified, non-racial, democratic South Africa.

As well as being a member of the SANAM Association, which helped the South African partner organisations to negotiate the strict funding guidelines under which EC support is administered, Oxfam is directly supporting many of the organisations in South Africa which also receive EC support.

Harassment and repression of the EC's South African partners

The operation of the EC Special Programme illustrates the repressive political context in which the Community's South African partners have to work, and shows how difficult it has been for an aid programme, uncoupled from a political programme, to achieve positive results.

The chronicle of harassment suffered by those administering funds through the Kagiso Trust illustrates only one aspect of the difficulties facing the Special Programme. It is entirely consistent with Oxfam's wider experience of the effects of repression on organisations working for a peaceful transition from apartheid to full democracy.

October 1986	Detention of Joyce Mabudafuzi, Kagiso Trust Regional Trustee in Transvaal.
December 1986	Detention overnight of Kagiso Trust Director.
January 1987	Police raid on KT's offices. Files removed and copied.
March 1987	"Inspection" of Resources and Advice Centre in Oudtshoorn by police, leading to investigation of KT funding.
August 1987	Bombing of COSATU offices in Cape Town.
October 1987	Ransacking of Detainees' Parents' Support Committee (DPSC) in Kimberley.
December 1987	Arrest of Eric Molobi, KT Trustee and founder of National Education Crisis Committee.
	Khotso Crutze, KT fieldworker in Transvaal, detained for five months.
February 1988	Official restriction of DPSC and 16 other organisations; protests by church leaders Archbishop Tutu, the Reverend Allan Boesak, and the Reverend Frank Chikane lead to their arrest.
March 1988	Announcement of the Promotion of Orderly Internal Politics Bill, proposing severe restrictions on overseas funding of anti-apartheid organisations
May 1988	*South* newspaper closed down.
August 1988	Khotso House, HQ of South African Council of Churches, bombed.
	KT Natal Regional Committee members questioned by police.
September 1988	KT offices in Johannesburg and Western Cape visited by police.
October 1988	SACBC office in Pretoria fire-bombed.
	Restriction order on Yunus Mohammed, KT Trustee.
November 1988	Police raid on KT offices in Johannesburg; project information confiscated.
January 1989	KT offices in Johannesburg raided by security police.
March 1989	Durban: KT Regional Projects Officer detained for questioning, keys confiscated; police illegally enter offices at night.
	False obituary notice for Yunus Mohammed in newspaper.
	Agency worker questioned by security police about European Scholarship Bursary Programme.
	KT Director given restricted passport for six months only.
June 1989	Poisoning of Frank Chikane, General Secretary of South African Council of Churches.
August 1989	Disclosure of Foreign Funding Act, to restrict foreign support for extra-parliamentary opposition, becomes law.
September 1989	South African government announces its intention to declare the KT a 'reporting organisation' under the terms of the Foreign Funding Act. KT appeals; no response as at the end of 1989.

*Cornfields, Kwa Zulu: Bongi Nene, a paralegal advice worker in the Natal region,
listens to a client whose goats have been confiscated by the manager of a nearby
white, commercial farm.*   (Rona Alexander / Oxfam)

It became virtually impossible for the 'positive measures' approach of the
EC Special Programme to lead to positive results when the State of
Emergency was tightened in 1988, with the restriction of 34 organisations in
two waves. A spokesperson for the Black Sash, a prominent anti-apartheid
organisation, concluded,

> Banning people, breaking organisations and silencing opposition does not
> guarantee submission — instead this creates divisions, hampers political
> education and discussion, and lays the foundations for increased frustration
> and violence.

Sir Geoffrey Howe, then British Foreign Secretary, declared that Pretoria's
action could lead to frustration, despair, and violence, and that it amounted to
"the suppression of non-violent activity".[37]

Cutting the lifelines

Community and development organisations working for change in South
Africa often rely on funding from outside the country. For some time they
have faced an increased threat that this funding will be blocked by the
government. The introduction of the Promotion of Orderly Internal Politics
Bill in February 1988 provided for a total ban on overseas funds for 'political
activities', a term which, in the South African context of repression, could be

Community leaders from Leeuwfontein and Braklaagte protest against their enforced incorporation into the 'homeland' of Bophuthatswana, February 1989. Oxfam provides support through the National Campaign Against Removals in South Africa, and by publicising their cause in the UK.

(Gill de Vlieg/Afrapix)

applied to much of the work funded by the EC Special Programme.

South African organisations, their partner NGOs in Europe, the European Commission, MEPs, and member state governments roundly condemned the proposals. A delegation of South African church leaders visited Foreign Ministers and EC officials to press their case for tough measures against South Africa should the Bill become law. International protest was credited with playing a large part in the South African government's decision to drop the Bill. But similar legislation — the Disclosure of Foreign Funding Bill — subsequently became law in August 1989, and no increased restrictive measures were adopted by the EC, although the Community did make a strong official protest.[38]

The British Foreign Office believed the new Bill to be a "considerable improvement on an already watered down Bill", in part due to the British Embassy's "frequent and direct" discussions on the issue with members of the South African Parliamentary Committee considering the Bill.[39] Yet one month after the Bill became law, the Kagiso Trust was among the first organisations to be singled out, when the South African government announced its intention to declare it a 'reporting organisation' under the new

Act, at a time when Mr de Klerk was promising significant movement towards negotiations.

With this move, the South African Government directly threatened the EC's Special Programme, and the ability of key democratic organisations to function. It highlights the futility of a policy which concentrates on aid to the victims of apartheid.

In a letter smuggled out from prison in January 1989, Eric Molobi of the National Education Crisis Committee, one of the organisations funded by the EC, summed up the senseless nature of the repression. He wrote:

> Around me there are many youngsters. Some have been here for over a year. I would like the EEC, the European Parliament and others to know that I am detained not for any unlawful act I have committed, but simply because I belong to an organisation which has stated on numerous occasions its opposition to Bantu education as a system of education ...

> My organisation is one that actually pressed for discussions with the Department of Education. Today, the South African government says, for media and overseas consumption, that it wants to talk. How can they talk to prisoners and detained persons? Are they not burning bridges by tormenting young black South Africans through detention without trial, through letting them rot under inhuman conditions?[40]

Section IV
Conclusions

Summary and key considerations

Development for the poorest in southern Africa is impeded by apartheid in South Africa, by the unjust economic relationship between the SADCC region and the industrialised North, and by the conspicuous failure of key SADCC governments to promote equitable development strategies. Throughout the 1980s, this combination of factors has resulted in brutal conflict, sharp economic decline, and increasing levels of poverty.

The key to a brighter future for the region lies in South Africa, where accumulated pressure on apartheid has resulted in an important shift in the National Party's outlook.

The end of apartheid and the establishment of democracy in South Africa would remove a central cause of regional instability. Furthermore, positive economic cooperation with a post-apartheid South Africa could boost the whole region's prospects for sustainable economic development.

However, all this is far from assured. South Africa is in a period of flux, and whether apartheid is abolished and replaced by democracy is a matter of history in the making. Much depends on the mainstream popular movement for a non-racial democracy and the international support it receives. If serious negotiations take place, the South African government will concede as little as it can, but as much as it has to. As the Commonwealth's 1989 Kuala Lumpur communiqué stated, the purpose of sanctions was the "pressure they created for fundamental political change. Their purpose was not punitive, but to abolish apartheid by bringing Pretoria to the negotiating table and keeping it there until that change was irreversibly secured".

The South African government has taken some important initial steps towards creating a political climate in which formal talks can take place, but (at the end of 1989) it is clear that more remains to be done before extra-parliamentary opposition can operate freely and before proper negotiations can begin.   Only then can work start on the central task of negotiating democracy in place of apartheid.   And only when substantial achievements are made on that front will it be possible to judge that change has indeed been 'irreversibly secured'.

International cooperation on a common strategy to end apartheid is essential.   During the 1980s, disagreement over sanctions has divided the Western nations, and reduced their potential for leverage.   A stalemate has grown up in place of a coordinated international approach.   Dispute over means has blocked effective action towards ends.   Now that the entire UN General Assembly has reached agreement on the steps which must be taken to create a suitable climate for negotiations, on the constitutional guidelines needed to establish a non-racial democracy in a unitary state, and on the need to maintain pressure on the South African government in pursuit of these objectives, there should be sufficient common ground for improved international cooperation.   The challenge facing the international community is that of summoning the collective political will to remove the remaining obstacles to democracy in South Africa.   The 1990s offer an unprecedented opportunity for international leverage.

In addition to the devastating economic consequences of South Africa's regional policy during the 1980s, the SADCC states also shoulder crippling burdens which have largely arisen as a result of economic trends in the industrialised North.   These external economic shocks, and the inability of key SADCC states to adjust to them, have seriously undermined development, creating a bleak future for the majority of the region's people. Development policy errors and failures within the SADCC states have also harmed the poor. Far-reaching measures on a number of fronts are needed.

Oxfam believes that the sheer scale of human suffering in southern Africa, and the opportunity which currently exists for international leverage demand a renewed international initiative.   Britain, the European Community, and the SADCC states all have a major role to play.   Britain is particularly involved in southern Africa's past, present, and future.   This involvement confers a strong obligation on the British government towards the people of the whole region, an obligation which, from Oxfam's perspective, is not recognised in present British policy.   More must be done, both to support the South African people's struggle for a non-racial democracy, and to promote the conditions for an assault on poverty throughout the region.

Key considerations

On hastening the abolition of apartheid and its replacement by democracy

Oxfam urges the British Government to:

● *Engage publicly with the MDM/ANC alliance*, recognising that it represents the major force for non-racial democracy in South Africa.

● *Maintain, rather than relax, pressure on the South African government.* Britain must honour the policy commitments it has entered into with the Commonwealth, European Community, and United Nations General Assembly, until the objectives of those agreements are secured.

● *Formulate British policy in a multilateral spirit*, so that it does not undermine other nations' efforts.

Oxfam calls on the European Community to take a number of steps:

● The EC must recognise that the South African people, including its partners in the Special Programme — the churches, the trade unions, and the community organisations — need more than aid if they are to win their struggle for a non-racial democracy. Differences between member states on the issue of sanctions have been reflected in the uneven implementation of the EC's 'dual-track' policy. Positive measures have effectively become uncoupled from restrictive ones. Yet international sanctions have proved to be a useful policy tool. They have played an important role in facilitating the process of initial change in South Africa. In practice as well as in official statements, there must be *a renewed, common commitment to the 'dual-track' nature of EC policy.*

● To keep up the pressure on apartheid, the emphasis on the 'positive measures' dimension of EC policy should be matched by maintaining and better enforcing the EC's programme of targetted sanctions. A number of specific measures should urgently be considered, which include:

— *The introduction of appropriate legal controls within the EC member states to strengthen and enforce existing measures.* In particular, the voluntary ban on new investment in South Africa should be made statutory, and redefined to cover the reinvestment of profits and the purchase of existing South African assets. Also, the statutory arms embargo (a UN Security Council sanction[1]) must be more rigorously controlled so that 'dual-purpose' goods and equipment do not reach South Africa. Further, the oil embargo (a non-statutory UN sanction[2]) should be backed up by enforcement legislation, and its terms should be extended to prevent shipping companies from delivering to South Africa.

— *A compulsory, blanket ban on the export of 'high-tech' and computer equipment.* The EC's existing ban on "the export of sensitive equipment destined for the police and armed forces of South Africa"[3] is not sufficient to prevent the government's apparatus of repression from gaining access to modern equipment. Computers and other 'high-tech' equipment which can be used for communications and surveillance are available from only a limited number of sources. Very few countries have the technology to manufacture this equipment, and South Africa is wholly dependent on imported supplies.

● If the momentum of progress towards the aims of the Harare Declaration falters, increased measures should be urgently considered. These should include:

— *A compulsory ban on all new loans, trade credits, and export credit guarantees.* For the time being, banks are not offering new loans, on the grounds that South Africa is a bad commercial risk, but trade credit is freely available and the British government, for example, encourages this form of lending through its export credit guarantee facility. The immorality of lending to apartheid will not therefore inhibit future lending unless loans are legally prohibited. Banks and finance companies should be actively discouraged from making new loans and trade credit available to South Africa, from operating revolving lines of credit, and from making further debt-rescheduling agreements. Governments should stop extending trade credits and export credit guarantees.

— *A compulsory ban on the import of coal and agricultural products.* Coal is South Africa's second largest export earner. Attempts in 1986 to establish an EC coal sanction were vetoed by West Germany, but some EC members have instituted their own coal boycotts. Their efforts would be greatly strengthened by a compulsory, Community-wide ban. Agricultural products are South Africa's fifth largest export earner, and have long been a target of consumer boycotts. Continuing imports into the EC undermine the ban imposed by other countries, including the USA, Ireland, the Nordic States, and the majority of Commonwealth countries (excluding Britain).

— *An end to all promotion of trade and tourism to South Africa, and a suspension of air links.*

— *An urgent examination of the possibility of a ban on gold exports from South Africa.* Gold is South Africa's largest export earner, accounting for some 40 per cent of total export revenue. The USA has taken the lead in applying a sanction against gold, and the EC should consider following suit.

● *Policy to maintain pressure on the South African government must be coordinated among all South Africa's economic partners,* especially with the nations of the G7 grouping, the UN Security Council, the Commonwealth, the ASEAN bloc, and Israel.

On helping the victims of conflict

● To give practical support to the initiatives for resolving conflict in Mozambique and Angola, and to end the terrible brutality suffered by civilians, there must be *a coordinated international policy to halt all military aid to the MNR and UNITA.* The EC could take a useful lead.

● To help the Mozambique refugees in South Africa, *the EC should urge the South African government to accord all refugees their full legal rights, and immediately stop forced repatriation.* If the South African government persists in its refusal to allow UNHCR to operate, then the EC should arrange for a special European commission to protect the refugees' rights. Further, the EC should press the South African government to dismantle the electrified fence along its border with Mozambique immediately.

● *More aid is needed for the victims of conflict.* In particular, the Mozambican and Angolan refugees and displaced people need more food and basic provisions. More resources should also be devoted to their longer-term social development needs, especially for those living in the crowded Zimbabwean and Malawian settlements with limited employment opportunities, and no access to land. More aid is also needed for children who have been traumatised by brutality, for the war-disabled, and for the people who have drifted into urban destitution as a result of the rural breakdown which war has caused.

● In the longer term, once conflict is resolved, *generous aid pledges for post-war reconstruction in Angola and Mozambique will be needed.*

On helping the SADCC states to strengthen their economies

● *Aid to compensate for destabilisation:* It has been estimated[4] that the SADCC region would need an injection of at least $2.5 bn. a year over four years in order to repair the economic damage created by destabilisation. Less than half of this amount is currently being provided. The international community must do much more.

● *External debt cancellation*: Among the SADCC region's creditors, there must be greater appreciation of the devastating economic costs of South Africa's regional policy during the 1980s. Now that the region faces the costs of reconstruction and economic reintegration, and given the urgent need for continuing emergency relief and development, special consideration should be given to the debt-distressed SADCC nations, Angola, Malawi, Mozambique, Tanzania, Zambia, and Zimbabwe. SADCC itself could do more to communicate these needs.

If the debt-distressed SADCC countries are to achieve sustainable economic growth and tackle poverty, their external debts must be cancelled outright. Among its member states and beyond, the EC should press for a number of immediate steps towards this goal:

— *Bilateral debt:* All creditor countries should cancel their aid debts. As regards non-concessional bilateral debt, a large proportion of which is export-credit debt, the Toronto Accord should be strengthened, and viewed as a first step towards the early cancellation of all bilateral debt.

— *Multilateral debt:* The EC should use its influence with SADCC's major multilateral creditors, the IMF and the World Bank, to press firstly for more concessional funds through the IMF's Enhanced Structural Adjustment Facility, and the World Bank's International Development Assistance facility, and then for a cancellation of all multilateral debt.

— *Commercial debt*: The repayment terms for commercial debt are particularly crippling. For example, Mozambique's annual commercial debt servicing consumes half its total export earnings. The EC should act immediately to promote a coordinated, mandatory debt-reduction programme. Commercial banks should be required to undertake immediate debt and debt-service reduction for all the debt-distressed SADCC states.

Some governments allow commercial banks tax relief on the provisions they set aside to safeguard themselves against debtor default. (In 1988, the British government allocated more money for tax relief on provisions for the four leading British banks than it did for its total bilateral aid programme to the Third World.[5]) However, in Britain, no measures have been taken to encourage the banks to use these provisions to reduce poor countries' debts. In Belgium, by contrast, the government does not allow such tax relief until an actual debt write-off or reduction is agreed by the bank. EC member states could significantly reduce the SADCC states' debt burden by insisting that a time limit is set, say of two years, by which time banks' provisions should be used for debt reduction or substantial interest rate relief, failing which, the tax relief would be clawed back.

On the SADCC region's deteriorating terms of trade

The economic relationship of the industrial North with the commodity-dependent South is fundamentally unequal, so although some palliative measures can help to a limited extent, real improvements depend on fundamental change.

The SADCC region's best hope lies in its proposals for regional economic integration, which could strengthen its productive base, realise its regional and export-trade potential, and give it greater bargaining power in the world's market place. In this respect, a majority-ruled South Africa could be a great asset to the wider region.

● *The EC should ensure that the advent of the Single European Market in 1992, and the new GATT global trading arrangements for the 1990s do not prejudice the precarious economic situation of its partner states in Africa, the Caribbean, and the Pacific, including the SADCC states.*

— Given the need to protect and develop the fragile export base of poor countries and to encourage their economic diversification, the EC should ensure *continued market access, more stable pricing of commodities, and the removal of protectionist market obstacles to the diversification of the region's productive base.*

— Given that the South will remain dependent on primary commodities for the foreseeable future, priority should be given to *funding research aimed at developing new uses for primary commodities.*

— *Investment in production*, rather than extraction, is a key SADCC initiative which *should be generously supported by EC governments and the private sector.* However, the unattractive investment climate, largely created by conflict and the economic decline it has aggravated, requires lasting political solutions.

— In line with UNCTAD's 'Common Fund' proposals, ways must be found for Third World countries, including the SADCC states, to participate more fully in the processing, marketing, and distribution of commodities — a domain dominated by Northern transnational companies.

On helping the SADCC region to adjust to changing global economic trends

The existing economic adjustment programmes being undertaken by the debt-distressed SADCC states, whether sponsored by the IMF and the World Bank or not, cannot overcome all the long-term constraints which have led to crisis in the first place, since many of these originated in the North. Furthermore, as with international debt-reduction policy, the structural adjustment model prescribed by the IMF and the World Bank lacks an appropriate regional perspective on the economic stress of destabilisation. At the very least, the EC should use its influence in the IMF and the World Bank to improve the terms of internationally-sponsored adjustment programmes.

● SADCC governments and Northern donors alike should adopt *a common strategy to ensure that nutrition, health service, and education imbalances are taken as seriously as fiscal and external account imbalances* and that raising the incomes of households below the absolute poverty line is given as high a priority as raising GDP and exports.

● *More aid should be made available for the development of essential social services in the debt-distressed SADCC countries.*

● Most importantly, structural adjustment programmes typically maintain the existing structures of debt-distressed countries' economic dependence on the North by promoting the production of primary commodities for export and perpetuating the unjust North/South trading relationships. Instead, *SADCC's plans for regional economic integration and industrialisation to boost production and trade should be supported by the international community, private and official.*

● In the long term, however, merely 'adjusting' to each new wave of adverse economic pressure will never enable poor countries to sustain sufficient economic growth for their development needs. *Far more radical changes in the North and South are needed.*

Promoting development in the interests of the poorest

In the storm of international outrage over South Africa's regional aggression, the fact that ruling elites within the SADCC states pursue their own interests at the expense of the poor has often been overlooked. It follows that the end of apartheid, the resolution of conflict, and the adoption of more appropriate international aid and trade policies are necessary, but not sufficient, to promote development in the interests of the poorest. A wide range of radical changes also need to be adopted by key SADCC states:

● As the SADCC states move towards a more integrated production and trading bloc, the governments and non-government institutions of the SADCC region must ensure that social equity is promoted through *the full participation of people in the production process and in every important sphere which affects their future well-being.*

● Where land shortage is creating problems for the poor, urgent priority must be given to *land reform.*

● *A more open and democratic social culture is needed,* whereby greater checks and balances create more accountability and responsiveness at all levels of government.

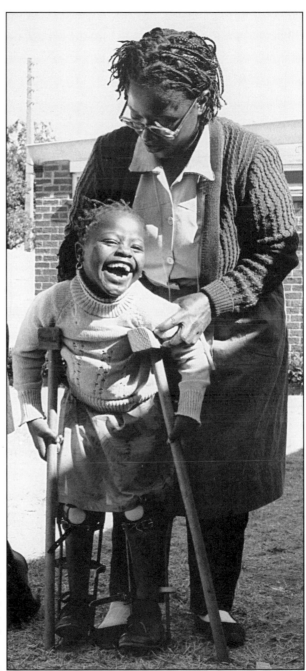

*Glenview Clinic,
Harare: reaping the
benefit of the Zimbabwe
government's extensive
investment in basic
services since
independence.*

(Chris Johnson/Oxfam)

Notes

Chapter 1

1. *Nyerere - Freedom and Unity (Na Umoja): A Selection From Writings and Speeches 1952—1965*, volume 1, Oxford University Press, Dar es Salaam, 1966, pp. 108-113.

2. The South African 'homelands' or bantustans are areas of (usually inferior) land set aside for black people to live on. They are based on what used to be called the 'native reserves', as formally constituted under the 1913 Natives Land Act, which restricted black people's right to acquire land legally to only 13 per cent of the country's land area. Following the National Party's accession to power in 1948, when apartheid was introduced as an extension of the former segregationist policies, the 'reserves' became an important basis for the apartheid concept that black South Africans do not really share a common national identity. Rather, it is held, "Throughout its history, South Africa has been a geographic designation rather than a reflection of a national unity. ... There is no basis for the common perception that South Africa's black population is a homogenous mass of individuals who could pass for Europeans but for the colour of their skins. In fact, they comprise nine major ethnic groups, each with its own cultural identity, including language ... Today the traditional territories of those Black peoples (or sections of peoples) ... are being developed and consolidated into cohesive geopolitical bases or national states as far as possible." ("Profile: population", a leaflet published by the Bureau for Information, Pretoria, distributed by the South African embassy in London in 1988.) Despite the lack of international recognition for the 'independent homelands' and the *de facto* demographic erosion of this classical notion of apartheid, this construct has enabled 'white' South Africa to be the place for 'white' citizens, thus maintaining white political and economic supremacy. It remains relevant to the current contention over 'group rights' of any sort being a part of a future South Africa.

3. Excerpts from a speech by General Magnus Malan, 3.9.80., cited by D. Geldenhuys, *The Diplomacy of Isolation: South African Foreign Policy Making*, Macmillan South Africa, Johannesburg, 1984, p.209.

4. Republic of South Africa, White Paper on Defence, 1977, Pretoria, p. 5.

5. "South Africa's Regional Policy - Regional Cooperation: The Record and Outlook", D. Geldenhuys, paper to the South African Institute of International Affairs' Golden Jubilee Conference, Cape Town, March 1984, pp. 19-22; "Total Strategy in Southern Africa: An Analysis of South African Regional Policy since 1978", R. Davies and D. O'Meara, *Journal of Southern African Studies*, Vol. 11 No. 2, April 1985, pp. 196-7; *The Diplomacy of Isolation*, Geldenhuys, op. cit., pp. 41, 103-4.

6. Davies and O'Meara, op. cit., pp. 197-8; Geldenhuys, "South Africa's Regional Policy", op.

cit., p. 24.

7. Beyers Naude, a leading UDF cleric, explained this view of the 'cycle of violence' in January 1989 to an Oxfam staff meeting, shortly after 32 anti-apartheid organisations had been restricted. He said, "Fully legitimate, peaceful forms of opposition against an undemocratic, criminal system are the target of repression. Some organisations have stopped operating, others have gone underground. Seeing how one form of peaceful action after another is being outlawed, people have increasingly come to believe that violent opposition is the only option left. You see, although state repression had affected the activities of opposition organisations, it has made no difference to people's commitment to end apartheid."

8. "Political Conflict in South Africa: Data trends 1984-1988", Indicator Project South Africa, University of Natal, South Africa, December 1988, p. 14.

9. Ibid.

10. Ibid, p. 93; *New Nation*, South Africa, 22-30.3.89.

11. "Race Relations Survey 1987/88", South African Institute of Race Relations, Johannesburg, 1988, pp. 817-30 lists all the restrictions introduced during 1986 and 1987, and details their implementation.

12. Excerpts from the White Paper on Defence and Armaments Supply 1986, Republic of South Africa, Department of Defence, 1986, p. 14.

13. See, for example, International Defence and Aid reports.

14. Interview with Oxfam fieldworker, 5 June 1989.

15. The nature of conflict in Natal, and Inkatha's role in South African politics, are complex areas of specialist study. For a range of views, see an interview with Chief Buthelezi in *Leadership* magazine's special edition on "Sanctions", 1988/89, pp. 102-4; *An Appetite for Power: Buthelezi's Inkatha and South Africa*, G. Mare and G. Hamilton, Ravan Press, Johannesburg, 1987; "Violence in Natal/Kwazulu: Results and Conclusions from a Survey of Residents of Durban", M. Sutcliffe, IDASA research report, South Africa, 1989; *and Gatsha Buthelezi: Chief with a Double Agenda*, Mzala, Zed Books, London, 1988.

16. Excerpts from a talk given by Alex Mbatha to Oxfam staff, Oxford, 17.11.82.

17. Excerpt from General Malan's preface to the White Paper on Defence and Armaments Supply 1986, Republic of South Africa, Department of Defence, 1986, p. iii.

Chapter 2

1. *Mission to South Africa - The Commonwealth Report: The Findings of the Commonwealth Eminent Persons Group on Southern Africa*, Penguin, Harmondsworth, 1986, p.126.

2. *The Diplomacy of Isolation: South African Foreign Policy Making*, D. Geldenhuys, Macmillan South Africa, Johannesburg, 1984, p. 145.

3. However, this is not to say that the military element - whether threatened or actual - will disappear over the coming, critical period. In its 1989 'Five Year Plan', the ruling National Party states that "Efficient security services are indispensable for an orderly and peaceful community, providing a sound climate for political, economic, and social development." It goes on to outline its intention to "... maintain the preparedness of the South African Defence Force in terms of both manpower and equipment to enable it to withstand internal, regional, and international threats against South Africa ..."

4. The Reverend Mcebisi Xundu, interview with author, Oxford, September 1989.

The April 1989 Commonwealth-commissioned "Independent Expert Study on the Evaluation of the Application and Impact of Sanctions" made the same point concerning the South African government's 1988 decision to concede the implementation of the UN Plan for Namibia's independence and withdraw the SADF from Angola. It stated, "After a decade of talking, negotiations became serious when Pretoria was under pressure. Thus sanctions were an essential part of the negotiations process, not an alternative to it." ("Final report to the Commonwealth Committee of Foreign Ministers on Southern Africa", Commonwealth Secretariat, London, p.2.)

5. *Africa Confidential*, 20.1.89, vol. 30 no. 2; 17.3.89, vol 30, no. 6; *Financial Times* 9.1.89; *Independent* 19.8.89, 24.89; *Daily Telegraph* 17.8.89.

6. *SouthScan*, vol. 4, No. 11, l5 March 1989. In point of fact, Mr Botha must have been referring to workers from the 'homelands', since there are few workers in the coal industry from outside South Africa. (Personal communication from Professor Green, August 1989.)

7. *SouthScan*, vol 4, no. 11, 15 March 1989.

8. Excerpt from "British Policy Towards South Africa", FCO paper, 1988.

9. Southern African Fact Sheet no. 97, July 1987, published by Southern African Editorial Services CC, Sandton, South Africa.

10. *Independent*, 9.2.89.

11. Ibid.

12. See the National Party's Five Year Plan. The political significance, of course, is that the essence of apartheid would remain, because 'white' South Africans would be able to retain a disproportionate share of political and economic power.

As far as protecting democratic rights is concerned, the ANC has proposed a Bill of Rights.

13. Excerpt from Thabo Mbeki's speech to the Southern Africa Coalition, London, 13.10.89.

14. See, for example, *Front File*, Southern Africa Brief, August extra 1989, vol. 3 No. 11.

15. Lynda Chalker, then Minister at the Foreign and Commonwealth Office with special responsibility for southern Africa, at the British Council of Churches London conference, February 1989.

16. For a fuller explanation of the National Security Management System, see: D. Geldenhuys, *The Diplomacy of Isolation*, op. cit., p 140; "The Power and Limits of the Emergency State", M. Swilling and M. Phillips, Centre for Policy Studies, University of Witwatersrand, paper given to the University of York Centre for Southern African Studies Research Seminar series, 1988/89; and "The Big Chill: From Reform to Counter-Revolution", M. Swilling, an article in "Political Conflict in South Africa: Data trends 1984-1988", Indicator Project South Africa, University of Natal, December 1988, pp. 92-4.

17. *Independent, Financial Times*, 29.11.89.

18. See, for example, "Political Economies in Conflict: SADCC and South Africa", R.H. Green and C.B. Thompson, Chapter 9 of *Destructive Engagement: Southern Africa at War*, eds. P. Johnson and D. Martin, Zimbabwe Publishing House, Harare, 1986.

19. "Mozambique and United States Policy", Hearing before the Subcommittee on African Affairs of the Committee on Foreign Relations, United States Senate, 100th congress, first session, 24.6.87.

20. Excerpt from the 1985 Nassau Commonwealth Accord on Southern Africa.

21. See, for example, J. Hanlon, *Beggar Your Neighbours*, CIIR, London, 1986, p. 252, and *Destructive Engagement*, eds P. Johnson and D. Martin, op. cit., p. 249.

22. South Africa is reported to have underwritten some $5,000 m. worth of investments in the region between 1986 and 1988. (*Work in Progress*, South Africa, June/July 1988.)

23. As clearly explained in the National Party's Five Year Plan.

24. Albeit by way of a complex offshore financing strategy which has been devised to overcome the 'problem' of official finance going to a project to benefit South Africa. (*Financial Times* 13.4.89.)

25. *Financial Times* 18.8.89; 28.8.89.

26. See *Work in Progress*, South Africa, June/July 1988.

27. Quoted in *The Southern African Economist*, April/May 1989 edition, Volume 2 no. 2. This

tallies with references made in the National Party's Five Year Plan unveiled in 1989.

28. *Resister*, Journal of the Committee on South African War Resistance, London and Amsterdam, no. 57, August/September 1988.

29. According to South African government claims.

30. "Southern Africa News and Views", quarterly publication by Quaker Peace and Service, London, October 1988.

31. However, clandestine South African support for rebel military/sabotage activities in Zambia, Zimbabwe, and Lesotho has also been reported.

In Zambia, South Africa is reported to have backed the 'Mushala Gang' during the 1970s. This was a group of bandits active in North Western Province from 1976 to 1982, when Mushala was killed by Zambian security forces. See, for example, *Kaunda and Mushala Rebellion*, P. Wele, Multimedia Publications, Lusaka, 1987, pp. 76-9.

In Zimbabwe, South Africa is reported to have exacerbated the mid-1980s 'dissident' conflict in Matabeleland, which was finally resolved following the December 1987 Unity Agreement between ZANU and ZAPU. See J. Hanlon, *Beggar Your Neighbours*, op. cit., pp. 173-83; J. Hanlon, section 4 of *Zimbabwe's Prospects*, ed. C. Stoneman, Macmillan, London, pp. 39-41; and "Zimbabwe: Apartheid's Dilemma", chapter 2 in *Destructive Engagement*, eds. P. Johnson and D. Martin, op. cit., pp. 43-72

In Lesotho, South Africa is reported to have backed the Lesotho Liberation Army which conducted a sabotage campaign against the government in the early 1980s. See, "Lesotho, Botswana, Swaziland: Captive States", R. Ajulu and D. Cammack, Chapter 5 of *Destructive Engagement*, eds. Johnson and Martin, op. cit., pp. 139-69.

32. "Principles for a Peaceful Settlement in Southwestern Africa", the official document initialled on 13.7.88 in New York by the USA, Angola, South Africa, and Cuba, which was incorporated both into the "Protocol of Brazzaville", signed on 13.12.88 by Angola, Cuba, and South Africa, and into the final "Agreement among the People's Republic of Angola, the Republic of Cuba, and the Republic of South Africa", signed on 22.12.88, at the UN in New York.

However, it has since been reported that South Africa continues to support UNITA clandestinely. See, for example, *SouthScan*, vol. 4 No. 34, 15.9.89; and the *Independent*, 13.2.89, which reported that South African forces made an incursion into Angola, reportedly to help a UNITA contingent.

33. A wide range of evidence for South African support of the MNR has been published. It consists of reports of border and airspace violations; reports of the capture of munitions, weapons, uniforms, documents, and other supplies originating from South Africa; confessions and testimonies from captured and defected MNR combatants; reports on the monitoring of radio transmissions   between South Africa and the MNR; eyewitness accounts; and international intelligence findings as reported by government spokespeople.

34. That is when the 'Gorongosa Diaries', which proved direct South African government support for the MNR in contravention of the 1984 Nkomati Accord, were discovered when the MNR's HQ at Gorongosa in Mozambique's Sofala Province were captured by Zimbabwean and Mozambican troops

'Casa Banana', the MNR's isolated mountain HQ, provided a base from which to attack the Beira corridor and to move northwards, cutting the rail link to Malawi and the road to Tete Province. The documents seized there revealed details of South African violations of the Nkomati Accord, including continued training, supply and direction of the MNR. They detailed South African air drops, the transmission of orders and strategies from the South African military, and visits to MNR bases in Mozambique by senior South African military officials and politicians, including the deputy Foreign Affairs Minister, Louis Nel.

The Gorongosa documents have been reproduced and published by the Mozambican government. See also MIO (Mozambican Information Office) News Review No. 62 October

1985, and *Destructive Engagement*, eds Johnson and Martin, op. cit., pp. 36-8.

35. Letter from the South African Embassy, London, to Oxfam's Director, dated 28.7.87.

36. "Mozambique and United States Policy", Hearing before the Subcommittee on African Affairs of the Committee on Foreign Relations, United States Senate, 100th Congress, first session, 24.6.87.

37. Reported to have been mediated through the British Ambassador to South Africa. (*Weekly Mail*, 24.3.89; *Herald Tribune*, 24.3.89.)

38. *Independent*, 13.9.89.

39. *Independent*, 11.3.89.

40. *Weekly Mail*, 18-24.8.89, reporting on a dossier compiled by the Eduardo Mondlane University in Maputo.

41. *New Nation*, South Africa, 5-11.5.89.

42. Excerpt from "British Aid to Southern Africa", speech to the SADCC Consultative Conference, Gaborone, 1987.

43. *Weekly Mail*, South Africa, 18-24 August, 1989.

44. *Independent* 18.7.89; *SouthScan* vol. 4 No. 28, 19.7.89.

45. *Weekly Mail*, South Africa, 18-24.8.89.

46. According to various newspaper reports, for example, the *Independent* 24.2.88; see also the appendix of "Terminators, Crusaders and Gladiators: Western (private and public) support for Renamo and Unita", P. Nesbitt, ROAPE no. 43, 1988.

47. For example, the debate about the extent to which MNR arms and equipment are supplied by external sources such as South Africa or by material captured from the Mozambican army is one area of specialised contention. Another feature of the debate relates to the type and kind of evidence advanced. For example, a recent report commmissioned by the Ford Foundation and the Swedish International Development Agency in March 1989 was based on field research undertaken in November and December 1988. The researcher interviewed ex-MNR combatants and concluded,

"It is clear ... that there was no dramatic change in the pattern of supplies, command, or communications at any time from the assumption of South African control in 1980 until the end of 1988." [i.e. when the field research work was completed]

"The Nkomati Accord of 1984 was described by combatants present before and after the Accord as producing a greater emphasis on secrecy, and slightly less regularity of supplies, but no basic change in the pattern of relationships. Continued South African involvement through late 1984, in violation of the Accord, was irrefutably documented by the Gorongosa documents.

"Some observers now argue that South African assertions of non-support for Renamo should be believed because no recent 'smoking gun' evidence has been uncovered. The author's interviews and Mozambican eyewitness reports, together with South Africa's well-documented past record of deception, make it hard to accept such an argument as credible."

("The Mozambican National Resistance (Renamo) as Described by Ex-participants", a report by William Minter, for the Ford Foundation and the Swedish International Development Agency, Washington DC, March 1989, p. 14.)

48. For a detailed discussion on this, see *Africa Confidential* 2.12.88; "The Mozambican National Resistance (RENAMO) as Described by Ex-Participants", Research Report submitted to the Ford Foundation and Swedish International Development Agency, W. Minter, Washington, March 1989; and "The World This Week", Channel 4's documentary programme, screened on 24.6.89.

49. That is the evidence for forced labour advanced in the Gersony report of 1988 ("Summary of Mozambican Refugee Accounts of Principally Conflict-Related Experience in Mozambique", R. Gersony, Bureau for Refugee Programs, US State Department, Washington).

50. See, for example, "The Mozambican National Resistance (RENAMO) as Described by Ex-

participants", Minter, op. cit., pp. 3-5.

51. See the *Southern Africa Review of Books*, April/May 1989, June/July 1989, and August/September 1989 editions.

52. William Minter, writing in the *Southern Africa Review of Books*, June/July 1989.

53. Particularly so within the context of the extreme colonial neglect of basic services for the black population. See Chapter 9.

54. "Angola to the 1990s, the Potential for Recovery", T. Hodges, EIU special report no. 1079, London, 1986, Chapter 1, pp. 4-17.

55. From 1966 to 1974, South Africa also provided intelligence and logistical support for the Portuguese 'counter-insurgency' forces during the struggle for Angolan independence.

56. Largely brought about by the politically embarrassing revelation that South Africa was involved 'on the same side', in the context of the contemporary climate of public distaste (following the Vietnam war) for involvement in foreign conflicts. ("Regional Security in Southern Africa: Angola", by J.A. Marcum, *Survival*, bi-monthly journal of The International Institute for Strategic Studies, 1988.

57. J.A. Marcum, op. cit., p. 6.

Chapter 3

1. It is also estimated that some 150,000 deaths of older children and adults have been caused by the collapse of medical services, together with malnutrition and/or not otherwise fatal diseases (in Mozambique and Angola). ("South African Destabilisation: The Economic Cost of Frontline Resistance to Apartheid", UN Economic Commission for Africa , ECA, 1989, p. 16.)

2. ECA, op.cit., p. 16; *Children on the Frontline: The impact of apartheid, destabilisation, and warfare on children in southern and South Africa*, UNICEF, New York, 1989, pp. 24, 38-40; an article entitled "Third World War" in *South* magazine, August 1986, p. 45; and "Summary of Mozambican Refugee Accounts of Principally Conflict-Related Experience in Mozambique" by Robert Gersony, Bureau for Refugee Programs, US Department of State, Washington, 1988, p. 25.

3. Gersony, op. cit., pp. 20, 21.

4. 100,000 in Mozambique during the 1983-84 famine, and 100,000 in Angola during the 1980-85 famine. (UNICEF, *Children on the Frontline*, 1989 edition, op. cit., p. 24.)

5. UNICEF, *Children on the Frontline*, 1987 edition, p. 10. In this report, UNICEF give the Under-5 Mortality Rate for Mozambique as between 325 and 375 per 1,000 live births, and the Under-5 Mortality Rate for Angola as 325-375 per 1,000 live births.

6. ECA, op.cit., p. 20.

7. Correspondence with R. H. Green, Professorial Fellow at the Institute of Development Studies, University of Sussex.

8. Information provided to Oxfam by SEAS (Angolan Social Services), April 1988.

9. Interview with Oxfam researcher, 'Lar Essanjo', Huambo, Angola, April 1988.

10. According to information given to Oxfam in April 1988. At the same time, the Angolan government estimated there to be 40,000. A proportion of the most severely wounded in Angola, known as the *mutilados* - those who have lost a limb - are officially registered. There were 10,000 officially registered war-disabled in 1987, but health and rehabilitation officials readily agree that the national total must be far higher.

11. ECA, op cit., p. 26. 1987 data estimate the total population of Angola to be 9 million. (*World Development Report*, World Bank, Oxford 1988, p. 233.)

12. "The Emergency Situation in Angola: Priority non-food requirements for the year 1988", document prepared by the UN Africa Emergency Task Force in collaboration with the

Government of Angola, April 1988, p. 51. Two Oxfam staff members were part of the fact-finding mission to Angola on which the findings of this document were based.

13. According to Africa Watch, a US-based non-governmental organisation concerned with human rights, refugees' testimonies held that FAPLA (the MPLA government army) indiscriminately used landmines in some northern, UNITA-held, areas of the country. (*Angola, Violations of the Laws of War by Both Sides*, Africa Watch, April 1989, New York, Washington, and London, pp. 65-9.)

14. "The Emergency Situation in Angola: Priority non-food requirements for the year 1988", op. cit., p. 4.

15. Interview with Oxfam researcher, Bomba Alta, Huambo, April 1988.

16. Information supplied by Bomba Alta staff to Oxfam researcher, April 1988.

17. In July 1989, an ACP-EEC Joint Assembly mission to southern Africa reported, "The major reason for such extensive population displacement in the region is fear of aggression resulting from the war situation in ... Mozambique and Angola. The conflict between the government forces in both countries and their respective 'bandit' or 'guerrilla' opponents has lasted for so long because other countries, notably South Africa, have continued to supply arms, equipment and logistic support with the hope of undermining internationally recognised governments." ("Refugees and Displaced Persons in Southern Africa", report of the Mission of Enquiry to Malawi, Zambia, Zimbabwe, Mozambique, and Angola, April 29 - May 12, 1989.)

18. The numbers of people directly affected by conflict in Angola and Mozambique have been calculated (as at 31.12.89) as follows:

a. *Internally displaced people*: officially registered displaced people (i.e. those receiving relief assistance in designated reception or resettlement areas, who are often only registered for a few months until they are considered to be self-sufficient) number 1.7 m. in Mozambique and 700,000 in Angola, total 2.4 m. However, it is estimated that there are a total of 6.1 m. internally displaced people altogether in Mozambique and Angola, taking into account those who are not officially registered and those who were once officially registered but who are no longer deemed in need of relief assistance. Of these, an estimated 1 m. people have drifted away from the insecure rural areas into the cities, where they are largely destitute. (Figures based on Oxfam field reports; statistical annex and background papers for the OAU/UNHCR international conference on the Plight of Southern African Refugees, Returnees and Displaced People (SARRED), August 1988, Oslo; ECA, op. cit.)

b. *International refugees*: a total of 1,897,000 is based on the following estimates: 632,000 Angolans and 1,265,000 Mozambicans. (Oxfam field reports; statistical annex to SARRED, op. cit.; UNHCR official estimates; and information bulletins produced by the Refugee Service of the League of Red Cross and Red Crescent Societies, Geneva.)

c. *Urban affected*: some 4 m. people living in towns and cities, without access to land, are now dependent on food aid, because their needs are no longer met from a rural surplus.

19. Using World Bank population estimates which give Mozambique's total population as 14.6 m. and Angola's as 9 m. (1987 figures given in *World Development Report 1988*). Estimates, breakdowns, and sources for numbers displaced and impoverished given in the statistical notes above.

20. Using the World Bank total population estimate for Malawi (1987 figures) of 7.9 m. (*World Development Report 1989*, p. 164) and an estimate of Mozambican refugees, as at December 1989, of 790,000.

21. Interview with author, Nsanje District Hospital, Southern Region, Malawi, June 1987.

22. "Angola to the 1990s: the Potential for Recovery", special report no. 1079 by T. Hodges, EIU *Economic Prospects* Series, London, 1987, pp. 15, 16.

23. Interview with author, Kayombo village, North West Province, Zambia, June 1987. However, the refugees were not living a problem-free life. Although they felt safe from the

threat of UNITA attacks, they expressed anxiety about the plans then proposed by the Zambian government to move all recent Angolan refugees away from the border areas to a large refugee settlement further into the province, at Maheba.

24. Information given to Oxfam by a fieldworker for the West German agency, Agro Action, Luanda, April 1988. Agro Action helps to run a resettlement programme for displaced Angolans near the coastal town of Sumbe.

25. There were 75,324 registered displaced in Waco Kungo town in April 1988, according to municipal records. (Oxfam research report, April 1988.)

26. Interview with Oxfam researcher, Kichocota (one of the displaced people's settlements in Waco Kungo), Kwanza Sul Province, April 1988. Maria's village was in the Kassongue area, on the border with Huambo Province.

27. Oxfam researcher's interview, Luanda, April 1988.

28. As at June 1987, when he was interviewed.

29. Interview with author, Muloza refugee camp, southern Malawi, June 1987.

30. According to "Refugees from Mozambique: Shattered Land, Fragile Asylum", an updated report by the United States Committee for Refugees (USCR), August 1988, Washington, p.20. In August 1987, it was reported in the South African Parliament that 31 people had died as a result of contact with the fence between 1 June 1986 and 3 August 1987. ("Race Relations Survey 1987/88", South African Institute of Race Relations, Johannesburg, 1988, p. 527.)

31. The following articles illustrate some of the problems refugees have encountered trying to cross into South Africa: *Refugees*, UNHCR's magazine, April 1987, pp. 27-9; article entitled "Ragged victims of a dirty war seek refuge in South Africa", *Independent* 16.10.86; and an article entitled "Police probe the case of a refugee shot on the wire", *Weekly Mail*, 18-24.8.89.

32. *Southscan* vol 4 No. 31, 25.8.89.

33. According to UNHCR's magazine *Refugees*, April 1987.

34. According to Oxfam field reports.

35. According to official South African government estimates. ("Race Relations Survey 1987/88", op. cit., p. 527.)

36. Early 1987, according to the South African Institute of Race Relations, "Survey 1987/88", op. cit., p. 854.

37. In April 1987, the deputy Minister of constitutional development and planning, and of public works and land affairs in South Africa, Mr Wilkens, said that refugees would be repatriated if they were found to be outside the particular 'homelands' where they are allowed to stay. ("Race Relations Survey 1987/88", South African Institute of Race Relations, op. cit., p. 17.)

38. Interview with Oxfam researcher, Ressano Garcia, Maputo Province, June 1987.

39. Ibid.

40. Which are supposed to be renewed every six months. However, Oxfam fieldworker reports indicate that there are no effective systems for ensuring re-registration; hence the task of estimating the numbers of refugees is further complicated. In view of this, Oxfam has based its working estimates on the numbers known to be registered and receiving relief assistance.

41. According to successive editions of the digest of The South African Institute of Race Relations.

42. 1989 figures, see above.

43. USCR, op. cit., pp. 25, 26.

44. As above. UNHCR was also criticised for not fielding sufficient staff along the border area, and in the capital Harare during such a difficult period.

45. USCR, op. cit., p. 26.

46. According to internal Oxfam reports, and official government statements at the time, the camps were very overcrowded. Oxfam also registered its concern to UNHCR that basic facilities

at the camps had been neglected.

47. USCR, op. cit.

48. According to the USCR, op. cit.

49. Unemployment is so widespread among South Africans in the 'homelands' that even this risky strategy creates additional problems. In October 1987, the Chief Minister of Lebowa said that the Mozambican refugees were being exploited by white farmers because the refugees were prepared to "work for nothing", which had led to increasing unemployment in Lebowa. ("Race Relations Survey 1987/88", op. cit., p. 855.)

50. As has been clearly pointed out by others, including the South African Council of Churches, and the United States Committee for Refugees, who have called for international action to get UNHCR fully operational in South Africa.

51. "The Emergency Situation in Mozambique: Priority requirements for the period 1989 - 1990", UN Office for Emergencies in Africa, New York, March 1989, p. 34. For an account of the background to food shortages in Angola, see Chapter 8.

52. 'Food security' is a term which has become commonplace in development work. Oxfam has chosen to give it the following working definition for the purposes of our fieldwork: lack of food security is the situation whereby "people are unable to obtain by production, gift, loan, or purchase enough food for survival". ("Food Emergencies in Sahelian Africa: Early Warning and Response. Alchemy or Science?", internal Oxfam paper, 1984.)

53. According to Oxfam field reports and press coverage.

54. Internal Oxfam field report on Gurue, Alto Molocue, Mocuba, and Lugela, February 1989.

55. Oxfam field report on the situation in Zambezia Province, 23.5.89.

56. Situation report from Oxfam emergency coordinator in Quelimane, Zambezia Province, 4.4.89.

57. Internal Oxfam report on food security and nutrition in Mozambique, 1987; UNICEF, *Children on the Frontline*, op. cit., p. 16.

58. Funding for the relief operation has been insufficient. The declining nutritional status has been documented by local surveys conducted by Médecins Sans Frontières, the International Refugee Committee, UNHCR, and the World Food Programme. (See, for example, "Food Provisioning Amongst Mozambican Refugees in Malawi. A Study of Aid, Livelihood, and Development", report prepared for the World Food Program by the Refugee Studies Programme, Oxford, 1989.)

59. Interview with Oxfam researcher, Zambezia Province, June 1987.

60. Oxfam report on Mankhokwe refugee settlement, Nsanje District, Southern Region, Malawi, June 1987.

61. Amnesty International have also documented human rights abuses by the Mozambican government, by the government of Angola, and by SWAPO, but these are few in number in comparison with those of their adversaries.

62. Extracts from the concluding section of Gersony, op. cit., pp. 25, 26. Following publication of the Gersony report, Phyllis Oakley (a State Department spokesperson) was quoted as saying "We are appalled by the findings", which she described as "horrifying". Another State Department official praised the report as "a careful, meticulous piece of investigation", adding "If anything, it understates the scope and magnitude of the problem." Another official said that the report "vindicates our reluctance to enter into any sort of relationship" with the MNR. (*New York Times*, 20.4.88.)

A RENAMO spokesperson in the USA reacted by dismissing the report as "politically commissioned and politically motivated". Mr Serapiao criticised the report's author for not visiting RENAMO zones in Mozambique and for not talking with RENAMO representatives. He argued that "traumatised refugees" can hardly be expected to speak "confidentially and candidly" with foreign researchers, suggesting that "unsophisticated villagers" would have trouble differentiating between RENAMO and other forces. He alleged that Mozambique's government "and its Marxist allies have embarked on a systematic program of psuedo-guerrilla operations to discredit RENAMO politically ... and to alienate the populace from RENAMO." (*The Christian Science Monitor*, 25.4.88.)

63. Chief Chitui, the traditional leader of the refugees at Kunyinda settlement. At the time this interview was conducted, June 1987, most of the people at this settlement had fled to Malawi in September and October 1986.

64. Interview with author, Kunyinda settlement, Chikwawa District, Southern Region, Malawi, June 1987.

65. Ibid.

66. Interview with Oxfam researcher, Becon, Waco Kungo, Kwanza Sul Province, Angola, April 1988.

67. Ibid.

68. Interview with Oxfam researcher, Waco Kungo transit centre for displaced people, Waco Kungo, Kwanza Sul Province, April 1988.

69. Ibid.

70. Interview with Oxfam researcher, Rushinga East District, Mashonaland East Province, Zimbabwe, October 1988.

71. Interview with Oxfam researcher, Chipinge District, Manicaland Province, Zimbabwe, October 1988.

72. Estimated by the UN Institute for Namibia.

73. The most commonly used figure; see for example, "Report on Standing Committee 11: the Military Situation in and relating to Namibia", UN Council for Namibia, 1984, p. 3.

74. For a fuller account, see S. Smith, *Namibia: A Violation of Trust*, Oxfam, Oxford, 1986.

75. See, for example, "Namibia: Amnesty International's Concerns", Amnesty International, August 1989.

76. Figure based on *Namibia: The Facts*, International Defence and Aid Fund, London, 1989, p. 70; *Brutal Force: the apartheid war machine*, G. Cawthra, International Defence and Aid, London, 1986, p. l79; and UNICEF, op. cit., 1989 edition, p. 58.

77. *Namibia: Apartheid's Forgotten Children*, Oxfam, Oxford, 1988, p. 35.

78. See Amnesty International reports; International Defence and Aid reports; and, most recently, "Koevoet Versus the People of Namibia: report of a human rights mission to Namibia on behalf of the working group Kairos", M. Hinz and N.G. Leuven-Lachinski, Kairos, Utrecht, October 1989.

79. Oxfam field report, 1988.

80. Namibia Communications Centre report from Oniipa, northern Namibia, 9.9.88.

81. Former estimates, ranging up to 100,000, were revised downwards when the transition period commenced, and some 41,000 returnees arrived in Namibia. Allowance is made for the children still at school in the former refugee settlements.

82. "The War in Namibia: Social Consequences", T. Weaver, in *Namibia in Perspective*, eds. G. Totemeyer, V. Kandetu, and W. Werner, Council of Churches in Namibia, Windhoek, 1987, p. 240; and UNICEF, op. cit., p. 50.

83. T. Weaver, op. cit., pp. 240-4l.

84. See S. Smith, op. cit.

85. UNICEF, op. cit., p. 58.

86. See S. Smith, op. cit.

87. See *Namibia: Apartheid's Forgotten Children*, Oxfam, op. cit., p. 42.

88. See T. Weaver, op. cit., p. 248; and UNICEF, op. cit., 1989 edition, p. 57.

89. Figures for the 1988/89 Financial Year.

90. That is, £2,740,872, during the 1988/89 financial year.

91.The total grants expenditure for the 1988/89 financial year in Malawi was £356,280.

92. £2.4 m. was spent on relief work in Mozambique during 1988/89, 92 per cent of total grants expenditure in Mozambique. The British government and the European Community, among other agencies, have generously matched many of our grants.

93.Oxfam internal reports. In January 1989, a field report stated that MNR attacks had occurred in Mueda, Nangade, and Palma Districts in December 1988.

94. For a full breakdown of Oxfam's relief grants in Mozambique, see the Oxfam Grants List produced annually.

95.UNICEF, *Children on the Frontline*, 1989 edition, op. cit., p. 23.

96. Interview with Oxfam researcher, at 'Lar Essanjo' children's home ('Home of Joy' in the Umbundu language), Huambo, Angola, April 1988.

97. Telex from Oxfam UK to the International Oxfams, March 1987.

98. Internal Oxfam telex, Maputo to Oxford, 27.7.87.

99. Interview with Oxfam's Zambezia-based emergency programme coordinator, February 1989.

Chapter 4

1. See Robert Gersony's report, "Summary of Mozambican Refugee Accounts of Principally Conflict-Related Experience in Mozambique" (Bureau for Refugee Programs, US State Department, Washington, 1988) for a full account of the MNR's methods of controlling and extracting goods and services from the civilian population.

2. Data on localised refugee influxes from internal Oxfam field reports.

3. Using Malawi Red Cross Society refugee statistics for June 1988, and data from the 1987 national population census ("Malawi Population and Housing Census, 1987, Preliminary Report", National Statistical Office of the Government of Malawi, Zomba, December 1987, table 1.1.) which gives the (Malawian) population for Nsanje District as 201,311.

4. In Dedza District, according to several interviews recorded by the author in June 1987. Of these, one refugee family reported that Mozambican government troops had stolen their crops.

5. Interview with author, Nsanje Boma, June 1987. The District Commissioner's fear of cholera was later to prove well-founded: outbreaks occurred in March 1988 in Mankhokwe, and subsequently in settlements at Tengani, Nyamithuthu, Kunyinda, and Mkhwayi. (Field reports from Médecins sans Frontières.)

6. Interview with author, Lilongwe, Malawi, June 1987.

7. As experience was later to prove, this was an underestimate of the numbers of people without Malawian kin.

8. Telex, 24.9.86, MAL 065.

9. *Financial Times*, 12.9.86, *Times* 12.9.86, *Guardian* 12.9.86, BBC Summary of World Broadcasts (SWB) ME/8363/ii and ME/8363/4-5 13.9.86, ME/8364/ii and ME/8364/B/1-2 September 1986, sourced in *Third World Quarterly*, vol. 9 no. 1, January 1987.

10. Because of the political uncertainty surrounding the situation of the Mozambican refugees at this time, relief workers in Malawi had been advised by government authorities to refer to the refugees as 'displaced people'. The term 'refugee' was not current inside Malawi until the Malawian government had signed the standard UNHCR protocol agreement (which was not to happen until 1987), thereby granting the Mozambicans who had fled their country under duress the full legal status of refugees.

11. Internal Oxfam correspondence, 4.3.86, MAL 065.

12. Funds were found, and the requested grant was sent straightaway. Field telex, 10.6.86, MAL 065.

13. Oxfam made an immediate grant for £73,000 in support of this appeal.

14. When President Banda signed Malawi's accession to the 1951 UN Convention and 1967 Protocol relating to the Status of Refugees (Malawi thus became the 104th state to accede to the UN Convention and Protocol), and the 1969 OAU Convention Governing the Specific Aspects of Refugee Problems in Africa. (UNHCR's monthly magazine, *Refugees*, February, 1988.)

15. See note 9 above.

16. BBC SWB ME/8434/ii 5.12.86, ME/8435/ii 6.12.86., ME/8445/ii 18.12.86, ME/8447/ii 20.12.86., ME/8448/ii 22.12.86. Sourced in *TWQ* vol.9 no. 3, July 1987.

17. BBC SWB, ME/8447/ii, 20.12.86., sourced in *TWQ* vol. 9 no. 3., July 1987.

18. Interview between Oxfam Regional Representative and the author, Malawi, June 1987.

19. Statistics of the number of people affected are based on press reports in Zimbabwe, and on the following:

a. Unpublished Zimbabwe Government reports (quoted in the *Independent* of 29.5.89), listing 375 raids attributed to the MNR, with 355 civilians and 22 Zimbabwean soldiers killed, 280 civilians and 44 soldiers wounded, 667 civilians kidnapped and more than 400 missing; reports also list 29 MNR rebels killed, 5 wounded, and 45 captured.

b. A speech by the Provincial Governor of Manicaland Province in November 1988, mentioning 130 victims of MNR atrocities.

However, Oxfam staff report that more atrocities were happening than were reported in the local media.

20. Districts in three border Provinces are affected, from the northernmost Rushinga District down to the southernmost Chiredzi District.

21. The issue is reported by the Zimbabwe press, although many say it is not comprehensively covered. However it is very under-reported in the British press, despite extensive British links with Zimbabwe in general, and with the commercial farms in the eastern border areas in particular.

22. Interviewees included village residents and leaders, health workers, a hospital matron, a doctor, school headmasters and teachers, and local government officials. To protect their identities, we do not give the names of individuals or their villages or places of work, except where names have already appeared in media reports.

23. Interview with Oxfam researcher, Rushinga District, Zimbabwe, October 1988.

24. See, for example, chapter 1 of *Destructive Engagement: Southern Africa at War*, edited by Phyllis Johnson and David Martin, Zimbabwe Publishing House, 1986, pp.1-42; *Serving Secretly*, by Ken Flower, John Murray, London, 1987.

25. "Southern Africa: The Price of Apartheid", by Roger Martin, EIU *Political Risk* series, Special Report no. 1130, 1988, p. 131.

26. "The Security Threat from South Africa", M. Evans, section 14 of *Zimbabwe's Prospects*, edited by C. Stoneman, Macmillan, London, 1988, pp. 227-8.

27. EIU Quarterly Report on Zimbabwe, No. 4, 1988.

28. Which stated, "We have concurred that an attack against Mozambique shall be regarded as an attack against Zimbabwe ...". (Evans, op. cit., p.227.)

29. Both Malawi and Tanzania have committed troops inside Mozambique. Malawi sent troops to Mozambique by early 1987. Tanzania began sending troops in late 1986, according to reports in the *Zimbabwe Herald* of 5.3.87. Tanzania's troop contingent was withdrawn in November 1988, as reported in Tanzania's *Daily News* of 1.12.88, and the *Guardian* of 2.12.88.

30. *The Herald* (Harare), 12.11.86.

31. The BMATT, composed of British Army personnel, was sent to Zimbabwe to assist the

unique and complex process of integrating the rival armies who had fought during the liberation war.

32. According to a report in *The Namibian*, 20.11.87, Tanzania was expected to use this aid to buy Land Rovers and radio equipment in Britain to equip its troops. According to an article in *New African* journal (May 1989, p.17), Britain's role in providing the governments of Zimbabwe and Mozambique with defence assistance is deeply resented by the MNR.

33. Interview between Oxfam researcher and the village headman of a village in Chipinge District of Manicaland Province, eastern Zimbabwe, October 1988.

34. Information provided by Oxfam researcher, November 1988.

35. Interview with Oxfam researcher, Rushinga District, Manicaland Province, Zimbabwe, October 1988.

36. Interview with Oxfam researcher, Chipinge District, October 1988.

37. From 1980 to 1988, Oxfam's total expenditure on health and disability programmes in Zimbabwe totalled £1,488,074. (Oxfam grants lists 1979/80 to 1988/89.)

38. Oxfam grants lists, Manicaland Province medical programme, 1983/84 to 1988/89.

39. EPI is a worldwide UNICEF/WHO strategy, and one of the key elements of effective preventive health practice.

40. The hospital records demonstrate the rising numbers of admissions and out-patients being treated as a result of the breakdown in outreach, preventive services.

Admissions:	Outpatients:
1986: 5,387 patients admitted	1986: 34,900 patients treated
1987: 6,606	1987: 42,696
1988: 5,158 (only up to September)	(1988 figures not available at the time of the field research)

41. Interview with Oxfam researcher, Manicaland Province, November 1988.

42. The clinic staffing situation in November 1988 for Chipinge District:

Clinic:	Population served:	Staff numbers:
Zamuchiya	6,924 people	One nurse
Mahenye	4,662	No qualified staff
Mabe	8,363	One nurse
Kopera	10,137	One nurse
Gwenzi	10,071	One nurse

43. Interview with Oxfam researcher, Manicaland Province, 1988.

44. UNICEF, "Children and Women in Zimbabwe: a Situation Analysis", 1985; "Farm Labour in Zimbabwe: a Comparative Study in Health Status", R. Lowenson, in *Health Policy and Planning*, No. 1, 1986, Oxford, Oxford University Press; "Labour insecurity and health: an epidemiological study in Zimbabwe", R. Lowenson, in *Social Science and Medicine*, Vol. 27 No. 7, 1988, Pergamon Press, Oxford, pp. 733-41.

45. Interview with Oxfam researcher, eastern Zimbabwe, August, 1987.

46. See "An Evaluation of the 1985-86 Chipinge District Health Plan in Rural Council Areas", R. Lowenson, Manicaland Provincial Medical Office, 1987.

47. The low rate of Mozambican migrant workers' participation in preventative programmes means that they account for up to 80 per cent of hospital admissions in the relevant border areas, according to Oxfam-supported health staff working in eastern Zimbabwe.

48. Interview with Oxfam researcher, Manicaland Province, Zimbabwe, November 1988.

Chapter 5

1. Interview with author, Lusaka, June 1987.

2. Botswana is dependent on South African transport routes only until the Limpopo line in Mozambique is reopened. Before 1965, this was its main route for exports and non-RSA imports. (Personal communication with Professor R.H. Green, August 1989.)

3. "Sanctions and South Africa's Neighbours", ODI Briefing Paper, May 1987, London.

4. See, for example, J. Hanlon, *Beggar Your Neighbours*, op. cit., pp. 199-218 for Zimbabwe's economic dependence on South Africa, 225-31 for Botswana's dependence on South Africa, and 248-54 for Zambia's dependence on South Africa.

5. E.W. Epstein, *The Death of the Diamond*, Sphere Books, Falmouth, and J. Hanlon, *Beggar Your Neighbours*, CIIR, London, 1986, p. 283. According to the *Times* of 1.6.89, de Beers and the Angolan government have also signed a new joint venture agreement.

6. "The Gold Mining Industry in the Transvaal, 1886 - 1899", P. Richardson and J.J. Van-Helten, one of the studies in a collection entitled *The South African War*, edited by P. Warwick, Longman, Harlow, 1980, p.22.

7. According to an Oxfam America study, UN trans-national companies invested three times as much capital in South Africa during the three decades after World War II as they had in the entire pre-war era. At the same time, the independent southern African states sought international investments to develop their economies in vain. By 1983, total US financial involvement in South Africa (including direct investment, bank loans, and stockholdings) had reached $14.6 billion - equal to roughly two-thirds of the total gross domestic products of all the neighbouring countries combined. US direct investment counted for some 20 per cent of all direct foreign investment in South Africa, and was surpassed only by UK investment. (*The Roots of Crisis in Southern Africa*, A. Seidman, Oxfam America Impact Audit No. 4, Africa World Press, New Jersey, 1984, p.41.)

8. See *The Roots of Rural Poverty in Central and Southern Africa*, eds. R. Palmer and N. Parsons, Heinemann, London, pp. 226, 227.

9. For a detailed description of these organisations' activities and interconnections, and those of the State Corporations, see *The Struggle for South Africa: A Reference Guide*, vol. 1, eds. R. Davies, D. O'Meara, and S. Dlamini, Zed Press, London, 1988 edition, pp. 65-129.

10. See *South Africa Inc.: The Oppenheimer Empire*, D. Pallister, S. Stewart, and I. Lepper, Simon Schuster, London, 1987; *Transnationals in Southern Africa*, eds A. Seidman, R. Seidman, D. B. Ndlela, and K. Makamure, Zimbabwe Publishing House, 1986; *Anglo American and the Rise of Modern South Africa*, D. Innes, Heinemann, London, 1984.

11. *Uprooting Poverty: The South African Challenge*, F. Wilson and M. Ramphele, W.W. Norton & Co., New York, 1989, p.199. The first "Report of the Carnegie Commission of Investigation on the Poor White Question in South Africa" was produced in 1932.

12. 'Tropicals' from north of the 22nd parallel were not recruited between 1912 and 1933, because the death rate among the workers who had marched on foot from their homes down to the mines was particularly high, and because the mines and white farms of Southern Rhodesia were crying out for black labour. To replace them, the Chamber of Mines established the Native Recruiting Corporation, to recruit black labour from within the Union of South Africa, Basutoland, the Southern Bechuanaland Protectorate, and Swaziland. Later, medical advances and the working of new mines in the Orange Free State led to the ban being lifted and WNELA re-scouring Nyasaland, Northern Rhodesia, and Tanganyika.

13. See *Gold and Workers: A People's History of South Africa, 1886 - 1924*, vol. 1, L. Callinicos, Ravan Press, Johannesburg, 1980, pp. 34-5.

14. For a clear summary of the South African government's 'internalisation' and 'stabilisation' labour policies and what they mean for the neighbouring labour-supplying countries, see section 3.2 of "The Comparative Sociology of Migration: Two Case Studies", C. Murray, contribution to *Global Aspects Of Human Migration*, a forthcoming United Nations University study, and the

other references cited therein.

'Internalisation' is the policy of increasing the proportion of South African workers in the mines, and its successful implementation has involved substantial wage increases. 'Stabilisation' is the policy of adapting to the very substantial increase in the proportion of skilled miners in a labour force whose overall numbers are diminishing.

15. According to *Children on the Frontline: The impact of apartheid, destabilisation and warfare on children in southern and South Africa*, UNICEF, New York, updated edition, 1989, p.18. UNICEF bases its estimate on the following: the total number of officially registered migrant workers is in the order of 300,000, and the South African government claims there are a further 1.2 million unregistered 'illegal' migrant workers. Given that the 'illegal' workers will include purely seasonal migrants, especially in the domestic and agricultural sectors, the total estimate has been rounded down for an accurate reflection of the numbers 'highly dependent' on remittances.

In Mozambique alone, 1987 Ministry of Labour/UNDP sources estimated that some 70,000 families (or 350,000 people) in southern Mozambique (Gaza, Inhambane, and Maputo Provinces) were dependent on remittances in Rand from menfolk working in the South African mines. December 1986 Ministry of Labour information estimated that, in addition, there were some 5,000 migrant workers at home in Mozambique in between contracts, plus another 30,000 Mozambicans working on South African farms, plus 3,500 in other sectors of the South African economy, and around 160,000 people working (or searching for work) as illegal migrants.

16. When the British government took over direct administration a few years before the copper mining industry took off.

17. "Zambia's Urban Situation", by H.J. Simons, the first chapter of *Development in Zambia: A Reader*, edited by B. Turok, Zed Press, London, 1979, p. 5. Of course, the turbulent pre-colonial history of this area, including the ravages of the slave and ivory trades, should not be overlooked.

18. See note 12 above.

19. However, there was also much competition of interests, especially for labour, as the surrounding colonial economies developed. In Nyasaland (Malawi) for example, white settlers had to petition the colonial authorities to channel migrant labourers on to the emerging commercial agricultural estates instead of down to South Africa.

20. FRELIMO had committed itself to the eventual ending of migrant labour, but the economic consequences of Mozambique's colonial inheritance, the failure of the collective farm system (adopted as a major agricultural development policy after independence), drought, and — worst of all — war mean it would be impossible to absorb migrant labourers rapidly into the domestic economy.

21. The *Southern African Economist*, April/May 1989.

22. According to information supplied by the Ministry to Oxfam's researcher.

23. Interview with Oxfam researcher at the FRELIMO Miners Welfare Committee centre at Ressano Garcia just by the Mozambican/South African border, Maputo Province, June 1987.

24. Interview with Oxfam researcher, Maxixe, Inhambane Province, Mozambique, May 1987.

25. Ibid.

26. Ibid.

27. Ibid.

28. *Beggar Your Neighbours*, J. Hanlon, op. cit., p. 77. The long-overdue wage increases to mine workers in the 1970s also increased dependence.

29. C. Murray, op. cit.

30. *Families Divided: The Impact of Migrant Labour in Lesotho*, C. Murray, Cambridge University Press, 1981, p. xi. Drought, a regular natural phenomenon affecting large areas of southern Africa, also played a role.

31. *Children on the Frontline*, UNICEF, 1987 edition, op. cit., p. 15.

32. 1987 TEBA figures.

33. Which policy was a key element in the subsequent political disaffection of the Lozi people of Western Province, who had woven migrancy into their economy. An Oxfam visitor to Western Province in May and June 1989 reported hearing Radio South Africa broadcasting in Lozi.

34. See note 12 above on 'tropicals'.

35. By 1920, some 50,000 Zambians were working outside their own country, mostly in South Africa and Rhodesia, more than the total number of waged workers inside Zambia/Northern Rhodesia. Ten years later, as the copper reserves were beginning to be exploited, some 113,000 Zambians had entered the waged labour market, 78,000 of them within Zambia. By 1969, five years after Zambia's independence, a third of all its citizens had moved away from their home district, most of them to Zambia's urban centres. (Statistics from Simons, op. cit., pp. 1-25.)

36. Even so, African farmers within reach of the urban centres found them to be a profitable food market. The colonial authorities took measures to rein back this trade in order to assist the European farmer settlers who were being established on prime land along the 'line of rail'.

37. *Children on the Frontline*, op. cit., 1989 edition, p. 18.

38. Foreign investment in South Africa is of three main types - direct investments, portfolio investments (purchase of stocks and shares), and loans. It has been and remains critical to the South African economy in a number of ways. Firstly, it generates foreign exchange which allows the imports of capital goods, on which the economy is highly dependent. Secondly, foreign investment gives the South African economy access to technology which it cannot produce itself. And thirdly, foreign borrowing finances government expenditure, state corporations, and the balance of payments deficit, as well as imports.

39. See J. Hanlon, *Beggar Your Neighbours*, op. cit., pp. 67-9; *Anglo American and the Rise of Modern South Africa*, D.Innes, Heinemann, London, 1984, pp. 232-41; *Transnationals in Southern Africa*, eds. Seidman et al., op. cit., pp. 21-2; *South Africa Inc.: The Oppenheimer Empire*, Pallister et al., op. cit, pp. 162-84.

40. See "Sanctions Against South Africa", R. Moorsom, a background research report prepared for Oxfam, July 1986, p. 19.

41. In 1987, over the period January to July only (due to official restrictions on trade data), South Africa's trade surplus with Africa was given as R662.9 m. (*Survey of Race Relations 1987/88*, op. cit., pp. 419-20.)

42. See note 78.

43. See note 74.

44. See *Beggar Your Neighbours*, J. Hanlon, op. cit., pp. 71-3.

45. See *Beggar Your Neighbours*, J. Hanlon, op. cit., p. 73-6, and "SADCC in the 1990s", J. Hanlon, op. cit., pp. 89-94.

46. See *SADCC in the 1990s*, J.Hanlon, op. cit., pp. 89-94, for an overview of the SADCC energy programme.

47. For an up-to-date, country-by-country account of the ways in which South Africa has used 'transport diplomacy', see *Apartheid Terrorism: The Destabilisation Report*, P. Johnson, and D. Martin, a report prepared for the Commonwealth Committee of Foreign Ministers on Southern Africa, James Currey, London, 1989.

Also, before South Africa's destabilisation took hold, other shortcomings were noticeable, including poor maintenance; inadequate rolling stock; breakdowns in cooperation between countries; and, until Zimbabwe was independent and sanctions could be lifted, its routes out through Mozambique were underutilised.

48. Based on data given in SADCC'S 1988/89 Annual Report.

49. Estimated by R.H. Green from background materials used in ECA study, op. cit. (Personal

communication with author, January 1990.)

50. With South Africa's volume of trade falling from over 14 m. tonnes in the early 1970s, to under 1 m. tonnes by the end of the 1980s. (R.H. Green, personal communication with the author, January 1990.)

51. Other international interests have also benefited from Namibia's colonial economy. In particular, business interests in the member states of the self-appointed 'Contact Group': Britain, the USA, Canada, France, and West Germany.

52. See, for example, *Namibia: A Violation of Trust*, S. Smith, Oxfam Public Affairs Unit, Oxford, 1986.

53. *SouthScan*, vol 4, no. 5, 1 February, 1989.

54. For South Africa's position, see "Question of Walvis Bay", press release from the Permanent Mission of South Africa to the United Nations, 18.11.88, New York.

55. UN Security Council Resolution 432 of July 1978, the Namibia SCR preceding 435 which, as a result of South Africa's conditions to the Contact Group, omitted to mention Walvis Bay (according to an official South African source, see note 54).

See, "Walvis Bay — An Integral Part of Namibia: Statements in Support of the Territorial Integrity of Namibia including Walvis Bay, by Representatives to the Ninth Special Session of the General Assembly on the Question of Namibia", Special Supplement no. 2, June 1978, of the *Objective: Justice* series of UN Public Information Office publications.

56. See "Walvis Bay: Namibia's Port", R. Moorsom, IDAF, London, 1984.

57. See "Transforming A Wasted Land", no. 2 in *A Future for Namibia* series, R. Moorsom, CIIR, London, 1982.

58. "Economic Prospects for Namibia", ODI briefing paper, August 1989.

59. *Profile Namibia*, CIIR, 1989.

60. And even less in terms of end-user share, probably between 15 and 20 per cent. By comparison, Switzerland accounts for 31 per cent. (Personal communication from R.H. Green, January 1990, ODI briefing paper, op. cit.)

61. Uranium concentrate accounts for 38 per cent of export earnings, and diamonds account for 31 per cent. (ODI briefing paper, op. cit.)

62. See S. Smith, op. cit., pp. 34-40.

63. Some black farmers were, however, able to market beef and karakul pelts through official channels.

64. Economic Policy Document of the Political Bureau of the Central Committee of SWAPO, November 1988, Luanda.

65. Of the TNCs in Namibia, South Africa hosts 35, the UK 25, West Germany 8, France 3, and Canada 2. (*Front File*, May 1989, vol. 3, no. 5.)

66. In 1987, the South African concerns' inshore fish quota was reduced from 91 per cent to 66 per cent. (EIU Country Profile, 1988/89.) The main South African parent companies involved (1983 data) were SANLAM, Liberty Life, Anglo American, Barlow Rand, Fisheries Development Corporation (state). ("Exploiting the Sea", R. Moorsom, no. 5 in the series *A Future for Namibia*, CIIR, London, 1984, p. 52.)

67. Ibid.

68. The figure of R892 is given in "Namibia: Fundamentals and Potential", H.A.R. Meiring, a paper compiled by the First National Development Bank, Windhoek, August 1989, p. 5. The official South African statistic for the debt is R549 m., an amount considered by the Administrator General to be "a truly healthy inheritance for the new government". (BBC World Summary of Broadcasts, ME/W0088 A2/1, 1.8.89.0)

69. United Nations Development Programme report, "Namibia: Fiscal and Financial Policies: Issues and Assistance Requirements. An Executive Summary", September 1989, p. 3.

70. H.A.R. Meiring, op. cit., p. 5.

71. BBC Summary of World Broadcasts, ME/W0088 A2/2, 1.8.89. Excerpts from the Administrator General's Budget presentation speech, 20.7.89, Windhoek.

72. According to Dr J. Faundez, of the Law Department of the University of Warwick, an expert on Namibia and international law. (Personal communication with the author, December 1989.)

73. The Rand Monetary Union was replaced by the Tripartite Monetary Agreement in 1986; the signatories are Lesotho, Swaziland nd South Africa (and formerly Botswana), with Namibia as an involuntary member. It links the countries of the RMA financially, although strictly speaking the Rand is no longer legal tender in Lesotho or Swaziland, and those countries are free to determine their own exchange rate policies. However, not least because of the common membership of SACU, in practice their currencies are tied to the Rand, with the result that South Africa retains some indirect control over their Central Banks.

SWAPO officials have said that it is SWAPO policy for Namibia, like Botswana, to leave the RMA and establish its own currency.

74. SACU is a regional arrangement involving Botswana, Lesotho, and Swaziland (the 'BLS states') and South Africa, with Namibia as an involuntary member. It dates back to 1910, when Britain and South Africa made arrangements for the surrounding territories (now the BLS states). SACU allows for unlimited free trade among its members. Because South Africa has the most developed economy, its export sector has benefited from there being no tariff walls blocking its access to these nearby markets. The BLS states have benefited financially from the way in which payments from SACU's central customs pool are divided. However, the World Bank and the Ford Foundation, for example, argue that Lesotho's membership of SACU has impeded economic growth because the high tariff walls around SACU oblige it to import goods from South Africa (often uncompetitive on a world market comparative basis), and prevent the development of a national industrial/ manufacturing sector. For a full account, see J. Hanlon, *Beggar Your Neighbours*, op. cit., pp. 81-90; and J. Hanlon, *SADCC in the 1990s*, op. cit., p. 32. SACU has been the main single vehicle which has integrated the BLS and Namibian economies with South Africa's. SWAPO's economic advisers are advising against independent Namibia's accession to SACU.

75. Estimated to be about US$170 m. in 1989/90 under present SACU arrangements, equivalent to about 22 per cent of 1988/89 government revenue.

76. ODI briefing, op. cit.

77. J. Hanlon, *SADCC in the 1990s*, op. cit., p. 122, citing SWAPO's economic advisers.

78. During the 1970s, South Africa's exports to the SADCC region (not then so-called, of course) expanded fivefold, while the SADCC region's exports to South Africa increased by only 126 per cent at current prices, raising South Africa's trade surplus with the SADCC states from $250 m. in 1970 to $1.8 bn. in 1979. (ODI briefing paper, "Sanctions and South Africa's neighbours", May 1987, p. 3.)

79. *Southscan*, vol. 4 no. 35, 22.9.89.

80. Ibid.

81. See "Race Relations Survey 1987/88", op cit., p. 419.

82. ODI briefing paper, "Sanctions and South Africa's Neighbours", May 1987. Statistics cited are from 1984.

83. Ibid., p. 3.

84. South Africa is also working to combat the restrictions which trading patterns place on it: through direct lobbying against sanctions, by establishing sanctions evasion mechanisms, through trying to diversify trading partners, by following import substitution programmes, stockpiling, etc.

85. Much has been published on this topic. For a cross-section of views and analysis see the

following: "Sanctions and South Africa's Neighbours", ODI briefing paper, op. cit.; "Sanctions Against South Africa", Oxfam background research report, R. Moorsom, op. cit., pp. 114-26; "Sanctions and South Africa: The Dynamics of Economic Isolation", M. Lipton, EIU Special Report no. 1119, London, January 1988, pp. 51-5 (see also the follow-up article by C. Stoneman in the *Southern Africa Review of Books*, Spring 1988 edition, pp. 32-4); *Economic Sanctions*, R. Renwick, Harvard University Centre for International Affairs, 1981, pp. 76-92; *The Sanctions Handbook*, J. Hanlon and R. Omond, Penguin, 1987, pp. 95-117; *Economic Effects of Sanctions on Southern Africa*, J. P. Hayes, Gower, Aldershot, 1987; "New Sanctions Against South Africa", R.C. Riddell, *Development Policy Review*, pp. 243-67; "SADCC in the 1990s", J. Hanlon, EIU Special Report no. 1158, op. cit., pp. 29-37.

86. See "Southern Africa: Apartheid and Sanctions, the SADCC View", an address given by Simba Makoni, Executive Secretary of SADCC, to the Annual General Meeting of the Anti-Apartheid Movement, Sheffield, November, 1987. Published by the Anti-Apartheid Movement, London, 1988.

87. See *South Africa: The Sanctions Report*, J. Hanlon, Penguin, Hardmondsworth, 1989.

88. See, for example, ODI briefing paper, 1987, op. cit., p. 3; J. Hanlon, "SADCC in the 1990s", op. cit., pp. 33-4; "The Effects of Sanctions on the Frontline States", B. Weimar, paper delivered to the West German Zimbabwe network seminar, Bonn, November 1987.

89. ODI briefing paper, op. cit., p. 3.

90. Excluding the proportion of SA/SADCC trade conducted with the countries in the Rand Monetary Area, of course.

91. ODI briefing paper, op. cit., pp. 3 and 4.

92. However, Zambia and Mozambique's experiences of international support to help them meet the costs of sanctions against Rhodesia are not encouraging. President Kaunda said that the international community had been "more generous with moral than with material support". (R. Renwick, op. cit., p. 83.)

93. A recent EIU report claims that all the other SADCC states could withstand the effects (of the predictable range of responses and effects) following increased sanctions against South Africa. ("SADCC in the 1990s", J. Hanlon, op. cit., pp. 29-38.)

94. That is, GDP loss, 1980-1988, at 1988 prices.

95. See "Skills and Sanctions against South Africa", mimeo, part of the independent expert study on the evaluation and impact of sanctions against South Africa, N. Swainson, January 1989, which concludes, "...The failure of the state education system to provide enough skilled black labour in the past was the result of an apartheid system committed to the policy and practice of 'separate development'. From the late 1970s corporate capital and the state came to realise that the only way to satisfy the current demand for certain types of skills was to expand the system of internal training, and supplement the local labour force with a small input of specialist immigrants. Despite some improvement, the serious shortcomings in existing formal and informal training systems are evident."

96. Hence the widespread contraventions of the old Pass Laws, and the present contraventions of the Group Areas Act and other influx control measures.

97. The following excerpts are from a Progressive Federal Party leaflet entitled "Nat Gravy Train ... How Much Government Can You Afford?", published in 1987.

"The Nationalist Party has created a government structure that has turned out to be the longest gravy train ever seen - and it's getting longer every year ... Because of the duplications of government along Nat apartheid lines, we have 4 Ministers of Health, 5 Ministers of Education, 4 Ministers of Agriculture, and 6 Ministers dealing with housing. And with the homeland policy we find ourselves with 5 Presidents, 5 Ministers of Foreign Affairs, 5 Finance Ministers, and 5 Ministers of Defence.

"And that's not all. Even these figures do not tell the whole story, since they do not include the six non-independent national states with their 46 Ministers and the 481 members of their Legislative Assemblies...

— R1 in every R6 spent by government goes on pay and

— 12c in every R1 is spent on apartheid structures.

— The Civil Service has grown by 20 per cent since President Botha took over the reins

— There is one civil servant to every 27 citizens (in Britain it's one to every 94,000).

— Government salaries, administration and allowances now cost R40.5 million — 500 per cent more than in 1981..."

98. In the 1989 Herman Cohen hearings, it was established that the US Administration believes that international sanctions have affected the white South African outlook

It is also held that the September 1989 election results have disproved the view that "sanctions would drive white South Africans into the laager".

In November 1988, South Africa's Finance Director General, Chris Stals, said that more than R20 bn. had left South Africa over the previous three years as a result of international economic pressure on the country. (*Southscan*, vol. 3 no. 11, 9.11.88.)

According to the International Chamber of Commerce, and the UN Centre on TNCs, more than 550 foreign companies have disposed of their South African holdings between 1985 and 1989.

99. Excerpts from Sir Geoffrey Howe's speech to the Royal Commonwealth Society entitled "South Africa: No Easy Answers", May 1988. Reproduced in *Perspectives on Africa*, HMSO, London, 1988.

100. War on Want Conference, "Peace and Development in the Frontline States", London, June 1988.

101. " South Africa: Building the Future. The Role of British Industry in South Africa", brochure produced by British Industry Committee on South Africa Limited (BICSA), London. BICSA was established in 1986, and states that its member companies represent the majority of British investment in South Africa. The Chairperson's Annual 1987/88 annual report stated, "We remain totally opposed to apartheid, but we shall continue to argue the positive case for maintaining British investment in South Africa and the importance of economic growth as a force for political change."

102. Excerpts from an address by the British Ambassador at the Annual General Meeting of the Urban Foundation, Johannesburg, 17.8.88. (Foreign and Commonwealth Office Press release.)

103. South Africa is already involved in the upgrading of Maputo port, for example, as it is in South Africa's economic interests to improve the port's efficiency. But even on this project, it is argued that there could be greater cooperation, for instance in the technical assistance field, if it were possible to have normal political cooperation.

104. As Professor Green points out, "The pattern of selling high-cost manufactured goods and transport services for cheap labour and hard currency is not a viable one even with a democratic South Africa." (Personal communication with author, August 1989.)

105. See, for example, "Post-apartheid South Africa and its Neighbours", J. Hanlon, *Third World Quarterly*, April 1987.

106. Excerpt from "One View on the Realities of SADCC", article by A.M. Babu, *Africa Analysis*, 9.6.89.

107. Concluding statement from Simba Makoni's address to the Annual General Meeting of the British Anti-Apartheid Movement, Sheffield, November 1987.

Chapter 6

1. Botswana is the key exception. Firstly because it has suffered relatively little from South Africa's regional policy, even though Gaborone has been the target of high-profile SADF attacks.

And secondly because Botswana has experienced high growth rates during the 1980s, and has had the ability to build up substantial foreign exchange reserves. See "Southern African Destabilisation: The Economic Cost of Frontline Resistance to Apartheid", UN Economic Commission for Africa (ECA), Addis Ababa, October 1989, p. 39.

2. For a full explanation of the different approaches to calculating the costs of destabilisation and warfare, see ibid., pp. 11-14.

3. According to UNICEF, "The share of the national budget that goes to recurrent defence costs in Mozambique is 35 per cent, one of the highest in the world. Angola's defence budget is much larger than Mozambique's in absolute terms and absorbs a comparable percentage of total spending as well as half of all imports. Tanzania, Zambia, and Zimbabwe also have large armed forces, and Zimbabwe is spending in the order of US$3 m. a week to defend its own and the region's trade routes through Mozambique." *(Children on the Frontline: The impact of apartheid, destabilisation and warfare on children in southern and South Africa*, UNICEF, New York, 1989 edition, p. 20.) For a full discussion of the diversion of scarce resources to defence, see also ECA, op. cit., and "Apartheid Terrorism: the Destabilisation Report", a report prepared for the Committee of Foreign Ministers on Southern Africa, James Currey, London, 1989.

4. Based on ECA, op. cit., p. 6.

5. ECA op. cit., p. 4.

6. ECA, op. cit., p. 30.

7. *World Development Report 1989*, op. cit., p. 164.

8. "Policy Reform and Adjustment in an Economy under Siege: Malawi 1980-87", J.G. Kydd, *IDS Bulletin*, vol 19, no. 1, January 1988, Sussex, p.36.

9. EIU Country Report, 1987/88, p. 15.

10. Zimbabwean politicians were reported to be particularly irritated by the fact that their army was often having to escort Malawian convoys carrying goods of South African manufacture. By the end of 1987, Zimbabwe had demonstrated its point by reducing the number of weekly convoys. Malawi responded in two ways, which have themselves added to the drain on scarce foreign exchange reserves. Firstly by paying a reported $4 m. p.a. in foreign exchange to Zimbabwe for the security of its convoys. And secondly by arranging for South African imports, and exports destined for the South African market, to be sent the long way round through Botswana and Zambia. (EIU Country Report on Malawi, no. 2, 1988, p. 34.)

11. EIU Country Profile for Malawi, 1987/88, pp. 22, 23.

12. Oxfam briefing paper, unpublished, on the effects of economic structural adjustment in Malawi (1988).

13. EIU Country Profile, 1987/88, p. 23.

14. *Africa Economic Digest*, vol. 9, no. 25, 1-7.7.88, p. 12.

15. Interview with the author, Blantyre, June 1987.

Chapter 7

1. See, for example, The International Freedom Foundation (IFF): "Diplomacy From A Position of Strength", *Freedom Bulletin* no. 10, 1988, published by the IFF's southern African branch in South Africa.

2. First articulated in the January 1987 publication of "A US Policy Toward South Africa: The Report of the Secretary of State's Advisory Committee on South Africa", US Department of State, Washington. In essence, this report found that the US policy of 'constructive engagement' had failed. However, no in-depth replacement was formulated by the US Administration until 3 October 1989, when Herman Cohen, Assistant Secretary of State for African Affairs, gave testimony to the Hearings of the Senate Foreign Relations Committee. Two key points emerging from the Administration's new position are (1) that the USA believes that the pressure of

sanctions has "played a key role in stimulating new thinking within the white power structure. It is now increasingly clear to that government that the well-being of the white minority cannot be sustained without a negotiated political settlement that results in political equality for all South Africans"; and (2) that the South African government should prove its seriousness of intent by beginning the process of creating a climate for negotiations, with substantial progress to be under way by February 1990.

3. *Leadership*, vol. 8 no. 1, March 1989.

4. Examples given are the South African role in ending the bus hi-jacking during the Pope's 1988 visit to Lesotho, and its role in Bophuthatswana during the 'attempted coup' of February 1988.

5. *Leadership*, March 1989.

6. Additionally, a number of other military capacities had been extended. See *SouthScan*, vol. 4 no. 8, 22.2.89, reporting on information made available by the World Campaign Against Military and Nuclear Collaboration with South Africa.

7. *Herald*, Zimbabwe 10.2.89; *The Chronicle*, Zimbabwe, 11.2.89.

8. See *Namibia: A Violation of Trust*, S. Smith, Oxford, Oxfam, 1986.

9. This widely held view should be contrasted with the analysis of South Africa's Director General of Foreign Affairs, Neil van Heerden, published in March 1989: "The Quiet South African", an article in *Leadership* magazine, Cape Town, March 1989.

10. For a balanced analysis of the complexities behind this development, see "Treacherous Crossing: Namibian Independence Debacle", *Southern African Report*, vol. 5, no. 1, July 1989, Toronto, pp. 15-17. Strategic errors of judgement by SWAPO, combined with poor UN/South African coordination on the ground, and the fact that SWAPO was excluded from the tripartite Namibia/Angola agreement, were the key factors behind this debacle.

11. See, for example, British press reports during the last two weeks of June 1989.

12. For a clear report, see "Background to Gbadolite", *Front File*, vol. 3, no. 11, August 1989 (extra edition), p. 8.

13. Internal Oxfam report, December 1988.

14. The South African Director-General of Foreign Affairs has said, "We have made Mozambique a high priority in our Department for the next year." (Interview in *Leadership* magazine, March 1989.)

15. Although the degree to which this occurs has been a matter of academic dispute.

16. M. Hall, op. cit.

17. *Independent*, 30.3.89.

18. In 1988, COSATU and NACTU organised joint actions, agreeing that they had common aims. And in 1989, there were further moves towards unity in action between the United Democratic Front and the Azanian People's Organisation (AZAPO). (*Guardian*, 17.8.89; *Independent*, 17.8.89.)

19. See, for example, an article entitled "W. Cape strategy aims to avoid mistakes of 1985", *SouthScan* 22.9.89.

20. For a full account of the various types of affiliation, and the various organisations connected with the MDM, see *Business Day*, South Africa, 30.8.89.

21. According to official statistics, 74.7 per cent of South Africa's population are 'African', 2.6 per cent are 'Coloured', and 14 per cent are 'White'. (Central Statistical Service data, given in "Race Relations Survey, 1987/88", South African Institute of Race Relations, Johannesburg, 1988, p.11.)

22. The high costs of running the apartheid state, and the high military costs incurred by South Africa's regional policy have also played a part in the country's economic difficulties.

23. According to *Africa Confidential*, 22.9.89, R25,000 m. have left South Africa since 1985. Of this, R15,000 m. have gone to service foreign debt obligations, and R10,000 m. have gone in

other ways: because South African investors prefer to invest abroad; because foreign companies have sold their businesses to local companies; because individual South Africans have prepared nest-eggs abroad; and because some fraudulent deals have been made by manipulating the dual exchange rate of the 'financial' and the 'commercial' Rand.

According to the United Nations 'Centre on Transnational Corporations' background papers for the September 1989 Geneva public hearings on transnational corporations in South Africa and Namibia, at least 88 South African transnationals have been identified as having controlling interests in 437 companies in 44 countries. The bulk of these investments are in Brazil, the USA, Britain and West Germany.

24. For example, this was evidenced shortly before the October 1989 Kuala Lumpur Commonwealth summit (at which a call for increased sanctions against South Africa was widely expected to be resisted by Mrs Thatcher), when President de Klerk — with ostentatious timing publicly advised London and Washington that he was about to release eight prominent political prisoners. An article in the *Sunday Telegraph* of 15.10.89 read, "... President de Klerk's government has apparently done everything in its power in the last few weeks to support the view that internal South African policy is being drawn up to please officials in London ... British officials find South Africa's rather obvious attempts to throw Mrs Thatcher a bone embarrassing and unnecessary."

25. According to the *Weekly Mail* (15-21.9.89), the ANC interpreted the election results as a sign that white South Africans had endorsed change.

26. This is a cumulative total; it includes subsidiary organisations and some which are probably defunct.

27. *Independent* 18.10.89.

Chapter 8

1. Entitled "South Africa: Quo Vadis?", Oxford, 6.3.85. Transcripts available from Oxfam.

2. See, for example, *Unconsummated Union: Britain, Rhodesia, and South Africa, 1900-45*, M. Chanock, Manchester, 1977; *Southern Africa Since 1800*, D. Denoon with B. Nyeko and J.B. Webster, Longman, London, second edition, 1984; *The Failure of South African Expansion*, R. Hyam, London, 1972; *Industrialisation and Social Change in South Africa*, S. Marks and R. Rathbone, Longman, London, 1982; *South Africa in Africa*, S.C. Nolutschungu, Manchester University Press, Manchester, 1975; *A New History of Southern Africa*, N. Parsons, Macmillan, 1982; *The Roots of Rural Poverty in Central and Southern Africa*, R. Palmer and N. Parsons, Heinemann, London, 1977; *Class and Colour in South Africa*, H.J. Simons and R.E. Simons, Penguin, London, 1969; *Capitalism and Colonialism in Mozambique*, L. Vail and L. White, Heinemann, London, 1980; *Magomero: Portrait of an African Village*, L. White, Cambridge University Press, Cambridge, 1987.

3. See *Namibia: A Violation of Trust*, S. Smith, Oxfam, Oxford, 1986.

4. *The Courier*, no. 116, July-August 1989, p. 59. There is some controversy over the comparative nature of commodity price decline: see "Sub-Saharan Africa: From Crisis to Sustainable Growth", World Bank, Washington, November 1989, pp. 24-5.

5. *Africa in History*, B. Davidson, Paladin, St Albans, 1978, pp. 207, 208. The Atlantic slave trade ravaged the peoples along the western African seaboard from the mouth of the Senegal river to southern Angola for over two centuries.

6. The Organisation for Economic Cooperation and Development (OECD) consists of Austria, Belgium, Canada, Denmark, France, the Federal Republic of Germany, Greece, Iceland, Ireland,

Italy, Luxembourg, the Netherlands, Norway, Portugal, Spain, Sweden, Switzerland, Turkey, the UK, the USA, Japan, Finland, Australia, and New Zealand.

7. However, it should be stressed from the outset that the SADCC region encompasses a wide range of economic circumstances ranging from comparatively successful Botswana, through debt-ridden Zambia, to devastated Mozambique.

8. "Statement on External Debt", South Commission, Kuala Lumpur, 3.3.88.

9. Normal strategies for this include increasing the range of primary exports and therefore spreading the risk; establishing processing industries to 'add value' to primary commodities; and setting up 'import substitution' initiatives.

10. EIU Country Report, 1988/89, p. 16.

11. Which does, however, centre on adding value to the country's agricultural produce, and on import substitution.

12. *Financial Times*, 28.6.89.

13. Tenant labourers on some of these estates (especially in the Central Region where the system of 'visiting tenants' was introduced to attract labour because casual migrant labour is more readily available in the land-hungry Southern Region) are also allowed to grow Burley.

14. Obviously, developments in Mozambique were also a likely factor.

15. According to UNCTAD, the US$ price in cents per lb., deflated in 1985 terms, was 117.9 in 1964 and 64.3 in 1985. ("Consideration of the Situation in, and Problems of, the World Market for Copper. A Review of Major Trends and Developments in the World Copper Market up to 1985." TD/B/C.1/RM/COPPER/2, November 1986, UN, p. 21.)

16. "Primary Commodities: Market Developments and Outlook", Commodities Division of the Research Department, IMF, Washington, July 1989, pp. 83-8.

17. See, *Zambia: Debt and Poverty*, J. Clark with C. Allison, Oxfam, Oxford, 1989.

18. "Angola to the 1990s: The Potential for Recovery", T. Hodges, EIU Special report No. 1079, January 1987, p. 52.

19. See EIU Country Review 1988/89.

20. For a good overview of these factors, see "Commodity Prices: Investing in Decline?", ODI briefing paper, London, March 1988. For data on how commodity prices have moved in relation to the Manufactured Goods Index, see, for example, ODA Commodity Price Charts, published regularly.

21. See *The Courier*, no. 116, July-August, 1989.

22. According to the Year Book of the International Sugar Organisation.

23. See "European Community Trade Barriers to Tropical Agricultural Products", M. Davenport, ODI Working Paper no. 27, London, 1988, pp. 91-6.

24. See, *The Hunger Crop: Poverty and the Sugar Industry*, B. Coote, Oxfam, Oxford, 1987.

25. *The Courier*, no. 116, July-August 1989, p. 63.

26. However, as some of the 'free trade' zones in the ASEAN bloc demonstrate, enclave industrial development and restrictive employment practices mean that countries in the South can produce for this lucrative market without having to attend to the development needs of the poor.

27. ODI, March 1988, op. cit., p. 2.

28. In 1969, the Pearson report pointed out the great importance of trade to the South, and how the need for aid often arises from the inadequacy of foreign exchange earnings and the difficulty of increasing them. It made a number of recommendations for changes in the North.

In 1980, the Brandt report concluded that countries in the South should be enabled to develop their commodity sectors and 'add value' to their products through a number of measures to be adopted by countries in the North.

In 1983, the Brandt Commission recommended a further set of emergency measures on world trade to be adopted by the North.

In 1987, the Brundtland report pointed out the disastrous environmental consequences that the commodity trade and the debt crisis were causing. A number of measures for international action were recommended.

29. "SADCC in the 1990s: Development on the Frontline", J. Hanlon, EIU special report no. 1158, 1989, pp. 60, 61, drawing on research done by the Christian Michelsen Institute.

30. Excerpt from a speech by Dr S.H.S. Makoni to the Southern Africa Political Economy Series (SAPES) Conference, Gaborone, October 1989.

31. Quoted in J. Hanlon, EIU 1989, op. cit., p. 65.

32. Excerpt from the conclusion of Nyerere's inaugural statement to the South Commission, Dar es Salaam, 27.7.87.

33. "Statement on External Debt", adopted by the South Commission, Kuala Lumpur, 3.3.88. While the World Bank and others highlight the role played by sub-Saharan Africa's rate of population growth, it should be noted that in most SADCC states (according to World Bank data) the projected rate of population growth for 1987-2000 is dropping.

34. *Sub-Saharan Africa: from Crisis to Sustainable Growth*, The World Bank, Washington, November 1989, p. 4. In addition, the IMF says, "On the assumption that there are no severe commodity shocks, sub-Saharan African countries pursue appropriate development policies, and the international economic environment improves, it is projected that during 1989-92 real GDP in sub-Saharan Africa could grow at an annual rate of close to 4 per cent ..." (*Finance and Development*, quarterly publication of the IMF and the World Bank, September 1989, p. 31.)

35. Growth in the SADCC region in 1988 averaged 4.5 per cent. According to SADCC, this was the first time since the 1970s that it had exceeded the rate of population growth in the majority of member states. This improved economic performance is thought to be due to economic growth in the industrialised North, some aspects of economic reform policies, and favourable weather conditions.

36. *World Bank Debt Tables, 1988/89*, World Bank. However, the total figure for sub-Saharan Africa's debt is greatly distorted by the inclusion of the debts of Nigeria and the Ivory Coast. Both of these countries have debts comparable to the world's Highly Indebted Countries, at $27,769 m. and $8,450 m. respectively. (World Bank, 1987 data.)

37. "African Debt: The Search for Solutions", T. Killick and M. Martin, UN Africa Recovery Programme Briefing Paper no. 1, June 1989, p. 1. The HICs are Argentina, Bolivia, Brazil, Chile, Colombia, Costa Rica, Ecuador, The Ivory Coast, Jamaica, Mexico, Morocco, Peru, Philippines, Nigeria, Uruguay, Venezuela, and Yugoslavia.

38. EIU Country Profiles, 1988/89.

39. Ibid., p. 41.

40. For a useful discussion of the way in which the economic consequences of conflict affect the wider economy, see "South African Destabilisation: The Economic Cost of Frontline Resistance to Apartheid", UN Economic Commission for Africa (ECA), pp. 11-14.

41. R. Renwick, "Economic Sanctions", *Harvard Studies in International Affairs* no. 45, Cambridge, Mass, 1981..

42. *Mozambique: A Cry For Peace*, J. Quan, Oxfam, Oxford, 1987, p. 3.

43. See *The Roots of Crisis in Southern Africa*, A. Seidman, Oxfam America, Africa World Press, New Jersey, 1984, Chapter 3.

44. "Debt in the SADCC region: Zambia Case Study", A. M. Mwanza, paper given to the SAPES Conference on SADCC Problems and Prospects for Regional Political and Economic Cooperation, Gaborone, October, 1989, p. 4.

45. After 1981, there was a substantial real reduction in net capital flows to sub-Saharan Africa, with a 30-40 per cent fall in 1984-85 alone. Much of this was the result of a virtual cessation of bank lending.

The SADCC region experienced a sharp decline in official resource flows at this time. In real terms, official flows dropped by 39.2 per cent between 1981 and 1983. (Statistics based on OECD data, "Geographic Distribution of Financial Flows to Developing Countries", OECD, 1984-1987, Paris.)

As far as aid levels are concerned, although global aid levels were stagnant throughout the 1980s, sub-Saharan Africa did better than the rest of the developing world, as its share of the total OECD aid flows rose from 32 per cent in 1980-82 to 39 per cent in 1987 (the USA was an exception, giving proportionately far less than the average for other OECD donors). Aid flows to the region have not, and would not anyway be expected to, compensate for the fall-off in other financial flows, just as they have not compensated for the economic costs of South Africa's regional aggression.

Private direct investment also fell away. For a thorough discussion of the declining levels of British TNC investment in English-speaking Africa, see "British Transnational Corporations in Sub Saharan Africa: Corporate Responses to Economic Crises in the 1980s", P. Bennell, mimeo, July 1989.

46. A.M. Mwanza, op. cit., p. 6.

47. See "Debt in the SADCC Region: A Case Study of Malawi", C. Chipeta, paper for a conference entitled "Debt in the SADCC Region", Brussels, January, 1989.

48. For a fuller account, see "The Problem of Official Debt Owed by Developing Countries", P.S. Mistry, paper produced for the FONDAD (Forum on Debt and Development) Conference, Brussels, August 1989.

49. The following recommended debt reduction and cancellation measures are in line with those urged on European governments and banks by two European NGO groups, the Forum on Debt and Development, and the British Overseas Aid Group.

50. The Council for Mutual Economic Assistance (CMEA) consists of Bulgaria, Czechoslovakia, the Democratic Republic of Germany, Hungary, Poland, Romania, and the USSR.

51. T. Killick and M. Martin, op. cit., p. 8. By the end of 1988, Britain, Canada, West Germany, and the Scandinavian Group had cancelled almost all aid debt owed to them by sub-Saharan Africa; total cancellation exceeded $3.2 bn. but will reduce debt service only by some $125 m. yearly, because these loans had soft terms. (Ibid.)

52. OECD debt tables.

53. P.S. Mistry, op. cit.

54. Sources: for concessional and non-concessional World Bank debt, *World Bank Debt Tables, 1989/90*; for IMF debt, OECD data.

55. *The Southern African Economist*, October/November 1989.

56. Ibid.

57. The World Bank and the IMF have argued that the poor would have been worse off had there been no structural adjustment. However, increasingly, they acknowledge that some groups in society are vulnerable to some adjustment measures in the short term.

58. See, for example, *Adjustment With A Human Face. Protecting the Vulnerable and Promoting Growth*, eds. G.A. Cornia, R. Jolly, and F. Stewart, 2 vols., UNICEF, Oxford, 1987; "The Social Consequences of Adjustment and Dependency on Primary Commodities in sub-Saharan Africa", UNICEF, New York, 1989, paper presented to the ACC Inter-agency Expert Meeting on Commodities organised by UNCTAD, May 1989, Geneva; *Zambia: Debt and Poverty*, J. Clark and C. Allison, Oxfam, Oxford, 1989; and an Oxfam-supported literature search of studies documenting the impact of economic adjustment programmes, undertaken during the 1980s, at household level in the nine SADCC states, mimeo, 1989.

UNICEF's study (Cornia et al., ibid.) is the most comprehensive study to date. It found evidence of rising malnutrition in ten African, six Latin American, and two Asian countries;

rising infant mortality rates in four countries (one in Africa); an end to the trend towards child health improvement in at least 21 countries; and an increase in the proportion of low-birthweight babies in at least ten countries.

59. Mozambique is omitted from this list because Oxfam's programme there concentrates almost wholly on relief.

60. *The World Bank: A Critical Analysis*, C. Payer, Monthly Review Press, New York and London, 1982, p. 153.

61. Interview with Oxfam researcher, Maputo, 2.9.87.

62. Because each member nation has, in addition to its voting power according to wealth, a block of votes which is the same size for each country.

63. World Bank Annual report, 1989, pp. 194-7; IMF Survey (Supplement on the Fund), August 1989.

64. Interview with author, Lusaka, 17.6.87.

65. For an account of this period in Zambia's adjustment history, see J. Clark and C. Allison, op. cit., pp. 17-25.

Programme Aid is the main form of non-project aid. It is used to finance vital imports, usually to assist countries with particularly acute balance of payments problems.

66. World Bank Annual Report 1989, p. 81.

67. "Adjusting to Recession: Will the Poor Recover?", ODI briefing paper, London, November 1988 edition, p. 1.

68. See, for example, "The Impact of the IMF/World Bank on the People of Africa with Special Reference to Zambia and especially on Women and Children", D.C. Muntemba, IFAA, London, 1987.

69. In 1982, 7.8 per cent of the national budget was spent on health, whereas by 1985 this proportion had dropped to 5.7 per cent. More dramatically, the foreign exchange value of the budget declined from $49.4 m. in 1982 to $19.7 m. in 1985, reflecting a substantial loss of purchasing power for the health service at a time when the national Primary Health Care programme was being established. ("Debt and Poverty: A Case Study of Zambia", J. Clark with D. Keen, Oxfam, Oxford, May 1988.)

Although recurrent PHC expenditure is designed to be far more cost-effective than, say, that for tertiary services, nevertheless the initial outlay on items such as motor cycles, drug kits, production of training manuals, etc. was affected by budget cut-backs. NGOs like Oxfam were therefore requested to fund PHC capital items.

70. Excerpt from a speech by Dr S.H.S. Makoni to the SAPES Conference, Gaborone, October, 1989.

71. See, for example, the "Brandt report", published in 1980, which stressed the fundamental, global nature of the economic crisis. (*North-South: A Programme for Survival, The report of the Independent Commission on International Development Issues under the Chairmanship of Willy Brandt*, Pan, London, 1980.)

72. According to World Bank data, 61.1 per cent of the national total of household income goes to the top 20 per cent of the population, while 3.4 per cent goes to the bottom 20 per cent of the population. (*World Development Report 1989*, op. cit., p. 222.)

73. See, for example, UNICEF, "The Social Consequences of Adjustment and Dependency on Primary Commodities in sub-Saharan Africa", op. cit.; and "The Politics of Adjustment Policy", A. Sawyerr, UN Economic Commission for Africa, ECA/ICHD/88/29, Addis Ababa, 1988.

74. See "Commodity Prices: Investing in Decline?", ODI, op. cit., p. 6.

75. See A. Sawyerr, op. cit.

76. UNICEF, May 1989, op. cit., pp. 28-9.

77. A good summary is to be found in *Africa: What Can Be Done?*, B. Turok, IFAA/Zed,

London, 1987.

78. However, this period was the time when Zambia was also having to meet the costs of the Rhodesian conflict and the international policies aimed at ending it.

79. See, for example, "Towards Another Development in Rural Zambia", R. Dumont, 1979, mimeo.

80. See "Elite Conflict and Socio-Political Change in Zambia", M. Szeftel, Ph.D. thesis, University of Manchester, 1978.

81. According to, for example, various articles by J. Kydd and R. Christiansen (for a bibliography of their work, see *IDS Bulletin* vol. 19, no 2, University of Sussex, Falmer, April 1988, p. 80); "Household Food and Nutritional Security in Malawi", V. Quinn, M. Chiligo, and J.P. Gittinger, paper presented to the Symposium on Agricultural Policies for Growth and Development, November 1988, Mangochi, Malawi.

82. Although it should be noted that some 66,000 'visiting tenants' (as estate labourers are sometimes called) on commercial estates are also permitted to grow Burley. *(Financial Times,* 28.6.89.)

83. M Hall, "The Mozambican National Resistance Movement (RENAMO): A Study in the Destruction of an African Country", forthcoming article in *Africa* 60 (1), 1990; J. Quan, op. cit., p. 6; see also the correspondence in the *Southern Africa Review of Books*, April/May, June/July, and August/September editions, 1989.

84. "Policy Reform and Adjustment in an Economy Under Siege: Malawi 1980 - 87", J. Kydd, *IDS Bulletin*, vol. 19 no. 1, 1988, Sussex, pp. 31,40. According to this source, among President Banda's policy and practice has been "a proclamation of fiscal conservatism, which was adhered to during the post-Independence 'austerity' when the fiscal effort had to be increased as the UK recurrent grant was phased out. But this stance was somewhat bogus, as an ambitious palace building programme was commenced in the late 1960s. From the mid-1970s Banda became profligate, as noted earlier."

85. According to an internal Oxfam Country report based on local press reports.

86. See, for example, T. Killick and M. Martin, op. cit., p. 3. For statistics on sub-Saharan Africa's falling volumes of exports during the 1980s, see *World Development Report 1989*, op. cit., p. 10.

87. *Guardian*, 10.11.88.

Chapter 9

1. During the 1980s, much of the South African investment has been bought out. For example, South African Breweries transferred its majority ownership of the Delta Corporation, the largest company in Zimbabwe, to the Zimbabwean Government. (*Zimbabwe: Politics, Economics, and Society,* C. Stoneman and L. Cliffe, Pinter, London and New York, 1989, p. 139.)

2. The World Bank is backing government initiatives to replace some old investment holdings with local and fresh international investment, in order to stimulate employment and the introduction of new technology.

3. "Growth with Equity" was the title of a 1981 paper which was the precursor of the First National Development Plan.

4. EIU Country Profile, 1987/88, p. 37.

5. See, for example, Lomé briefing no. 4 December 1988, op. cit.

6. For a full account of the human rights abuses of this period, see "Zimbabwe: Wages of War", Lawyers Committee for Human Rights, New York, 1986; and "Zimbabwe: A Break With the Past?: Human Rights and Political Unity", Africa Watch, London, 1989.

7. The *Independent*, 28.10.1989.

8. *Financial Gazette*, Harare, 8.9.89.

9. For example, the 'standstill' July 1988 government budget reduced the year's allocation to the Ministry of Lands, Agriculture, and Rural Resettlement by 13.5 per cent, among other spending cuts aimed at reducing the budget deficit, projected at the time to reach a new record of Z$1,149.7 m. (US$ 618.2 m.). (*Africa Economic Digest*, vol. 9. no. 30, 5 - 11.8.88, p. 2.)

10. The peasant sector's contribution to crop sales rose dramatically from Z$12 million in 1979 (4.5 per cent of the total) to over Z$300 million in 1988 (22 per cent of all crop sales). (*Financial Times*, 21.8.89.)

11. See "Land and Agricultural Development", D. Weiner, Chapter 6 in *Zimbabwe's Prospects: Issues of Race, Class, State, and Capital in Southern Africa*, ed. C. Stoneman, Macmillan, London, 1988, pp. 63-89.

12. *Independent*, 28.10.1989.

13. For example, in November 1989 — reportedly with an eye on the following year's parliamentary elections — President Mugabe pledged to complete the unfinished business of the liberation struggle with a renewed resettlement programme.

14. *Financial Gazette*, Harare, 10.8.89.

15. *Africa Confidential*, 22.9.89.

16. Ibid.

17. Ibid.

18. The EIU, for example, suggests that negotiations with the World Bank to expand Zimbabwe's Export Revolving Fund (which was originally established in 1983 to promote manufactured exports, and became self-financing by 1985) have been made conditional on Zimbabwe liberalising its trade through removing the import tariff walls it has erected to protect its manufacturing industry.

19. 28.10.89.

20. For academic summaries of this view, see C. Stoneman and L. Cliffe, op. cit., pp. 129-34; and D. Weiner, op. cit.

21. According to 1986 FAO data, quoted by Stoneman and Cliffe, op. cit., p. 132.

22. See "Indigenous conservation in Zimbabwe: soil erosion, land-use planning, and rural life", K.B. Wilson, mimeo, paper submitted to African Studies of the UK Conference, Cambridge, September 1988; "Trees and Fields in Southern Zimbabwe", K.B. Wilson, *Journal of Southern African Studies*, vol. 15, no. 2, January 1989.

23. Unlike Malawi, Zimbabwe did well from tobacco in the 1989 auctions. This was due to a number of factors: the highest output for 25 years, a good quality crop, and high prices (partly assured by Zimbabwe's preferential access to the EC market, which was expected to take 46 per cent of output). (*Financial Times*, 26.10.89.)

24. Excerpt from an Oxfam report, "Rural Development in Zimbabwe: proposals for a new strategy", S. Nyoni, November, 1980.

25. According to "Planning for Equity in Health", Ministry of Health, Harare, 1984, p. 4, quoted in "The political economy of health and nutrition", R. Lowenson and D. Sanders, section 9 in C. Stoneman, op. cit., p. 134.

26. See, for example, a report submitted to the Rhodesian Bishops' Conference, "Some Aspects of the Dehumanising Effects of the War", August 1978.

27. Oxfam report on its Zimbabwe medical programme, 1980.

28. Called "Planning for Equity in Health".

29. By mid-1981, an estimated 100,000 undernourished young children and their mothers were receiving supplementary foodstuffs. The programme had to continue for a second year because of widespread drought.

30. In 1979/80, the two main hospitals in Salisbury (now Harare) consumed 31 per cent of the

total health budget, while only 8 per cent was allocated for preventive health care services for the whole of the country. (C. Stoneman and L. Cliffe, op. cit., p. 173.)

31. The minimum wage at the time was Z$70 per month. However, as part of the economic stabilisation measures, the Z$150 limit has remained fixed, while the minimum wage has risen to Z$158, largely an inflationary adjustment. By the end of the 1980s, most people were having to pay for health care. See "The Economy, The Health Sector, and Child Health in Zimbabwe Since Independence", R. Davies and D. Sanders, mimeo, 1986, p. 15.

32. See "Planning For Equity in Health", Ministry of Health, Harare, 1984.

33. "The Struggle for Health", J. Gilmurray, R. Riddell, and D. Sanders, no. 7 in the series *From Rhodesia to Zimbabwe*, CIIR, London, 1979, pp. 22,23. These are academic assessments, made with caution, since comprehensive, accurate, and time-series data were very scant. These figures represent the estimated IMR rates among the 'African' population; in comparison, the IMR for whites was estimated at 17 per thousand live births. However, even this wide range of estimated IMR statistics for the black population masks regional disparities. For example, according to a 1976 report from the Provincial Medical Officer of Health for Matabeleland, IMR figures were up to 300 per thousand live births in the Binga District. (Ibid.)

34. R. Davies and D. Sanders, op. cit., p. 21. This figure was based on a nationwide survey and was calculated according to population data from the 1982 Population Census. Again, the lack of hard time-series data at this point means the statistics should be used with caution.

35. Ibid., p. 16.

36. C. Stoneman and L. Cliffe, op. cit., p. 174.

37. C. Stoneman et al., 1988, op. cit., p. 140.

38. Real government health expenditure rose 27.5 per cent in 1980/81, and a further 47 per cent in 1981/82, but then fell slightly and has since more or less stabilised.

39. R. Davies and D. Sanders, op. cit., p. 6.

40. For details of how economic stabilisation policies during the 1980s have affected health in Zimbabwe, see "The Political Economy of Health and Nutrition", R. Loewenson and D. Sanders, chapter 9 in *Zimbabwe's Prospects*, op. cit., pp. 133-52; "Adjustment Policies and the Welfare of Children: Zimbabwe, 1980-1985", R. Davies and D. Sanders, case study no. 10 in *Adjustment with a Human Face*, UNICEF, vol. 2, op. cit., pp. 272-99; C. Stoneman and L. Cliffe, op. cit., pp. 172-5.

41. Extract from an internal report, "Oxfam Primary Health Care Project in Manicaland Province, Zimbabwe. A Report of the four years in Chimanimani District, December 1983 - December 1987", pp. 45, 46.

42. Translated from Sindebele, from "Development and Underdevelopment, Participation and Self Reliance: as defined by villagers and experienced through ORAP programmes", ORAP report on a seminar held at Vusisuzwe Development Centre, Silobela, Zimbabwe, April 1984 (ZIM 069). Oxfam is among the donor organisations which support ORAP.

43. ORAP is registered with the Ministry of Social Services as a non-profit making organisation, and is a non-governmental, non-party political association. An early statement of ORAP's function and orientation declares: "ORAP member group projects promote local production, generate income, circulate local capital and goods, reduce urban dependency and are cooperative in nature. These characteristics are in conformity with the Government of Zimbabwe's policies for rural development." A number of other foreign NGOs have also supported ORAP, and ODA has contributed towards Oxfam grants to ORAP as part of the 'co-funding' scheme run in conjunction with British NGOs.

44. In 1988, an ORAP worker explained, "In ORAP, we have been through and are still working at a long process of debate about our development and what it means to us. We find, for example, that a lot of the current 'development jargon' is confusing. We have learned that we need to define our own meanings of such widely used terms as 'participation', 'self-reliance', and

'underdevelopment'. We have come to learn that they are meaningless as slogans unless rural people themselves have met to define what they understand and mean by these terms." (Interview with ORAP coordinator, Birmingham, September, 1988.)

See also, for a discussion of the need for local definitions of 'participation', "Participation in the Context of Rural Development in Zimbabwe", S. Nyoni, chapter 12 of *The Importance of People: Experiences, lessons and ideas on rural development training in Zimbabwe: Hlekweni and Beyond*, ed. M. de Graaf, Hlekweni FRSC, Bulawayo, 1987, pp. 121-6.

45. Interview with Sithembiso Nyoni, ORAP coordinator, September 1988.

46. See *Africa Analysis*, 28.4.89, which warns that the raising of the EC beef quota may lead to the Cold Storage Commission encouraging the over-culling of cattle stocks held in the Communal Areas. This is because, in addition to their commercial value in terms of marketed meat and milk, cattle provide valuable draught power and manure. It is thought that cattle holdings for rural families in the CAs are already below subsistence levels, yet also above sustainable carrying capacity, unless more land can be secured for drought-year use.

47. Excerpt from "ORAP's First Four Years: An Overview of the Work", J. Khabo, C. Mzaca and M. Ndiweni, ORAP, Bulawayo, April 1984, p. 6.

48. Excerpt from Vusisizwe seminar report, ORAP, op. cit.

49. S. Nyoni, op. cit. p. 124.

50. At 1988 prices. ("South African Destabilisation: The Economic Cost of Frontline Resistance to Apartheid", UN Economic Commission for Africa, Addis Ababa, p. 6.)

51. Ibid., pp. 27-9.

52. At the CBI/CZI conference, "Zimbabwe: Opportunities for Trade and Investment", London, 12.5.1989.

53. According to UNICEF (1987 data), Malawi has the sixth highest (national average) Under-5 mortality rate in the world, at 267 per 1000 live births. From the mid-1980s, Malawi's rank in the world table has dropped from fourth place, because warfare in Mozambique and Angola have pushed those countries into third and fourth places respectively. (*The State of the World's Children* 1989, UNICEF, Oxford University Press, Oxford, p. 64.)

54. "Policy Reform and Adjustment in an Economy Under Siege: Malawi 1980-87", J. Kydd, *IDS Bulletin*, January 1988, p. 38. Projection based on the findings of the 1980/81 National Sample Survey of Agriculture.

55. Ibid. According to a survey in central Malawi (Liwonde Agricultural Development Division), only 33 per cent of the farming families surveyed had large enough land holdings on which to produce enough for their subsistence needs and a little surplus produce for sale. In this survey area, land holdings of at least one hectare per family were necessary to achieve subsistence and a small cash income. Among the survey sample, 29 per cent of the households surveyed had holdings of less than 0.5 ha. and could produce, on average, only 37 per cent of their basic food requirements (assuming that they devoted all their land to food crops). (Malawi Country Review, 1985, internal Oxfam document.)

56. Extract from Oxfam's 1987/88 Annual Report for Malawi: case-study from Oxfam's village research programme in Mulanje District of southern Region, Malawi.

57. "Malawi's Export Crop Boom: A Reappraisal", J. Kydd, *IDS Bulletin*, vol. 19 no. 2, Sussex, April 1988, p. 71, quoting World Bank data and the results of air photo surveys. According to this source, it is hard to be precise about the amount of land held by the commercial estates, because complete statistics are not published by the government.

58. For detailed studies on the land issue during the colonial era, see: "The State and the Creation of Colonial Malawi's Agricultural Economy", L. Vail, Chapter 3 of *Imperialism, Colonialism, and Hunger: East and Central Africa*, ed. R.I. Rotberg, Lexington Books, 1983; "Johnston and Jameson: a comparative study in the imposition of colonial rule", R.H. Palmer, chapter in *The*

Early History of Malawi, Longman, Harlow, 1971, pp. 311-13, 314-15; "Working Conditions and Worker Responses on Nyasaland Tea Estates, 1930 - 1953", R.H. Palmer, *Journal of African History*, 27, 1986, pp. 105-8, 125-6; and "Land Policies in Malawi: An Examination of the Colonial Legacy", B. Pachai, *Journal of African History*, XIV, 4, 1973.

59. L. Vail, op. cit., p. 44.

60. "Malawi's Agricultural Export Strategy and Implications for Income Distribution", R.E. Christiansen and J.G. Kydd, US Department of Agriculture, Staff report no. AGES870224, Washington, 1987, p. 6.

61. See *The Story of an African Famine: Gender and Famine in Twentieth Century Malawi*, M. Vaughan, Cambridge University Press, Cambridge, 1987.

62. See, for example, Chapter 10 of *Land and Politics in Malawi, 1875-1975*, B. Pachai, The Limestone Press, Ontario, 1978, pp. 186-204. By the mid-1960s, when Malawi became independent, employment data show that the dominant sector was smallholder agriculture. In contrast, by 1977, 50 per cent of the male labour force was engaged in waged employment in the expanding estate sector, with a consequent reduction in male labour available for domestic production.

63. For a thorough discussion of the economic and developmental implications of this period, see "Malawi's Export Crop Boom: A Reappraisal", J. Kydd, *IDS Bulletin*, vol. 19, no. 2, April 1988, pp. 71-80; and "Malawi's Agricultural Export Strategy and Implications for Income Distribution", R. Christianson and J. Kydd, op. cit., p.6.

64. ADMARC has since been drastically restructured as part of Malawi's structural adjustment programme.

65. From 1971 to 1980, ADMARC made profits of MK 182 m. on its handling of peasant sector tobacco, groundnuts and cotton. In 1978, ADMARC invested 68 per cent of its profits in estate production, 4.3 per cent in peasant production, and the remainder in financial investments which gave it a controlling interest in the country's two commercial banks of the time, which in turn were directed by government to make substantial loans, beyond the limits of financial prudence, to the estate sector, including estates owned by the President's company. (1981/82 internal Oxfam report, based on the work of Christiansen and Kydd, op. cit.)

66. See "Structural Adjustment, Agricultural Development and the Poor: Some Observations on Malawi", U. Lele, World Bank, 1988.

67. This section is based on briefings from Jonathan Kydd and an internal Oxfam report, both of 1981/82.

68. Over half of the country's 1978-81 borrowings were on non-concessional terms, according to the EIU 1988/89 Country Profile, p. 33. By the late 1980s, most of the debt was on concessional terms, according to OECD debt tables and "African Debt: The Search for Solutions", UN Africa Recovery Programme briefing paper no. 1, June 1989.

69. The London Club is the annual meeting of the commercial banks who have lent to Third World countries. The Paris Club is the annual meeting of nations (normally OECD countries) who have lent to Third World countries.

70. It is estimated that, if Malawi continues with its economic reform programme, its debt-service ratio (as a proportion of the export of goods and services) will decline to 27.3 per cent in 1992. ("Debt in the SADCC Region: A Case Study of Malawi", C. Chipeta, paper given to a conference of NGOs on "Debt in the SADCC region", Brussels, January, 1989.)

71. For a summary, see EIU Country report 1989/90, p. 10.

72. A useful chronological summary of Malawi's economic reform initiatives over the period 1979-1988 is given in a recent unpublished report by the Overseas Development Institute, London.

73. As the World Bank has admitted (see U. Lele, op. cit.).

74. The rates for workers in the three main urban centres of the country, Blantyre, Lilongwe, and Mzuzu, rose to MK 2.17 ($0.82). Rates in smaller District towns were raised to MK 1.74 ($0.65), and rural rates rose to MK 1.74.

75. *Africa Economic Digest*, 8.5.89.

76. According to *Africa Economic Digest*, 30.10.89, average input prices for fertiliser rose between 23 per cent and 47 per cent, while the producer price for maize was to be increased by 8 per cent.

77. For a thorough discussion of the complex issue of food security in Malawi, see "Household Food and Nutritional Security in Malawi", V. Quinn, M. Chiligo, and J.P. Gittinger, paper presented to the Symposium on Agricultural Policies for Growth and Development, November 1-4, 1988, Mangochi, Malawi.

78. Oxfam reports indicate that this was also due to two other factors: firstly drought in the 1986/87 agricultural season and the 'grain borer' pest, which together affected the national harvest; and secondly the extra drain on national food stocks caused by the influx of Mozambican refugees, before international food aid for the refugees had been requested.

79. Oxfam fieldworkers reported that a bag of maize was selling at prices from MK60 to MK90 during October-December 1987. According to a recent, unpublished report by ODI, which compared 1987/88 prices in four different areas, prices reached their peak in December/January — the start of the hungry season — and declined in March/April.

80. According to a recent, unpublished report by ODI, ibid.

81. According to the World Bank's Head of its Southern Africa Department's Agriculture Division in a letter to Oxfam of 2.2.89.

82. Oxfam undertook its action research programme because it was felt to be essential to any future development support in the area. Our experience is that if people are to participate actively in identifying and acting upon the development constraints they face, they must first be directly involved in assessing their own needs and analysing their own problems. Malawian researchers were fielded to facilitate community debate and to undertake 'listening surveys'. The results were reported directly to the village people concerned, so that they had full access to the information gathered, and were able to comment on and improve the analysis.

83. Final Report, Oxfam Action Research Programme, Mulanje District, July 1988, pp. 38, 86.

84. Ibid., p. 43.

85. EIU, Quarterly Report, no. 2, 1988, pp. 31, 32, and World Bank press release.

86. Action Research Final Report, op. cit., pp. 37, 46, 47.

87. See *In the Eye of the Storm: Angola's People*, B. Davidson, Longman, Harlow, 1972; *Africa in Modern History: The Search for a New Society*, B. Davidson, Penguin, Harmondsworth, 1978; *The African Slave Trade From the Fifteenth to the Nineteenth Century*, volume 2 of *The History of Africa* series, UNESCO, Paris, 1985.

88. However, it has to be noted that the relationship between production and equitable access to food is a very complex one. Exporting food crops does not of itself entail equitable food security.

89. UNICEF estimates that the Under-5 Mortality Rate for both Angola and Mozambique is between 325-375. (*Children on the Frontline*, 1989 edition, pp. 38-40.)

90. "The Emergency Situation in Angola: Priority non-food requirements for the year 1988", UN African Emergency Task Force in collaboration with the Government of the People's Republic of Angola, 1988, p. 71.

91. Angola was 'discovered' by the Portuguese voyager Diogo Cao in 1483. It became independent in 1975, after the fall of Portugal's military dictatorship in 1974.

92. For example, the EIU special report, op. cit.; a joint UN/NGO emergency needs assessment mission of late 1987; a joint USAID/US NGO mission of 1988; and various internal Oxfam reports.

93. According to T. Hodges, op. cit., p. 86.

94. UN report, op. cit., p. 3. It has also to be noted that the Angolan government did not then place top priority on getting food aid.

95. 1985 data.

96. The USA has insisted on its right to continue support for UNITA, even right through the delicate 1988 negotiations when the USA sponsored agreement to Namibia's independence and the withdrawal of South African and Cuban troops from Angola.

97. Hansard, Oral Answers, 8.2.89, col. 977.

98. The average harvest is 600 kg per hectare for maize. (Final Report, US Government Assessment Team to Angola, October 1988.)

99. In the 1988 Geneva Appeal background document.

Chapter 10

1. Legally, the UK was the colonial power in Namibia from 1920, when Namibia was placed under a League of Nations mandate to be administered by South Africa on behalf of the British Crown, until 1966 when the UN General Assembly revoked the mandate.

2. Britain does, of course, acknowledge its special relationship to its former colonies, as demonstrated by the formation and continued importance given to the Commonwealth, and by the British Overseas Aid Programme, which expressly focuses on Commonwealth countries.

3. See, for example, *The Third Portuguese Empire*, G. Clarence-Smith, Manchester University Press, Manchester, 1985; and *In The Eye of the Storm: Angola's People*, B. Davidson, Longman, London, 1972.

4. Appendix to item no. 29, under "Correspondence respecting Terms of Surrender of the Boer Forces in the Field on the Conclusion of the War in South Africa, March-June, 1902", State Papers 95, 1901-02, p. 146.

5. Report of the Select Committee on Foreign Affairs on South Africa, 1986, Volume I. HMSO, London, p. x.

6. Eurostat data from "External Trade, Monthly Statistics", Eurostat no. 5, 1989. Note that Eurostat data give aggregate figures for Namibia and South Africa.

7. As compared to between 20 and 40 per cent for the industrialised countries of the OECD. (UN Commission on TNCs (UN CTC), "The South African Economy and TNCs", Public Hearings on the Activities of TNCs in South Africa and Namibia, Geneva, September 1989, E/C.10/AC.4/1989/5, p. 7.)

8. For a full analysis of the relative changes in the pattern of South Africa's main trading partners, see *South Africa: The Sanctions Report*, report prepared for the Commonwealth Committee of Foreign Ministers on Southern Africa, Penguin, Harmondsworth, 1989.

9. UN CTC, op. cit., E/C.10/AC.4/1989/5, p. 7.

10. Ibid.

11. "External Trade, monthly statistics", no. 5 1989, Eurostat.

12. Which give £808 m. as the value of imports from South Africa in 1988.

13. According to R.H. Green (personal communication, January 1990).

14. The *Times* and the *Herald Tribune*, 21.8.89.

15. *South Africa: The Sanctions Report*, op. cit., p. 256.

16. "Key Facts", ECGD promotional leaflet, DTI, London.

17. Hansard, col. 203, 28.11.89.

18. "The Role of Transnational Banks in South Africa", paper no. 6 tabled at the UN Commission of Transnational Corporations Public Hearings on the Activities of TNCs in South Africa and Namibia, September 1989, p. 22.

19. "Sanctions, loans, and the South African economy", A. Hirsch, chapter 21 of *Sanctions Against Apartheid*, ed. M. Orkin, CIIR, London, 1989, pp. 282,323.

20. "Sanctions Against South Africa", R. Moorsom, a background report prepared for Oxfam, Oxford, July 1986, p. 23.

21. "List of TNCs with interests in South Africa and Namibia", report of the UN CTCs, Public Hearings on the Activities of TNCs in South Africa and Namibia, Geneva, September 1989, E/C.10/AC.4/1989/8, pp. 19-31.

22. See R. Moorsom, op. cit., pp. 25, 26.

23. *Africa Economic Digest*, 11.9.89. The UN Commission on TNCs puts the figure at 277 between 1984 and mid-1989. (UN CTC Public Hearings 1989, op. cit., report no. E/C.10/AC.4/1989/2, p. 3.)

24. UN CTC, Public Hearings 1989, op. cit., E/C.10/AC.4/1989/2., pp. 4, 5.

25. Ibid., pp. 9-16.

26. Ibid., pp. 17-20.

27. The UK government produces only broad estimates every few years, and the South African Reserve Bank does not break down investment figures on a country-by-country basis.

28. The UK South Africa Trade Association, British Industry Committee on South Africa, South African Reserve Bank, and the Department of Trade (UK).

29. Direct investment is that put into subsidiaries, associates, plant, branches, and long-term ventures, etc. Indirect investment is portfolio investment in government securities and private sector stock, etc.

30. *Apartheid in Crisis: a compilation of information on trade and investment in South Africa*, 5th edition, May 1989, Anti-Apartheid Movement, London, p. 6.

31. Using the estimates given above and information provided by the South African Reserve Bank Quarterly Bulletin. (*Apartheid in Crisis*, op. cit., p. 9.)

32. UN CTC, Public Hearings September 1989, op. cit., E/C.10/AC.4/1989/8, pp. 12, 24-8.

33. UN CTC, Public Hearings, September 1989, op. cit., E/C.10/AC.4/1989/5, p. 12.

34. UN CTC, Public Hearings September 1989, op. cit., E/C.10/AC.4/1989/8, pp. 8-11, 34, 35.

35. "Apartheid for Export", ICFTU, Geneva, 1989.

36. As reproduced in *Banking on Apartheid: the Financial Links Report*, prepared for the Commonwealth Committee of Foreign Ministers on Southern Africa, James Currey, London, 1989, p. 6.

37. "No Credit", J. Hanlon, Standing Committee of European NGOs, 1989.

38. Based on "The Role of Transnational Banks in South Africa", UN CTC, Public Hearings of September 1989, op. cit., E/C.10/AC.4/1989/6, p. 7.

39. "No Credit", J. Hanlon, Standing Committee of European NGOs, 1989.

40. UN CTC, op. cit., E/C.10/Ac.4/1989/6, p. 11.

41. South Africa's moratorium covered $13.6 bn., mostly short-term debt owed to banks and not covered by government guarantees. (J. Hanlon, "No Credit", op. cit.)

42. *Guardian* 4.6.87.

43. UN CTC, Public Hearings September 1989, op. cit., E/C.10/AC.4/1989/5, p. 19.

44. See ibid., p. 11, for fuller details on the breakdown of loans made from UK banks and those made from UK branches of banks incorporated outside the UK.

45. Ibid., p. 8.

46. Ibid., p. 21.

47. For fuller details, see ibid., pp. 21-4.

48. See *Outposts of Monopoly Capitalism: Southern Africa in the Changing Global Economy*, A. Seidman and Makgetla N. Seidman, Zed Press, London, 1980; and *The Roots of Crisis in*

Southern Africa, A. Seidman, Oxfam America, Africa World Press, New Jersey, 1984.

49. According to a speech to SADCC in February by Chris Patten, then the Minister for Overseas Development. In addition, by the end of 1988, the Commonwealth Development Corporation had committed a cumulative total of £267 m. in the SADCC region. (Ibid.)

50. According to Department of Trade data, published in Census of Overseas Assets, 1984. Calculations based on the South African Reserve Bank's data would put the figure at 1.85 per cent.

51. For an account of falling UK direct private investment levels throughout sub-Saharan Africa, see "British Transnational Corporations in sub-Saharan Africa: Corporate Responses to Economic Crisis in the 1980s", P. Bennel, mimeo, July 1989.

52. Based on *Beggar Your Neighbours*, J. Hanlon, CIIR, London, 1986, pp. 282-306.

53. For details of Zimbabwe's foreign investment profile, see, *Zimbabwe: Politics, Economics and Society*, C. Stoneman and L. Cliffe, Pinter, London and New York, 1989, pp. 138-41.

54. This excludes UK multilateral aid for refugees given through UNHCR and ICRC.

55. UK delegation's statement to SADCC's 1989 Annual Consultative Conference.

56. For a full discussion of the role of the 'Aid and Trade Provision', see the Foreign Affairs Select Committee's second report, 1986-7, on bilateral aid.

57. "British Aid Statistics, 1984–1988", ODA, London, 1989, p. 26.

58. "Britain's Voice in South Africa", FCO, London, 1989, p. 23.

59. See the communiqué of the EC Foreign Ministers, Luxembourg, 10.9.85, and the European Council's statement of 27.6.86.

60. Until Namibia's independence, and therefore its 'statehood', Britain could not have a fully accredited diplomatic representation there. However, shortly after the internationally recognised transition process to independence began, the Foreign and Commonwealth Office were able to open a Liaison Office in anticipation of independence. Before independence, therefore, British diplomatic affairs regarding Namibia were directly controlled by the British Embassy in Pretoria. However, Namibia's colonial status did not prevent successive British governments from permitting substantial British business operations in Namibia, even in defiance of the United Nations' Council for Namibia's Decree for the protection of Namibia's natural resources. (See *Namibia: A Violation of Trust*, S. Smith, Oxfam, Oxford, 1986, pp. 69-72.)

61. Excerpt from her speech to the British Council of Churches conference, London, 28.2.89.

62. Britain's historical 'kith and kin' legacy forms an important part of white South African society. It is impossible to estimate the extent to which this has shaped British policy towards South Africa over the years, but it has undoubtedly been significant, as has, more recently, the issue of British citizens in South Africa.

There is an estimated 1 million white South Africans holding, or entitled to, British passports (according to the Foreign Affairs Select Committee's 1986 report on South Africa). Although the prospect remains remote, the British government is keen that any future political changes in South Africa should not be so dramatic as to precipitate a mass influx of refugees to the UK.

It is still sometimes argued that the Cape sea route is strategically important to Britain. However, in the nuclear era, it is now widely thought that this view is obsolete.

63. FCO memorandum, as quoted in the Foreign Affairs Select Committee's 1986 report on South Africa, op. cit., p. vii.

64. Excerpt from an interview in *Leadership*, vol. 8 no. 3, Cape Town, May 1989.

65. As quoted in *Britain and South Africa: The Way Forward*, British Council of Churches, February 1989, p. 19.

66. This section is limited to Britain's relationship with those countries which have been discussed in this book. British links with Botswana, Lesotho, Swaziland, and Tanzania are therefore not examined. For a discussion of Britain's links with Namibia, see *Namibia: A*

Violation of Trust, S. Smith, Oxfam, Oxford, 1986.

67. "Southern Africa: The Price of Apartheid. A Political Risk Analysis", R. Martin, EIU special report no. 1130, London, July 1988, p. 99.

68. Information made available to Oxfam researcher, Harare, November 1989.

69. "Geographical Distribution of Financial Flows to Developing Countries, 1984-1987", OECD, p. 198.

70. Although the Malawi/Tanzania part of the 'northern corridor' helps Malawi only, Britain pressed for its inclusion in the SADCC portfolio. The reconstruction of the Nacala line also assists provinces within Mozambique, and the Beira line mainly assists Zimbabwe, but also helps Malawi, Zambia, and Mozambique.

71. Programme Aid is an official category specifically available to help with balance of payments support while a country is following an IMF-approved structural adjustment programme. Zambia could, therefore, have calculated that its break with the IMF would entail this result. Nevertheless, in the face of the rapidly declining economic situation in Zambia and its adverse effects on the urban poor, Oxfam argued that the British government could use the withheld Programme Aid resources for specially targeted assistance to those worst affected by the short-term economic results of structural adjustment. ODA, however, refused to agree to this suggestion for change of use.

72. Because of the widely held view that Britain, in insisting on an EC mission so shortly after rejecting the findings of the Commonwealth Eminent Persons mission (which recommended sanctions), was deliberately trying to undermine the Commonwealth's effort to form a coherent and coordinated international policy on ending apartheid in South Africa.

73. As of end November 1989, see Hansard, col. 203, 28.11.89.

74. *Financial Times* and *Guardian*, 3.1.89.

75. Hansard, 16.12.87. Britain's total gross bilateral aid to Angola for 1986 was £317,000.

76. Excerpt from the Prime Minister's interview with the South African newspaper *Beeld*, 29.11.89.

77. Excerpt from Sir Robin Renwick's speech to the Urban Foundation, Johannesburg, 17.8.89.

78. Speech to the Royal Commonwealth Society, 17.5.88.

79. See, for example, *Britain's Voice in South Africa*, FCO, London, 1989.

80. On this issue, however, the British government has often been criticised for not doing enough. For example, it was widely noted that the British government failed to intercede over the Delmas trial, in which extra-parliamentary opposition was effectively judged to be a treasonable offence, whereas other western governments strongly signalled their disapproval.

81. According to the *Independent*, 16.12.89.

82. See para. 21.5, section III, of the Harare Declaration, appendix 2.

83. Although SWAPO agreed to abide by its terms, they were not directly party to the negotiations, and nor was the UN, which, in international law, is the body responsible for the administration of the territory up to independence.

84. The UN's Special Representative and South Africa's Administrator General were constantly in dispute over transition issues. These disputes included the establishment of conditions under which refugees could safely return; the delayed repeal of discriminatory legislation; and the establishment of electoral registration and balloting law for free and fair elections.

85. *British Policy Towards South Africa*, FCO, London, 1988.

86. *Beeld*, op. cit.

87. See point 3 of the draft declaration to the UNGA sixteenth special session, 15.12.89, which was unanimously accepted. It differs slightly from the Harare Declaration's para. 16.3, section II, but stands none the less firmly against 'Group rights' being enshrined in the constitution.

88. Excerpt from her speech to the BCC conference, London, 28.2.89.

89. From Sir Geoffrey Howe's speech to the Royal Commonwealth Society, London, 17.5.89.

90. This point was addressed to Mrs Chalker during the plenary session of the conference of the British Council of Churches, London, 28.2.89.

91. *Anti-Apartheid News*, February 1989, p. 4.

92. *Observer* 21.5.89.

93. Hansard, col. 975, 8.2.89.

94. *Anti-Apartheid News*, March 1989, p. 4.

95. Excerpt from her speech to the BCC conference, London, 28.2.89.

96. British statements on the ANC have highlighted objections to its policy of armed struggle, and minimised the role it plays in South African political affairs. At the Vancouver Commonwealth summit of October 1987, Mrs Thatcher dismissed the ANC as a "typical terrorist organisation". Later, and less publicly, the Foreign Office stated, "We acknowledge that the ANC is an important focus for black opinion in South Africa, and one of the representative organisations of the opposition. A central purpose of our Ministerial and other contacts with the ANC has been to seek to persuade them that violence and acts of terrorism are not the right approach." (FCO statement on British policy towards South Africa, 1988.)

When asked to reconcile these two positions, Mrs Thatcher explained, "As a political movement, the ANC undoubtedly is a factor in South African politics. The question is how to get it to give up the politics of violence. The best approach is by offering the possibility of negotiations." (*Beeld*, 29.11.88.)

97. The highest official level at which the British government had met the ANC as at the end of 1989 was Ministerial level, as demonstrated by the contacts Mrs Chalker had as a Minister of State at the FCO. Sir Geoffrey Howe met ANC representatives in late 1986, but Mrs Thatcher later played this down, telling the House of Commons that he had met them in his capacity as the President of the European Community Council of Ministers, and not in his capacity as the British Foreign Minister. (*Guardian* 23.10.87.)

98. Excerpt from the UDF delegation's statement of 13.7.89.

99. In his speech to the Royal Commonwealth Society, May 1988.

100. For example, it has been estimated that R20 billion left South Africa as a result of financial sanctions between mid-1984 and mid-1988, a figure estimated to rise to R25 billion by 1990. International sanctions are also thought to have been a key factor responsible for South Africa's falling national economic growth rate. ("Facing the Nineties: Business Amidst Sanctions and Disinvestment", a speech given to the 8th national congress of Chartered Accountants in Durban, by Chris van Wyck, Managing Director of the Trust Bank of Africa Ltd., June 1988.) The author estimates that without sanctions and disinvestment, the 1988 economic growth rate could have been 4.5 per cent instead of 2.5 per cent.

101. See "Southern Africa: the Way Ahead, the Kuala Lumpur Statement", and "Southern Africa: The Way Ahead: Britain's View", both of 22.10.89.

102. See "South Africa: The Sanctions Report", Commonwealth Secretariat, op. cit., p. 211.

103. Interview with Jay Naidoo, *SouthScan,* vol 4 no. 20/21, 24.5.89.

104. See "British Aid to Southern Africa: A Force for Peaceful Development", FCO, London, 1987.

105. For example, successive Ministerial statements in parliament referred only to Britain's diplomatic requests to Pretoria to "abide by the terms of the Nkomati Accord".

106. When in September of that year, a few days after State President Botha had pledged to cease supporting the MNR, Sir Geoffrey Howe, then Foreign Secretary, said he hoped Pretoria would indeed cease its support. (FCO transcript of the press conference given by Sir Geoffrey Howe at Maputo airport, Mozambique, 19.9.88; *Independent* 19.9.88; *Financial Times* 21.9.88.)

107. *Leadership* magazine, Cape Town, May 1989. Indicating that UK diplomatic pressure lay

behind the September 1988 meeting of Presidents Chissano and Botha, Sir Robin Renwick stated, "We have worked hard to contribute to the process of attempting to normalise relations between South Africa and Mozambique, which culminated in the meeting between President Chissano and President Botha." (*Weekly Mail*, South Africa, 24.3.89.)

108. "Britain and International Debt Relief", paper produced by the Reference Services of the Central Office of Information, London, February 1989.

109. *Financial Times* 10.6.88.

110. Hansard, col. 204, 28.11.89.

111. See, for example, Chris Patten's statement (as ODA Minister) on behalf of the UK delegation, to SADCC's 1989 Annual Consultative Conference.

112. See, for example, "Aid and the Private Sector: The British View", C. Patten, *Development International*, May/June 1987.

113. Excerpt from Chris Patten's statement on behalf of the UK delegation to SADCC's 1989 annual meeting.

Chapter 11

1. Consisting of Belgium, Denmark, France, Greece, Ireland, Italy, Luxembourg, the Netherlands, Portugal, Spain, United Kingdom, and West Germany. The EC's key decision-making bodies are the Council of Ministers and its administrative arm, the European Commission, based in Brussels. The European Parliament has the important power of budget approval.

2. These are approximate figures only. Official EC trade figures combine data for South Africa and Namibia. A notional allowance has been made for this.

3. Comparing export levels in the early 1980s with those of the later 1980s. ("Lomé Briefing", monthly review published by the Liaison Committee of the Development NGOs to the European Communities, Brussels, no. 4, December 1988, p. 2.)

4. EC members plus Austria, Switzerland, and Turkey. (*South Africa: The Sanctions Report*, Commonwealth, op. cit., p. 77.)

5. UN CTC report E/C.10./AC.4/1989/5, p. 8, and "Statistics on trade with South Africa", Commonwealth news release, 5.8.88.

6. UN CTC, op. cit., E/C.10/AC.4/1989/5, pp. 10, 11.

7. "No Credit", J. Hanlon, Standing Committee of NGOs, Brussels, 1989, table 1.

8. Table compiled by Dr P. Goodison, Fonds voor Ontwikkelingssamenwerking (FOS)/Holland Committee on Southern Africa, Brussels, from EC sources.

9. Although expenditure on SADCC projects has sometimes been drawn from National Indicative Programme funds. Under Lomé III (1985-1990), 141 m. ECU was allocated to SADCC's Programme of Action.

10. Source: South Africa/Namibia Association (SANAM) internal memo, 12.1.89.

11. See "The European Community and Southern Africa: Looking Towards Lomé IV", AWEPAA, The Hague, 1989, pp. 8-11.

EC funds for structural adjustment are available via two routes under Lomé IV. The bulk will be drawn from a special fund which will be available as and when required by eligible ACP (African, Caribbean, and Pacific) states. In addition some programmable NIP funds, which are normally used for traditional project aid, can be retained for import support. ("Negotiating the Fourth Lomé Convention", ODI briefing paper, London, October 1989.)

12. STABEX was first introduced under Lomé I, and SYSMIN under Lomé II.

13. "The European Community and Southern Africa: looking towards Lomé IV", The Association of West European Parliamentarians for Action Against Apartheid (AWEPAA), The Hague, 1989, p. 6.

14. Sugar prices fell from a free-market price peak of 28.7 US cents per lb. in 1980 to a low of 4.1 US cents per lb. in 1988.

15. Its quota is 21,500 tonnes.

16. *Financial Times*, 10.10.89.

17. See "Developing Countries and 1992", ODI briefing paper, London, 1989.

18. "Negotiating the Fourth Lomé Convention", ODI briefing, London, October 1989, pp. 3, 4.

19. The Treaty of Rome does not give the EC a direct mandate to act on debt issues, because it does not have competence to deal with financial policy. How this will be affected by moves towards European Monetary Union is not clear.

20. One technical reason for this is that not all EC member states have their own single-country representation on the IMF and World Bank boards.

21. IMF and World Bank annual reports for 1989.

22. Statement by EC Foreign Ministers, 10 September 1985.

23. Statement by the European Council, The Hague, 27 June 1986.

24. Statement by Foreign Ministers, Brussels, 16 September 1986.

25. *Weekly Mail*, South Africa, 30.6.89.

26. Excerpt from the EPC press release, Luxembourg, 10.9.85.

27. Excerpt from the Simons Report, European Parliament, 1987, compiled on behalf of the External Relations Committee and adopted by the European Parliament in 1987.

28. This trend is accentuated by the internal organisation of EC structures whereby the implementation of restrictive measures falls within the scope of the all-powerful European Political Cooperation (EPC), while the implementation of the Special Programme falls under the Commission for Development and Cooperation.

29. Excerpt from the Commissioner's speech to the SADCC Annual Consultative Conference, Gaborone, February 1987.

30. Excerpt from the speech of the Director General for Development, Arusha, January 1988.

31. Excerpt from the speech of the EC's Development Commissioner, Luanda, February 1989.

32. *Weekly Mail*, South Africa, 30.6.89.

33. Hansard, 19.1.89, col. 270.

34. ODA Press Office.

35. Internal memo for FOS 7.3.88, and SANAM Secretariat figures, September 1989.

36. Although Oxfam does not channel EC Special Programme funds to South Africa.

37. *New Nation*, South Africa, 25.2.88.

38. EPC press release, 6.9.89.

39. FCO letter to War on Want, 9.3.89.

40. *Guardian*, 29.1.89.

Chapter 12

1. UNSCR 418 of 1977, acting under Chapter VII of the UN charter.

2. UN General Assembly Resolution 41/35 F, of 1986.

3. EC Council of Ministers Statement, September 1985.

4. By the UN Economic Commission for Africa, in its publication, "South African Destabilisation: The Economic Cost of Frontline Resistance to Apartheid", 1989. The ECA estimates that the first year of a four-year reconstruction programme would need $3.475 bn., with the annual amount declining to $2.6 bn. in the fourth year.

5. Submission to the Treasury and Civil Service Select Committee on Management of Third World Debt, Oxfam, December 1989.

Appendix 1

Proposed Five Year Action Plan of the National Party

This Five Year Plan of Action is based on the Programme of Principles and the 1987 Election Manifesto of the National Party, as well as the complete Plan of Action of 1989, all of which remain relevant and valid and, indeed, opened the way for this Five Year Plan of Action.

THE GOAL:

The National Party aims to create

A *new South Africa* in which every South African can live in safety, prosperity and dignity, as an individual and as a member of a group.

The new South Africa must
* be a *democracy* in which
* no individual or group *dominates or is dominated,*
* the *independence of the judiciary* is upheld and honoured,
* *civilised norms* apply,
* a dynamic economy thrives, based on *free enterprise,*
* everybody lives in *safety* and *harmony,* and
* *as good neighbours* to the international community.

In short

A South Africa to be proud of!

COMMITMENT:

We, as the National Party, commit ourselves

* to *pursue energetically* each of the cardinal points of this ideal for the future;
* to show *real progress* within *the next five years* in respect of each of the key objectives contained in this Plan of Action;
* to uphold all the commitments contained in our Programme of Principles and our Manifesto of 1987;
* to put to the electorate any new constitutional principles before implementation, and to submit constitutional changes to Parliament for approval.

1 A DEMOCRACY: PARTICIPATION FOR ALL

Every South African has the right to participate in decision-making at all levels of government that affect his interests, subject to the principle of non-domination.

The National Party will, within the next five years

* promote those values that unite us;
* engage the leaders of groups who are committed to peaceful solutions in talks and negotiations;
* start institutions in which these leaders can participate in the creation of a new South Africa;
* review the position of the Head of State, his functions and powers, and the manner of his election.

NEGOTIATED PARTICIPATION FOR EVERYONE WILL CREATE A JUST SOUTH AFRICA OF WHICH WE ALL CAN BE PROUD.

2 NO DOMINATION: PROTECTION FOR INDIVIDUALS AND GROUPS

The diversity of the South African population necessitates the protection of individuals and of minorities. Domination, of whatever nature, will bring bloodshed, poverty and misery.

To ensure continued democracy, the participation of all groups and individuals must be permanently protected, with checks and balances to prevent domination.

The National Party will, within the next five years

* promote the peaceful settlement of political disputes, and non-domination, as exalted values;
* promote, by continued action, self-determination regarding own

affairs, along with joint decision-making on general affairs, by means of division and devolution of power in a non-discriminatory manner;

* inject a new dynamic into the process of negotiation to seek agreement among leaders on:

—a basis for eliminating and preventing domination,

—an objective and depoliticised deadlock-breaking mechanism to take final decisions in case of disputes,

—a more just and meaningful basis on which groups may be defined for political participation;

give constitutional expression to the protection of human rights — both individual rights and group values;

* give content to the overall juridical and structural protection of groups in constitutional structures;

* reinforce the process of negotiation with independent expert research and advice.

JUST AND EFFECTIVE PROTECTION OF MINORITIES IN SOUTH AFRICA WILL PROVIDE THE BASIS FOR COOPERATION BY ALL.

3 THE JUDICIARY AND EQUALITY BEFORE THE LAW

A strong, independent judiciary is an essential guarantee for the protection of individual rights and group values, and to ensure stable democracy and justice for all.

The National Party will, within the next five years

* continue with law reform in order to ensure the availability of full justice to all;

* guarantee the inviolability of judges and officers of law to ensure the independence of the judiciary;

* ensure the conduct of proper and lawful public administration by constant review of the jurisdiction of the Advocate General.

A SOUND, STRONG AND INDEPENDENT ADMINISTRATION OF JUSTICE IS THE CORNERSTONE OF A JUST AND FREE SOUTH AFRICA.

4 CIVILISED NORMS; SOCIAL WELFARE

Each individual and each group must have the freedom to enjoy a community life of his choice. Because of the diverse needs of the people of South Africa, this must be embodied in the principle of 'live and let live'.

The practical application of this principle must eventually be in the form of a set of arrangements mutually acceptable to all groups, arrived at through negotiation.

The National Party will, within the next five years

* negotiate with leaders to find a mutually acceptable basis for maintenance of own community life, own residential areas and own schools for those who so wish, and for the provision and utilisation of public amenities;

* within means, promote effective education on all levels;

* promote home ownership and appropriate welfare housing;

* make progress in respect of the housing needs of rapidly urbanising groups, within the limits of affordability;

* make available new and established residential areas, after thorough consultation with the inhabitants, to provide for people who prefer living in free settlement areas;

* maintain own residential areas according to the Group Areas Act in a firm, yet sensitive manner until an acceptable alternative method can be put into practice;

* show progress in the provision of public amenities in order to provide, as far as possible, for the needs of the various communities;

* open up amenities where necessary and where this can take place without causing serious conflict; amenities which have been successfully opened shall not be closed again;

* ensure the prevention of health hazards and poor social conditions caused by over-population and illegal squatting by the proper implementation of local by-laws and other applicable measures.

THE PRINCIPLE OF 'LIVE AND LET LIVE' WILL BRING SATISFACTION BECAUSE IT OFFERS AN ORDERLY EXISTENCE TO ALL ACCORDING TO THEIR OWN CHOICE.

5 A DYNAMIC ECONOMY

A healthy and dynamic economy is essential for stability, peace and prosperity.

Adversities such as the worst drought in living memory, a prolonged slump in the gold price, and the most vicious international attempt — over more than two decades — to destroy the South African economy by boycotts, sanctions and disinvestment, have strained the economy of the country and of every business and household.

A concerted effort by the government and the people of South Africa is necessary to restore the health and prosperity of our economy and the well-being of all our people.

The National Party will, within the next five years

* lower personal income tax, reducing marginal rates to a maximum of 40 per cent at the income level of R100,000 (as far as possible in terms of 1989 values) instead of the present 45 per cent at R80,000;
* reduce company tax from 50 to 40 per cent, together with the phasing out of tax abatements as recommended by the Margo Commission;
* reduce the deficit before borrowing to attain an acceptable level of around 3 per cent of the Gross Domestic Product in order to relieve pressure on interest rates;
* reduce inflation;
* follow a continuous programme of privatisation and deregulation;
* implement an industrial strategy focussed on export promotion and import replacement;
* promote the further beneficiation of South Africa's raw materials;
* continue to reconstruct the agricultural sector;
* promote the vast tourism potential of our country.

THIS REALISTIC ECONOMIC PLAN PLACES SOUTH AFRICA ON THE ROAD TO SUSTAINED ECONOMIC GROWTH AND PROSPERITY.

6 SECURITY

The first duty of a state or government is to protect people and their property against enemies and criminal elements. Efficient security services are indispensable for an orderly and peaceful community, providing a sound climate for political, economic and social development.

The National Party will, within the next five years

* equip the South African Police adequately with manpower and resources to enable them to counter crime even more effectively;
* maintain the preparedness of the South African Defence Force in terms of both manpower and equipment to enable it to withstand internal, regional and international threats against South Africa;
* limit the involvement of the Citizen Force and Commando members, especially as far as annual camps are concerned, with due regard to the security situation;
* enable the South African Prison Service to carry out its role of custody and rehabilitation even more efficiently.

A STRONG DEFENCE FORCE AND A STRONG POLICE FORCE WILL REMAIN THE BASIS FOR A STRONG AND JUST SOUTH AFRICA.

7 THE INTERNATIONAL COMMUNITY

The Republic of South Africa must regain its rightful place in the international community, while maintaining the honour and dignity of our country.

The National Party will, within the next five years

* promote the successful conclusion of the independence process for South West Africa/Namibia;
* promote peace and stability in all the countries of the southern African region, and particularly Angola and Mozambique;
* promote economic cooperation among all the countries of southern Africa;
* counter boycotts and sanctions while working to improve the image South Africa.

THE NATIONAL PARTY CAN BE ENTRUSTED WITH THE FUTURE OF SOUTH AFRICA IN SOUTHERN AFRICA AND IN THE REST OF THE WORLD BECAUSE THE NATIONAL PARTY PUTS SOUTH AFRICA FIRST.

Appendix 2

Declaration of the OAU Ad-Hoc Committee on Southern Africa on the Question of South Africa

Harare, Zimbabwe: August 21, 1989

I PREAMBLE

1.0. The people of Africa, singly, collectively, and acting through the OAU, are engaged in serious efforts to establish peace throughout the continent by ending all conflicts through negotiations based on the principle of justice and peace for all.

2.0 We reaffirm our conviction, which history confirms, that where colonial, racial and apartheid domination exists, there can neither be peace nor justice.

3.0 Accordingly, we reiterate that while the apartheid system in South Africa persists, the peoples of our continent as a whole cannot achieve the fundamental objectives of justice, human dignity and peace which are both crucial in themselves and fundamental to the stability and development of Africa.

4.0 With regard to the region of Southern Africa, the entire continent is vitally interested that the processes, in which it is involved, leading to the complete and genuine independence of Namibia, as well as peace in Angola and Mozambique, should succeed in the shortest possible time. Equally, Africa is deeply concerned that the destabilisation by South Africa of all the countries of the region, whether through direct aggression, sponsorship of surrogates, economic subversion and other means, should end immediately.

5.0 We recognise the reality that permanent peace and stability in Southern Africa can only be achieved when the system of apartheid in South Africa has been liquidated and South Africa transformed into a united, democratic and non-racial country. We therefore reiterate that all the necessary measures should be adopted now, to bring a speedy end to the apartheid system, in the interest of all the people of Southern Africa, our continent and the world at large.

6.0 We believe that, as a result of the liberation struggle and international pressure against apartheid, as well as global efforts to liquidate regional conflicts, possibilities exist for further movement towards the resolution of the problems facing the people of South Africa. For these possibilities to lead to fundamental change in South Africa, the Pretoria regime must abandon its abhorrent concepts and practices of racial domination and its record of failure to honour agreements, all of which have already resulted in the loss of so many lives and the destruction of so much property in the countries of Southern Africa.

7.0 We reaffirm our recognition of the right of all peoples, including those of South Africa, to determine their own destiny, and to work out for themselves the institutions and the system of government under which they will, by general consent, live and work together to build a harmonious society. The Organisation of African Unity remains committed to do everything possible and necessary to assist the people of South Africa, in such ways as the representatives of the oppressed may determine, to achieve this objective. We are certain that, arising from its duty to help end the criminal apartheid system, the rest of the world community is ready to extend similar assistance to the people of South Africa.

8.0 We make these commitments because we believe that all people are equal and have equal rights to human dignity and respect, regardless of colour, race, sex or creed. We believe that all men and women have the right and duty to participate in their own government, as equal members of society. No individual or group of individuals has any rights to govern others without their consent. The apartheid system violates all these fundamental and universal principles. Correctly characterised as a crime against humanity, it is responsible for the death of countless numbers of people in South Africa. It has sought to dehumanise entire peoples. It has imposed a brutal war on the whole region of Southern Africa, resulting in untold loss of life, destruction of property, and massive displacement of innocent men, women and children. This scourge and affront to humanity must be fought and eradicated in its totality.

9.0 We have therefore supported and continue to support all those in South

Africa who pursue this noble objective through political, armed and other forms of struggle. We believe this to be our duty, carried out in the interest of all humanity.

10.0 While extending this support to those who strive for a non-racial and democratic society in South Africa, a point on which no compromise is possible, we have repeatedly expressed our preference for a solution arrived at by peaceful means. We know that the majority of the people of South Africa and their liberation movement, who have been compelled to take up arms, have also upheld this position for many decades, and continue to do so.

11.0 The positions contained in this Declaration are consistent with and are a continuation of those elaborated in the Lusaka Manifesto, two decades ago. They take into account the changes that have taken place in Southern Africa since that Manifesto was adopted by the OAU and the rest of the international community. They constitute a new challenge to the Pretoria regime to join in the noble effort to end the apartheid system, an objective to which the OAU has been committed from its birth.

12.0 Consequently, we shall continue to do everything in our power to help intensify the liberation struggle and international pressure against the system of apartheid until this system is ended and South Africa is transformed into a united, democratic and non-racial country, with justice and security for all its citizens.

13.0 In keeping with this solemn resolve, and responding directly to the wishes of the representatives of the majority of the people of South Africa, we publicly pledge ourselves to the positions contained hereunder. We are convinced that their implementation will lead to a speedy end of the apartheid system and therefore the opening of a new dawn of peace for all the peoples of Africa, in which racism, colonial domination and white minority rule on our continent would be abolished for ever.

II STATEMENT OF PRINCIPLES

14.0 We believe that a conjuncture of circumstances exists which, if there is a demonstrable readiness on the part of the Pretoria regime to engage in negotiations genuinely and seriously, could create the possibility to end apartheid through negotiations. Such an eventuality would be an expression of the long-standing preference of the majority of the people of South Africa to arrive at a political settlement.

15.0 We would therefore encourage the people of South Africa, as part of their overall struggle, to get together to negotiate an end to the apartheid system and agree on all the measures that are necessary to transform their country into a non-racial democracy. We support the position held by the majority of the people of South Africa that these objectives, and not the amendment or reform of the apartheid system, should be the aims of the negotiations.

16.0 We are at one with them that the outcome of such a process should be a new constitutional order based on the following principles, among others:

16.1 South Africa shall become a united, democratic and non-racial state.

16.2 All its people shall enjoy common and equal citizenship and nationality, regardless of race, colour, sex, or creed.

16.3 All its people shall have the right to participate in the government and administration of the country on the basis of universal suffrage, exercised through one person one vote, under a common voters' roll.

16.4 All people have the right to form and join any political party of their choice, provided that this is not in furtherance of racism.

16.5 All shall enjoy universally recognised human rights, freedoms and civil liberties, protected under an entrenched Bill of Rights.

16.6 South Africa shall have a new legal system which shall guarantee equality of all before the law.

16.7 South Africa shall have an independent and non-racial judiciary.

16.8 There shall be created an economic order which shall promote and advance the well-being of all South Africans.

16.9 A democratic South Africa shall respect the rights, sovereignty and territorial integrity of all countries and pursue a policy of peace, friendship and mutually beneficial cooperation with all peoples.

17.0 We believe that agreement on the above principles shall constitute the foundation for an internationally acceptable solution which shall enable South Africa to take its rightful place as an equal partner among the African and world community of nations.

III CLIMATE FOR NEGOTIATIONS

18.0 Together with the rest of the world, we believe that it is essential, before any negotiations take place, that the necessary climate for negotiations be created. The apartheid regime has the urgent responsibility to respond positively to this universally acclaimed demand and thus create this climate.

19.0 Accordingly, the present regime should, at the very least:

19.1 Release all political prisoners and detainees unconditionally and refrain from imposing any restrictions on them;

19.2 Lift all bans and restrictions on all proscribed and restricted organisations and people;

19.3 Remove all troops from the townships;

19.4 End the state of emergency and repeal all legislation, such as, and including, the Internal Security Act, designed to circumscribe political activity; and,

19.5 Cease all political trials and political executions.

20.0 These measures are necessary to produce the conditions in which free political discussion can take place — an essential condition to ensure that the people themselves participate in the process of remaking their country. The measures listed above should therefore precede negotiations.

IV GUIDELINES TO THE PROCESS OF NEGOTIATION

21.0 We support the view of the South African liberation movement that upon the creation of this climate, the process of negotiations should commence along the following lines:

21.1 Discussions should take place between the liberation movement and the South African regime to achieve the suspension of hostilities on both sides by agreeing to a mutually binding ceasefire.

21.2 Negotiations should then proceed to establish the basis for the adoption of a new Constitution by agreeing on, among others, the Principles enunciated above.

21.3 Having agreed on these principles, the parties should then negotiate the necessary mechanism for drawing up the new Constitution.

21.4 The parties shall define and agree on the role to be played by the international community in ensuring a successful transition to a democratic order.

21.5 The parties shall agree on the formation of an interim government to supervise the process of the drawing up and adoption of a new constitution; govern and administer the country, as well as effect the transition to a democratic order including the holding of elections.

21.6 After the adoption of a new Constitution, all armed hostilities will be deemed to have formally terminated.

21.7 For its part, the international community would lift the sanctions that have been imposed against apartheid South Africa.

22.0 The new South Africa shall qualify for membership of the Organisation of African Unity.

V PROGRAMME OF ACTION

23.0 In pursuance of the objectives stated in this document, the Organisation of African Unity hereby commits itself to:

23.1 Inform governments and inter-governmental organisations throughout the world, including the Non-Aligned Movement, the United Nations General Assembly, the Security Council, the Commonwealth and others of these perspectives, and solicit their support;

23.2 Mandate the OAU ad-hoc committee on Southern Africa, acting as the representative of the OAU, assisted by the Frontline States, to remain seized of the issue of a political resolution of the South African question;

23.3 Step up all-round support for the South African liberation movement and campaign in the rest of the world in pursuance of this objective;

23.4 Intensify the campaign for mandatory and comprehensive sanctions against apartheid South Africa: in this regard, immediately mobilise against the rescheduling of Pretoria's foreign debts; work for the imposition of a mandatory oil embargo and the full observance by all countries of the arms embargo;

23.5 Ensure that the African continent does not relax existing measures for the total isolation of apartheid South Africa;

23.6 Continue to monitor the situation in Namibia and extend all necessary support to SWAPO in its struggle for a genuinely independent Namibia;

23.7 Extend such assistance as the Governments of Angola and Mozambique may request in order to secure peace for their peoples; and

23.8 Render all possible assistance to the Frontline States to enable them to withstand Pretoria's campaign of aggression and destabilisation and enable them to continue to give their all-round support to the people of Namibia and South Africa.

24.0 We appeal to all people of goodwill throughout the world to support this Programme of Action as a necessary measure to secure the earliest liquidation of the apartheid system and the transformation of South Africa into a united, democratic and non-racial country.

Appendix 3

Declaration on Apartheid and its Destructive Consequences in Southern Africa (A/RES/S-16/1)

PREAMBLE

We, the States Members of the United Nations, assembled at the sixteenth special session of the General Assembly, a special session on *apartheid* and its destructive consequences in southern Africa, guided by the fundamental and universal principles enshrined in the Charter of the United Nations and the Universal Declaration of Human Rights, in the context of our efforts to establish peace throughout the world by ending all conflicts through negotiations, and desirous of making serious efforts to bring an end to the unacceptable situation prevailing in southern Africa, which is a result of the policies and practices of *apartheid*, through negotiations based on the principle of justice and peace for all:

Reaffirming our conviction, which history confirms, that where colonial and racial domination or *apartheid* exist, there can be neither peace nor justice;

Reiterating accordingly that, while the *apartheid* system in South Africa persists, the peoples of Africa as a whole cannot achieve the fundamental objectives of justice, human dignity and peace which are both crucial in themselves and fundamental to the stability and development of the continent;

Recognizing that, with regard to southern Africa, the entire world is vitally interested that the processes in which that region is involved, leading to the genuine national independence of Namibia and peace in Angola and Mozambique, should succeed in the shortest possible time, and equally recognizing that the world is deeply concerned that destabilization by South Africa of the countries of the region, whether through direct aggression, sponsorship of surrogates, economic subversion or other means, is unacceptable in all its forms and must not occur;

Also recognizing the reality that permanent peace and stability in southern Africa can only be achieved when the system of *apartheid* in South Africa has been eradicated and South Africa has been transformed into a united, democratic and non-racial country, and therefore reiterating that all the necessary measures should be adopted now to bring a speedy end to the *apartheid* system in the interest of all the people of southern Africa, the continent and the world at large;

Believing that, as a result of the legitimate struggle of the South African people for the elimination of *apartheid*, and of international pressure against that system, as well as global efforts to resolve regional conflicts, possibilities exist for further movement towards the resolution of the problems facing the people of South Africa;

Reaffirming the right of all peoples, including the people of South Africa, to determine their own destiny and to work out for themselves the institutions and the system of government under which they will, by general consent, live and work together to build a harmonious society, and remaining committed to doing everything possible and necessary to assist the people of South Africa, in such ways as they may, through their genuine representatives, determine to achieve this objective;

Making these commitments because we believe that all people are equal and have equal rights to human dignity and respect, regardless of colour, race, sex or creed, that all men and women have the right and duty to participate in their own government, as equal members of society, and that no individual or group of individuals has any right to govern others without their democratic consent, and reiterating that the *apartheid* system violates all these fundamental and universal principles;

Affirming that *apartheid*, characterized as a crime against the conscience and dignity of mankind, is responsible for the death of countless numbers of people in South Africa, has sought to dehumanize entire peoples, and has imposed a brutal war on the region of southern Africa, which has resulted in untold loss of life, destruction of property and massive displacement of innocent men, women and children and which is a scourge and affront to humanity that must be fought and eradicated in its totality;

Therefore we support and continue to support all those in South Africa who pursue this noble objective. We believe this to be our duty, carried out in the interest of all humanity;

While extending this support to those who strive for a non-racial and democratic society in South Africa, a point on which no compromise is possible, we have repeatedly expressed our objective of a solution arrived at by peaceful means; we note that the people of South Africa, and their liberation movements who felt compelled to take up arms, have also upheld their preference for this position for many decades and continue to do so;

Welcoming the Declaration of the *Ad Hoc* Committee of the Organization of African Unity in Southern Africa on the Question of South Africa, adopted at Harare on 21 August 1989, and subsequently endorsed by the Movement of Non-Aligned Countries at its Ninth Summit Conference held in Belgrade in September 1989, as a reaffirmation of readiness to resolve the problems of South Africa through negotiations. The Declaration is consistent with the positions contained in the Lusaka Manifesto of two decades ago, in particular regarding the preference of the African people for peaceful change, and takes into account the changes that have taken place in southern Africa since then. This Declaration constitutes a new challenge to the Pretoria regime to join in the noble efforts to end the *apartheid* system, an objective to which the United Nations has always been committed;

Noting with appreciation that the Commonwealth Heads of Government, at their meeting in Kuala Lumpur in October 1989, noted with satisfaction the strong preference for the path of negotiated and peaceful settlement inherent in the Harare Declaration and considered what further steps they might take to advance the prospects for negotiations;

Also noting with appreciation that the Francophone Summit in Dakar in May 1989 likewise called for negotiations between Pretoria and representatives of the majority of the people with a view to the establishment of a democratic and egalitarian system in South Africa;

Consequently, we shall continue to do everything in our power to increase support for the legitimate struggle of the South African people, including maintaining international pressure against the system of *apartheid* until that system is ended and South Africa is transformed into a united, democratic and non-racial country, with justice and security for all its citizens;

In keeping with this solemn resolve, and responding directly to the wishes of the majority of the people of South Africa, we publicly pledge ourselves to the positions contained hereunder, convinced that their implementation will lead to a speedy end of the *apartheid* system and heralding the dawn of a new era of peace for all the peoples of Africa, in a continent finally free from racism, white minority rule and colonial domination;

DECLARE AS FOLLOWS:

1 A conjuncture of circumstances exists, which, if there is a demonstrable readiness on the part of the South African regime to engage in negotiations genuinely and seriously, given the repeated expression of the majority of the people of South Africa of their long-standing preference to arrive at a political settlement, could create the possibility to end *apartheid* through negotiations.

2 We would therefore encourage the people of South Africa, as part of their legitimate struggle, to join together to negotiate an end to the *apartheid* system and agree on all the measures that are necessary to transform their country into a non-racial democracy. We support the position held by the majority of the people of South Africa that these objectives, and not the amendment or reform of the *apartheid* system, should be the goals of the negotiations.

3 We are at one with the people of South Africa that the outcome of such a process should be a new constitutional order determined by them and based on the Charter of the United Nations and the Universal Declaration of Human Rights. We hold therefore the following fundamental principles to be of importance:

(a) South Africa shall become a united, non-racial and democratic State;

(b) All its people shall enjoy common and equal citizenship and nationality, regardless of race, colour, sex or creed;

(c) All its people shall have the right to participate in the government and administration of the country on the basis of universal, equal suffrage, under a non-racial voters' roll, and by secret ballot, in a united and non-fragmented South Africa;

(d) All shall have the right to form and join any political party of their choice, provided that this is not in furtherance of racism;

(e) all shall enjoy universally recognized human rights, freedoms and civil liberties, protected under an entrenched bill of rights;

(f) South Africa shall have a legal system that will guarantee equality of all before the law;

(g) South Africa shall have an independent and non-racial judiciary;

(h) There shall be created an economic order that will promote and advance the well-being of all South Africans;

(i) A democratic South Africa shall respect the rights, sovereignty and territorial integrity of all countries and pursue a policy of peace, friendship, and mutually beneficial cooperation with all peoples.

4 We believe that acceptance of these fundamental principles could constitute the basis for an internationally acceptable solution that will enable South Africa to take its rightful place as an equal partner among the world community of nations.

A. *Climate for negotiations*

5 We believe that it is essential that the necessary climate be created for negotiations. There is an urgent need to respond positively to this universally acclaimed demand and thus create this climate.

6 Accordingly, the present South African regime should, at the least:

(a) Release all political prisoners and detainees unconditionally and refrain from imposing any restrictions on them;

(b) Lift all bans and restrictions on all proscribed and restricted organizations and persons;

(c) Remove all troops from the townships;

(d) End the state of emergency and repeal all legislation, such as the Internal Security Act, designed to circumscribe political activity;

(e) Cease all political trials and political executions.

7 These measures would help create the necessary climate in which free political discussion can take place — an essential condition to ensure that the people themselves participate in the process of remaking their country.

B. *Guidelines to the process of negotiations*

8 We are of the view that the parties concerned should, in the context of the necessary climate, negotiate the future of their country and its people in good faith and in an atmosphere which, by mutual agreement between the liberation movements and the South African regime, would be free of violence. The process could commence along the following guidelines:

(a) Agreement on the mechanism for the drawing up of a new constitution, based on, amongst others, the principles enunciated above, and the basis for its adoption;

(b) Agreement on the role to be played by the international community in ensuring a successful transition to a democratic order;

(c) Agreed transitional arrangements and modalities on the process of the drawing up and adoption of a new constitution, and of the transition to a democratic order, including the holding of elections.

C. *Programme of action*

9 In pursuance of the objectives stated in this Declaration, we hereby decide:

(a) To remain seized of the issue of a political resolution of the South African question;

(b) To step up all-round support for the opponents of *apartheid* and to campaign internationally in pursuance of this objective;

(c) To use concerted and effective measures, including the full observance by all countries of the mandatory arms embargo, aimed at applying pressure to ensure a speedy end to *apartheid*;

(d) To ensure that the international community does not relax existing measures aimed at encouraging the South African regime to eradicate *apartheid*, until there is clear evidence of profound and irreversible changes, bearing in mind the objectives of this declaration;

(e) To render all possible assistance to the front-line and neighbouring States to enable them: to rebuild their economies, which have been adversely affected by South Africa's acts of aggression and destabilization; to withstand any further such acts; and to continue to support the peoples of Namibia and South Africa;

(f) To extend such assistance to the Governments of Angola and Mozambique as they may request in order to secure peace for their peoples, and to encourage and support peace initiatives undertaken by the Governments of Angola and Mozambique aimed at bringing about peace and normalization of life in their countries;

(g) The new South Africa shall, upon adoption of the new constitution, participate fully in relevant organs and specialized agencies of the United Nations.

10 We request the Secretary-General to transmit copies of the present Declaration to the South African Government and the representatives of the oppressed people of South Africa, and also request the Secretary-General to prepare a report and submit it to the General Assembly by 1 July 1990 on the progress made in the implementation of the present Declaration.

Further reading on southern Africa

Donald Denoon and Balam Nyeko: *Southern Africa Since 1800* (Harlow: Longman, 1984)

Joseph Hanlon: *Beggar Your Neighbours* (London: James Currey, 1986)

Phyllis Johnson and David Martin (eds.): *Destructive Engagement: Southern Africa at War* (Harare: Zimbabwe Publishing House, 1986)

Phyllis Johnson and David Martin: *Apartheid Terrorism — The Destabilization Report:* A Report on the Devastation of the Frontline States, prepared for the Commonwealth Committee of Foreign Ministers on Southern Africa (London: Commwealth Secretariat and James Currey, 1989)

Tom Lodge: *Black Politics in South Africa since 1945* (Harlow: Longman, 1983)

William Minter: *King Solomon's Mines Revisited: Western Interests and the Burdened History of Southern Africa* (New York: Basic Books, 1986)

Robin Palmer and Neil Parsons: *The Roots of Rural Poverty in Central and Southern Africa* (London: Heinemann Educational Books, 1977)

Neil Parsons: *A New History of Southern Africa* (Basingstoke: Macmillan, 1983)

Colin Stoneman (ed.): *Zimbabwe's Prospects* (Basingstoke: Macmillan, 1988)